D0065238

DATE DUE

Undeclared War and the
Future of U.S. Foreign Policy

Undeclared War and the
Future of U.S. Foreign Policy

Kenneth B. Moss

Woodrow Wilson Center Press
Washington, D.C.

The Johns Hopkins University Press
Baltimore

EDITORIAL OFFICES

Woodrow Wilson Center Press
One Woodrow Wilson Plaza
1300 Pennsylvania Avenue, N.W.
Washington, D.C. 20004-3027
Telephone 202-691-4010
www.wilsoncenter.org

ORDER FROM

The Johns Hopkins University Press
Hampden Station
P.O. Box 50370
Baltimore, Maryland 21211
Telephone 1-800-537-5487
www.press.jhu.edu/books/

2 4 6 8 9 7 5 3 1

Library of Congress Cataloging-in-Publication Data

Moss, Kenneth B.
    Undeclared war and the future of U.S. foreign policy / Kenneth B. Moss.
      p. cm.
    Includes index.
    ISBN 978-0-8018-8856-4 (cloth : alk. paper) — ISBN 978-0-8018-8857-1
(pbk. : alk. paper)
    1. War and emergency powers—United States. 2. War, Declaration of—United
States. 3. Executive power—United States. 4. United States—Foreign relations.
5. Intervention (International law) I. Title.
KF5060.M67 2008
342.73'062—dc22
                                      2008002496

**Woodrow Wilson
International
Center
for Scholars**

The Woodrow Wilson International Center for Scholars, established by Congress in 1968 and headquartered in Washington, D.C., is the living, national memorial to President Wilson.

The Center is a nonpartisan institution of advanced research, supported by public and private funds, engaged in the study of national and world affairs. The Center establishes and maintains a neutral forum for free, open, and informed dialogue.

The Center's mission is to commemorate the ideals and concerns of Woodrow Wilson by providing a link between the world of ideas and the world of policy, by bringing a broad spectrum of individuals together to discuss important public policy issues, by serving to bridge cultures and viewpoints, and by seeking to find common ground.

Conclusions or opinions expressed in Center publications and programs are those of the authors and speakers and do not necessarily reflect the views of the Center staff, fellows, trustees, advisory groups, or any individuals or organizations that provide financial support to the Center.

The Center is the publisher of *The Wilson Quarterly* and home of Woodrow Wilson Center Press, *dialogue* radio and television, and the monthly newsletter "Centerpoint." For more information about the Center's activities and publications, please visit us on the web at www.wilsoncenter.org.

Dedicated to the memory of my father,

Basil B. Moss, Master Sergeant, U.S. Army
(1921–1981)

Wounded in combat in declared and undeclared wars
World War II and Korea

Contents

Acknowledgments

All authors know the immense gratitude they owe to those who have inspired, supported, and criticized their work. Elements of this book stirred in my mind for several years before I began writing. However, the opportunity of a full one-year sabbatical offered to me by the Industrial College of the Armed Forces in the National Defense University (NDU) allowed me to take my interest in this subject in a serious direction. The then-commandant of the Industrial College, Major General Frances C. Wilson, USMC, and the dean of faculty, Dr. John Yaeger, arranged and supported my sabbatical from March 2005 to March 2006. As president of the National Defense University, General Wilson (now a lieutenant general) has continued to foster an environment conducive to open study and teaching of all aspects of national security. The book that has resulted from this sabbatical solely reflects the author's judgments and in no way represents a stated policy or position of the U.S. government, the Department of Defense, or the National Defense University.

Others in the Industrial College also made the sabbatical and completion of this book possible. Dr. Benjamin F. Cooling, chair of the Department of Grand Strategy supported my application. Three subsequent deans of faculty made sure that I had the time for the sabbatical and enabled me to get a good start on the writing before I returned to the classroom. Thus, I owe my lasting gratitude to Captain Walt Kreitler, USN; Colonel John Boggs, USMC, and particularly to Dr. Alan Whittaker. As a department chair, Alan told me to keep on writing when I returned in March 2006. I did so, and was able to find the time even after he became a dean and I succeeded him as department chair. The commandant of the Industrial College, Rear Admiral Gerard M. Mauer, USN, has given endless hours of inspired devotion to the

College and its students and faculty to promote the analytical study of national security issues.

Many in academic life take sabbaticals as part of their professional custom, but, as one who worked over a decade in congressional and private sector settings, I found the opportunity to have an entire year on my own almost astonishing. Having lived in and worked in Washington, DC since 1981, I thought I needed to get outside of Washington to avoid the tendency to succumb to a "crisis *du jour*" approach that would have me largely chasing headlines but not thinking as much about broader factors that affect how the United States has authorized and used military force in undeclared conflicts. I wanted extensive freedom and access to a good library system. To that end I ended up spending eight months of the sabbatical at Indiana University in Bloomington and over three months at the Stiftung Wissenschaft und Politik (German Institute for International Security and Policy) in Berlin.

My career in Washington began with the support of Representative Lee H. Hamilton of Indiana, who was willing to hire a Hoosier with no congressional experience to work on the professional staff of the House Subcommittee on Europe and the Middle East that he chaired. I turned to Rep. Hamilton again in late 2004 with an inquiry as to whether I could work in the Center on Congress at Indiana University, which he directs along with his substantial responsibilities as director of the Woodrow Wilson International Center for Scholars in Washington. He and Ken Nelson arranged with the Bloomington director of the Center, Wayne Vance, to offer me office space where I could research and write when not in the library. Kathy Haney and Vicky Myer provided much help and support in the Center, especially when I was fumbling around with the fax machine or had e-mail problems. Jessica Gerrity, who was working on her own doctorate in political science at Indiana, offered me invaluable tips on the literature dealing with the influence of American religious groups in recent U.S. politics. When my research came to a temporary halt, Wayne Vance and I could always swap serious and irreverent comments about politics.

Another part of my stay at Indiana University was graciously backed by the Department of History. When I contacted Nick Cullather in the department, he immediately sought the assistance of John Bodnar, then chair of the department, on my behalf. The department could not offer me office space, but it gave me access to things that were even more important—a university ID card, faculty privileges at the library, and the right to purchase a parking permit. Ms. Rebecca Bryant in the department guided me through the steps I had to take to accomplish all of this. Nick Cullather's own work in the history of American foreign relations often intersected with my interests, and he and his family provided intellectual and moral support to a geographic bachelor. John Bodnar and I shared thoughts based on my work and his ongoing work on war and public memory. In January 2006 several members of the Department of History, joined by graduate students, listened to a presentation of an early version of my argument and made several very helpful comments.

Libraries are a scholar's real home during part of a book's preparation. Three libraries in particular were critical for my work. The American taxpayer should be immensely proud of the support provided to the study of national security by the staff of the library at the National Defense University. Indiana taxpayers ought to know that they have one of the nation's major research libraries right in the limestone hills of south central Indiana. In Virginia, the Law Library at George Mason University Law School kindly permitted me to use its collections when I needed to do additional work in some legal resources.

For just over three months, I worked in the Security Group at the Stiftung Wissenschaft und Politik in Berlin. Much of my work there involved research on the German constitutional framework and laws that govern the use of force. I used that research in support of a course I teach on the use of force and political accountability as well as for a separate shorter work I am still preparing. However, working in a foreign setting and examining other political and legal considerations that affect how a government sanctions the deployment of its military opens questions related to U.S. law. It was in Berlin where the framework of my argument and its organization began to take shape. Professor Volker Perthes and the entire staff of SWP made me feel like a full member of this outstanding policy institute. Dr. Oliver Thraenert, who heads the Security Group, graciously arranged to bring me into his section and acted as a helpful mentor and friend. Tanja Thiede, who was working on her own dissertation, provided me with critical help and suggestions for resources. Many in the group and elsewhere in SWP listened to parts of my work and, in particular, had to suffer through some of the most mangled German they had probably ever heard. I would like to thank Dr. Peter Rudolf, Dr. Jens van Scherpenberg, Benjamin Schreer, Dr. Markus Kaim, Anthony Seaboyer, Sascha Lange, Roland Hiemann, Frank Kupferschmidt, Lieutenant Colonel Detlev Justen (Bundeswehr), Dr. Ronja Kempin, and Dr. Christian Schaller. Dora Lindemann answered my many questions about office policies and practices in the SWP and also followed my research with interest.

Having to explain U.S. policies and institutions to foreign audiences requires one to rethink and examine these subjects differently. Recurrent travel to Germany has often given me a chance to explore my thinking at different stages, and there are four scholars to whom I owe particular thanks for allowing me these opportunities. At the University of Goettingen, I had repeated opportunities to speak on aspects of this book's subject before classes and seminars arranged by Werner Heun and Peter Loesche. Stephan Bierling provided a similar venue as well as years of friendship and insight from his own extensive scholarship in U.S. foreign policy. Rainer Praetorius with the University of the Bundeswehr in Hamburg (now Helmut Schmidt University) sponsored lectures for me and critiqued my work through his own knowledge and experience with U.S. political institutions and processes.

Several colleagues, friends, and scholars discussed issues with me or read through the entire manuscript or parts of it and made invaluable suggestions. Jim Currie, a colleague in the Industrial College of the Armed Forces, read through the manuscript with a keen eye based on his years of work in and teaching about Congress. A former student who then became a colleague at the National War College, Colonel Tom Trobridge, saved me from some embarrassing comments related to limited war and special operations. Steve Randolph, another colleague in the Industrial College, read parts of the manuscript and became a sounding board for ideas as he and I discussed the Nixon presidency and the Vietnam War. Sandra F. VanBurkleo with Wayne State University, a close friend from our days as graduate students at the University of Minnesota, referred me to several important sources concerning the federal courts and the foreign policy of the early American Republic. David Fidler at the Indiana University School of Law spent a morning with me to discuss international law, especially as it relates to the use of non-lethal weapons. Reaching all the way back to my undergraduate years at Indiana University, Robert H. Ferrell, now professor emeritus, read through the entire manuscript with his remarkable attention to style and content. I stand in a long line of educators and scholars who have benefited from his support and encouragement. To my two outside readers I owe immense gratitude. Both wrote assessments of the manuscript that were strongly encouraging and at the same time truly instructive through proposed additions, revision, and reassessment. Louis Fisher with the Library of Congress provided a number of suggestions that he knew would strengthen my interpretation. To all of them I owe boundless thanks.

Of course, any errors in fact or judgment are my responsibility and certainly not theirs. They saved me from many more.

Inevitably, there are books that appear so late in the preparation of one's own that it becomes difficult to consider their interpretations fairly. Readers should be aware of Charles A. Stevenson, *Congress at War: The Politics of Conflicts Since 1789* (Washington, DC: National Defense University Press and Potomac Books, 2007); William G. Howell and Jon C. Pevehouse, *While Dangers Gather: Congressional Checks on Presidential War Powers* (Princeton, NJ: Princeton University Press, 2007); and Michael D. Ramsey, *The Constitution's Text in Foreign Affairs* (Cambridge, MA: Harvard University Press, 2007). The literature on presidential use of power domestically in relation to the war on terror grows daily, and some of this has a bearing on the argument in this book. However, the three books cited above relate most directly to portions of this volume.

The Wilson Center Press was very encouraging throughout the process. Its director, Joe Brinley, saw potential merit in the second draft of the manuscript and sent it to the outside readers for comment. Yamile Kahn and others on the editorial staff of either the Wilson Center or Johns Hopkins University Press worked on the manuscript to improve its clarity and organization.

At home, my wife, Debbie, was a true bastion of support. She encouraged me in moments of self-doubt, willingly accepted lost afternoons and evenings as I retreated to research or write, supported my decision to take my sabbatical away from Washington even though it meant being apart much of the time, and then acted as my first critic and editor. She read the entire manuscript as an editor—her professional calling—and the marriage still survived! When the manuscript went to the editors, I knew it was in far better shape than it would have been if I had sent it without her attentive eye. Her love made this book possible, and now it is my turn to try to do the same as she embarks on her own book.

Finally, during the last fourteen years it has been my honor to work with colleagues and students in professional military education. Over 60 percent of the students in the Industrial College are officers from all services of the U.S. military. And they come here as lieutenant colonels and colonels or commanders and captains if they are in the Navy or Coast Guard. The rest of the students comprise international officers, a handful of private sector students, and government-employee civilians who are from departments and agencies devoted to foreign policy and the national security of the United States. I hope that they have learned from me as much as I have from them, but I am certain I have learned more. Each year widens and deepens my understanding of national security thanks to their knowledge and insight. Not every educator is lucky enough to meet students that he or she actually admires, but here at the NDU that occurs every year. This book is certainly about these students in some ways, and it reflects concern about their welfare and dependence on government institutions and processes that do not always do the best job of fulfilling constitutional obligations when sending them in harm's way. I could easily dedicate this book to them, but I think that all of them—particularly those in uniform—would understand why I have dedicated it instead to the first soldier I ever knew.

Undeclared War and the
Future of U.S. Foreign Policy

Introduction

In 2007 the United States once again found itself in a debate about war and the balance of power between the president and Congress. After the September 11, 2001, terrorist attacks and again in October 2002, the president obtained from Congress the authority to use military force against Taliban and Al-Qaeda groups in Afghanistan and beyond, and then to invade Iraq, remove the regime of Saddam Hussein, and destroy his alleged weapons of mass destruction. As most Americans probably understand their Constitution, the president had done what is required. Although not seeking a formal declaration of war in either situation, he had turned to Congress to obtain legal authority to use military force. Few Americans probably expected an actual declaration of war, a practice that had begun to fall out of favor even before the delegates assembled in Philadelphia in 1787 to write the Constitution. Outwardly, it seemed that the process of going to war laid out in the Constitution over two centuries before still worked.

Yet, had it? Five years later, as the successful outcome of operations in both Iraq and Afghanistan is questionable, public and congressional criticism of the president's policies and actions has increased. Like presidents before him, particularly since the beginning of the Cold War, President George W. Bush had ordered military forces into the region before obtaining Congress's approval. He cited authority given the president in the Constitution as commander-in-chief of military forces. It was a claim with strong historical precedent. President Bill Clinton had claimed that he did not need congressional authorization to send U.S. forces into Somalia or Haiti or against Serbia for its actions in Bosnia and Kosovo, since these operations—according to the administration—did not have characteristics of a war. The right of presidential control over the use of military force based

1

on the constitutional designation of commander-in-chief has been a mainstay of every presidential administration since World War II. Therefore, turning to the Constitution, whose position is correct? Is it the president's (using force rests on the office's authority as commander-in-chief) or Congress's (originating from its authority to declare war)?

The controversy is at its greatest during an undeclared war. The Constitution restricts the power to declare war to Congress, but it is not as instructive absent a declaration: The Constitution does not explicitly recognize a condition between peace and declared war. What branch of government has final authority over the decision to use force in a limited war or operations that fall under a variety of labels, such as small wars, "brushfire" or guerrilla warfare, insurgency and counterinsurgency operations, low-scale military operations, military operations other than war, special operations, contingency operations, or the eighteenth-century term "imperfect war"? All may involve armed force, combat, injury and death, and success or failure. They may be short in duration or last longer than some declared wars. Military operations in Afghanistan and Iraq now have lasted longer than any declared war in U.S. history. Such limited conflicts occurred throughout history, and the last half of this book examines factors that may make them more frequent and constitutionally problematic.

Most scholars and politicians have tried to answer these questions by closely analyzing the Constitution itself; other contemporary documents, such as *The Federalist Papers;* exchanges of correspondence or printed debates between important principals, such as James Madison and Alexander Hamilton; and other key letters or speeches from the American republic's early years. After studying these sources, scholars investigate historical actions, debates, congressional committee hearings, and court cases through the following two centuries. As this approach depends on interpreting a few key clauses in the Constitution, it is no surprise that the majority of serious work on this question has been written by lawyers, legal scholars, political practitioners, and historians and political scientists specializing in this subject or executive–congressional relations.

The Constitution must be the starting place for serious examination of this subject, but if seeking a final, definitive answer from the U.S. Constitution itself, one reaches a dead end. The first three chapters of this book discuss the diverse range of opinion on what the Constitution and U.S. law may or may not say about which branch of government has authority to send U.S. forces into hostilities, conflict, or war. They illustrate that presidents and legislators during the early years of the American republic largely accepted Congress's dominance in decisions to use military force. However, even during those years an alternative view was emerging in instances that favored independent presidential authority, and, as the interest in using military force as an instrument in foreign policy grew, so too did the proclivity to decide and act without prior congressional approval. This trend continued during the first decades of the twentieth century, and since the start of the Cold War the president has been even more ascendant.

A fundamental problem in the entire debate over who has control in using force is that the variety of military operations at the limited level has increased. Presidents have a larger menu of options to consider using against an adversary. For example, the development and enhancement of recent forms of weapons, such as precision-guided munitions, and the continuing emergence of information technologies that actually may substitute for more traditional weapons have opened new possibilities for limited forms of war. The Constitution's language, though, is grounded in the late eighteenth century. This book suggests to this very day almost all U.S. laws about the appropriate constitutional control over using force face serious challenges from such developments.

If there are more options to select from when using force, thanks to the global scale of U.S. strategic interests, there are also a large number of circumstances in which resorting to force may be worthwhile or tempting. To appreciate why disagreements over presidential and congressional control of military force have become so frequent since the Korean War, one has to understand how presidents have wanted to use military force. What situations favor limited military force versus a formal declaration of war? Furthermore, if a president wishes to use force in such circumstances, he or she may want to recruit and shape the military in ways that best advance national objectives. Limited wars for less clearly defined objectives than defense against attack are unpopular in the United States if they become long and costly in human and financial terms. Particularly since Vietnam, presidents have tried to find ways to make limited uses of force politically acceptable to accomplish foreign policy objectives in locations as diverse as Lebanon, Central America, the Balkans, Somalia, Afghanistan, and Iraq. Why and how presidents have done so are instrumental to understanding the historical debate over the control of military force as well as the troubling future facing the United States and other democracies in this arena.

The next three chapters examine both the debates over the criteria for using armed force as well as several developments that have made the United States more prone to exercising limited military force. A significant amount of the debate over criteria for using force has occurred between branches of the U.S. military (especially the Army) and presidential cabinet members and advisers. The method or form of force chosen often influences the position that presidents take toward the role of Congress in the decision. The historical record from the first three chapters illustrates this as well.

The debate over war powers and the Constitution often has been part of a debate over how a government can keep military force as a usable instrument in national policy. One appeal of a war purposely limited in scale is that it can be a form of military force which can accomplish strategic and political objectives without seriously disrupting our economy or population. Long before Carl von Clausewitz famously wrote "War is a continuation of policy by other means," early American statesmen grasped the same point, including examples such as the successful quasi-war against France in 1798–1800 and the rationale behind some of the thoughts and actions that brought the United States to its first declared war in 1812.

What answers, though, did supporters of usable military power advocate when more recent experience seemed to suggest that war was no longer a viable alternative for governments, thanks to two world wars' massive destruction, the emergence of atomic weapons, and the "lessons" drawn from Vietnam? Did differences between the professional military and civilian leadership emerge over the appropriate, timely use of military force? The answers to all these questions played greatly into the executive–congressional balance in war powers. The final chapters briefly illustrate how debates over American strategy and force and the desirable characteristics of military operations have influenced, or will affect, the struggle over war powers in the American system.

Certainly some factors dispel the notion that armed force still could be a usable instrument in national security policy. Demographic trends and parallel changes in public values made it harder to consider sending the nation's sons and daughters into armed conflict. Moral doubts about the value of war increased during the nuclear arms race and the years spent in Vietnam and afterward. After both Korea and Vietnam, many in the military vowed that the United States must never commit itself to limited wars with such poorly defined or open-ended aims.

However, other trends eventually outweighed these constraints. Circumstances arose in several settings in which presidents believed the United States had to use force for reasons of national interest. The postwar consensus shaped around the founding of the United Nations, collective security, and international law increasingly was attacked in the United States.

Humanitarian catastrophes invited American critics and others to question some of the restrictions and processes of international law. Was it not more important for nations to do what is right for other human beings than permitting international law to determine what nations could or could not do? Is not outcome in moral and political terms more important than adherence to process? Development of military capabilities resting on information technologies, private sector contractors, and special operations presented ways of conducting operations that could limit the numbers of dead and wounded in uniform but still accomplish the objective. Chapters 5 and 6 examine how these developments contribute to a president's ability to use force without Congress's consultation or approval.

Even in the wake of congressional disillusionment with U.S. operations in Iraq, the imbalance between the president and Congress seems nearly impossible to correct. Iraq and Afghanistan are the latest chapters in the debate over the role and applicability of military force in U.S. policy, but sometime in the future a president assuredly will want to use force again. It is not just the existence of a large standing military since World War II that has strengthened the president's position compared to Congress's, but rather the long-developing trend that military force is used less for traditional concepts of defense and more to advance foreign policy goals supporting national security. In the Constitution, the president's authority in foreign policy is stronger than it is in conditions of declared war and control of the military. The conduct and the very objectives of foreign policy, which seek to influence a state's conduct rather than defeat it, depend on the ability to employ military force on a limited scale if used. This trend emerged in U.S. policy during the nineteenth century; it is not a result of the Cold War. Presidents frequently have used military force in this context, and Congress has largely found itself in agreement, regardless of which party controlled either branch of government. Unless Congress finds different frameworks to deal with the challenge to its role, it will continue repeatedly to yield to presidential prerogative. Whether it has the will power to right the imbalance is uncertain. This entire study shows a pattern of congressional deference since World War II that may have become so entrenched that it is irreversible.

My own development and professional experience have played a role in this study. As a youth who grew up in the shadow of World War II, I believed, like many, an overly assertive Congress that defeated the Treaty of Versailles and passed the Neutrality Laws of the 1930s had impeded the ability of the United States to respond to the threats of fascism and National Socialism. The Vietnam War reversed that bias against Congress, replacing it with suspicion of the presidency's concentrated power. During most of the 1980s, I worked with the majority staff of the House Committee on Foreign Affairs and other staff and members on presidentially initiated military operations in Lebanon and Grenada and against Libya. Teaching a course on Congress and national security policy at the National Defense University for nearly a decade demanded closer examination of these convictions, but they have largely remained in the congressional camp.

Capitol Hill experience leaves me disturbed with judgments and biases that appear in discussions of war powers and the Constitution. There is a troubling tendency to sometimes treat one or the other side as acting from conspiratorial, almost villainous, or naïve motives. Yes, elements of those types of behavior occasionally occur. Having worked closely around politicians and both parties' staff for over a decade, including more than four years as a lobbyist for a large multinational corporation, I fully realize political actors sometimes strive for personal power and gain. So do some of their military and academic counterparts. Several founding fathers were very cognizant of this desire for power and reputation. James Madison, in particular, regarded the structure of government in the Constitution as a check on the quest for fame, the subject of a famous essay by the historian Douglass Adair.[1] However, a sizable extent of the struggle over war powers and control over the use of military force also reflects the circumstance of a particular time and the perceived threat or danger, the demands of government process, congressional deference and unwillingness to challenge the president, and a cautious stance by the federal courts on this subject in recent decades. Political ambition is only one part of the story.

Furthermore, all can justifiably question the rationale or wisdom behind certain military operations or interventions, but the discussions leading up to them usually have shown a conscientious, calculated effort to determine the best numbers and characteristics for the military force to be deployed, no matter how misinformed national leaders may appear in hindsight. Political leaders may make poor decisions, but they do not intentionally make bad ones. They know there is a price to be paid at the polls. Searching for heroes or villains in the history of war powers and military force will not offer very helpful answers as to why more power has gravitated into presidential hands at Congress's expense.

Nevertheless, the willingness to accept personal and political responsibility is a significant part of the process and decision to authorize using military force. A disturbing contemporary trend is both congressional and respective presidents' diminished accountability. Each has taken advantage of options and ways that make it harder for either side to hold the other accountable. In civil–military relations, accountability often means the ability of civilian leadership to retain control of the military and the decision to go to war. In a governmental system with separate branches, however, constituents must be assured that all branches fulfill the expectations set out in a constitution and subsequent law. If it is the legislative branch's responsibility, for example, to "approve the existence of the military," as is the case in the United States, then it should do so in as public a setting as possible. Such openness fulfills the Congress's duty to the public and the Constitution, and also reminds the president to which branch the military is ultimately accountable. Thus, when U.S. military officers testify before Congress, they must give Congress their personal professional judgments, as they have sworn an oath to uphold the Constitution and the laws of the United States.[2] This book does not examine the process of approving and supporting the military's existence, but it is clear that in terms of meeting constitutional obligations, the Congress does a better job of fulfilling that duty than it has in controlling the use of military force. Admittedly, some of the explanation is not hard to figure out. The Constitution explicitly states the Congress's role in the military's creation and support, unlike issues in using military force, where the initiative rests more in the president's hand while Congress awaits to respond. An additional contemporary reason partly examined is the complexity of military operations and the adoption of new technologies that have made it harder for civilian authorities to review and act on decisions on the use of force. Whether the military has taken this route to intentionally diminish civilian control is a serious question, but one this book explores only indirectly.[3]

Accountability also involves the citizen as well. To whom or to what body do Americans on the street, and ultimately people throughout the rest of the world, turn when they seek to identify who shoulders responsibility for using U.S. military forces overseas? On whom can those in uniform rely to ensure the strongest legal justification and authority support their deployment? From whom do they have a guarantee their actions have a clear legal basis within U.S. law, and to what extent is the military accountable to international law and the organs responsible for administering and enforcing it? To whom does the American public turn to know the dispatch of U.S. forces into harm's way and ensuing field operations comply with the U.S. Constitution and subsequent laws? Accountability is more than assigning blame or preventing illegality; rather it guarantees both a clear line of responsibility for decisions and a protective base of law to stand on that ensures public and governmental support. Without such assurances, public debates about the legitimacy or legality of military operations may develop if events turn unfavorable. Without congressional attention to the aim and conduct of operations, legal and ethical ambiguities that enable incidents like those in Abu Ghraib to happen will continue.

The simple answer to these questions is the U.S. Congress. Even though the chain of command runs all the way to the Oval Office, the authority in that chain originates from the Constitution. A restrictive condition governs a president's powers to use the military, as stated in Article II, Section 2 of the Constitution: "The President shall be Commander in Chief of the Army and Navy of the United States, and of the Militia of the several States, *when called into the actual Service of the United States*" (emphasis added). However, this stipulation clearly reflected a world when a permanent American army was small. While not defining or elaborating on the title commander-in-chief, the Constitution did so with powers for creating and paying the military, as well as deciding to declare war, all of which are matters of holding responsibility and ensuring accountability, these powers clearly rest with the Congress.

Whether it is necessary and important to worry about the expansion of presidential power in the twentieth and early twenty-first centuries is a fair question. The founders did not experience learning about events elsewhere while they actually occurred, but the delegates in Philadelphia had anticipated circumstances in which a president might have to act and not be able to gather Congress quickly. A common argument today is the rapid speed of events and consequent decisions no longer easily permit the type of deliberative process implied in the Constitution. Some even argue that Congress's power is too great and that its tendency not just to legislate, but to deliberate, procrastinate, equivocate, and pontificate can cost precious time in a period of national emergency and also divulge sensitive information. Arguments about excessive congressional interference in national security rely on claims about the unconstitutional nature of the War Powers Resolution of 1973 or decry alleged congressional micromanagement and overly intrusive control and limitations on key weapons programs. Lastly, some insist the Congress's complaints about expanded presidential power are its own fault. The Congress has hesitated or deferred to the president when it could have better protected its powers and even asserted them more.

Yet, if accountability of decision and action is to be strongly maintained, it must be Congress and the courts that do so in accordance with the Constitution. No branch should have the responsibility of policing itself and validating its own record in ensuring accountability to the citizenry, to the other branches of government, to the States, and, in some instances, to the international community. Through free speech, a free press, and elections, the Constitution also provided forms of accountability beyond the government's control. Thus, the Constitution actually recognizes a system of multiple checks to strengthen accountability, not just the triangular set existing among the three branches of government.

How to ensure the best process for accountability exists and is practiced in the area of national security is one of the questions that this book tries to examine and answer. No answer, including any of those in the conclusion, will be absolute or final. I merely hope that readers will find thoughtful suggestions, perhaps a partial answer to these questions, and encouragement to look further.

Ultimately, the answers to questions about war powers and accountability may rest beyond the confines of law, the characteristics of Congress and the presidency, or the nature of military operations. The fundamental consideration is how a society and its government define themselves in terms of national priorities and the role they wish to exercise in the international community. Those concerns significantly influence why, how, and when a government decides to turn to military force. The Constitution written in 1787 defined a purpose and mission that matched the concerns and assumptions of its time. The processes agreed on then now must operate in a world set on its own head from that of over two centuries ago. A much-feared permanent, large standing military now exists, and presidents have found ways to use that force quickly and intrusively, if needed, to protect American interests. The 9/11 attacks and proof of American vulnerability further reinforced that inclination. If we really could return to the original constitutional intentions in questions of using military force, the United States probably would have to return as well to the international environment of its founding.[4] While it may be desirable to seek to retreat from the frequency and justifications for U.S. use of military force, that is unlikely to occur. Successfully retaining the constitutional framework will demand the continued endeavor of all governmental branches and press and public attention to take the necessary steps to guarantee that accountability is alive and working.

This book tries to combine traditional scholarship and thought about the Constitution and war with some lines of inquiry and study not commonly considered by specialists on the subject. By seeing the topic in some different contexts, perhaps one may better understand not only the historical and current issues that have shaped the current status of war powers, but also future trends and technologies that will affect this issue in new ways. If in the past the course of most events has pushed in the direction of presidential power, those of the future may do so even more.

Chapter 1

Where Is Limited War in the Constitution?

The Constitution's writers would have done later generations a favor if they had elaborated their intentions in those provisions dealing with the Congress's power to declare war and the president's role as commander-in-chief. At one time or another, most politicians, writers, and lawyers have shared the frustration of the noted constitutional scholar Louis Henkin: "The web of authority they created, from fear of too much government and the need for contemporary political compromise, virtually elevated inefficiency and controversy to the plane of principle, especially in foreign relations."[1] The Constitution provides extensive instructions about raising and supporting the military but fewer definitions or at least some clarification on when or how it can be used. What did the delegates mean exactly by "war," "declare," and "commander-in-chief"? What did their reference to "letters of marque and reprisal" signify? There are few definitive answers. Aside from one fairly short debate in the Constitutional Convention itself, several *Federalist Papers,* debates in some of the state conventions to ratify the Constitution, and the writings and correspondence of several major participants, we have little explicit guidance.

The prospect of war worried the authors of the Constitution and their contemporaries. In one way the new republic was a product of the recurring violent struggle affecting the balance of power between Great Britain and France.[2] John Jay believed the hostility of the international environment was a certainty; in *The Federalist, No. 4,* he wrote, "Nations in general will make war whenever they have a prospect of getting any thing by it, nay . . . absolute monarchs will often make war when their nations are to get nothing by it, but for purposes and objects merely personal . . ."[3]

Two hundred and twenty years later it is easy to overlook the fear that war also could originate from the lack of unity among the thirteen states. Reflecting on the causes of war, Jay observed in the previous *Federalist* essay, "Whether so many *just* causes of war are likely to be given by *United* America, as by disunited America." If a "united America" provided the "fewest, then it will follow that . . . the Union tends most to preserve the people in a state of peace with other nations."[4] In fact, a major part of the debate about the Congress, president, and war powers would result from the federal assumption of the power to declare and make war from that of the states. The new nation had to become unified enough so that outside actors, whether European powers or Native Americans, could not divide it. That meant a lot of things besides being able to muster a standing army. It included the power to collect revenue as well as to rein in the abilities of the individual states in several areas, such as agreements with foreign countries or issuing letters of marque and reprisal. If fragmented, what had been the United States could end up like Europe, a collection of warring states.[5] In 1781, as the Revolution headed towards its climax at Yorktown, Jay's fellow New Yorker, Alexander Hamilton, had worried that Congress had left so many war-related functions, such as finance and recruiting, to the states; he strongly urged congressional assumption of these powers in the new Articles of Confederation. Hamilton remained dissatisfied afterward with the Articles, fearing that the states still retained too much power and would ignore their responsibilities in national defense. Congress remained too weak in national security and related matters of wellbeing.[6] Writing six years later, Jay reminded his readers of the consequences of disunity that Hamilton had so feared, and warned that without a national government the states would not be capable collectively of raising enough money and personnel to defend themselves. They could succumb to "specious promises" from foreign powers and compromise their immediate neighbors' safety.[7] The need for national unity and a stronger government, especially a more effective Congress, was critical for national survival.

Whether the United States might be able to shun war in favor of a different way of interaction with foreign states was a matter on which the founders disagreed. Some French Enlightenment writers had questioned Thomas Hobbes's premise that war reflected man's natural state. One factor promoting greater harmony among people and nations was commerce, which was expanding globally during the eighteenth century and building mutually beneficial relationships. Writers such as the Abbe de Saint-Pierre, Montesquieu, and the German philosopher Immanuel Kant stressed that commerce's growth would diminish the prospects of war.[8] Contemporary political and economic works by Thomas Paine and Adam Smith restated that argument. In *The Federalist, No. 4,* Jay had suggested commerce could contribute to a greater unity among the American states, while acknowledging increased American competition in other markets might lead to war.[9] James Monroe forcefully advocated the calming effects of commerce in the Virginia Constitution ratification convention.[10]

However, others sharply disagreed with this entire premise. Hamilton firmly objected in *The Federalist, No. 6* and *No. 7.*[11] He warned that commerce in fact could be a cause or objective of war; the United States could not rely on commerce and harmony for its security. Possessing a military and potentially using force was a reality the United States had to accept. The darker side of human nature ensured war's survival. Thus, the Framers initiated debate that has lasted to the present day—a clash between "realists" who thought distrust, avarice, and the quest of states for power and security would forever govern the international system, and reformers, be they "liberals," "internationalists," or "idealists" who believed their values and efforts could change the rules of the international system.

Much of the debate in the Constitutional Convention or surrounding it actually focused on the question of whether the United States needed a standing military, especially an army, rather than on any prospective use of force. However, some insight emerges from these discussions on the subject of when and how the United States might have to use force. The requirement for a military originated from three realities—the threat to commerce from foreign rivals and pirates, protection as well as action against the Native American tribes, and the danger of actual foreign attack. Here was a mixture of defense against external threats combined with internal dangers and military actions supporting territorial expansion. Today's debates about congressional or presidential control of war powers revolve around scenarios between the United States and foreign actors, partly reflecting the influence of scholars who traditionally have treated actions in North America against Indians and foreign states as part of westward expansion rather than measures supporting foreign policy.[12] However, the founders also drew similar distinctions. War against foreign governments or non-state actors, such as pirates, most influenced the founders' deliberations over war powers.

Just how large a military force, navy or army, the new country needed was unclear. Due to cost, fear of military intervention in internal politics, and a desire to avoid foreign wars, most founders hoped to keep the mili-

tary as small as possible. In 1785 while serving as secretary for foreign affairs under the Articles of Confederation, John Jay initially believed arming American merchant vessels would be an adequate interim solution to
deter the Barbary pirates from Algiers, who had declared war against the
United States. The Americans had hoped Great Britain would agree to continue to protect their commerce on the high seas as part of the 1783 treaty
ending the Revolution, but, not surprisingly, London was not so interested
in offering the Royal Navy's services to a country that had just established
its independence from the empire. Jay's refusal to regard war with Algiers
as "a great evil" probably made it easier for the Americans to believe that
arming merchant ships might be a sufficient response. In the long run, he
hoped—vainly—that the individual states would provide Congress with
enough money to build a genuine navy. This experience no doubt reinforced
Jay's belief that national security depended on a stronger form of government than the Articles provided.[13] Jay's assessment of the threat and the
proposed initial response also suggested this was a war that did not justify
a full-scale response even if the United States had had that capability. Nevertheless, without any really effective military instrument, America ultimately had little choice but to resume negotiations with the Barbary states
and pay ransom for captured Americans.[14]

In 1781, while serving as governor of Virginia, Thomas Jefferson believed that his country would need a navy to deal with threats. It is interesting that Jefferson saw this navy as a military instrument for fighting opponents in a limited fashion. Writing in *The Notes on the State of Virginia,*
Jefferson observed a young nation had no need to waste its resources "in
efforts of mutual destruction." Jefferson trusted the beneficial value of
commerce in shaping the relationship between the emerging United States
and the world around it; he even hypothesized to avoid war "it might be
better for us to abandon the ocean altogether." Yet he was enough of a realist to know this was neither possible nor desirable. Americans could prevent half of future wars by avoiding their "own follies," but must prepare
themselves as much as possible for the other half. An army "would be useless for offence, and not the best or safest instrument of defence. For either
of these purposes, the sea is the field on which we should meet a European
enemy." To try to match the strength of the major European navies would
be a "wicked waste of the energies of our countrymen." As he estimated
the situation, the country needed a navy strong enough "to prevent insults
from those nations of Europe which are weak on the sea." More importantly, Jefferson believed there were factors that even made the "stronger

ones weak to us." In short, because of other interests and obligations no European power would commit the entirety of its military might against the new United States. "They can attack us by detachment only; and it will suffice to make ourselves equal to what they may detach." Consequently, all the United States needed was a "small naval force," which would be "sufficient."[15]

Here was an insightful commentary on one very influential American's thinking about war. Jefferson did not wrestle with the question as to what branch of government should decide to authorize this use of force. Nor did he confront the question of whether such conflicts should be "declared." Clearly, he anticipated most American actions would be defensive, thus diminishing the importance of the question of who decides to use force. Yet, when he acknowledged that force could be used for either purpose, it is obvious Jefferson entertained the possibility of Americans being on the offense. Full-scale war aimed at defeating an enemy was out of question; the means were to be limited but strong enough to protect American interests on the high seas.

Writing at almost the same time in *The Continentalist No. 6,* Hamilton largely concurred with Jefferson's assessment of the role of a navy. "As commercial people," Hamilton wrote, "maritime power must be a primary object of our attention." If the American states remained united, they would face fewer prospects of foreign wars, but Hamilton that worried internal enemies, such as the tribes on the frontier, made it impossible to "dispense with the usual precautions for our interior security."[16] In short, there would be need for military capabilities on land as well.

After the Constitution was ratified, Jefferson and his fellow Virginian James Madison retreated from their support for the navy due to its possible cost, its potential to draw the United States into war, and its support among Federalists like Hamilton. With Congress instead of the states now controlling licenses for privateers, in 1790 Madison argued that privateers would be an adequate instrument for disrupting European shipping and asserting American interests.[17] As described in Chapter 2, Jefferson became increasingly suspicious of the navy as an instrument of military force, but that prejudice probably never equaled that he held against a standing army.

The debate over whether the United States would need a standing army or could rely on the state militias can illuminate some contemporary thinking about how the American republic might use military force. In 1783, Congress received a series of papers from General George Washington, several of his senior generals, and Secretary at War Benjamin Lincoln recommending a national standing army and arguing that the nation could not depend on state militias, which essentially could not fulfill any function, especially protecting the frontier. Whether the threat came from Indian tribes, continued activity by British agents and their allies in contested parts, such as the Ohio River area, or potential attacks from British or Spanish colonies near the newly independent states, a professional army— Washington ultimately recommended one of 2,600 men—was necessary. While he and his supporters intended much of this army's activity to be defensive, as Richard Kohn has observed in his study of U.S. military policy during this period, they obviously expected that the United States would engage in expansionist acts that could bring the nation into conflict with various tribes as well as foreign governments holding competing claims on the desired territory.[18]

Another dimension of the argument over a standing military revolved around the potential need to use it to pressure the thirteen states or maintain domestic order. James Madison, who later became highly critical of a standing army or navy as Hamilton and the Federalists advocated, was more positive while serving in the Continental Congress. Madison thought that giving Congress control over the military might enable Congress to use it to coerce reluctant states to contribute to the national defense. The navy, in fact, might prove more useful than the army because of the states' geographical positions, which rendered the states vulnerable to pressure from just two or three ships.[19] To twenty-first century sensibilities, the prospect of using the military instrument in this way seems alien, but it certainly was not the under the Articles of Confederation, when states still could refuse congressional requests for troops, equipment, or money.

The serious weakness of the Articles system painfully emerged in 1786 with Shay's Rebellion. Angered by their debts, a lack of currency, and increased taxes, western Massachusetts farmers rebelled and took over several counties' courthouses and legal systems. Congress had no real power to intervene, and when it did, it had to justify raising troops with claims referring to an Indian conflict. State constitutions also could make raising troops difficult. Faced with unrest on its own frontier, in raising troops to deal with the situation Pennsylvania directly violated its own constitution, which prohibited a standing army during periods of peace.[20] Hamilton feared both the consequences of citizens' identity with their state governments rather than the national government when faced with requests for troops, as well as the implications of those states that violated their own constitutions when responding to internal disturbance. The best solution to avoid this was a standing army placed under the control of a majority vote in Congress.[21] Hamilton did not believe a large army was necessary, as he explained to his New York readers in *The Federalist Papers, No. 8.* Seeing parallels between the fledgling United States and the relative security of its former British master from invasion, Hamilton claimed that America would not need a large standing army, showing how Britain relied on the strength of its navy. Clearly, the British example was the one to emulate, for Hamilton explained that it was in nations where the danger of invasion seemed recurrent that armies became ascendant in internal affairs: "The continual necessity for their services enhances the importance of the soldier, and proportionately degrades the condition of the citizen. The military state becomes elevated above the civil."[22]

However, Hamilton thought it was vital to establish a system that would not enable the United States to be drawn easily into war, due to the fear many had because of the prospect of a standing army and national rather than state control over decisions to raise armies, authorize use of force, or declare war. One obvious consequence of this fear was the decision in Philadelphia to separate the power of the purse from that of the sword—the retention of budget authority in the Congress. No president can easily go to war without money. An intense suspicion of concentrated power in the hands of the executive branch drove much of this concern. In a famous exchange of letters in 1793 between "Helvidius" (James Madison) and "Pacificus" (Alexander Hamilton), Madison wrote:

> War is in fact the true nurse of executive aggrandizement. In war, a physical force is to be created; and it is the executive will, which is to direct it. In war, the public treasures are to be unlocked; and it is the executive hand which is to dispense them. In war, the honours and emoluments of office are to be multiplied; and it is the executive patronage under which they are to be enjoyed. It is in war, finally, that laurels are to be gathered; and it is the executive brow they are to encircle. . . . Hence it has grown into an axiom that the executive is the department of power most distinguished by its propensity to war; hence it is the practice of all states, in proportion as they are free, to disarm this propensity of its influence.[23]

Proponents of a standing army and the need to use force could dismiss the suspicion of both war and executive power in Madison's statement as alarmist. Although Hamilton regarded using military force as a positive for a state and government because it showed resolve and created respect among both enemies and friends, others, such as Washington's first secretary of war, Henry Knox, viewed it as "moral bankruptcy," in Richard Kohn's characterization, especially when used against Indian tribes.[24] In Hamilton's eyes, the rhetorically violent opposition to a standing army of Antifederalists like Virginia's Patrick Henry would have left the United States almost defenseless.[25] To prevent dangerous executive or presidential adventurism and ensure public acceptance of the need to use force, Hamilton argued that the United States must place this decision in the hands of a majority in Congress, whose elected members would decide whether using force was offensive or defense, justified or unjustified. Congress would check or restrain the "executive aggrandizement" that Madison so feared during both the constitutional debates and well afterward.[26] If only Congress could declare war, the Constitution appeared to offer adequate obstacles to easy political access to the battlefield.

Speaking to the ratifying convention of his home state, Pennsylvania, James Wilson, who had been a delegate in Philadelphia, explained the advantages of congressional control: "This system will not hurry us into war; it is calculated to guard against it. It will not be the power of a single man, or a single body of men to involve us in such distress."[27] By stressing that not just a "single body of men" would make the decision, Wilson was pointing out both the Senate and House of Representatives would vote on the declaration, not just the Senate, which had received power to ratify treaties.

Dividing control over the military between the president and Congress also created a better system of accountability. As Richard Kohn has written, "Accountability to the legislature implies accountability to the people, forcing public discussion and scrutiny of defense policy, budgets, and cases of military mistakes or malfeasance."[28] Consequently, any decision to go to war would result not only from checks and balances between these two governmental branches but also public scrutiny and participation in the debate between both the president and the Congress and the proponents and opponents of war. If such a process worked to its best, it would ensure the greatest extent of public and congressional support for the decision to go to war.

For some, like Madison, the proposed congressional control over the purse—the budget supporting the military and war—was especially important. Given his distrust of a standing force, Madison nonetheless believed if potential adversaries knew that Congress had the authority "to raise and support an army," this could deter their attack. As he stated in the Virginia convention to ratify the Constitution, "If sir, Congress be not invested with this power, any powerful nation . . . will be invited by our weakness to attack us . . ."[29]

Others were not as confident that knowledge of Congress's power to raise and support a military would be an adequate defense. Writing as "Aristides," Alexander Contee Hanson, a judge on the Maryland General Court, warned, "There can be no perfect security, without both a land force, and naval armament." Congress would have to make the decision about the situation facing the United States, Hanson argued, and it would "be expedient to declare war, at the instant in which the danger shall be conceived, or order that it may be lawful to prepare for only a just defense."[30] Hanson focused on a critical point discussed later in this chapter—namely, raising an army apparently had to await a declaration of war. That seemed reckless, even at the slower pace of eighteenth-century wars. The United States had to be able to prepare for its defense before war could occur. The same problem greatly disturbed a North Carolina attorney, James Iredell, who as "Marcus," wrote in the *Norfolk and Portsmouth Journal* in neighboring Virginia, "The absurdity of or being prohibited from preparing to resist an invasion till after it actually [took] place" was "so glaring that no man can consider it for a moment without being struck with astonishment." Furthermore, as Iredell noted, declarations of war had "been for some time out of fashion."[31]

Critics observed that the world did not operate as cleanly as some thought it should. Wars were not always declared. Governments could not risk leaving themselves defenseless in the absence of a declaration. More problematic, as Aristides had told his Maryland readers, Congress possibly could even declare war at an early stage based on its assessment of another's intention. While one does not want to infer too much from Hanson's words, this nevertheless resembled an early resort to war that later generations would regard as preventive or preemptive. Obviously, the Constitution's treatment of war was somewhat ambiguous. To the founders, war was not just a violent phenomenon that occurred among states, it was a political condition that invited possible aggrandizement of power by the president. In a sense efforts to define just what is meant by war began during the first years of the history of the United States and have continued to the present day.

War and Imperfect War

By its very nature limited war is a challenge to accountability, which in its purest, most enforceable form depends on the *process* of Congress declaring war. While Congress has never declared limited *war,*[32] Congress repeatedly has authorized a limited *use of force.* Later in Chapter 2, I will examine a critical example, the quasi-war against France that began in 1798—a conflict in which the president purposely relied on authorization rather than a declaration to avoid major political unrest at home.[33] More recently, in some cases presidents have argued the extent of military activity was not a use of force and therefore there was no need even for congressional review and approval. The desire to avoid political controversy both in Congress and the public seems to have been an important motive, as was the case with the unilateral action by President Clinton in Haiti and against Serbia.[34]

A declaration of war clarifies a government's action and both foreign and domestic perceptions of it. The public learns the reasons for such action by announcing the declaration and stating military goals, a breadth of knowledge that may not occur in instances of undeclared war, particularly if limited in both scale and objective. In the early 1980s, Edward Keynes aptly titled his book on this subject *Undeclared War: Twilight Zone of Constitutional Power.*[35] "Twilight zone" probably invoked in readers' minds a state of light between night and day as well as a famous American television series depicting characters' responses to a disorienting, alien, and sometimes psychologically frightening environment. Keynes suggested that Congress and the president had entered an area of war and warfare not explicitly addressed in the Constitution. The types of conflict occurring in the last half of the twentieth century blurred the distinctions between war and peace and defensive and offensive war. Keynes concluded the president's powers were strongest in cases of actual or imminent attack, where he would not need congressional authorization for military operations. However, in situations in which the United States was initiating action by taking the offensive, the president needed congressional authorization or a declaration of war.

To try to clarify this debate over the Constitution and war powers, we must ask how the writers would have defined "war." Assuredly the authors held their individual opinions on what might constitute war. All had lived through the American Revolution; many had experienced it firsthand. Nevertheless, notions of war in 1789 might differ from those arising from the Civil War, World War II, Vietnam, or the peacekeeping missions of the

1990s. Chapter 4 focuses on the characteristics of limited war and its conduct in U.S. history to better understand its implications for the struggle between congressional and presidential control over the use of force, but a short discussion here must examine the meanings of the word that might have influenced thinking in Philadelphia.

Although most Western thinkers in the eighteenth century regarded war as part of the climate between states and rulers, that same century had witnessed an effort to limit the scale of war and not repeat the mass destruction of the seventeenth century's religious wars. Many eighteenth-century European wars were not as "horrific" as those in the centuries preceding or following it. With some Enlightenment thinkers challenging the universal, inevitable nature of war, the desire to limit war and to regulate it expanded and found a following among several influential writers. International agreements to outlaw war or to restrict its conduct were still in the future, but even from the time of the early seventeenth century and thus into the eighteenth, a body of thought was emerging on how to govern war and make its destruction more specific and limited.[36]

Some delegates might have read partly or completely pertinent works on war by Cicero, Hugo Grotius, Samuel Pufendorf, and J.J. Burlamaqui, among others. From their readings and experience, Michael Ramsey argues that the founders assigned war a "broad reading."[37] They would have agreed with Grotius's acknowledgement to Cicero in the beginning of the former's *On the Law of War and Peace* war is "a contending by force."[38] Samuel Johnson's definition described the situational nature of war as "the exercise of violence under sovereign command." One of Johnson's British contemporaries, Richard Lee, defined it as "the state or situation of those . . . who dispute by force of arms."[39] These definitions were not that different from Carl von Clausewitz's later one that dominates modern military and strategic literature: "War is thus an act of force to compel our enemy to do our will."[40]

Some writers distinguished among different types of war. J.J. Burlamaqui's *The Principles of Political Law,* published in 1748 and translated into English in 1752, summarized some of these definitions and also provided additional explanations.[41] He described just and unjust wars and then discriminated between defensive and offensive wars, describing the latter as wars that "are made to constrain others to give us our due . . . or to obtain satisfaction for a damage unjustly done us, and to force them to give caution for the future." He advised his readers not to conclude from these definitions all defensive wars could be just or offensive ones unjust. Another differentiation among wars relied on Grotius's earlier categories: public, private, and mixed wars. Public wars were "made on both sides by the authority of the civil power." Private war occurred among "private persons . . . without any public authority," and, not surprisingly, mixed war was when one side acted under civil power and the other privately.[42]

Burlamaqui then added elaborations that come closer to the question of undeclared and limited war. He wrote of "solemn" war as war "made by the authority of the sovereign" and accompanied with certain formalities, such as a formal declaration. War that was not "solemn" was "made either without a formal declaration, or against mere private persons." Finally, he differentiated between "perfect" and "imperfect" war. The former "entirely interrupt[s] the tranquility of the state, and lays a foundation for all possible acts of hostility." Imperfect war "does not entirely interrupt the peace, but only in certain particulars, the public tranquility being in other respects undisturbed." Burlamaqui added that this form of war "is generally called reprisals," which he described as "acts of hostility, which sovereigns exercise against each other, or, with their consent, their subjects by seizing the persons or effects of the subjects of a foreign commonwealth . . . with a view to obtain security, and to recover our right, and in case of refusal, to do justice to ourselves, without any other interruption of the public tranquility."[43]

Burlamaqui clearly distinguished between both declared and undeclared wars as well as wars fought on an intentionally limited scale to avoid disrupting "public tranquility." To a modern ear, the latter would mean no mobilization of the population or the economy in ways that would affect the daily lives of the population. The reference under "perfect" war to "all possible acts of hostility" suggested, as well, that "imperfect" wars or reprisals intentionally avoided certain forms of response or action Burlamaqui's contemporaries would have regarded as unconditional and entailing very destructive measures. The objective of "imperfect" war would not be an enemy's total defeat, but rather securing satisfaction and changing the adversary's behavior to conform to the other party's desires.

It is impossible to know how well the delegates knew Burlamaqui's writings, but in a 1782 appeals court ruling (*Miller v. The Ship Resolution*) during the Articles of Confederation period, and later in 1800 in a decision by the Supreme Court in *Bas v. Tingy,* Burlamaqui's influence seems to be noticeable. The latter case resulted from an undeclared war fought between France and the United States from 1798 to 1801. Angered by the American declaration of neutrality in 1793, when the French republic entered into war against Great Britain, and then by trade and political concessions the United

States made to Great Britain in Jay's Treaty in 1795, France ordered the seizure of American merchant ships. In 1799, an American naval vessel, the *Ganges,* captured a former American merchant ship that had been seized by a French privateer. On getting to port, Tingy, the captain of the *Ganges,* sought compensation for his restoration of the American vessel from its original owners.[44] Meanwhile, efforts to find a diplomatic solution to the Franco-American struggle were still unsuccessful.[45] The Court had to rule on the legality of the hostilities. Tingy argued that he should receive compensation, for which a declaration of war was unnecessary; his opponents argued that Congress had not declared war and they owed Tingy nothing.[46]

Commenting on the character of the war, Justice Bushrod Washington used Burlamaqui's concepts of solemn and perfect war and imperfect war that was not solemn. Washington thought the latter a "public war, because it is an external contention by force between some of the members of the two nations, authorized by the legitimate powers. It is a war between the two nations, though all the members are not authorized to commit hostilities such as in a solemn war, where the government restrain[s] the general power." Also writing in the ruling was Justice William Paterson, who commented, "An imperfect war, or a war, as to certain objects, and to a certain extent exists between the two nations; and this modified warfare is authorized by the congressional authority of our country. . . . As far as [C]ongress tolerated and authorized the war our part, so far may we proceed in hostile operations. It is a maritime war, a war at sea as to certain purposes." The third justice, Samuel Chase, stated, "Congress is empowered to declare a general war, or [C]ongress may wage a limited war; limited in place, in objects, and in time." The Court's opinion had recognized the right of Congress to authorize an undeclared war. A war of a "certain extent" was clearly "limited," the term Justice Chase chose to use.[47]

Declared and Undeclared War

This ruling, made only thirteen years after the Constitution was written, illustrates the court's understanding of some categories of war discussed in past or contemporary literature. Justice Paterson also had been a delegate in Philadelphia. Yet the Constitution does not differentiate among types of war to try to guide future presidents and congresses. The absence of any definition or elaboration on war has been a factor in arguments on congressional and presidential authority. If war had an all-inclusive meaning when used in the words "declare war," it would seem all wars would require a declaration, but it is hard to think the delegates really expected this. The authors of the Constitution possibly thought this was an issue that would have to be resolved case by case, dependent on both Congress's and the president's assessment of each situation and its requirements. No definition or criterion could resolve everything. The actual process of deciding whether to declare war would be a logical setting for that assessment to occur, including the possibility and utility of waging the conflict in an undeclared status. Some scholars, such as John Yoo, have argued that the Congress's actual power rested not in declaring war, but in its control over appropriations for the military and spending to support war-related operations; if so, the establishment of a permanent standing military like today's would seriously undermine that power.[48]

On August 6, 1787, the Committee on Detail at the Constitutional Convention circulated among the delegates a draft containing this wording about war: "The legislature of the United States shall have the power . . . [t]o make war. . . ."[49] This proposal was met with unease. The Articles of Confederation essentially had retained executive authority in the hands of the Congress, including the authority to "make" war. The conclusions drawn from that experiment did not encourage the continuation of this practice.[50] Nevertheless, the delegates disagreed over the extent to which the Congress should be removed from the responsibility of making war. Charles Pinckney of South Carolina thought the deliberative process of the Congress as a whole "too slow," and favored giving this power to the Senate, which would have more expertise in foreign affairs. His fellow South Carolinian, Pierce Butler, argued that the president should have the sole authority in making war. This stunned Elbridge Gerry of Massachusetts, who answered that "he never expected to hear in a republic a motion to empower the Executive alone to declare war."[51] Gerry and James Madison proposed to drop the word "make" in favor of "declare." Many scholars have seen this as both a decision both to remove Congress from the war-making task but also to define more clearly Congress's actual role. In 1986, Francis D. Wormuth and Edwin B. Firmage wrote, "The meaning of the motion was clear. The power to initiate war was left to Congress, with the reservation that the President need not await authorization from Congress to repel a sudden attack on the United States."[52] A decade later, David Gray Adler commented, "The debate and the vote on the war clause make it clear that Congress alone possesses the authority to initiate war."[53] More recent scholars on this subject, such as Peter Irons, have agreed with these views.[54]

Yet is the answer that definitive? What exactly did "declare" mean in the late eighteenth century? Did it require that every time a president wanted to use force, whether in a "perfect" or "imperfect" war, a declaration of war must follow? The preceding discussion suggests that was not the understanding or conviction of many contemporaries. Is declaration synonymous with Congress's formal authorization for the president to use military force, or could the Congress exercise authorization from other powers given to it in the Constitution, such as appropriations? The final words in the Constitution were not as clear on this as some, like Yoo, claim. However, the lack of clarity does not automatically mean that the Congress did not have any foundation to exercise a role in deciding to use military force aside from declaring war. After all, the Constitution rested on strong suspicions of both concentrated power in the presidency and a fear of standing militaries. What is left unstated in the Constitution about war powers is intriguing. A fundamental difficulty is that it was already a challenge by the end of the eighteenth century to reconcile the Constitution's words and goals with political practices and realities of the time in relation to war and warfare.

Proponents of the view that the word "declare" places power in the hands of Congress emphasize the word actually meant to "commence" hostilities.[55] This interpretation relies on the distinction between defensive and offensive war that was already recognized in the literature on war. Offensive war would require a congressional declaration. Madison's recommendation to substitute "declare" for "make" was an extra precaution because it would prevent the possibility a president could not act in the nation's defense against an attack until given authority by the Congress. The president did have the authority to engage in defensive war for the nation's welfare. Whether an authorization or declaration was necessary in case of war following an attack remained an open question. Nor did the Constitution provide any answer to the concern that Congress might declare war at an earlier stage in order to begin raising a military. However, the clear assumption in the Constitution is that initiating war requires congressional approval.

Yet it is worth looking at some of the other prevalent notions about the meaning of "declare" that might have influenced the discussion in Philadelphia. In interpreting the delegates' intentions, scholars inevitably draw attention to the strong influence of William Blackstone's *Commentaries on the Laws of England,* a work well-known to many delegates. Hamilton, for example, cited Blackstone in *The Federalist No. 69,* when he explains the differences between the powers of the British king and the president in war.[56] As will be seen later, those like John Yoo who defend executive primacy rely especially on Blackstone, but here the focus is also on the meaning of declaring war. This great British legal commentator believed that a declaration of war was not necessary before starting hostilities against another nation. Yoo relies greatly on this quotation from Blackstone to support his case for executive power.

> [The reason] [Yoo's wording] why according to the law of nations a denunciation of war ought always to precede the actual commencement of hostilities, is not so much that the enemy may be put upon his guard (which is matter of magnanimity than right), but that it may be certainly clear that the war is not undertaken by private persons, but by the will of the whole community; whose right of willing is in this case transferred to the supreme magistrate by the fundamental laws of society. So that, in order to make a war *completely effectual,* it is necessary with us in England that it be *publicly declared and duly proclaimed* by the king's Authority; and, then, all parts of both the contending nations, from the Highest to the lowest, are bound by it [Yoo's emphasis].[57]

Yoo's key point is that such a declaration distinguishes "between limited hostilities and an all-out conflict," and moreover adds, that "in the eighteenth century . . . a 'declared' war was only the ultimate state in a gradually ascending scale of hostilities between nations."[58]

Yoo's point about the distinctions in categories of war is important, even though he ultimately cites it to support the case for stronger presidential control over using force. Hamilton, for example, would not have been comfortable with the direction of Yoo's remarks. A congressional decision to use force or declare war was a check on executive power that Hamilton realized needed to be in place to ensure public confidence and trust in the decision itself. When contrasting presidential power in war with that of the king, Hamilton stressed the American president would be only the commander-in-chief, but not responsible for declaring war or raising a military force—powers the British monarch held.[59]

In this interpretation, a declaration was more an announcement or notification, not unlike the Declaration of Independence, intended for an audience both domestic and foreign. As the early nineteenth-century American legal scholar Chancellor James Kent wrote, a declaration of war "should announce to the people at home, their new relations and duties growing out of a state of war, and which should equally apprize neutral nations of the fact, to enable them to conform their conduct to the rights belonging to the new state of things. . . . Such an official act operates from its date to legalize all hostile acts . . ."[60]

Kent's reference to legalizing all subsequent actions by a declaration echoed a fundamental concern that John Jay raised in *The Federalist, No. 4,* who wrote that "[a]bsolute monarchs will often make war when their nations are to get nothing by it." A king's ability to "engage in wars not sanctified by justice, or the voice and interests of his people" troubled Jay. Without elaborating more about a declaration in his essay, Jay went on to explain how the American system was intended to make war more difficult by avoiding a monarch's arbitrary whims.[61] Nearly a half-century later, one of the republic's most prominent legal commentators, Supreme Court Justice Joseph Story, wrote:

> It should therefore be difficult in a republic to declare war; but not to make peace. The representatives of the people are to lay the taxes to support a war, and therefore have a right to be consulted, as to its propriety and necessity. The executive is to carry it on, and therefore should be consulted, as to its time, and the ways and means of making it effective.[62]

Even though Story's dissent in a case, *Brown v. United States* (1814), defending a president's power to seize property without a declaration of war marked him among some legal scholars and jurists as a defender of strong executive power, the importance of a declaration as a means to prevent making resort to war easy remained central to Story's concerns.[63] What a president could do about property without a declaration of war is a seriously related issue; however, defense of presidential action there does not inevitably cancel out the case for a declaration or authorization before force is used. Elsewhere in his *Commentaries,* Story wrote, "The power to declare war is exclusive in [C]ongress." More importantly, he drew a pivotal distinction when he stated this power existed for "general" or "partial" hostilities: "The power to declare war may be exercised by congress, not only by authorizing general hostilities, in which case the general laws of war apply to our situation; or by partial hostilities, in which case the laws of war, so far as they actually apply to our situation, are to be observed."[64] Story then cites the war of 1812 as an example of "general" hostilities and the "qualified war of 1798 with France" as an example of "partial" hostilities, "which was regulated by divers (*sic*) acts of congress, and of course was confined to the limits prescribed by those acts."[65]

If Kent and particularly Story are correct, the president and Congress should deliberate beforehand and determine whether an actual declaration would be in the national interest. Yet if there was no declaration would the United States have no other recourse or options to permit or justify using military force? Clearly not. Obviously, one choice was to authorize a more limited form of conflict that would resemble "imperfect war" and not require a formal change in relations between both the adversary and potentially neutral governments, as would be the case with a declared war.

By the eighteenth century, there was a pattern of undeclared wars or wars declared only after hostilities had begun. George Washington had played a role in bringing about one of them in 1754 when French soldiers and Native American allies defeated forces that he commanded. The subsequent disastrous 1755 expedition led by General Edward Braddock destroyed near Fort Duquesne occurred during a period of undeclared hostilities. Great Britain's actual declaration that formally began the Seven Years War did not occur until 1756.[66] It is interesting to consider this British reaction to more irregular forces—some today would call them non-state actors (even though many of the tribes fighting were allied with either the French or British). It was state-to-state conflict that customarily generated formal declarations of war and not tribes, pirates, or others.

Just how greatly the matter of undeclared wars entered into discussions in Philadelphia is hard to say. Many conversations inside the convention and elsewhere never became part of the historical record, so we must rely on contemporary discussions and correspondence to suggest some of the views that probably influenced the debate on the use of force. It is difficult to imagine the delegates in Philadelphia conceived their thoughts about war and declarations only in terms of law and not through recent, sometimes personal, experience. However, we must be careful when interpreting some parts of the debate or other contemporary statements and not automatically read our current concerns into the historical record. Some writers have strongly noted Alexander Hamilton's observation in *The Federalist, No. 25,* "the ceremony of a formal denunciation of war has of late fallen into disuse."[67] The remark is accurate as far as it goes, but Hamilton was not trying to make a case for undeclared war, rather emphasizing the importance of retaining enough of a standing army to defend the country against an external or internal attack and not depend on a subsequent raising of troops or state militias.[68]

Another argument about a declaration of war is it can be by either word or action. This draws upon John Locke's *Second Treatise on Civil Government,* in which he writes, "The *State of War* is a state of Enmity and Destruction; And therefore declaring by Word or Action, not a passionate and hasty, but a sedate settled Design, upon another Mans Life, *puts him in a State of War*" (emphasis added by Michael Ramsey).[69] Citing Locke on war powers is problematic because he believed there were five powers—executive, legislative, judicial, federative, and prerogative—not the three defined in the Constitution. Federative power involved making war, forming alliances, and finding peace; these rested in the hands of the executive. Prerogative was a separate power allowing the executive to act in the interests of public welfare without the approval of law and in select circumstances even against the law. American writers such as Hamilton were thinking of federative powers when they described the executive.[70] Yet Hamilton ultimately rejected this concept of federative or executive power (as he called it) because he believed that Congress had to authorize using force.

Locke's claim that a declaration of war can be word or action produces two problems. First, given the military weakness of the United States at the time of the Convention and the opposition to offensive war most delegates shared, it is hard to imagine they really would have perceived or defined a declaration in terms of taking an action like a surprise attack. Doing so would have been the form of offensive war that most wanted to avoid. An unannounced attack certainly would be a president's use of Locke's federative power—possibly even one of prerogative. A declaration had to follow deliberation and then be announced. Also, only modest resources were available to use against any major power like Great Britain, France, or Spain, the three sources of foreign concern, and a declaration, surprise or not, at this time in history almost assuredly would have resulted in defeat. Second, any Congress independently legislating a declaration would have to convince the president to execute it.[71] Here, one has to be thankful for the separation of powers and the authority of the president. In 1896, President Grover Cleveland actually told a congressional delegation that he would not pursue war against Spain over Cuba even if Congress declared war (admittedly not as a surprise attack), thus raising an interesting question of how he could veto it.[72] A more recent example would have occurred in 1998 if the Congress had made binding the provision expressing its sentiments in favor of overthrowing Saddam Hussein's government in Iraq, arguably tantamount to a declaration of war. Would President Clinton have executed the declaration by attacking Iraq?

In modern vocabulary, a declared war automatically means combat. In his study on the origins, meanings, and uses of declarations of war, Brien Hallett has cautioned against this, rightly warning that this is a disturbing distortion which may overshadow possible advantages that might be obtained by a declaration.[73] A declaration can exist as a statement or signal without inevitable recourse to armed combat. Hallett makes this case to support an argument for a much stronger congressional understanding and use of declarations as a measure or step in foreign policy. To find war declared against oneself is a strong signal. The fact declared war need not always occur hand in hand with violence is illustrated by the formal states of war that remain after cease-fires and surrenders. The formal state of war between Japan and the United States, for example, did not end until 1950.

One final factor that possibly influenced deliberations in Philadelphia, but would not have been expressed in today's leaders' and strategists' vocabulary, is that wars sometimes are fought more for foreign policy aims than for national survival and defense. Without question, any appreciation of the differences between "perfect" and "imperfect" war probably depended somewhat on understanding this dimension of war. Late eighteenth-century thinkers realized that war is a means, that is, an instrument of policy used to accomplish political objectives. Absolute wars usually sought complete victory over the adversary, but the reference to "imperfect war" implied that war goals, like the means used, might be more limited. As wars moved increasingly into the realm of foreign policy rather than defense, the questions of both whether to declare war and Congress's and the president's roles in doing so became murkier and harder to resolve.[74] The first twenty years of history following the Constitution quickly illustrated these problems, and they were glaringly evident after the beginning of the Cold War.

War and the Foundations of Congressional Power

Depending on the "declare war" provision of Article 1, Section 8, no one can ever totally solve the dispute between Congress and the president in the areas of undeclared war, unless we argue that all conflicts should be declared, a solution that while clean and absolute does not look any more realistic today than it did in 1787. The foundations for congressional power in the area of undeclared or limited war arguably descend more from a comprehensive consideration of all powers given to Congress related to the military and defense as well as a consideration of contemporary remarks about the nature and role of war for the new nation.

However, following the words "declare war," the same article and section gave Congress one additional authority, letters of marque and reprisal. This provision is part of the clause dealing with the declaration of war, thus indicating that the Framers regarded the issuance of these letters to be a war-related issue. Viewed from the perspective of delegates such as Hamilton, Jay, and others who feared that a weak, fragmented United States actually could make war a greater likelihood, including letters of marque and reprisal in this clause would have been easy to understand. The constitutional solution was a matter of national control over actions related to war. Before the Constitution, issuance of these letters rested with the states, which meant Massachusetts or New York could put on the high seas a licensed private agent whose actions might pull the United States into war. This was not acceptable for a new nation so sensitive to the dangerous consequences of war for its survival. While still serving as secretary of state in 1793, Jefferson stressed the power of reprisal, the act of retaliation to compensate for an injury, rested with Congress, not the president. Five years later, Alexander Hamilton argued the authority to allow reprisals required the approval of Congress, as it was the branch responsible for declaring war.[75]

The authority to "grant Letters of Marque and Reprisal" has drawn renewed interest in recent years; several scholars argue that it is proof the Congress has the power to authorize limited wars—that, in fact, it must do so. The highly respected Library of Congress expert on these issues, Louis Fisher, claims, "The phrase 'letters of marque and reprisal' came to refer to any use of force short of a declared war."[76] Hallett argues that from the sixteenth through the early nineteenth centuries, "the law of war stipulated that 'solemnly perfect' 'big' wars were to be initiated with a formal declaration of war, whereas 'unsolemn imperfect' 'little' wars—what are known as 'armed conflicts'—were to be initiated by issuing letters of marque and reprisal."[77] Jules Lobel, perhaps the leading exponent of this view in recent years states, "the Marque and Reprisal Clause . . . provides Congress the power to authorize a broad spectrum of armed hostilities not rising to the level of declared war."[78]

Within the legal literature the Framers would likely have known, judgments and interpretations supported such a view. The seventeenth-century legal scholar Sir Matthew Hale had written, "Special kinds of wars are that which we usually call marque and reprisal." Blackstone's *Commentaries* provided further support by noting granting letters of marque and reprisal "is nearly related to . . . making war; this being indeed only an incomplete state of hostilities."[79]

It was possibly from these sources and others Elbridge Gerry proposed adding after the phrase "declare war" language "concerning letters of marque, which he thought not included in the power of war."[80] Twenty years later, Thomas Jefferson observed in a letter, "General letters of marque and reprisal" could be more desirable "because on a repeal of their edicts by the belligerent, a revocation of the letters of marque restores peace without the delay, difficulties and ceremonies of a treaty."[81]

Story's *Commentaries* also discussed letters of marque and reprisal as forms of limited military force.

> [I]t is often a measure of peace, to prevent the necessity of a resort to war. Thus, individuals of a nation sometimes suffer from the depredations of foreign potentates; and yet it may not be deemed either expedient or necessary to redress such grievances by a general declaration of war. . . . In this case the letters of marque and reprisal (words used as synonymous, the latter (reprisal) signifying, a taking in return, the former (letters of marque) . . . passing . . . frontiers in order to [execute] such taking) contain an authority to seize the bodies or goods of the subjects of the offending state, wherever they may be found. . . . This power of reprisal seems indeed to be a dictate almost of nature itself, and is nearly related to, and plainly derived from that of making war. It is only an incomplete state of hostilities, and often ultimately leads to a formal denunciation of war.[82]

In short, these measures could be part of a phased set of measures moving from a state of peace to a formal state of war, but as Story noted they also could serve as a recourse to avoid an actual declaration of war while still obtaining compensation for losses.

The evidence certainly suggests that the Philadelphia delegates regarded letters of marque and reprisal as something not covered in the "declare war" clause. Gerry's recommendation implied that the "declare war" clause did not seem to cover forms of hostilities or actions that were not "perfect" war. Yet it may be a stretch to conclude letters of marque and reprisal were *the* constitutional foundation that unquestionably granted Congress the right and power to authorize all limited conflicts. To claim so assumes most would have understood the use of letters of marque and reprisal in this way and no other, and there is no evidence of such unanimity. That claim rests on inference rather than explanation.

It is certain that all would have understood letters of marque and reprisal as a distinctly maritime measure. With the beginning of the American Revolution, American shipping became vulnerable to British attacks on the high seas. Merchants and shippers suffered noticeable losses, and such letters served as a type of reprisal by which aggrieved parties could obtain a license to conduct privateering, seize vessels and the property thereon, and bring them into port for compensation. A special court determined the amount to be paid.[83]

There are important factors to consider here, especially in light of the present renewed interest in this constitutional provision. Those who received letters were private parties seeking monetary compensation and, they hoped, profit. Privateers financed their own operations; they did not receive government money. Given the navy's small size during the Revolution and even after the Convention, it would be understandable some might regard privateers as supplementing American naval strength. Their actual military value was debatable.[84] Also, after two hundred years, we are justified in asking whether Congress intended privately funded parties to fight limited wars, which is why scholars' interest in letters of marque and reprisal clause has revived in relation to the roles of private military firms and covert operations supported by the United States but funded by other sources.[85] However, our focus is on whether this clause is *the* basis for Congress's authority over limited wars and other forms of low-intensity operations, or whether the same clause is just one specific authority.

Given some of the historical context, it is hard not to see this clause as confined to a specific type of measure rather than as the foundation for an entire set of powers related to congressional control of limited war. Yet letters or marque and reprisal were a form of limited or "imperfect" war, although not representative of all of it.[86] What the Constitution suggests rather than literally states is important here. With a form of limited military operations well known to most delegates, the Constitution gives control over their authorization to Congress and not the president, and certainly not state governments. The applicability of such letters today is compromised by the fact that most nations renounced privateering in the Declaration of Paris in 1856; although interestingly, the United States held out because it regarded the practice as a way of reinforcing its naval capabilities. Only a century ago, in The Hague Convention, did the United States officially renounce privateering and letters of marque and reprisal.[87]

Why does the Constitution fail to elaborate other examples of such limited measures? Doing so would have greatly helped later generations in understanding the delegates' view of war and the extent of their efforts to place it under congressional control. Clearly, many examples of limited war and other operations involving land forces then existed to which reference to letters of marque and reprisal would have made no sense.[88] On the other hand, we must acknowledge, as the United States had no effective standing army at the time to fight a foreign power, naval action was about the only form of hostilities the Framers could envision being used against a foreign power. They addressed one form of limited war they did know and thereby set a precedent or basis for Congress's implied power to act in other forms of limited war.

Concentrating too much on the letters of marque and reprisal clause in Article I, Section 8, results in underestimating the importance of other powers there and elsewhere in the Constitution that have the cumulative effect of establishing Congress's role in the use of military force. A case for congressional authorization of limited conflict emerges not just from a variety of powers in the Constitution, but also from a set of arguments after the Convention that favored the Congress and several decisions related to military force that Congress made during the first decades of U.S. history. Chapter 2 suggests that the latter may have been more critical than the Constitution itself in defining and creating a role for Congress in limited war.

Listing congressional powers related to national defense and the uses of military force in the Constitution is admittedly an elementary exercise, but it also should remind us of just how far and wide Congress can arguably reach. In Article I, Section 8, alone, aside from the power to "declare war" and "grant Letters of Marque and Reprisal," the delegates also considered the following powers:

> Provide for the common Defence;
>
> Define and punish Piracies and Felonies committed on the high Seas, and Offenses against the Law of Nations;
>
> Make Rules concerning Captures on Land and Water;
>
> Raise and support Armies, but no Appropriation of Money to that Use shall be for a longer Term than two Years;
>
> Provide and maintain a Navy;
>
> Make Rules for the Government and Regulation of the land and naval Forces;
>
> Provide for calling for the Militia to execute the Laws of the Union, suppress Insurrections and repel Invasions;

Provide for organizing, arming, and disciplining, the Militia, and for governing such Part of them as may be employed in the Service of the United States,

Make all Laws which shall be necessary and proper for carrying into Execution the foregoing Powers, and all other Powers *vested* by this Constitution in the Government of the United States, or in any Department or Officer thereof [author's emphasis].

Section 9 contains the following clauses related to the military or national defense:

The Privilege of the Writ of Habeas Corpus shall not be suspended, unless when in Cases of Rebellion or Invasion the public Safety may require it,

No Money shall be drawn from the Treasury, but in Consequence of Appropriations Made by Law.

In Section 10, these clauses have implications for Congress and war:

No State shall enter into any Treaty, Alliance, or Confederation; grant Letters of Marque and Reprisal,

No State shall, without the Consent of Congress, . . . keep Troops, or Ships of War in time of Peace, enter into any Agreement or Compact with another State, for with a foreign Power, or engage in War, unless actually invaded, or In such imminent Danger as will not admit of delay.

Yet Article II, which actually identifies the powers of the president, gives to or implies important powers for Congress. Both of the following are from Section 1; the first sentence begins the section.

The executive Power shall be vested in a President of the United States of America.

[In the oath of office, a president swears to:] ". . . faithfully execute the Office of President of the United States, and will to the best of my ability, preserve, protect and defend the Constitution of the United States."

Although Section 2 pivotally defines presidential power, within that section is an arguable link to congressional power:

> The President shall be Commander in Chief the Army and Navy of the United States, and of the Militia of the United States.

Furthermore, this same section provides a power with unintended possible implications for using military force:

> He shall have Power, by and with the Advice and Consent of the Senate, to make Treaties, provided two thirds of the Senators present concur.[89]

Section 3 formally states a relationship with Congress:

> He shall from time to time give to the Congress Information of the State of the Union, and recommend to their Consideration such Measures as he shall judge necessary and expedient.

However, this section also declares that the president:

> Shall nominate, and by and with the Advice and Consent of the Senate, shall appoint Ambassadors,

> Shall take care that the Laws be faithfully executed.

Many of these provisions deal not only with the military, foreign affairs, and national defense capabilities, but also create a structured system of accountability to both the public and Congress. Consider, for example, the words in the oath of office to "preserve, protect and defend the Constitution," or the implications of the first sentence in Article II, Section I. The oath subordinates the president to the Constitution and its contents. While presidents do have a foundation to argue for strong executive authority in national security from constitutional language as well as arguments external to it, the bulk of the document clearly points the president in the direction of the Congress. The word "vest" in that first sentence in Section 1 underlines the presence of an authority to which the president, as well as the Congress, is accountable. Of course, that authority rests with the people of the United States. However, it is the members of Congress who are the people's elected representatives, and through the powers given to the Congress to legislate both funding and actions in areas related to national defense, such as raising armies, Congress enables the president to serve and defend the nation's interests. The latter are among those powers vested by the people and Congress in him, and sometimes reviewed by the courts and revised based on their constitutionality.

Two decisive stipulations in Article I, Section 8 link the president inseparably to Congress: no money can be removed from the Federal Treasury unless it has been appropriated and military appropriations must be no longer than two years. Those restrictions require a president and his officials to discuss with the Congress the provision of funds and to explain and justify the necessity for providing another two-year cycle of money for the military. Congress should examine the specific requirements requiring the continuation of military funding. Yet when Congress agrees that the funding is necessary for whatever purposes, is that decision the exercise of a war power? Yoo has argued that in the eighteenth century the appropriating power was the war power, as was evident from the British record. Prime ministers and their kings could not legally fight unfunded wars.[90] Yoo is correct in pointing out that a Parliament unhappy with the course of a war could halt funding but, while such votes may have served as a decisive act for the British government, was that to be the modus operandi of the American system as well? The answer is "no."

Through its exercise of the power of the purse, the Congress would retain a way of preventing easy entrance into war and maintaining a stricter accountability and control over future presidents' actions. The Framers hoped not to have to shoulder the role and behavior of traditional actors in the international system of that day. They strongly wanted to avoid continual wars that demanded cycles of funding and congressional votes. Armies would be raised as needed. The large standing military of today and the role of the United States as the dominant world and military power would have been a distressing shock rather than a fulfilled vision. The appropriation powers given Congress were to restrain not just a president but any impulse that could push the United States into the treacherous world of European power politics. If the appropriations process contained the war power, that process customarily would deter the desire to use force rather than to approve it. Given the suspicion with which much of late eighteenth-century America viewed the outside world, perhaps this obstacle-filled path to authorization and American involvement in foreign matters was how the Constitution intended war powers to work. Yet even in its historical context, it seems almost unnecessarily restrictive in stacking the odds against the use of force. If authorization was tied more to the "declare war" or "letters of marque and reprisal" clauses, that approval would be more a calculated act based on objectives sought, relations with other countries, and, yes, the availability of resources. The object of the appropriations power was as much to ensure that Congress closely supervised a president and the use of the instruments of war and to hold a president accountable for decisions made during the course of the conflict.[91]

The word "authorization" appears nowhere in the Constitution. Today "authorization" means to provide the authority by law to create or establish something. Nevertheless, the concept of authorization runs throughout the powers assigned to Congress. When the Constitution refers to raising an army, it is essentially authorizing its creation and existence. This is clear. Nevertheless, we cannot find any words for war powers explicitly providing the power to act or use military force in undeclared wars in such an authorization, unless so stated. By doing so, the Congress could both authorize using force as well as begin the process providing the actual funding to support the operation.[92] Military officers and civilian officials who work on the defense budget have told the author that requests reflect either existing or anticipated operational needs. The language in the budget request contains no statutory authority to use the funded equipment; instead, the Congress is supposed to authorize only the existence or continuation of the military force and various weapons and support systems. The fundamental question is money and not prior authorization for a use of force. Presidents can put such requests in a budget request, or more often in a supplemental request for money, as has been the case with the Iraq and Afghanistan wars, but these are not included in the legislation seeking congressional approval for use of force. Obviously, if Congress provides the money, it supports the well-being of deployed forces, but that is not an automatic equivalent to authorizing the use of force.[93]

However, in other places in the Constitution, the authorization of limited force is arguably is more explicit. Besides the clause related to letters of marque and reprisal another provision gives Congress the power "[t]o define and punish Piracies and Felonies committed on the high Seas, and Offences against the Law of Nations." In *The Federalist, No. 42,* James Madison explains the purpose here was to elevate these powers to the Federal level and not leave them with the states, where they had resided during the Articles of Confederation. The meaning of "punishment" seems to extend only to the creation of courts to deal with "Piracies and Felonies." Yet Madison adds an interesting observation when he notes the Articles contained "no provision for the case of offences against the law of nations," which would "consequently leave it in the power of any indiscreet member to embroil the confederacy with foreign nations."[94] Again, the dominant concern is independent state government action or possibly the acts of private individuals, but Madison's remark about embroiling the nation seems to imply if any recourse or measures are taken, Congress must undertake, meaning authorize, them.

Another implicit authorization, in this case for wars on American soil, seems to rest in the clause empowering Congress to call "forth the Militia to execute the Laws of the Union, suppress Insurrections and repel invasions." Calling forth or summoning the militia is for domestic order and defense. The Congress must do this, and it is hard to imagine the Framers would have provided this power for domestic purposes and defense only and not for cases when offensive measures were needed to support that defense. Yet to allow any president such independent authority over the militia would have significantly strengthened that office's war powers at the cost of the Congress's. Of course, the expectation was that the fledgling United States would have no need for such offensive actions unless attacked or provoked. Even if the president assumed the position of commander-in-chief, that would occur only after congressional mobilization.

Finding the power of authorization and the lines of accountability for undeclared or limited war in these clauses admittedly requires a degree of liberal interpretation. We can infer the power from these provisions but not assert it in an ironclad claim. Perhaps the strongest foundation for the claim of war powers in the Constitution, as many scholars have seen, actually comes in the immediate aftermath of the Constitutional Convention, in this case from Hamilton's discussion of the president's powers during war in *The Federalist No. 69*. Writing of the president's role as commander-in-chief, Hamilton states:

> In this respect his authority would be nominally the same with that of the King of Great Britain, but in substance much inferior to it. It would amount to nothing more than the supreme command and direction of the military and naval forces, as first General and Admiral of the confederacy: while that of the British King extends to the *declaring* of war and to the *raising* and *regulating* of fleets and armies; all of which by the Constitution under consideration would appertain to the Legislature [Hamilton's emphasis].[95]

Here seems to be the answer. Case closed. Hamilton leaves no doubt as to who has the authority to declare war. It is Congress, and the president shoulders the task of commander-in-chief only after Congress has declared war. Congress's control over "raising" and "regulating" armies and fleets seemingly guarantees that no president can wage imperfect war without Congress's authorization. Yet, keep in mind that Hamilton is the same defender of the Constitution who had observed that declaring war had fallen somewhat out of use by this time.[96] No one, as seen earlier, seemed to argue that every war must be declared, but Hamilton's argument in *The Federalist, No. 69* really suggests that Congress has a permanent role in the decision to use military force. Given all the powers over the military enumerated in Article I, Section 8, it is hard not to think otherwise. Congress would not raise and fund military forces and then just let a president do whatever he desired with them. The constitutional process implies that the president must justify raising or the continuing existence of military forces. Doing so requires consulting with the Congress.

Just what consultation means has become an endless debate between Congress and each president. No standard explanatory language can be inserted into legislation when the Congress states that the president shall consult with Congress. The gamut of understandings runs from just being informed, through the president's active solicitation of opinions and perspective from Congress before making a decision, to full collaboration in the decision. This author's own experience with members of Congress indicated that most definitions fell in the middle category, which would require learning about a tentative or proposed decision with enough advance notice to give the president timely analysis of congressional views and the best options that would both serve the national interest and enjoy the broadest congressional and public support. In so doing, Congress also secures the president's accountability to it and U.S. statutes, and simultaneously fulfills its duty of actions that enable the public to hold Congress accountable as the collective decision-making body.

Some have decried the role of consultation in the arena of war powers because Congress has allowed consultation to become a substitute for a more active role in determining the best course and then authorizing the use of military force.[97] It is not an unfair criticism, particularly in instances where the Congress subsequently has failed to give an authorization or has delayed acting to the point where it has served little constitutional or political value. Nevertheless, consultation is a critical prerequisite in the path to decide to use military force. Imagine a scenario—seemingly remote in today's environment—of worry about unchecked presidential power, when Congress would provide the authority to use military force without consulting with the president. This would return the United States to the situation that the Framers feared due to their experience with the Articles of Confederation, when the Congress managed both foreign and defense policies. No president should be put in a position in which he or she would have to act. It would be as unilateral an act as a presidential order to use military force without consulting at all with Congress. Consultation is a critical part of the process to decide to use military force, and it is there to make both the Congress and president accountable for their actions.

After consultation, though, the Congress should provide or deny the appropriate legal authority to a president to use military force. Being involved in the formulation of a policy before its actual adoption implies accepting partial responsibility for the decision that results. Failure to do so is a failure of accountability to the citizens of the United States and arguably even many in the international community who depend and rely on the United States to show leadership and demonstrate the political values of its system of government. The Constitution says nothing about the latter form of accountability, but its meaning surely prevails throughout that document. Voting for or against an authorization to use force is the ultimate act of responsibility.

The President and War

To understand the congressional perspective on war powers, it is critical, though, to consider just briefly some of the salient arguments made to support a president when ordering use of force without a declaration or authorization from Congress. The longest-standing argument for this position is that of executive prerogative, which John Locke supported in his *Second Treatise on Civil Government.* Certainly many delegates would have known Locke's position. In foreign affairs, which Locke placed under the authority of federative power related to "the security and interest of the public without," he argued that it was important not "to bind the prince in every instance to 'antecedent, standing, positive laws.'" Since no one could foresee all the crises or scenarios that could unfold in the world arena, "the executive must be permitted to do 'many things . . . which the laws do not prescribe.'" In fact, as Donald Robinson has noted, "prerogative includes the power to act" *against* law.[98] Certainly, here was a case for independent presidential authority and action in circumstances of war when it appeared an "imperfect" course without congressional approval was better than a "solemn" or "perfect" one.

Locke's line of argument did not find strong support in Philadelphia. The phrase in Article II, Section 3, stating the president "shall take Care that the Laws be faithfully executed" seeks to exclude the option that presidents in critical times could bypass or act against the law.[99] However, an activist president arguably could turn elsewhere in the Constitution to find language offering discretion over whether to report to Congress or seek legislation providing necessary authority, which might come from the same sentence that today is affiliated with the required State of the Union address, which instructs the president to "recommend to their [Congress's] consideration such Measures as he shall judge necessary and expedient." From today's vantage point, the word "expedient" is particularly prominent, as it clearly connotes presidential choice in informing and involving the Congress. The founders did not identify how much discretion the president should have in deciding to inform the Congress. Yet they thought a president needs an independent ability to determine which laws he needs from Congress. The relationship between president and congress requires accountability, but here it is a more open-ended accountability.

Cases will occur in which presidents must act and use force without congressional approval. If so, what should be done? For Congress to allow such an act to go unchallenged creates a troubling precedent for expanded presidential power. When presidents so act they must be willing to return to Congress to seek the authorization, which, if provided, will only enhance the strength and constitutional basis of the earlier action. In April 1861, faced with the growing rebellion in parts of the South, President Abraham Lincoln initiated several sweeping measures without congressional approval—declaration of a blockade, raising troops, and suspension of the writ of habeas corpus, to mention just a few. Congress had not been in session in April, and Lincoln thought he had to act, but, as he explained to Congress on July 4, 1861, he thought he had done so within the bounds of the Constitution and law. His speech sought retroactive congressional approval of these actions, which Congress gave on August 5, 1861. In March 1863, in a 5–4 decision in the *Prize Cases,* the Supreme Court ruled in Lincoln's favor.[100] Nearly ninety years later (1952), President Harry S. Truman seized control of the steel industry to avert a strike and continue production of materiel to support the Korean war. Truman exercised his power vigorously and made no effort to seek subsequent congressional approval. He apparently had tested the idea with Supreme Court Chief Justice Fred Vinson, but it was not Vinson's place to lend the president a favorable interpretation of his authority. That authority had to come from Congress, and in June 1952, by a 6–3 decision, the Court ruled that the seizure had been unconstitutional.[101] When a president must act without congressional approval, Lincoln's path is the way to take, not Truman's.

One frequently cited source of presidential authority is the argument that the president is the sole voice of the United States in foreign policy. Some important figures in the early history of the United States seemed to suggest this broad authority.[102] For example, Secretary of State Thomas Jefferson wrote in 1790:

> The transaction of business with foreign nations is Executive altogether. It belongs then to the head of that department, *except* as such portions of it as are submitted to the Senate. *Exceptions* are to be construed strictly. The Constitution itself indeed has taken care to circumscribe this one within very strict limit; for it gives the *nomination* of the foreign Agent to the President, the *appointment* to him and the Senate jointly, the *commissioning* to the President.[103]

Yet Jefferson's comments did not represent a philosophy about the whole scope of presidential authority. In fact, he had written this about a dispute over diplomatic nominations and appointments. President Washington had asked whether the Senate could reject both a nominee as well as the level or grade of the U.S. mission that he desired. Jefferson answered that the latter was interference in a president's ability to conduct relations with other countries.[104]

A similar overreach in interpretation rests on remarks by then Representative John Marshall, a Virginia Federalist, in the House in 1800, when he stated in an often-quoted speech just before his nomination to the Supreme Court, "The President is sole organ of the nation in its external relations, and its sole representative with foreign nations."[105] Again, it is important to consider the context of Marshall's observation. He intended to make the point that the president was the voice for the United States in foreign relations. Marshall's concern was a question of communication between governments and nations, not a statement providing any foundation for presidential prerogative to bypass Congress when the Constitution or law required otherwise, including the constitutional requirement on Congress and the use of force.[106]

Nevertheless, supporters of a strong presidential role in war powers have relied on Marshall's words again and again. Modern presidents do often use armed force for foreign policy purposes. Since it is often impossible to separate the use of military force from foreign policy, a president must decide whether it is necessary to turn to Congress for approval to use military force for limited or defined political purposes rather than to fight a full-scale war.[107] Within a decade of the ratification of the Constitution, national leaders were struggling with the question of the appropriate procedure to authorize military force for foreign policy goals in relation to France. Today this question is at the heart of the struggle over war powers in the Constitution and the use of force.

The Constitutional Convention gave little guidance on how expansive or limited a commander-in-chief's powers were. Interestingly, during the First Congress in August 1789, Representative Thomas Tudor Tucker of South Carolina proposed a constitutional amendment to limit the president's power by dropping the title commander-in-chief in favor of granting the president "'power to direct (agreeable to law) the operations' of the armed forces," which would have required the president to conduct "operations ordered by Congress in the manner specified by Congress." The resolution did not even make it into a committee.[108] It is curious why this effort to make the president so accountable to Congress failed. Perhaps it reflected a congressional conviction that not every form of military force or activity required authorization. In what remains the best study of the war powers issues in this period, Abraham Sofaer briefly examines the fate of an initiative by a Georgia representative that same year to seek an authorization for the president to raise troops to protect his state from Creek Indians. James Madison persuaded the sponsor to drop this motion since troops already had been raised for frontier defense, and the president could assign troops where he thought they were most needed.[109] Obviously, Madison thought that the Congress should not be managing military operations and that presidents must have some flexibility in making decisions about the nation's security without congressional intrusion. Yet where the line existed between presidential discretion and congressional authorization remained invisible.[110]

The title commander-in-chief itself provided little reason for a president at this time to think he could act independently of the Congress. Created just before the English Civil War, it was clear the title's powers were contingent on actions and instructions from Parliament. On June 12, 1775, the Continental Congress designated George Washington "General and Commander in chief, of the army of the United Colonies" in terms that made it clear he was to respond to orders from the Congress and report to it as well. After the Revolution and their later experiences with the Articles of Confederation, the Framers had little desire to leave Congress in such sweeping control of the military. However, when deliberating the actual command of the military, the title remained provisional. James Madison noted that Hamilton's proposal to create the position of commander-in chief specified "to have direction of war when authorized or begun," which implied the title's authority stopped when the situation generating its designation did. Whether the president should directly command troops was a matter of some concern with critics, like Patrick Henry, who feared such power in a president's hands could be a step towards military dictatorship.[111]

The Constitution provides little guidance for either president or Congress about using limited force or implementing "imperfect war." Some of this ambiguity was probably intentional, a realistic hesitation to tie future generations to contemporary definitions or notions. Then too, the Framers recognized the existing reality and their vision for the United States. The delegates had crafted a document for a nation that would not wage offensive wars fought by standing armies led by a princely commander-in-chief, as did European monarchs, an objective that runs throughout the discussions surrounding the Constitution. Scholars who disagree over congressional or presidential control over using force nonetheless agree on the strategic objective set by the founders of the United States. The founders did not elaborate on governmental powers to conduct war because they did not think they needed to. As the first years of the new nation's history unfolded, the Americans hoped they could interact with Europe and the rest of the world primarily through commerce. The nation faced several internal problems, it needed to solve questions about national growth and expansion, and it did not want to spend its limited resources on military means. Within a decade of the Philadelphia convention, though, circumstances had emerged requiring the first generation of leaders to rethink some of their assumptions and hopes about the United States and the outside world.

Chapter 2

Imperfect War and the Fragile Balance

In late June 1793, under the name "Pacificus," Alexander Hamilton wrote that the president in "certain cases" could "determine the condition of the Nation, though it may consequentially affect the proper or improper exercise of the Power of the legislature to declare war." Hamilton added, "The Executive indeed cannot control the exercise of that power. . . ." He wrote, "The Legislature is free to perform its own duties according to its own sense of them—though the Executive in the exercise of its constitutional powers, may establish an antecedent state of things which ought to weigh in the legislative actions." Reflecting on how the Constitution's authors had divided the executive power to prevent it from being unchecked, he nonetheless added, "There results, in reference to it, a *concurrent* authority."[1]

Republican France declared war against Great Britain and Holland on February 1, 1793, setting into motion events that generated Hamilton's essay. President George Washington and his cabinet had to decide whether the nation's Revolutionary War alliance with France obligated it to assist a government that was now a republic, not a monarchy, and also an arguable aggressor. After consulting with his cabinet, Washington issued a proclamation of neutrality on April 22. Both before the proclamation and right after it, an argument occurred over its constitutionality. If only Congress could declare war, some, like Thomas Jefferson, argued such a proclamation could be issued only after congressional action. Deciding not to go to war was as much a decision as going to war. Taking up Jefferson's argument, his fellow Virginian James Madison, writing as "Helvidius," acknowledged that a president had the responsibility to keep the nation at peace until Congress decided otherwise. But a presidential proclamation, Madison argued, was going too far; it was unconstitutional.[2]

Hamilton's reference to "an antecedent state of things," in which the president might use force without prior authorization from Congress, identified a challenge that repeatedly has tested the Constitution. Situations might well occur when, due to circumstances and urgency, a president would need to decide for the sake of the nation's welfare to use force before turning to Congress. Hamilton rested his case on the vesting of executive powers in the executive branch and a duty to maintain peace until a declaration of war, but he had openly suggested the possibility of dispatching military force that Congress subsequently would have to approve or override. Nevertheless, Hamilton in no way suggested that a president could use force without any consultation and action from Congress at some stage: "[T]he right of the Legislature to declare war includes the right of judging whether the Nation be under obligations to make War or not." But at the same time "it will not follow that the Executive is in any case excluded from a single right of Judgment. . . ." Hamilton realized that prior presidential use of force could influence what Congress might do or not; the "antecedent state" could "weigh" or shape a congressional decision. It almost assuredly would increase the likelihood Congress would concur with the president's actions and decrease any possibility of overriding them.[3]

The next century would show how seriously presidents and congresses would follow the text of the Constitution. By the War of 1812, the historical record had validated Congress's role in authorizing military force in limited or undeclared wars. Equally important, presidents during this time agreed with this interpretation of the Constitution. Although in some instances presidents initiated military measures before formal congressional action, they did not base these actions on any inherent power to do so, and they subsequently involved Congress in the continuation of the policy and the use of military force. Nevertheless, a contradictory pattern of presidential behavior asserting a more independent control over some forms of armed or military force also had begun to appear. A practice of using private or covert agents emerged, disagreements developed over how far a president could go in a defensive war without turning it into an offensive one, and arguments arose for claims that a president could use military force without congressional consent in order to conform to the law of nations. Also, there were repeated reprisals against countries or parties who had violated U.S. citizens' rights, especially by the navy, without congressional authorization. When the Mexican War began in 1846, the United States was acting through a perspective of presidential power that believed the president was better qualified than any other elected representatives to act on behalf of the entire nation, including decisions to use force.

Congress Secures Its Role in Authorizing Limited Force

The requirement for limited military actions against either Indians or foreign governments quickly faced the new U.S. government, and it was here that Congress first defined its role. Indian tribes' raids and anticipated problems in the Old Northwest moved President Washington to press for authorization to increase the size of the army inherited from the Articles of Confederation and renew his authority to call out the militia to deal with the problem. During the first half of 1790, Congress took a series of steps to raise troops from the state militias and create a small number of regular forces.[4] While not a declaration of war—Congress never formally declared war against any Native American tribe—Congress's action provided authority to use force against these particular tribes.

Yet it was in the arena of war with foreign nations or their agents where the debate about using force and limits on presidential control over it had focused. Continued problems with Great Britain, the split with republican France, and the costly nuisance of Algerian pirates fueled a debate in late 1793 and 1794 over the need to create a defensive capability. Some thought privateers might be a way of dealing with the pirates, but the fear of an army and tyranny and the reality of costs made most of this discussion just talk, aside from a provision in 1794 to fund construction of four warships to deal with the Algerian pirates. War on a large scale was out of the question. As secretary of the treasury, Hamilton believed the populace would sacrifice only for a defensive war. To deal with Britain, he thought the United States could resort to war only as a last resort, but interestingly he listed reprisals before war, thus indicating the middle course of a limited war on the high seas might be pursued first. Two years later he suggested privateers would be effective at disrupting British trade.[5]

The Quasi-War against France in 1798–1800 became a major illustration of this approach to limited war for two reasons. Besides establishing the fact that the United States intentionally could choose to fight an undeclared war, it also recognized a constitutional place for Congress's role in the absence of a formal declaration of war. The conflict's origins had rested in the Franco-American Alliance during the American Revolution and the French Revolution a decade later. When Republican France entered war against other European powers, particularly its archenemy Great Britain, France thought that the United States was obliged to come to its aid based on the terms of the alliance. President Washington's declaration of neutrality angered the French, as did America's continued trade with France's European enemies. The French capture of over three hundred American ships on the high seas was extremely damaging to both American exports as well as American vessels' ability to carry foreign goods from one port to another. Diplomatic efforts to resolve the crisis went nowhere.[6]

To stop French attacks on and seizure of American vessels, the United States purposely chose the path of limited, undeclared war, due to concerns about American capabilities to wage a larger war, fear of harsh French retribution, and alarm about the divisiveness of the issue in the United States, as Americans seemed to move into pro-British or pro-French camps. Some Federalists wanted to declare war against France, but other key Federalists, like Hamilton, no longer in the cabinet, opposed it. He thought the Federalist majority in Congress was too small; instead, he a favored "a mitigated hostility" that would not preclude chances for a negotiated settlement. If war came, it would result from a French decision to escalate it to a higher level. Hamilton favored arming merchant vessels, building twenty sloops, and completing three frigates. He seems to have feared the prospect of major French retaliation if the United States overstepped by declaring war. Perhaps more than any contemporary he understood the extent of mass mobilization of resources and manpower undertaken by France as it moved to a more total form of war.[7]

At different times, Adams and Hamilton seemed to think that France might declare war, or conditions perhaps had come to the point where a declaration was necessary. After learning the French foreign minister, Talleyrand (Charles Maurice de Talleyrand-Périgord), had sought a bribe from the American delegation before meeting with them, and also learning that France would seize all neutral vessels containing British goods, Adams drafted a message for a declaration, but then withdrew it. Adams arguably thought that it was too great a risk, both domestically as well as diplomatically, to pursue. He largely regarded the conflict as a naval one, and as most of the preparatory measures discussed above had been taken, it does not seem that he wanted to expand its scope. Some scholars, like Alexander DeConde, think Adams believed he needed to wait for more serious French actions that would unite the American public. That said, Adams never requested a declaration, and those Federalists who wanted authorization of more aggressive and offensive measures against France failed to get a majority in Congress in July 1798. For Adams, the conflict remained a "half-war."[8]

President Adams consistently demonstrated a strong respect for Congress's role in decisions related to any form of force, although it would be a distortion to suggest he was thoroughly deferential to Congress. Taking advantage of the expiration of a 1794 act prohibiting the arming of merchant vessels, in 1797 Adams issued such an order, basing it on the right to use force against pirates, cautiously adding in a letter that this order did not apply to vessels engaged in commerce in the West Indies or with Europe.[9] After the collapse of negotiations with France, Adams and some in Congress, as noted, considered an actual declaration. From May through July 1798, several congressional acts empowered the president to order the navy to seize French armed vessels operating along the U.S. coast or to give commissions to private citizens to arm vessels and capture French ships or to recapture vessels taken by the French. These actions, combined with a treaty signed in September 1800 that formally ended the Franco–American alliance from the American Revolution, ended the hostilities.[10]

In many ways Adams's "half-war" had been the type of limited war most envisioned by the founders and recognized in the Constitution—a maritime war also involving use of the letters of marque and reprisal clause. As discussed in Chapter 1, a claims case from this war, *Bas v. Tingy,* provided a basis for the Supreme Court to recognize the legality of a limited or undeclared war. In 1801 in another claims case, *Talbot v. Seeman,* the recently installed Chief Justice John Marshall affirmed both the place of limited war and a role for Congress in decisions about the use of limited force.

> The whole powers of war being, by the constitution of the United States, vested in congress, the acts of that body can alone be resorted to as our guides in his enquiry. It is not denied, nor in the course of the argument has it been denied, that congress may authorize general hostilities, in which case the general laws of war apply to our situation; or partial hostilities, in which case the laws of war, so far as they actually apply to our situation, must be noticed.[11]

Congress's role in authorizing limited war was now more firmly established than it had been in the Constitution. After President Thomas Jefferson entered the White House, events would occur that both reinforced and challenged Congress's role in imperfect war.

For more than a century the Barbary pirates along the northern shore of Africa from modern Morocco to Libya had been one of the most vexing problems for commerce in the western Mediterranean before they became an issue for American commerce.[12] By the time that George Washington entered office, the four Barbary states—Morocco, Tripoli, Algiers, and Tunis —recurrently threatened war against any country that did not pay tribute or money for hostages. The Washington and Adams administrations had tried negotiating with them, paid tribute, and even built warships to give to them, but with no lasting success. Peace treaties with Morocco and Tunis did not last, and the pirates working from these states continued to seize American vessels, declare the crews slaves, and demand increasingly higher payments for their release.[13]

On taking office Thomas Jefferson had hoped to eliminate the little U.S. Navy, but the continued attacks on shipping, topped off by Algeria's impressment of the U.S. frigate *George Washington,* was too much for the new president to bear, who interestingly had consistently opposed tribute and ransom. Jefferson ordered a squadron of three cruisers and a tender to the Mediterranean to protect American commerce. Specifically, these ships' commanders were ordered to determine the Barbary states' stance toward the United States, and if any one of them was at war with the United States, the U.S. commander could attack and sink that state's shipping. Jefferson regarded this action as a measure not to defeat the Barbary states, but rather a limited, measured act to change their behavior to what he regarded as the international norm.[14] Subsequently, Jefferson turned to Congress in December 1801 to obtain its authority to protect American shipping in the Atlantic and Mediterranean and act against vessels controlled by Tripoli, which had attacked American shipping. Louis Fisher points out that Jefferson in fact ultimately turned to Congress ten times for various authorities to use force against the Barbary pirates.[15] Jefferson also considered a declaration of war, but his secretary of the treasury, Albert Gallatin, argued against it. While pointing out that the president could not create a state of war, Gallatin added that war could result from either act of Congress or aggression by another nation. Tripoli in this case seemed to solve the question by announcing it was at war against the United States. Jefferson's personal view on Congress's role was perhaps more colorfully expressed years later in another letter to Gallatin when he observed, "[That a] body containing 100 lawyers in it, should direct the measures of a war is, I fear, impossible."[16]

Whether the president needed a declaration of war or even an authorization to use military force against the pirates irritated his political rival Alexander Hamilton, whose views on presidential power and military force had moved more into the executive branch's camp since he wrote a sizable share of *The Federalist Papers.* While some scholars debate about the defensive nature of the orders provided the squadron's commander, when Jefferson did turn to Congress in December 1801, he believed he needed its authorization for "measures of offense." Hamilton, writing as "Lucius Cras-

sus," disagreed, arguing that the Constitution "has only provided affirma-
tively, that,

> 'The Congress shall have power to declare War;' the plain meaning of
> which is, that it is the peculiar and exclusive province of Congress, *when
> the nation is at peace* to change that state into a state of war; whether
> from calculations of policy, or from provocations, or injuries received:
> in other words, it belongs to Congress only *to go to War.* But when a for-
> eign nation declares, or openly and avowedly makes war upon the United
> States, they are then by the very fact *already at war,* and any declaration
> on the part of Congress is nugatory; it is at least unnecessary [Hamilton's
> emphases].[17]

Some recent historians have tried to see in Jefferson's initial actions before he turned to Congress an antecedent in the unstopped march of presidential power at Congress's expense.[18] However, this seems to read too
much recent or current perspective into a president's motives just over two
hundred years ago. Louis Fisher, whose work is quite critical of unrestricted
presidential power, credits Jefferson for recognizing the constitutional role
of Congress and working with it.[19] While Jefferson provided graphic instances of being an activist president in relation to the office's constitutional
powers (e.g., his entire treatment of the Louisiana Purchase, which was a
foreign policy, not a war powers issue), the third president of the United
States reaffirmed Congress's place in limited war. It would require wars
with different objectives than that against the Barbary pirates to elicit more
aggressive interpretations of presidential power and military force.

   The events leading to the declaration of war that formally commenced
the War of 1812 reaffirmed Congress's central role in the decision to use
force. It was the first time the United States officially declared war, and, regardless of the controversy surrounding the war's benefits, as John Adams
wrote in 1815 it "proved that an administration, under our present Constitution, can declare war."[20] Both Jefferson and his successor James Madison had wrestled with the question of whether the United States needed to
declare war against Great Britain to force it to recognize what they believed
were the rights of American ships and goods on the high seas. Jefferson
thought the United States needed to explore a diplomatic solution first from
London; only if that failed did it appear probable that a declaration of war
might obtain support in the Northeast, where most American shipping was
owned.[21]

Jefferson and Madison approached the prospect of war against Great Britain very gingerly—after all both were highly suspicious of the threat of military power in politics, but neither president wanted to defeat Britain. Their objective was to pressure the British to recognize American rights to trade on the high seas as a neutral power and compensate for British violations and impressments of sailors from American vessels.[22] Jefferson and Madison had hoped commercial pressure through embargoes and other measures would change London's perspective. Threatening to use force and actually using it were acts of escalation that just might produce the changes these two presidents wanted. In November 1811, Madison turned to Congress to approve preparatory steps for war—raising more troops, organizing the militia, procuring more munitions, and issuing letters of marque and reprisal. Madison hoped these actions would catch London's attention and win more support in Congress and the public for a war that also could include an invasion of British-held Canada. Madison now resembled later presidents who hoped that a few more troops, additional bombing, or other measures would turn the tide in favor of their policies.[23] His secretary of state, James Monroe, told several interested members of Congress that the administration would seek a declaration of war if Britain did not respond favorably by the following spring. In March 1812, Monroe recommended an embargo for sixty days to remove U.S. ships off the high seas before war; Madison sent the formal request for the embargo to Congress on April 1, 1812.[24]

Much of the discussion leading up the actual war suggested a limited scale of conflict fought to protect maritime and commercial rights, not unlike the Barbary wars, in which no declaration had been necessary. As noted, Madison desired a declaration to maximize his domestic political support and to try to coerce change in British policy. Unlike some of the Barbary states, Great Britain had not regarded itself in a state of war with the United States. However, the American threat to Canada raised the attendant question of "offensive war," with troubling constitutional implications. Madison sent a request for a declaration of war to Congress on June 1, 1812. Nothing in it mentioned invading Canada, but the reference to British agitation of the Indian problem in the West was an invitation to justify such an action. The declaration was hardly unanimous—79 to 49 in the House, and 19 to 13 in the Senate. Opponents to the war sometimes argued that the entire war was unconstitutional because, they insisted, the Constitution had anticipated the United States would fight only "defensive" war. The "declare war" clause certainly had been intended to make any resort to offensive war more difficult. Supporters of the war argued that even "defensive" wars required "offensive" measures, thereby posing an argument that would recur to the current day as subsequent presidents and congresses tried to determine whether, based on the causes of the conflict, approval from Congress was necessary to use military or armed force.[25]

Possibly aside from the War of 1812, these early limited wars were fought primarily for commercial reasons and protection of perceived rights—freedom of trade and transit of American property and nationals on the high seas or neutral rights of commerce during times of war. They conformed to the international vision that had guided the United States since the Revolution—a vision of commercial engagement with the world but restraint and avoidance when risking involvement in the major political rivalries and conflicts of that era. They were a form of imperfect war and use of military force that seemed to fit most comfortably the constitutional framework. They were definitely foreign policy–related wars, although with more of a defensive mantle. However, when the objective turned to other types of national ambition, such as territorial expansion, presidential challenges to the Congress's role in controlling the use of armed force increased.

A Presidential Challenge Emerges

Expansionist policies inevitably pushed initiative more toward the direction of the president. While anyone could read openly about America's expansionist ambition in newspapers or the speeches of many a representative or senator, the actual initiation of many of the measures contemplating or using force had to originate from a small number of people. Obviously, it might not be desirable for a foreign government to know certain intentions beforehand, and open knowledge of some details also could spur unwanted public political debate, since the country was divided as to whether territorial expansionism was a positive step. Consequently, presidents sometimes relied on covert or private agents, minor deployment of ships or troops, and emphatic statements of the right of presidents to make such use of military force for national interests.

American ambition to acquire Florida proved an early example of wide presidential interpretation of legal authority provided by Congress as well as a president's asserted right of independent initiative. Jefferson and his secretary of state, James Madison, believed that the Louisiana Purchase included much of West Florida. In October 1803, Congress gave Jefferson the authority to occupy the land sold by France and to use the army and navy to do so. In relation to West Florida, Jefferson did nothing, but he never relinquished the American claim to it, even though Florida then was under Spanish control.[26] After Madison became president in early 1809, the governor of the Orleans Territory, William Claiborne, told the new administration that West Florida was ready to be plucked, setting in motion a very complex set of maneuvers that initially fell much more into a president's powers over foreign affairs. Apparently at Madison's order, Claiborne wrote a parish judge in Louisiana, William Wykoff, Jr., to see if the latter could act as an American agent and prompt a request by West Florida's inhabitants for American possession. Madison thought the aforementioned authorization to occupy lands from the Louisiana Purchase gave him the power to take such actions, and he did not consult Congress before issuing a proclamation to take possession in late October 1810. Congress learned the details in December.[27]

Here the story moves closer to questions of actual war powers because some critics argued that the president had committed an act of war when he directed troops to occupy West Florida. Whether war with Spain was actually likely was not the point—Madison had ordered U.S. troops not to take any position occupied by Spanish troops; the constitutional question rested on deploying troops and bypassing Congress, which in fact approved adding this area to the Mississippi Territory in May 1812. American expansionists had little discomfort with Madison's secret tactics. The president used similar tactics to seek control over East Florida, which the Spanish were much more reluctant to cede. Madison had selected two army officers to oversee the occupation of West Florida; he also ordered them to work to occupy East Florida. The United States provided guns and supplies to the "patriots" there and later enlisted "volunteers" from the regular U.S. Army to assist. Arguably, Madison had clearer congressional authorization for this due to the Non Transfer Act in early 1811, which gave him the authority to use troops in East Florida if an agreement was reached with a "local authority" or if another foreign country tried to take possession.[28]

Admittedly, Congress played a part in authorizing the use of military force in parts of the Florida affair, but in other instances it was not consulted or informed of actions that fell within its jurisdiction. Some of Madison's actions intentionally avoided clear accountability. The same could be said for General Andrew Jackson's invasion of Pensacola in late 1814 during the War of 1812, an action that rested on a mixture of Jackson's worries about the British presence there and the U.S. desire for Florida. Congress was not consulted before Jackson's attack, although he had corresponded with Secretary of State James Monroe about his concern. Jackson's attack ultimately was his own decision.[29] Arguably the president could have claimed that this was more of an operational decision determined by concerns in the field and thus not an action needing congressional authorization. However, the status of Florida was still an open question and remained so until 1819, when the United States obtained final control by treaty with Spain. Many in the Congress, especially in the trans–Appalachian West, were expansionists, and their support of and cooperation with these policies showed that, like their modern successors, congressional supporters of a policy will often yield to a president who backs and implements their aspirations rather than acting to protect Congress's constitutional powers.

The role of the military in such affairs—in Florida, the American squadron near the California coast before the Mexican War, or John C. Fremont's expedition into California's interior when that war began—illustrated how nineteenth-century presidents could quietly or covertly use small amounts of armed force to prepare for or even prompt a state of hostilities. However, a more frequent pattern for using limited force during this century was in defending the rights of American nationals or seeking reprisals. Unlike many expansionist actions during the nineteenth century, these measures relied on an interpretation of international law, not just the rightness of American vision. Presidents and their backers argued that when force "is in defense of what international law itself recognizes as *rights of person and property* and is not excessive, it is not an *act of war* or a legitimate cause for warlike retort by the country suffering it."[30] In 1837, Secretary of State Daniel Webster took this line of argument in the *Caroline* affair, involving British destruction of a vessel of that name used in American waters by some Americans to promote an insurrection in Canada.[31] The distinguishing point that should determine whether such a measure was an act of war was whether it involved using force against a government to protect the rights of American nations. If so, Congress should authorize such action. Using force against politically unorganized groups or "riotous or rebellious citizens in a foreign state" was not an act of war.[32] A prominent example of the latter at the beginning of the twentieth century was U.S. intervention alongside Japan and key European powers in suppressing the Boxer Rebellion. In 1901, the imperial Chinese government conceded that this was not an act of war; although Congress did not authorize the president to use armed force, interestingly, President William McKinley kept Congress informed on his use of force.[33]

Clearly, these types of limited military actions created a gray area subject to differing interpretations as to whether a president needed to justify congressional authorization. Piracy was one example where congressional authorization did occur. After the War of 1812 ended, piracy increased in the Caribbean and along the Latin American coasts, thanks partly to the anti-Spanish revolutions simultaneously occurring there. In March 1819, Congress provided President James Monroe the authority to attack the pirates and seize their vessels. This authority became permanent U.S. law in 1823. Just three years later in his famous *Commentaries on American Law,* James Kent wrote, "Every nation has a right to attack and exterminate them without any declaration of war [because] they are not considered as a national body, or entitled to the laws of war, as one of the community of nations." However, Kent reminded his readers that Congress retained the authority "to define and punish piracies and felonies committed on the high seas, and offences against the law of nations."[34]

Since naval officers often had to act immediately on the scene against various non-state actors, to use the current term, or groups tied to governments and states, many officers' decisions often occurred without clear congressional sanction. Finally in 1862, in the midst of civil war, Congress authorized the secretary of the navy to prepare regulations governing such actions for the president's approval. The ensuing 1865 regulations, along with the manual written for U.S. consular officers in 1863, gave naval officers on location authority to decide based on personal assessment and responsibility. Not surprisingly, such power could conflict with the role of the Department of State, but throughout much of the nineteenth century, U.S. diplomatic officials were not always near at hand. Even though a revised naval regulation in 1893 required explicit consultation with U.S. diplomatic representatives, the decision still rested largely with the senior naval officer.[35] By the 1880s, however, the global spread of the telegraph made it easier for a president and other governments to make the actual decisions about intervention. What had been a delegation of executive authority to a commissioned officer now became a presidential decision, and decisions that often had been made based on an estimate of a local situation now became more entangled in larger concerns of global politics as the twentieth century progressed.[36]

Reprisal was another common use of limited American military force during the nineteenth century. This was not the concept of reprisal meant in the letters of marque and reprisal, but a broader response to an "an official act of retaliation" by one state against another or even its nationals for injuries they had caused the former. Reprisals can take a variety of forms, but in whatever form they are arguably acts of war. Secretary of State Thomas Jefferson had so characterized them in 1793 and added that they required congressional authorization—an opinion Alexander Hamilton echoed five years later when the United States was weighing its options in the Quasi-War.[37] Presidents Monroe and Andrew Jackson's efforts to obtain congressional authorization for reprisals failed because of Congress's concern about their repercussions and its protection of its war-making authority.[38]

Reprisals and which branch of government really controlled them became a controversy in the 1854 Greytown Affair. This incident, which had almost operatic moments of melodrama, originated from competing British and American plans to establish a canal from the Pacific to the Caribbean at the isthmus along the Mosquito Coast of modern-day Nicaragua. In 1850, the two nations agreed in the Clayton–Bulwer Treaty that any canal would be a joint effort and unfortified. In 1852, Great Britain announced that it and "His Mosquito Majesty," the British-selected ruler, would relinquish control over the port of Greytown.

In the meantime, the U.S. Minister to Nicaragua, the southern expansionist Solon Borland, had resigned his position because of his open disagreement with the Clayton–Bulwer Treaty and a subsequent rebuke from the secretary of state. A sullen Borland made his way to Greytown in May 1854 and boarded a small private craft commanded by an American to take him to a steamship sailing back to the United States. While heading to the steamship, the small vessel collided with a local boat in the water. The captain of Borland's craft became so infuriated at the protests of the local captain that he announced he had no choice but to kill him. Borland agreed. Not surprisingly, this act angered Greytown's inhabitants, who wanted Borland arrested. He returned to town to meet with the U.S. commercial agent there to discuss his situation, and a crowd gathered to apprehend him. Borland confronted them, and someone threw a bottle at him, slightly cutting his face. The injury had been done. On returning to Washington, Borland met with a sympathetic secretary of the navy, James Dobbin, who believed that the United States could not tolerate such behavior, and ordered Captain George N. Hollins, commanding the *Cyane,* to sail to Greytown and try to rectify the situation peaceably. On arriving, Hollins found that Greytown would neither apologize to Borland nor pay damages for property owned by Commodore Cornelius Vanderbilt's Accessory Transit Company. Issuing an ultimatum over the objections of a British naval officer whose vessel was also in the harbor, when the deadline passed, Hollins flattened Greytown with gunfire. No one was killed.[39]

The significance of this episode from the Age of Bluster in American foreign policy was the question it posed about presidential responsibility and control. Somewhat to their surprise, members of President Franklin Pierce's administration came under strong press criticism, including accusations that Pierce himself violated the Constitution by authorizing an act of war. The Congress was not consulted, and even though the president and his cabinet tended to agree Hollins had exceeded his orders, they decided to stand behind him. In a message to Congress in December 1854, Pierce argued that this action could not fall into the category of war because Greytown was not an organized society but "a piratical resort of outlaws." Nearly sixteen years later, a federal circuit court upheld the president's interpretation against a lawsuit by an American citizen who had lost property in the affair.[40]

The issue of reprisals raises a whole array of questions, some of which resurface later. Obviously, the extent to which a president can use military force with congressional approval is foremost. Seventy years later, President Woodrow Wilson turned to Congress for authority to use reprisals after Mexico arrested a group of U.S. soldiers who had gone ashore to pick up supplies in the port of Tampico. Wilson claimed that he had the authority to act without congressional consent, but the magnitude and seriousness of the problem made it necessary to turn to Congress.[41] Some argue that in the Gulf of Tonkin Resolution in 1964 President Lyndon Johnson sought, among other goals, congressional approval of reprisals (air strikes) that he had ordered right after reported North Vietnamese attacks on U.S. warships.[42] Similar questions about reprisals exist about congressional authorization to use military force against the Taliban government and Al-Qaeda members in Afghanistan. Like Wilson, both Presidents Johnson and Bush believed they had the constitutional power to act on their own, but chose to turn to Congress for additional reasons.

The argument over presidential authority and reprisals poses as well the difficult question of just what is required to define a situation as war. If a president can argue that the circumstances do not meet the standards of a definition of war, then independent presidential power is greatly enhanced. For example, President Bill Clinton claimed the situations in Haiti and the Serbia/Kosovo crisis in 1999 were not in this category, thereby making a request for congressional authorization unnecessary. None of these, though, involved reprisals. Scholarly publications, military writing and doctrine, and international law contain abundant definitions of war; however, no particular definition guides presidents and lawmakers. If anything, the definition of war, a word shunned even in the United Nations Charter in favor of "use of force," probably would be harder to reach today than it was in 1787.[43]

In reality, it is left to the president and Congress to decide what war is, then to try to agree among themselves, and then with the international community. Obviously it is much easier for one official, supported by his cabinet and advisors, to make a claim about the status or lack thereof of war than it is for the entire U.S Senate and House of Representatives.

That lesson was illustrated by the Mexican War, when President James K. Polk told Congress in May 1846 that a state of war existed between Mexico and the United States because Mexican troops had invaded U.S. territory.[44] Just how Congress ended up recognizing a state of war rather than declaring war is still troubling to study and consider some 160 years later. In Polk, Congress dealt with a president who held views of presidential power closer to today's than to many of his nineteenth-century counterparts. Although he did not rely on the commander-in-chief clause to justify his actions, Polk believed the president had a singular responsibility to guide the nation's direction. Part of his philosophy reflected that of his political mentor and fellow Tennessean Andrew Jackson. The president alone was elected by a national vote, and only he really had the perspective, vision, and legitimate foundation to decide what national interests were. Senators and representatives represented more narrow constituencies and perspectives. While not oblivious to the powers of Congress, Polk believed that he could and must act in the national interest, even if there was no consensus on it. Given the power of American sectionalism, Polk probably thought consensus on key expansionist measures was impossible. From a singular and personal view of the nation's interests, Polk was prepared to resist Congress.[45]

To understand Congress's actions before May 1846 it is important to remember the president was not alone in his conviction that war with Mexico was likely, possibly unavoidable. Several of Polk's fellow Democrats shared his expansionist ambitions. Yet exactly when Polk thought he would have to use force is unclear. In late May 1845, it appears that Polk believed he had a right to defend Texas once the Texas republic approved annexation to the United States. In early June 1845, before Texas's congress approved annexation, he ordered General Zachary Taylor to move U.S. troops into Texas, specifically into the region between the Rio Grande and the Nueces River. This was a provocative act, as Mexico claimed the correct boundary was the northern river, the Nueces, while Polk held to the Texan position that it was the Rio Grande. That same month he ordered Commodore John D. Sloat, who commanded the Pacific Fleet, to be prepared to seize San Francisco and other key points in California.[46]

This pre-positioning of U.S. soldiers and ships showed a potentially hostile intent. A Congress defensive of its constitutional powers would have been completely justified in exploring the president's intention to seek a request for authorization to use force, but like later Congresses, scrutiny was lax, partly because many shared Polk's convictions about expansionism, whether into Texas or Oregon, and Polk also secretly conducted some affairs. In fact, some scholars argue that all Polk's acts to this point were intended to pressure Mexico into a negotiated settlement rather than to prepare for war.[47] Polk's last attempt to find a solution, dispatching John Slidell to Mexico City, ended fruitlessly. In late March 1846, after Slidell learned that Mexico would not negotiate with him as the U.S. minister as long as U.S. troops were on its border and ships just off its coast, but before Polk knew about it, the president ordered reinforcements to Taylor, who now had begun to build fortifications on the north side of the river opposite Matamoros.[48]

Polk probably thought he was justified in seeking a declaration of war after he learned of Mexico City's rejection of Slidell. On May 9, 1846, Polk told his cabinet he thought he had reason to seek a declaration and that "it was my duty to send a message to Congress very soon and recommend definite measures." The catalytic event, it seemed, would be "any act of hostility on General Taylor's forces" after which Polk would "immediately send a message to Congress recommending an immediate declaration of war."[49] Unknown to Polk, General Taylor had written a dispatch on April 26 reporting a Mexican attack on a reconnaissance party. That news arrived in Washington on May 9, just four hours after the cabinet meeting ended. They met again that evening, and on May 11 Polk sent a "war message" to Congress stating war "exists by the act of Mexico herself."[50]

Polk immediately faced challenges in Congress for his unilateral announcement of a state of war. Numerically, the battle was not that problematic for the president in the House; ultimately, the declaration received 174 votes with 14 against. However, a handful of Whigs led by John Quincy Adams never gave up, and one, Representative Garret Davis (Kentucky), asked the president a pointed question. Had the war begun on American or Mexican soil? In the Senate, Polk faced not only the opposition of the Whigs but also from a few Democrats led by Senator John C. Calhoun (South Carolina). Calhoun believed a distinction existed between defensive hostilities, which the president could direct, and war, which required a declaration. Calhoun wanted to know whether Taylor's operations had been defensive or offensive; if the latter, the president should have obtained congressional authorization. However, the Senate then fell into a quandary resembling that faced by congressional opponents of the Iraq war 160 years later. Troops already were in harm's way, they needed reinforcements, and Congress had to raise troops and provide money. Senator John M. Clayton (Delaware) said he had to " 'go for the soldiers and the millions at once, to support the honor of the country and the army.'" Senator Lewis Cass (Michigan) defended the president's position by observing, "No authority but Congress can commence a war. But another country can commence a war against us without the co-operation of Congress." Ultimately, many critics swallowed their misgivings and voted to support the declaration by 40 to 2, with three, including Calhoun, abstaining.[51]

The controversy surrounding Polk's actions grew and fed mounting political division, thanks to growing criticism of the war and the entanglement of the desire for territorial expansion with the question of slavery. Toward the end of the Mexican War, Calhoun told the Senate he had opposed the president's policy not only because he believed the latter's "allegations" were "untrue," but out of concern about the political problems this war and expansionism would bring to the country. Serving his one term in the House of Representatives, Representative Abraham Lincoln (Illinois) again raised the question of exactly where the engagement involving Taylor's troops had occurred. While considering a resolution to praise General Zachary Taylor or his victory at Buena Vista in February 1847, the House voted 85–81 for an amendment adding the words "in a war unnecessarily and unconstitutionally begun by the President of the United States." That caused the Taylor resolution to be dropped, but it later was reintroduced and passed without the troubling amendment.[52]

The Mexican War produced the strongest assertions of executive authority in war powers against a foreign country made in the nineteenth century. Polk created the "antecedent" situation that Hamilton had warned of and pulled the Congress right along. The combination of Polk's secrecy and the wide base of support he thought he had for expansion to Oregon and also through Texas to the Pacific Coast and California created a climate in which Congress did little to understand or anticipate Polk's actions. Claims of the Congress of 1846 being radically different from that of 1964, 2002, or 2007 really do not matter. Many members understood the constitutional implications of Polk's actions when they had to confront his request to recognize the existence of a state of war. Like their successors in the twentieth and twenty-first centuries, they ended up trying to rectify the situation after the fact through their statements and resolutions about the war against Mexico rather than shaping the president's decision and actions beforehand.

Interestingly, Polk did not rely on an argument that his relatively obscure predecessor, John Tyler, a Whig from Virginia, had used for his own interpretation of presidential powers. Seeking to press for the annexation of

Texas, a prominent issue in the election of 1844, Tyler and his secretary of state, John C. Calhoun, supported moving naval ships off Texas's coast and troops to the border with Texas. Tyler explained that he did so out of concern about an imminent Mexican attack on Texas, which the president regarded as American territory, but more importantly, he told the Senate he had done this under his constitutional authority as commander-in-chief.[53] That claim of an inherent power in the Constitution's commander-in-chief clause became a fixture in presidential statements about the use of military force, especially in limited operations, after 1950. It is curious that Polk did not rely on it, but his interpretation of singular presidential power in the national interest, versus legislators' fragmented interests and constituencies probably provided a concept that made specific reliance on the commander-in-chief provision unnecessary. It would require different presidential personalities and a different international climate for the United States, operating with a standing military, for the commander-in-chief clause to become so central in justifying the use of force.

Lincoln, of course, used the commander-in-chief clause as one of the justifications for his actions in April 1861 that involved raising troops, imposing a blockade, and suspending the writ of habeas corpus. For the latter he also stressed what he saw as his greatest objective and concern—not to allow the Union to be destroyed for the sake of preserving that same law. Yet, as discussed in Chapter 1, Lincoln never once argued that the commander-in-chief clause provided him authority to go beyond or circumvent congressional authority. As sweeping and intimidating as Lincoln's actions were, he did turn to Congress for its approval in July 1861. In March 1863, the Supreme Court announced in *The Prize Cases* its agreement that the president had the right to declare a blockade in the absence of Congress, which had not been in session in April. Arguing for the president before the Court, Richard Henry Dana, Jr. defended both the president's actions and Congress's powers. He stressed in a case of "foreign war," when the United States had been attacked, there was not a need for "a preceding act of Congress declaring war." Several sentences later Dana added, "It is not as to the right to initiate war, as a voluntary act of sovereignty. That is vested only in Congress." Writing for the 5–4 majority, Justice Robert Grier agreed: "Congress alone has the power to declare a national or foreign war," but "[i]f a war be made by invasion or a foreign nation, the president is not only authorized but bound to resist force by force." He does not wait for "special legislative authority," and that situation, Grier added, included both foreign invasion or "States organized in rebellion." Congress itself approved all

Lincoln's actions, except the suspension of the writ of habeas corpus, in August 1863.[54] Lincoln definitely created "antecedents" that placed Congress in a situation of having to concur or reject his actions after the fact, but equally importantly he had acted while still recognizing Congress's ultimate power. A president could justify many actions as commander-in-chief, but he could not use that clause to justify using force for offensive operations.

Even though presidential power clearly increased between 1789 and the end of the Civil War, events showed in the recognition and practice of perfect and imperfect war Congress's relatively consistent retention of power. In these examples, arbitrarily selected to try to illustrate certain subjects and themes rather than to be comprehensive, Congress was involved from the beginning or fairly early in key decisions except in Florida and the Mexican War. Part of the respect for Congress's role reflected the reasons for which wars were fought and how they were conducted, as illustrated by the deliberations occurring during the wars to protect commercial rights or to change foreign governments' policies (revolutionary France and the Barbary pirates). Historians have pointed to other influences as well. Policies on territorial expansion and legal measures necessary to enable land settlement and building a transportation infrastructure greatly involved Congress, and this involvement logically spilled over into Congress's role in defense and foreign affairs.[55] Yet as the Mexican War revealed, there could be exceptions to that involvement. Cycles between presidential and congressional strength were emerging in U.S. history. For example, after the Civil War, Congress reasserted its role, both in domestic policy and in exercising its powers in foreign policy, and regained some of the jurisdiction it lost during the war and the early phase of Reconstruction.[56]

The extent of congressional control over war powers during most of the nineteenth century probably startles most modern readers. Perhaps the best example was the unique record of President James Buchanan, to whom Congress denied approval to use force six times in just one term! Buchanan wanted to use military force to protect freedom of movement over the Isthmus of Panama or seek redress for U.S. vessels seized in harbors in South and Central America.[57] The only congressional approval he obtained was a conditional declaration of war involving the use of military force to respond to Paraguay's shelling of a U.S. warship in 1858. In most instances, his aspirations to use military force collided with a growing suspicion in the North of expansionist actions that might benefit the South.[58]

Reviewing the entire century, Frances Wormuth and Edwin Firmage identify three other conditional declarations—the first dealing with Venezuela's seizure of three U.S. ships that resulted (nineteen years after the incident!) in an authorization to use "such power as may be necessary" to obtain indemnity. Two more actions targeted Spain: the first in 1895 dealt with paying property losses to a naturalized American, and the second in April 1898 demanded Spain withdraw from Cuba and directed the president to use military force to enforce this ultimatum. Spain broke off relations with the United States on April 21, 1898, and four days later Congress declared a formal state of war.[59]

The controversy with Spain over Cuba, in particular, produced a situation in which, in some opinions, a war-minded Congress pressured a reluctant president into war. As mentioned earlier, President Cleveland said that he would not act if Congress declared war against Spain. His successor, William McKinley, sometimes sounded as though he was reluctant to go to war, but did little to stop or thwart the push for war in the Congress. Lewis Gould argues that McKinley wanted to pursue a series of "incremental steps" short of war that would compel Spain to relinquish its control of Cuba. Another scholar of the period, H. Wayne Morgan, acknowledges McKinley's repugnance for war but adds that his policies always left open its eventuality. McKinley could not easily retreat from that. Yet, McKinley did not turn to war when some thought he should have—namely, in the immediate aftermath of the explosion of the *Maine* on February 16, 1898, which nearly all attributed to sabotage. Even in early April, McKinley seemed to want to give diplomacy a last opportunity, and he told congressional leaders he would postpone sending a war message to Congress. On April 11, McKinley sent a message to Congress asking for authority "to take measures to secure a full and final termination of hostilities between the Government of Spain and the people of Cuba."[60]

McKinley's reluctance to seek a declaration of war infuriated some in Congress. Some in Republican circles talked of initiating a vote for a declaration of war, but proponents learned that their Republican president might veto such an action, which could have tremendously damaged McKinley's political coalition. His April 11 message sought intervention as a neutral. He did not recognize the Cuban insurgents, and he wanted to intervene for humanitarian purposes, to protect U.S. citizens and commerce on the island, and to end a strategic problem in the Western Hemisphere. Congress agreed to McKinley's terms on April 20, but Spain immediately rejected them, and four days later McKinley requested a declaration of war.[61]

McKinley's actions were part of a struggle with Congress as to which branch decides to go to war. He did not disagree with congressional power over the decision to use force, but his interpretation of constitutional responsibilities showed that he believed Congress could not force a president to go to war. Afterward, he spoke of the declaration of war as a source of grief, and it is important to remember that McKinley personally had seen the human costs of combat during the Civil War.[62] After the declaration, some of his actions in relation to Hawaii and the Philippines imply that his grief may have quickly subsided. Nevertheless, it is fair to argue McKinley responded to pressure from Congress more than leading it, unlike Polk in the Mexican War.[63]

Global Ambition, Power, and the Presidency

The emergence of the United States as a power prepared to use military force world-wide changed the calculus for both the justifications and methods in using military force and the nature of the struggle between the president and Congress over control of that force.[64] A new framework for U.S. foreign policy emerged by the end of the nineteenth century, although its antecedents became visible particularly after the Civil War.[65] Presidential power increased over foreign policy alongside greater reliance and control over the use of armed force, especially in limited form. Between the Spanish-American and Second World Wars, reliance on armed force ebbed and flowed, but after World War II and the beginning of the Cold War, the pattern moved almost consistently in direction of greater presidential use and control of military force and often ineffective efforts by Congress to assert and regain its position.

New criteria for interventions and limited war developed while older reasons took on a different context. For example, the clamor for war against Spain included concern about humanitarian and human rights. The cause of human rights rested partly on the sense of special mission and convictions about the universality of the American system of government that has existed throughout U.S. history, but it also reflected a trend shared especially with the British, who used such arguments to oppose policies of the Ottoman Empire and earlier against the slave trade. A heightened Christian social conscience, combined with domestic reform movements, reinforced interest in human rights in both countries.[66]

Probably more important was a global perspective shaped by expanding commercial commitments that assigned more importance to stability. Protecting foreign nationals and property rights and preventing economic and political turmoil could invite other foreign powers to intervene and potentially undermine U.S. interests. From the beginning of the twentieth century, when the United States joined the ranks of the formal imperialists, into the 1930s, new criteria developed to justify using limited military force in such areas. Increasingly, presidents regarded the military as an instrument of foreign policy and justified its use as necessary through their role as the nation's voice in foreign policy and as commander-in-chief. Even though by then few American statesmen would have read von Clausewitz, other contemporary strategic writers, such as Alfred Thayer Mahan, heightened appreciation of how military force could be a critical instrument in advancing and protecting national interests.[67] Displays of force or actual intervention now served as a means of protecting U.S. interests against regional and global probes or actions by the traditional powers (Great Britain and France) or the more recent insurgent powers (Germany and Japan).

Theodore Roosevelt justified such actions by arguing that a president was a "steward" of the people; the Constitution or the Congress limited his powers only in specific ways.[68] In one sense, Roosevelt's view acknowledged accountability to the American public, but vested with that accountability he thought he held extensive power to do what he believed was right and necessary. Roosevelt brought to the White House a conviction shared by other contemporary reform-minded politicians that state intervention could prevent the abuses of either organized labor or expansionist corporations. Government could be a neutral regulator of the nation's domestic system, and Roosevelt carried this assumption into the international system, where he believed the United States, in the absence of an international body, could act for the sake of peace and stability. In this context, as James R. Holmes has pointed out, in world affairs Roosevelt perceived "little distinction between the military and police functions."[69] Furthermore, if Roosevelt believed limited uses of military force could advance U.S. interests, he did not hesitate to act without consulting Congress, such as in November 1903 when he ordered U.S. Marines to land in Panama to prevent Colombia from using force against a rebellion there—a vital step in preparing to build the Panama Canal. Blurring police and military functions, Holmes notes, almost guaranteed expanded presidential claims over using force.

In Roosevelt's annual message to Congress in 1904, he very explicitly linked the use of military force to advance the foreign policy goal of regional stability, unveiling what became known as the Roosevelt Corollary to the Monroe Doctrine. Unlike the United States of 1823, which had no effective military power to prevent the transfer of colonies or territories in the Western Hemisphere from one European power to another, the situation eighty-one years later had changed radically. Roosevelt warned that the United States would intervene directly in the sovereign affairs of other nation-states in the hemisphere if they did not handle their internal affairs with "reasonable efficiency and decency" and failed to keep order and pay their obligations. The consequent danger of such misbehavior was European intervention and that the United States could not accept. Intervention would be a "last resort," but Roosevelt showed he would follow through with his threat when he later deployed troops to the Dominican Republic.[70]

This new willingness to intervene in other countries' sovereign affairs appeared different from many interventions undertaken since 1789. In 1912, the solicitor general of the State Department, J. Reuben Clark, proposed a new legal framework for such actions. Clark wrote that an appreciated distinction between "interposition" and "intervention" existed. The former was simply sending in troops to protect lives and property, and, Clarke argued, as it was accepted by international law and not aimed at the actual foreign government, Congress did not need to authorize it. The power to do so came from the executive power of the president, who in this instance would not need to invoke the power of commander-in-chief. "Intervention," however, meant intruding in another state's sovereign affairs and, as it suggested an act of war, Congress must authorize it.[71] Clark's proposal was an important step in an emerging trend in the twentieth century to find constitutional and legal grounds for using military force in ways not requiring congressional approval.

Roosevelt's successor, William Howard Taft, who intervened with military force twice in Nicaragua and once in Honduras, commented after leaving the White House that he believed a president could order troops anywhere "if the appropriations furnish the means of transportation." If those means had been funded earlier, this suggested an "instrumentality which this power furnishes [that] gives the president an opportunity to do things which involve consequences that it would be quite beyond his power under the Constitution directly to effect." Taft acknowledged in a book written on the presidency in 1916 that this meant a president could use the powers of commander-in-chief to go beyond the office's delegated constitutional powers and involve the United States in a war Congress would retroactively have to declare or recognize as already existing.[72] This very sweeping statement implied that Congress's real power was intended to be in appropriations, but if the means of transporting military personnel already existed, which was Taft's caveat, how necessary was subsequent congressional action? Appropriations for weapons and transportation are seldom tied to any specific military operation, although to some degree Taft made his observation in a period before a large, permanent standing military. However, during Taft's single term, 1909–1913, the U.S. Navy was a sizable standing permanent force.

It was not that individual representatives failed to oppose or criticize the interventions that occurred during the first decades of the twentieth century. The problem, and it is now perennial, is their efforts usually occurred in the wake of presidential action. When a presidential decision is made, overriding it to force another course is a major undertaking that Congress can attempt only in rare circumstances when a sizable portion of the president's own party no longer supports the White House. Such a development almost inevitably reflects the public rejection or failure of a policy significantly affecting the United States, the two major parties, and the reelection prospects of those in Congress. The constitutionality of the decisions made to use military force probably will be a second-tier issue in the debates. For example, in 1912 Senator Augustus Bacon (Georgia) proposed legislation that would have denied appropriations for military forces deployed without Congress's consent outside the United States, an attempt to use the appropriations power as an actual political and constitutional hurdle. However, Secretary of War Elihu Root responded, as could any of his successors to the present day, by arguing that no law prohibits a president from ordering troops "into any country where he considers it to be his duty as Commander-in-Chief of the Army to send them, unless it be for the purpose of making war, which of course, he cannot do." If Congress "attempted to deprive the Commander in Chief of the power to protect American citizens," Root added, "[it] would hear from the American people." Arthur Schlesinger, Jr. notes Root's choice of words seemed to concede that the president could not commit troops into combat, but this assumes Root would have regarded the words "combat" and "war" as interchangeable.[73] Root's emphasis on protecting citizens was a context Americans would have understood, but by the time of his rebuttal to Senator Bacon, the protection of nationals became a justification for action that also could involve larger political or strategic objectives. Not surprisingly, Bacon's proposal went down in defeat.[74]

Most of the instances when Presidents Woodrow Wilson and Calvin Coolidge intervened with limited force—in Mexico, Haiti, the Dominican Republic, and Nicaragua—as well as the continuation of gunboat diplomacy, followed the rationale developed during the Roosevelt and Taft administrations. Wilson, of course, entertained universalistic assumptions about the transferability of American democracy and a sense of divinely guided purpose that permeated his policies. He cited such justifications prominently in his use of limited force in Mexico, and, obviously, in his approach to declaring war in Europe in April 1917. Wilson, however, appeared to treat the need for Congress's participation individually. As noted, he chose to request congressional authorization for the right of reprisal after the Tampico incident.[75]

Possibly of even greater significance was his intentional rejection of pressure from many in Congress to demand full-scale war with Mexico if it did not attempt to punish Pancho Villa and his band after their raids into New Mexico in January and March 1916. Wilson feared war against Mexico because of its possible tragic, destructive aftermath; he also viewed Mexico as largely defenseless. Perhaps too he recognized that the eventuality of American involvement in World War I was becoming more likely. Instead, Wilson chose to act on his own and ordered a more limited response, a punitive expedition into Mexico led by General John J. Pershing to try to capture Villa.[76] Although this affair now often serves as a case of American bullying of Mexico, it also can stand as an example of how presidential freedom to make decisions to use military force can limit the impact of public emotion that would precede a congressional declaration of war. While America's handling of Villa and his supporters was a sovereign matter for Mexico, based on cross-border raids into the United States, Wilson also arguably had reasons to take some action, even if it was a stretch to justify sending troops into Mexico. Here he had a series of historical precedents involving Indian raiders to rely on, if he wished.[77] The key point, though, is that Wilson chose to use limited military force because he believed it would best serve overall U.S. national interests.

Setting the Stage for Presidential Power

Before World War II, Congress's role in authorizing the use of limited military force and involvement in undeclared war clearly was eroding, although not because of any decisive court ruling or specific action in which Congress chose to limit or narrow its role. The problem was that the Constitution had not provided definitive guidance about the types of military operations which had become more common. A constitution written for a new, weak nation trying to avoid the intrigue and wars of the major powers was now in a very different international environment, and most of the nation's political leadership accepted, if they did not embrace, the fact that the United States was a global power requiring different priorities and means to accomplish and support its international objectives. Changes in America and abroad raised new questions about how military force could be used to serve U.S. interests. The strong disillusionment following World War I created among many a determination that the United States should never let itself be pulled into such a war again, resulting in a heightened congressional activism in the form of neutrality laws to prevent American intervention in another fruitless European war. During the peak years of this isolationism and aversion to total war, the Supreme Court would make a ruling that some argue justifies presidential use of military force independently without congressional concurrence.

The background of *U.S. v. Curtiss-Wright Corporation et al.* had nothing to do with war powers and using force but rather with the question of whether Congress had ceded legislative authority to the president by giving him power to impose an arms embargo. After war between Paraguay and Bolivia broke out in 1932, Congress, true to the contemporary strong inclination toward U.S. neutrality in conflicts (1934), authorized the president to stop arms traffic between the United States and the two belligerents. Curtiss-Wright, the company in question, was later found a party in a conspiracy to violate the embargo. It filed a suit on the grounds that Congress had unconstitutionally delegated its authority to the president.[78] An additional factor in the timing of the Court's actual ruling (1936) was the Court ruling only the year before in two cases critical to New Deal programs that an unconstitutional delegation of constitutional authority to the president had occurred. However, could Congress transfer more of its authority in international affairs than in domestic ones?[79]

The central question was whether Congress had delegated power too broadly to the president.[80] However, the majority opinion, written by Justice George Sutherland, addressed the more open-ended question as to whether all presidential actions must be grounded in constitutional authority. Because the Constitution does not elaborate much on foreign policy and war powers, this lack of explicit direction creates many potential constitutional issues. Sutherland stepped far beyond the issue under consideration when he wrote a lengthy dictum—a judicial statement on a legal issue other than the central question in the case—on a president's authority over foreign policy that went beyond the Constitution.[81] Sutherland was a former senator from Utah and member of the Senate Foreign Relations Committee, and based on that experience and some earlier scholarship on constitutional powers, he seems to have thought that he had the basis to make a more sweeping statement.[82]

The core of Sutherland's argument took the issue back to the Declaration of Independence and through the Articles of Confederation. The transfer of sovereignty and authority from Great Britain to the new American government took two different paths. Sutherland described "two classes of powers." In domestic affairs, these powers and rights went to the thirteen states and then in the Constitution to the federal government. However, in foreign affairs "the powers of external sovereignty passed from the Crown not to the colonies severally, but to the colonies in their collective and corporate capacity as the United States of America." Moving from that claim, Sutherland then made his key argument about the nature of executive power.

> It results that the investment of the federal government with the powers of external sovereignty did not depend upon the affirmative grants of the Constitution. The powers to declare and wage war, to conclude peace, to make treaties, to maintain diplomatic relations with other sovereignties, if they had never been mentioned in the Constitution, would have vested in the federal government as necessary concomitants of nationality.

This was a concept of external sovereignty that essentially dismissed the Constitution.[83] Sutherland elaborated his argument with a controversial assertion of the concept of the president as "sole organ" in foreign affairs.

Another part of the opinion particularly strengthened the president's hand.

> It is important to bear in mind that we are here dealing not alone with an authority vested in the President by an exertion of legislative power, but with such an authority plus the very delicate, plenary and exclusive power of the President as the sole organ of the federal government in the field of international relations—a power which does not require as a basis for its exercise an act of Congress, but which, of course, like every other governmental power, must be exercised in subordination to the applicable provisions of the Constitution.[84]

Sutherland's claims rested on very arbitrary, misleading interpretations. First, the British had not seen themselves as transferring sovereignty from the Crown to the United States but to the individual states, which Britain regarded as independent sovereign states. He seemed to dismiss the fact that the Constitution's advocates argued in its favor to have a stronger national government over the states, and that the writers of that document purposely divided sovereign powers between the Congress and president after the problems during the Articles of Confederation when the Continental Congress held all government powers.[85] His reliance on the "sole organ" argument referred to a speech that John Marshall gave in 1800 while serving in the House of Representatives; taking Marshall's words of out of historical context, Sutherland asserted a far more sweeping interpretation of "sole organ" than Marshall intended.[86]

Proponents of strong presidential authority and the commander-in-chief provision cite Sutherland's interpretation of the nonconstitutional foundations of executive power to defend using force without previous congressional approval as well as executive actions, such as the Reagan administration's in the Iran–Contra Affair. More recently, the same arguments supported Department of Justice justifications for using force after the 9/11 attacks and intercepting international communications.[87] The important thing is its legacy, especially in questions about using limited military force and other small-scale operations. A president can claim the right to use force without congressional consent, and, although this pattern of justification began to emerge by the early twentieth century, it became quite standard, almost routine, during the last half of that century and the first years of this one.

The historical context of Sutherland's famous opinion was unsettling, since events in Europe and Asia pointed toward another world war, and a major political debate about increasing presidential power in domestic politics was also under way. Ultimately the Curtiss-Wright case with Sutherland's opinion was not the principal cause of greatly expanded presidential powers in war, especially imperfect war, in the last half of the twentieth century, even if it supplied a controversial justification for that development. Constitutional arguments over presidential power, Congress, and the use of force were part of a much larger debate in the United States over the nation's international goals, the appropriate strategy and supporting policies necessary to reach those goals, and the utility of military force as part of that strategy. The constitutional balance between Congress and president in war was irrevocably changed after the peace ending World War II in 1945.

Chapter 3

The Rise of Imperfect War and Presidential Power

Even more than the terrible conflict a generation before, World War II witnessed a mobilization of populations, economies, and ideologies, and a cataclysm of destruction most of the contemporary world has vowed never to repeat. As so many civilians became involved in war-related activities in industry and elsewhere, the distinction blurred between warrior and civilian for both their leaders as well as their enemies. The war's requirements demanded strong leadership to focus the war effort and make the complex array of decisions necessary to support and direct those fighting. It was war on a scale far from most of the conflicts discussed in this book.

In the United States, the war concentrated decision- and war-making powers in the president's hands to an unprecedented degree and helped create government institutions and policies still existing today. Franklin D. Roosevelt relied extensively on his authority as commander-in chief to make key decisions about the strategic and operational direction of America's role in the war. The creation of the combined chiefs of staff increased the military's advisory capacity to the president and simultaneously strengthened presidential control over the armed forces.[1]

After the war ended, the American dream of returning quickly to a peacetime economy with less government control and a smaller military quickly reasserted itself, and the country rapidly began to demobilize its military. This situation did not last very long. By 1946, the tenuous cooperation of the United States and Great Britain with the Soviet Union during the war turned more confrontational over the political fate of Central and Eastern Europe and the extent of Western versus Soviet influence there. By February 1947, the United States was assisting Greece and Turkey to limit expansion of Soviet influence and becoming more involved in the Mediter-

74

ranean and Middle East as Great Britain yielded its historic role in the region to the United States. In June 1947, the United States proposed the Marshall Plan, a framework for European economic recovery encompassing all of Europe. The Soviets saw this proposal as a threat to their influence. Two years later the division of Europe into Western and Eastern spheres was so entrenched that an alliance security structure emerged in both areas to defend against attacks from the other. That same year on the other side of the world, the communist Chinese took control of the mainland and installed a government under Mao Tse-tung in Beijing. The Soviets also detonated their first atomic bomb in 1949, much earlier than Western analysts had anticipated. Faced with two communist regimes in Europe and Asia sharing a threatening ideology that apparently erased any historic differences between them, the United States thought that it had little choice but to gird itself and its allies for a global confrontation. Soviet possession of long-range bombers and the atomic bomb meant that for the first time the United States faced the prospect of direct attack by air from a major power.

The first occasion the United States thought it had to respond with direct military force against a communist challenge occurred in late June 1950, when communist forces from North Korea invaded the South. The United States believed that such an attack could not have occurred without cooperation and support between both the Soviet Union and People's Republic of China.[2] However, to respond to this crisis, the United States resorted to the newly established United Nations, created at the end of World War II. Considered in the context of U.S. history and the nation's aversion to alliances and long-term international commitments, this turn to the UN was a pivotal development.

Unlike the fateful decisions after World War I, in 1945 both president and Congress committed themselves to the creation of an international security organization dedicated to rejecting aggressive war as a means to settle differences between nation-states. In 1919, Congress began to try to restore a balance in executive and congressional relations that had grown during the previous two decades and become personified in the actions of President Woodrow Wilson to build a new international system. Some in the U.S. Senate strongly opposed Wilson's vision of a League of Nations and U.S. membership in it, but others were prepared to accept it if the president recognized that League membership would not circumvent Congress's right to authorize the use of military force.[3] Wilson stubbornly opposed a compromise formula and thus contributed to the Senate's rejection of his plan for a postwar order. Many Americans later concluded their own short-

sightedness in 1919 and the defeat of the Treaty of Versailles had contributed to World War II.

Unlike the aftermath of World War I, Congress did not have an interval
after 1945 to reassert its role in war powers against those of a presidency
made immensely stronger by wartime mobilization and the necessities of
being commander-in-chief. The Second World War and events of the early
Cold War forced Congress and president toward greater unity in controlling
military force, even if they sometimes disagreed over foreign policy goals
and means. These developments created a climate inviting presidential activism and congressional deference. Roosevelt's successor, Harry S. Truman,
emphasized a notion of presidential prerogative that became permanent—
especially from John F. Kennedy to the present.[4] Relying on the commander-in-chief clause literally created "an alternative interpretation of the
Constitution" in the eyes of some; although, hopefully, the previous chapters have showed that there was some shift in that direction during the first
half of the twentieth century.[5]

Cold War and Imperfect War:
Finding the Appropriate Instruments

Just what role limited military force had in this new security environment
now operating with an international security organization was unclear.
While the next chapter looks at some strategic and military operational issues that affected decisions to resort to limited uses of force, this one continues to examine how and where limited or imperfect war fit into discussions about war powers and congressional and presidential controls over
using force. For the first time, Congress and the president had to weigh both
the U.S. Constitution and also the issue of how an international body, the
United Nations, might affect or justify a congressional vote or presidential
decision dealing with military force.

Even during the middle of World War II, advocates of the future UN argued it needed the ability to support the use of limited forms of military
force to deter or stop aggression. But also right from the start, congressional
backers of the UN wanted to ensure that it would not become a means by
which presidents could use U.S. troops without previous congressional
agreement. In late July 1945 while attending the Potsdam Conference, Truman sent a note assuring Congress that both chambers would first have to
approve any agreement about commitments of U.S. troops.[6] If the United
Nations determined nonviolent measures could not block or prevent ag-

gression, Article 43 of the UN Charter gave it the authority to obtain through "special agreements" with member-states the military forces and other means to use. In Section 6 of the UN Participation Act of 1945, Congress inserted a provision that the United States could provide troops in such agreements only with congressional consent.[7]

However, it was unclear whether such an authorization was necessary for *every* UN use of U.S. troops. Even back in 1943, when Congress debated legislation to support negotiations to establish the UN, Senator Claude Pepper (Florida) argued that U.S. troops could be sent as a "police force" against smaller acts of aggression without congressional authorization.[8] This potentially opened the door to independent presidential use of force. Two years later in a hearing before the Senate Foreign Relations Committee, John Foster Dulles, who had been a legal adviser to the U.S. delegation in San Francisco where the UN treaty was signed, told the committee that the "policing powers" attributed to the UN might allow a president to contribute U.S. forces to a UN mission without Congress's approval.[9] In 1949, Congress added an amendment to the UN Participation Act to allow the president to contribute up to 1000 troops for "cooperative action" as non-combatants serving as guards or observers.[10]

President Truman quickly responded to the North Korean invasion on June 25 and the UN Security Council's subsequent request for assistance to stop the aggression, thanks to a Soviet boycott, by announcing on June 27 that he was providing U.S. air and sea forces to support South Korea, although he actually gave the order a day earlier. He did not formally consult with Congress, but in all fairness, Truman realized he might need congressional authorization. On June 26, he spoke with his friend Senator Tom Connally, the Texas Democrat who chaired the Senate Foreign Relations Committee, who told Truman he had the power to send troops based on the UN Charter and his authority as commander-in-chief. Consulting Congress might result in a debate that would tie the president's hands.[11] Connally essentially had told the president to ignore what Congress sought to avoid in the UN Participation Act—the UN Charter could not be a basis for using force without congressional approval. As to the commander-in-chief provision, it is not certain that Congress would have blocked Truman's wishes, given the prevalent anti-Soviet and anti-Chinese climate, and Truman could have resorted to Lincoln's approach by acting and then seeking subsequent congressional approval. Since the United States had not been attacked, that would have been a debatable course, but nonetheless one that would have placed the president's actions on arguably stronger grounds.

On June 27, Truman told the press that the United States was not at war but involved in a "police action" under United Nations authority.[12] During the next few days, Truman faced some criticism for not having sought congressional approval for ordering U.S. air and sea forces to Korea, primarily from Senator Robert A. Taft (Ohio), but not nearly as much as the constitutional magnitude of the issue should have generated. Indeed, some senators thought Truman's course preferable. In early July another Democrat, Senator Paul Douglas (Illinois) commented, "[I]t may be desirable to create a situation which is half-way between complete peace, or the absence of all force, and outright war marked by the exercise of tremendous force on a wholesale scale. . . . It would be below the dignity of the United States to declare war on a pigmy state."[13] Douglas's remarks implied that if a declaration of war was not at stake, Congress could step aside and let the president use force without an authorization. That was not the understanding of discussions during and after the Constitution's adoption or much of the nineteenth century in cases of limited or imperfect war, but with the emergence of notions of policing powers and new criteria for intervention stated earlier in the twentieth century, such views of presidential power became more evident. Douglas's assertion provided any president with open-ended authority. Armed with legal analysis from his secretary of state, Dean Acheson, Truman decided on June 29 to send ground troops to Korea and famously claimed that he could issue this order without congressional authorization based on his powers as commander-in-chief.[14]

As the Korean War grew more unpopular, debate intensified over Truman's justifications for his orders to U.S. forces. Few probably anticipated it fully at the time, but his reliance on the commander-in-chief clause established a critical precedent for nearly all his successors. In addition, his reference to the UN Charter raised questions about whether presidents could use it or any other part of the growing body of international law to justify the use of military force without congressional authorization. Forty years later, the same issue surfaced during the first Gulf War in early 1991 and then again in 1993–1994 over Haiti. The arguments made in both examples were similar to Truman's.

In the case of the first Gulf War, the desire to turn to the UN to authorize using force rather than making an initial request to Congress seemed to reflect President George H.W. Bush and his advisers' desire to reinforce the UN's role in the post–Cold War environment and avoid accusations that the United States wanted to deal with Saddam Hussein on its own. UN Security Council Resolution 678, approved on November 29, 1990, provided that authorization.[15] In *The New York Times,* prominent legal scholar Thomas Franck subsequently wrote that congressional authorizations did not apply to "police actions" waged under the UN Charter's authority.[16] If so, how could Franck's assertion be reconciled with what Congress wanted to prevent in the UN Participation Act? To allow the UN Charter to become a distinct justification for presidential use of military force without congressional consent guaranteed that future presidents would rely on it to try to bypass Congress. President Bill Clinton invoked authorization provided by the UN Security Council to initially justify not requesting Congress for consent to send troops to Haiti to restore its government, which was toppled by a coup. Congress repeatedly balked at asserting its authority, preferring instead to pass a nonbinding sense of Congress measures to discourage funding for using forces in Haiti without congressional approval or adding waiver language allowing the president to do so if national security concerns were at stake. Proponents of strong presidential activism, such as John Yoo, argue that President Clinton did not even need to rely on a treaty (the UN Treaty in this case) for authority to act.[17] Truman's rationale for ordering U.S. troops to Korea built a framework for presidential activism to the present day.

During the 1950s and later as the Cold War seemed to head toward a full-scale nuclear showdown, anxieties about atomic bombs overshadowed questions of military force and Congress more than the utility of limited or low-scale military operations and their constitutional justification. The adoption of the policy of strategic deterrence with nuclear forces required the existence of a standing nuclear force and a president who could act within minutes.[18] President Dwight D. Eisenhower, who succeeded Truman in 1953, in many ways highly respected Congress's constitutional responsibility. Furthermore, as the worst effects of McCarthyism began to subside, Eisenhower was able to build a fairly far-reaching degree of bipartisanship in foreign policy and national security matters, due in part to the cooperation of House Speaker Sam Rayburn and Senate Majority Leader Lyndon Johnson.[19] Eisenhower turned to Congress twice—in 1955 over Formosa and the Pescadores Islands and in 1957 over the prospect of Soviet intervention in the Middle East—to obtain statutory authority to use military force if necessary. Congress was not totally supine when the president approached it, especially in 1957, but it gave the president the authority he wished. Eisenhower relied partly on the Middle East resolution when he sent Marines into Lebanon in 1958.[20] Both were significant steps in using military force as a foreign policy tool to send signals to both Beijing and Moscow.

However, Eisenhower turned to other forms of force or military support that hardly attracted Congress's attention, but later would become contentious areas between presidents and Congress—intelligence operations and mutual security agreements. Eisenhower's reliance on intelligence operations was a particularly murky option in terms of U.S. law. What today we would call intelligence, covert, or even special operations was a small but important facet of U.S. policy since the Revolution. Examples from agents sent into Spanish-controlled Florida or the timely presence of Captain John C. Fremont's force in California at the beginning of the Mexican War serve as reminders that this is a long-standing practice. Yet, if undeclared or imperfect war did not have an explicit constitutional status, the status of intelligence operations was even less clear. Their very ambiguity could make such operations a valuable dimension of imperfect war.

The use of intelligence operations also opened another question that became increasingly problematic. The constitutional and congressional understanding of use of force generally meant military force, that is, uniformed personnel in the service of their government. Exceptions existed, such as the letters of marque and reprisal, meaning private citizens licensed by the government, but this practice fell out of use by the mid-nineteenth century. The Neutrality Act of 1794 also prohibited private persons under U.S. jurisdiction from assisting military actions against a state with which the United States was at peace.[21] Yet what guidelines existed for actions that might be regarded as a use of force by the United States that did not involve military personnel? Other government offices or agencies, such as parts of the growing intelligence community, might be involved. Such a question meant that Congress faced not just a question of control over the use of military force but the more open-ended issue of control over use of force involving civilian actors.

Just where did the president's authority originate to conduct intelligence operations, and did Congress have any inherent constitutional authority to control them? Presidential authority could derive from the same arguments used to justify independent dispatch of U.S. forces without congressional authorization—the executive authority given the president, the power to execute the laws, the president's role as the sole organ in foreign affairs, and the commander-in-chief clause. Congressional powers over intelligence operations relied on the same clauses cited for limited war—the declare war clause, the power over appropriations, and restrictions on presidential monetary expenditure, and, some scholars argue, the clause on letters of marque and reprisal.[22]

The legal foundations of Eisenhower's actions in Iran and Guatemala, where the Central Intelligence Agency participated in coups that toppled two governments, largely rested on provisions in the National Security Act of 1947 and the Central Intelligence Act of 1949. Obviously Congress enacted both laws, but it was unclear whether in so doing it intended to provide the president power to wage covert war; although besides assigning the CIA the power to collect and analyze information, the National Security Act also gave it authority "to perform *such other functions and duties related to intelligence affecting the national security* as the National Security Council (NSC) may from time to time direct."[23] Congress obviously appropriated the money for such operations, but it really managed to write itself out of any role in the way the money was spent in the 1949 law, which stated that the CIA could expend money appropriated to it "without regard to the provisions of law and regulations relating to the expenditure of Government funds."[24]

The desire to ensure that covert operations were conducted in ways making U.S. responsibility difficult to trace ("plausible denial") probably reinforced a congressional desire not to want to know what was happening. As the *Iran-Contra Report* observed some thirty years later, most of the oversight was based on close "personal relationships" between the CIA's director and key congressional committee chairs.[25] Congress appropriated intelligence money through the defense budget, which meant that the House and Senate Armed Services Committees were responsible for the sporadic congressional review of intelligence community activities that did occur during those years. However, by the 1950s the NSC was evolving into a policy-executing body, not just the advisory body intended in the National Security Act establishing its existence. In 1955, Eisenhower created a coordinating committee within the NSC, the "5412 Committee," to approve covert actions.[26] Although it had representatives from departments whose heads had received congressional approval, such as defense and state, the overall process was not easily within Congress's reach, since the evolving NSC was part of the president's White House staff and traditionally not required to testify before Congress on grounds of separation of powers and executive privilege. An additional impediment to congressional accountability was the operational necessity in many instances of relying on foreign surrogates or organized insurgents to conduct these operations. Congress had no effective control over the expenditure of the money it provided, and, of course, private or other monetary sources also could support operations.[27]

The fact that in their defenders' opinion intelligence operations were foreign policy initiatives rather than measures using military force gave the president the advantage. In 1948, President Truman defined covert action in ways closely tying such measures to war-related activities, such as "sabotage," "demolition," "subversion against hostile states," or "assistance to underground resistance movements."[28] In 1981, President Ronald Reagan apparently defined covert operations far more loosely in Executive Order 12333, stating they are "special activities conducted in support of national foreign policy objectives abroad which are planned and executed so that the role of the United States Government is not apparent or acknowledged publicly."[29] Congress used similar language a decade later in the Intelligence Authorization Act of 1991.[30] Moving covert operations into the foreign policy corner complicated oversight because these means did not inevitably have intentions or characteristics, such as uniformed, armed personnel, that enabled Congress to control them through war powers mechanisms.

Toward the end of his administration, Eisenhower pursued other covert operations, such as in the Belgian Congo, and initiated the planning of an operation to use Cuban exiles to try to topple the government of Fidel Castro, culminating in the Bay of Pigs debacle in April 1961. Wherever their location, all such actions were part of a global strategy to contain or possibly push back the tide of communism and governments sympathetic to Moscow's and Beijing's views of the United States.[31]

Using covert operations for foreign policy ends became even more important for President John F. Kennedy, who criticized his predecessor for over-reliance on threatened nuclear retaliation, and then urged a more nuanced, tiered choice of responses to deal with populist revolutions and insurgencies in the developing world.[32] Covert operations relying on limited uses of military force and discrete or concealed American involvement occurred without any congressional consultation or authorization. The Bay of Pigs fiasco, which involved CIA-trained Cuban insurgents, lacked congressional foreknowledge. Had any occurred, the CIA probably would have tried to convince Congress that the entire operation was a bad idea.[33] The global struggle against communism also moved the Kennedy administration to begin a war in Laos that remained largely covert until 1969. At the onset of the Laos operation, which involved military advisers, agents, and U.S. Air Force pilots who had been "resigned" to fly for a CIA-run airline, Congress knew very little. As the 1960s progressed, and Laos operations became more entwined with the Vietnam War, some in Congress began to learn more or parts of the story.[34] The presence of U.S. military personnel, even in a temporary capacity as CIA agents or private citizens, posed legitimate war powers issues, but no clear U.S. legal framework existed to address this in 1962 or 1963. In fact, the 1962 Geneva Agreement on Laos prohibited the presence of U.S. military personnel in that country.[35]

The continuation of covert actions in Cambodia and particularly in Chile finally spurred Congress to establish a system of accountability over covert operations between the president and Congress. A 1974 amendment to the 1961 Foreign Assistance Authorization Act by Senator Harold Hughes (Iowa) and Representative Leo Ryan (California) prohibited expending funds

> [b]y or on behalf of the Central Intelligence Agency for operations in foreign countries, other than activities intended solely for obtaining necessary intelligence, unless and until the President finds that each such operation is important to the national security of the United States and reports, in a timely fashion, a description and scope of such appropriate Committees of the Congress.[36]

Of course, the amendment contained loopholes, such as the words "timely fashion." Also through the 1970s, the number of committees involved, including the two newly established intelligence committees that could receive such presidential findings, as they came to be known, was arguably too numerous to ensure secure treatment of such sensitive information. Congress resolved that question in the Intelligence Oversight Act of 1980 by limiting such findings to the two intelligence committees.[37] Both chambers assigned members from other key committees—Foreign Relations (Foreign Affairs or International Relations in the House), Armed Services, and Appropriations—to the intelligence committees. Although within several years Congress would find its review and control of intelligence operations challenged from a very different direction in the Iran-Contra Affair, it nonetheless established a system of oversight and accountability that, flawed as it may be, surpasses anything about war powers and the authorization of presidents to use military force that it has enacted into law to the present day.[38]

A different channel through which a president could send military personnel into hostile or potentially hostile situations was through mutual security agreements. In Vietnam during the final years of the Eisenhower administration and throughout the short Kennedy administration, U.S. military advisors with military assistance or advisory groups worked alongside South Vietnamese units fighting against the Viet Cong.[39] Congress reviewed none of the bilateral agreements with Vietnam. They were not negotiated as treaties, which would have required Senate consent; in fact, they generally did not even have the status of executive agreements. The Senate Foreign Relations Committee in 1969 created a special committee chaired by Senator Stuart Symington (Missouri) to investigate these agreements, and the committee found that they deeply committed the United States to the security of Southeast Asia. Often resting on commitments within the Southeast Asia Treaty Organization (SEATO), the secretary of state or other senior department official frequently negotiated or signed these agreements. U.S. military assistance to Thailand, the Philippines, and South Vietnam included not just money and equipment but also personnel. As the war in Vietnam expanded in the late 1960s, U.S. money also often paid for troops sent to Vietnam from SEATO members and other countries.[40]

Arthur Schlesinger, Jr. has observed that Congress largely had itself to blame for the troubling downstream results in Southeast Asia resulting from its own inattention. While that is arguably true, Schlesinger himself contributed to the growth of presidential power at Congress's expense when he defended Truman's decisions on Korea. However, when Secretary of State Dulles asked Congress about whether foreign base agreements should be negotiated as treaties, the answer from Capitol Hill was "no," since the funds for such commitments would have to be appropriated by Congress. In short, Congress would have to approve money for maintenance of the bases anyway.[41] Perhaps that answer depended on a technical explanation or on the type of bipartisan trust prevalent in the 1950s when Congress sometimes was overly deferential to the executive branch, but it was tantamount to saying that if no money was needed then Congress did not really need to know—an attitude that deserves no high marks for its defense of congressional responsibility or for maintaining accountability between Congress and the president in both defense and foreign policy. Obviously, as seen, U.S. money was being spent in ways that would have major repercussions for the United States by the mid-1960s.

From the Gulf of Tonkin Resolution to the War Powers Resolution

In hindsight, Congress's willingness in the 1950s and early 1960s to give the president such open-ended, loosely restricted provisions about various limited deployments or uses of military force appeared astonishing. In truth, these types of authorizations and congressional deference eroded congressional power as much as did presidential efforts to claim an independent right as commander-in-chief to issue such orders. The prolonged sense of crisis created by East–West rivalry largely surmounted most partisan differences during this time, and also contributed to a decision to escalate the Vietnam War based on false evidence. Whether the exact facts would easily have come to light in late summer 1964 is unclear; it would probably have been harder to verify them than the allegations about Iraq's weapons of mass destruction in 2002–2003. But Congress could have done much more to examine the scenario than it did. By 2002, Congress appeared to have forgotten the lesson from 1964.

In early 1964, President Lyndon Johnson approved a covert operations program against North Vietnam that included some attacks by South Vietnamese patrol boats on the night of July 30 on islands in the Gulf of Tonkin from where, it was thought, North Vietnamese were infiltrating into the South. On the afternoon of August 2, North Vietnamese patrol boats attacked the *Maddux,* a U.S. destroyer on patrol in the Gulf. The *Maddux* returned fire and the aircraft carrier *Ticonderoga* launched its aircraft. What followed on the evening of August 4 was much more unclear. The *Maddux* and another destroyer, the *C. Turner Joy,* reported that an attack was imminent due to radar indications of surface ships and aircraft in the area. In reality, there was no second attack, a fact confirmed in 2005 by a National Security Agency study that revealed signals intelligence analysts had combined elements of reports about the first attack into analysis of the second incident. McNamara, Johnson, and others operated from their understanding of this first analysis, although a subsequent request from the *Maddux*'s commander advised caution about the sequence of events before ordering any additional measures. The secretary of defense and Johnson found the evidence compelling enough to order air strikes against North Vietnam.[42]

As the Senate majority leader, Lyndon Johnson had worked to support this type of executive–congressional cooperation, and in 1964 he wanted to have the same support from Congress.[43] Thus, Johnson turned to a draft resolution that had existed in various forms since early 1964 but that he had hesitated to introduce because he feared it might distract Congress's work on the Civil Rights Act of 1964. On the morning of August 3, Johnson told McNamara that he wanted to meet with the speaker, the Senate majority leader, and key Armed Services and Foreign Relations committee members to inform them of what had happened. He commented that he did not think he needed the resolution, but, remembering the criticism Truman had undergone because of Korea, he still wanted a resolution from Congress.[44]

The resolution, which passed in the House by 410–0 and in the Senate by 88–2, declared, "Congress approves and supports the determination of the President, as Commander in Chief, to take all necessary measures to repel any armed attack against the forces of the United States and to prevent further aggression." The next section of the resolution used the words "all necessary steps" to include members or protocol states "of the Southeast Asia Collective Defense Treaty. . . ."[45] During consideration of the resolution, several senators asked questions about the resolution's intent, especially whether it was part of a presidential plan to greatly increase force levels in and near South Vietnam. In hindsight, it is staggering to read Senator J. W. Fulbright's answer that it most likely was not—a response Fulbright would deeply regret within a few years.[46] To understand why the House and Senate willingly could support this resolution requires us to remember how widely most members in both parties shared a common assessment of the need to respond wherever necessary to stop an expanding communist movement headed by Moscow and Beijing. In his memoirs, President Johnson also added an important clue when he observed that it was important to have such a resolution on hand if necessary in the future.[47] Johnson saw the resolution as comparable to the area resolutions President Eisenhower obtained from Congress during the 1950s to have in his pocket if needed. Many in Congress had worked on those as well, and therefore the president's request did not seem that portentous or misleading. Having no previous "Gulf of Tonkin"–like resolution that had gone seriously awry in congressional memory, this resolution failed to switch on caution lights for most senators and representatives.

Some have argued that the resolution was unconstitutional or illegal on grounds that it was hurriedly approved, did not actually give the president the authority to increase forces to the high levels ultimately deployed by Johnson, or the president and others based it on false information provided to Congress. However, as harsh a critic of the resolution as John Hart Ely has correctly argued that Congress essentially did its job and gave the president its authorization.[48] Just because legislation is poorly considered and approved does not invalidate it. Without question, Congress acted on false or misrepresented evidence; a calculated effort by more members to demand the time to more comprehensively examine the president's version of the Gulf of Tonkin and other assessments and the administration's long-term objectives might have ferreted out more of the truth. That is what Congress must do to make the best-informed judgment alongside the president's.

The Gulf of Tonkin Resolution was an example of honoring strict process and requirement, but failing to do the substantive investigation and inquiry that must be part of that process. Strictly speaking, Congress had not been a rubber stamp, but it failed to use its powers of oversight to examine the president's claims and intentions more thoroughly. Congress faces no decision of greater magnitude than to give a president the authority to use military force. Doing so requires, among other things, scrutiny of the justifications given, the strategic objectives sought, the levels of forces required to accomplish the mission, and whether other means could accomplish the same end as well with less human and financial cost. President Johnson found a setting in which, because of the reported incidents in the Gulf of Tonkin, Congress felt pressured to act.[49] Yet delaying the resolution by a week or month would not have had any operational impact on the war. Johnson likely would have used executive authority he believed he had, but Congress might have sought a more prudent, less open-ended resolution and examined more vigorously at an earlier stage the relationship between U.S. objectives in the war and its conduct.

As the war in Southeast Asia became less popular, the Congress resorted to several measures to end it. It repealed the Gulf of Tonkin Resolution in 1971, an act that in itself had no bearing on President Richard M. Nixon's conduct of the war. Nixon argued that he had constitutional authority to protect U.S. troops and secure a "just peace" in Vietnam. These expansionist views of the commander-in-chief's role clearly circumvented congressional efforts to stop the U.S. role in the war. As Congress repeatedly reinforced its 1964 authorization with numerous appropriations measures, it proved necessary for Congress to reverse course. In 1971, in a supplemental appropriations bill the Senate approved an amendment by Senators Frank Church (Idaho) and John Sherman Cooper (Kentucky) prohibiting the use of authorized or appropriated funds to introduce ground troops into Cambodia, although it did not prohibit money for bombing missions. Two years later on July 1, 1973, President Nixon signed an appropriations bill containing a provision introduced by Senator Thomas Eagleton (Missouri) to halt funding for U.S. military operations in Southeast Asia as of August 15, 1973.[50]

The war in Southeast Asia evolved in a decade from very limited, low-scale operations into a conflict scarcely limited in most operational meanings of the term, except for ultimate numbers of U.S. forces, choices of targets, and avoidance of nuclear weapons. Strategically, the war's objective was not so much to defeat North Vietnam and absorb it into South Vietnam, but to coerce North Vietnam to accept South Vietnam, although some Americans would have welcomed the demise of the Hanoi government.[51] The war's conduct and outcome raised fundamental questions about the utility of limited war, limited military operations, and their role in U.S. strategy. That debate had a major impact on both presidents and Congress in subsequent decades.

The congressional legacy after Vietnam was to consider how such a small-scale conflict that began with minimal congressional concern or review developed into a struggle that literally tore at the country's social, cultural, economic, and political fabric. Charges of imperial or monarchical presidents became the popular explanation, but likewise some observers realized that Congress's own inattention or deference during the 1950s and early 1960s contributed to this tragedy. Consequently, Congress acted on several fronts. Its members now sought better information and the power to review security assistance packages, mutual security agreements, and executive agreements reached with other countries. Covert operations now came under stricter review with reporting requirements, and Congress tried to impose stricter control and discipline over the entire budgetary process. However, the endeavor that most directly focused on Congress's role in limited war was the War Powers Resolution of 1973.

This resolution tried to establish a legal framework for congressional control over limited military force. However, the various versions approved in either the House or Senate from 1970 to 1973 acknowledge the president's prerogative to use military force in specific instances without prior congressional authorization. The original House version of the bill, passed in 1970 and then again in 1971, was weak because it allowed the president authority to act without prior congressional approval, but failed to specify just where the president could do so. It provided Congress the power to legislate the recall of U.S. forces, but sought to restrain the president by stressing consultation between Capitol Hill and the White House. The bill introduced by Senator Jacob Javits (New York) in 1972 and 1973 and approved by the Senate identified four instances in which the president could exercise such authority without congressional approval. The first three were the defense of U.S. territory, military forces, and U.S. citizens, and each of these had the Constitution or historical precedent to support presidential action. The fourth embraced the defense of treaty partners if the president previously obtained a regional authorization similar to what Congress legislated in the 1950s for Formosa and the Middle East. The Senate bill finally offered the power of presidential initiative in all four cases where there was a "direct and imminent threat of attack."[52]

These terms, especially those relating to treaty partners and imminent attack, restricted presidential power less than one would have expected after Vietnam. Even under the newly proposed Senate version, any president could have done much of what Eisenhower, Kennedy, and Johnson did before the Gulf of Tonkin Resolution. The two chambers negotiated and then passed a version of the resolution, but President Nixon vetoed it on grounds that the resolution imposed unconstitutional restrictions on the president and a realistic settlement of this dispute would require revising the Constitution itself. Both the House and Senate overrode the president's veto.[53]

The first major paragraph in the final Resolution, Section 2(a), starts impressively enough with the declared purpose

> to fulfill the intent of the framers of the Constitution of the United States and insure that the collective judgment of both the Congress and the President will apply to the introduction of United States Armed Forces into hostilities, or into situations where imminent involvement in hostilities is clearly indicated by the circumstances.

Section 2(c) recognizes the president's right to introduce military forces as commander-in-chief "pursuant to (1) a declaration of war, (2) specific statutory authorization, or (3) a national emergency created by attack upon the United States, its territories or possessions, or its armed forces."[54] Absent is provision of authority to attack due to a treaty, unless the Congress approves it in legislation to implement the treaty, or in case of imminent attack.[55] Otherwise, the provision acknowledges what had been historical practice since the early days of the United States.

Section 3 puts into legal language what always had been implied for an effective congressional–presidential decision to occur—the necessity of consultation. It requires a president "in every possible instance . . . to consult with Congress before introducing" forces "into hostilities, or into situations where imminent involvement in hostilities is clearly indicated by the circumstances." Consultation should continue "regularly" until the hostilities are over or the troops removed.[56] The legislative history or report accompanying the legislation as finally approved in the House Committee on Foreign Affairs clarifies several important terms. The choice of "every possible instance" tried to reinforce the committee's conviction that consultation should occur *before* commitment, although the committee obviously realized in some cases that might not be possible, such as a missile attack.[57] The committee report made it clear that consultation was not "synonymous with merely being informed," but rather "means that a decision is pending on a problem and that Members of Congress are being asked by the President for their advice and opinions and, in appropriate circumstances their approval of action contemplated."[58]

The likelihood that limited or low-intensity operations would be central to many deliberations involving authorization was clear to the committee. The paragraph in the report dealing with the term "hostilities" demonstrates that and is worth reading in full.

> The word *hostilities* was substituted for the phrase *armed conflict* during the subcommittee drafting process because it was considered to be somewhat broader in scope. In addition to a situation in which fighting has actually begun, *hostilities* also encompasses a state of confrontation in which no shots have been fired but where there is a clear and present danger of armed conflict. "*Imminent hostilities*" denotes a situation in which there is a clear potential either for such a state of confrontation or for actual conflict.

The committee's goal was to be as inclusive as possible in envisioning scenarios in which

> limited force might be used. Nonetheless, the report did not explicitly define these terms, which disturbed several Members, such as Senator Eagleton, who wanted the Resolution to deal more directly with various paramilitary options. These were speculative types of concerns, though, and Congress generally does not like to legislate in the speculative arena. Among other reasons, it is not easy to explain to constituents, and it is admittedly impossible to legislate for everything that could occur.[59]

The real problem in this resolution starts in Section 4, especially in Section 4(a). To understand why, it is important to read through this subsection:

> In the absence of a declaration of war, in any case in which United States Armed Forces are introduced—
>
> (1) into hostilities or into situations where imminent involvement in hostilities is clearly indicated by the circumstances;
>
> (2) into the territory, airspace, or waters of a foreign nation, while equipped for combat, except for deployments which relate solely to supply, replacement, repair, or training of such forces; or

(3) in numbers which substantially enlarge United States Armed Forces equipped for combat already located in a foreign nation . . ."

The language then states that the president must submit a report within forty-eight hours to the speaker of the House of Representatives and the president pro tempore of the Senate to explain the circumstances requiring the deployment, the constitutional and legal authorities used, and the projected length of time and size of the operation.[60]

One could say, "So far, so good," as the resolution addresses many of the types of deployments in Vietnam that enabled a limited, low-scale operation to escalate into a full-scale war. The critical problem arises in Section 5, which has the perhaps unintentional effect of giving the president *the choice* of whether the White House will submit a report under Section 4(a). If the president does so, he or she is obligated to end the use of armed forces within sixty days unless the Congress has declared war, given another authorization, extended the sixty days, or cannot meet due to attack. The president actually can request a thirty-day extension of the sixty days. The resolution is silent about what happens if the president does not report under this provision; although later the bill provides the option of a legislative veto through a concurrent resolution passed by the House and Senate, a process that the Supreme Court ruled unconstitutional in *Immigration and Naturalization Service v. Chadha*.[61] Consequently, Congress would have to pass a joint resolution, which requires presidential signature and thus is subject to a possible veto.

Legislators, congressional staff, scholars, and journalists have all puzzled at times over this loophole in Section 4(a), which leaves the president so much freedom of action both in deploying force and reporting to Congress. Scholars, including Louis Fisher, Michael Glennon, Harold Koh, and others, have all pointed to its problems. Koh even says it apparently just went unnoticed while staff and members tried to reconcile the House and Senate versions of the bill.[62] What is even more troubling in the nearly thirty-three years since the War Powers Resolution became law is that this loophole remains. One cannot sympathize greatly with Congress when it fails so consistently to correct a problem while complaining so vocally about not being consulted or respected by presidents. It is almost as if members prefer to retain the provision because by leaving the president so much freedom to use force without adhering to the War Powers Resolution, they are better insulated from criticism of the policy and president that may follow if the use of force turns out badly. However, this cynicism does not fairly explain the reason why this opening for the president remains.

The more likely truth is that any president would almost assuredly veto an amendment to the resolution about this provision, since it would weaken presidential authority. The status and effectiveness of the entire War Powers Resolution would be in question. It is unlikely that Congress would have the veto-proof majority it had in 1973 against a president who was already weakened by the emerging Watergate scandal. Thus, the War Powers Resolution continues to dwell in a type of political purgatory, where its legality and status remain only conditionally recognized. It is not every day that we find a law regarded as unconstitutional by adherents of both the presidential and congressional sides of the issue. Presidential supporters believe it unduly infringes on presidential powers, and no president has recognized it as constitutional. Constitutional scholars like Louis Fisher believe the resolution is unconstitutional because it delegates to the president powers the Constitution gives the Congress in matters of war.[63]

It is unfair to suggest everything about the War Powers Resolution is a failure. Sections 8(a) (1) and (2) try to close avenues that presidents had used to introduce military force without authorization. The first states no provision of law, including an appropriations measure, can provide such authority, unless the Congress specifically has provided the authorization in that law. Second, as noted earlier, treaties cannot serve as a justification for introducing military force, except when the treaty "is implemented by legislation specifically" giving that authorization. The purpose here is to rule out arguments treaty obligations can justify military intervention so congressional approval is unnecessary.[64] Yet to the present day presidents still cite UN Security Council resolutions when convenient, and NATO treaty obligations continue to serve as another source for presidential action.[65]

Who Respects the War Powers Resolution?

Even though presidents challenge the legality of the War Powers Resolution, they largely have dutifully reported to the Congress; by April 2006, presidents had done so 118 times.[66] Section 4(a) of the Resolution had been cited only twice. President Gerald Ford did so in the rescue operation related to the *Mayaguez,* and in October 1983, in extending the deployment of U.S. Marines in Lebanon in the Multinational Force in Lebanon Resolution, Congress stated that the authority of this section had become effective on August 29, 1983.[67] Otherwise, presidents have avoided officially recognizing the authority of the War Powers Resolution. By President Jimmy

Carter's administration, the preferred language when reporting to the Congress was "consistent with the reporting provisions of the War Powers Resolution," or just "consistent with the War Powers Resolution."[68] These words effectively said the president respected the resolution's intention and the position of the Congress but would not recognize the resolution as constitutionally binding.

The War Powers Resolution has had a very unhappy history since its passage thirty-four years ago. Hampered by vague language and a major opening for independent presidential action, the legislation never became the check on presidential use of military force as intended. By recognizing the president's power to determine why, when, how, and with what numbers military force should be used, and then conceding to the White House the choice of acting first and reporting later, Congress put itself in a disadvantageous position from the start. Yet given the increased reliance of U.S. policy on limited military force and the remote likelihood of a full-scale war that might justify a declaration, Congress has little choice but to function in an environment with priorities and methods that clearly favor the president. The post-Vietnam military and the Congress understandably feared that limited wars could develop into large, costly, unlimited commitments, but by the beginning of the 1980s President Ronald Reagan and his successors were faced with situations in the Middle East, Central America, and the Caribbean and, later, in Europe, in which the need for limited military intervention seemed critical for U.S. foreign policy interests.

We need not examine each and every episode during the last three decades to understand how the authority of the War Powers Resolution eroded. The Reagan administration did not notify Congress when it introduced military personnel into El Salvador in early 1981, although it assured the chair of the Foreign Affairs Committee, Representative Clement Zablocki (Wisconsin), "The requirements of the War Powers Resolution will be complied with in a timely manner should they become applicable."[69] The requirements did not become applicable. Ultimately the Central American situation would take a very different direction, as U.S. policy came to rely on covert operations funded by non-U.S. sources, a problem examined later in determining the effectiveness of congressional control over the uses of military force through the appropriations process.

A pattern of informing Congress after the fact emerged during these years. The letter to the speaker of the House of Representatives, Representative Tip O'Neill (Massachusetts), notifying the House, apparently arrived two hours after the invasion of Grenada began on October 25, 1983.[70] The author remembers a Foreign Affairs Committee colleague phoning to ask whether he knew anything to confirm TV stories on U.S. forces landing in Grenada. The notification had not yet arrived in Committee offices.[71] A similar scenario followed in March 1986 with U.S. air strikes against Libya. The president invoked his constitutional role as commander-in chief to justify this action.[72] Louis Fisher suggests in these cases, especially Grenada, that the Reagan administration seemed attentive to the War Powers Resolution's sixty-day limit, even if it did not accept the law as constitutional. As to Grenada, the House approved 402–23 a resolution declaring that the clock began ticking on October 25, 1983; the Senate was working on its counterpart when the president withdrew U.S. forces. For Libya, the point was moot because the action consisted of air strikes.[73]

The resolution that Congress negotiated with the Reagan administration to extend the length of deployment for U.S. Marines in Lebanon specifically depended on the authority and terminology of the War Powers Resolution. The immediate background of this extension involved two situations in that country. The first was the arrival on August 24, 1982, of 80 Marines to assist a multinational force removing Palestine Liberation Organization leaders and members from Lebanon. The second was the deployment of 1,200 Marines a month later, also as part of a multinational force, to create an environment enabling the Lebanese Armed Forces to stabilize the situation in and around Beirut. Administration representatives and congressional members and staff had discussed these deployments, but no formal attempt emerged from them to press the administration to request a formal authorization. The president reported the deployments to Congress, but not in total compliance with the War Powers Resolution. The terrorist bombing of the U.S. Embassy in Beirut that killed sixteen Americans, and the deaths of Marines in late August and early September 1983, moved several members to try to get the White House to begin the sixty-day clock required by Section 4(a)(1). When the president refused, Congress initiated legislation to make that Section effective as of August 29, 1983, the date the first Marines were killed, and to give the president an eighteen-month extension.[74]

Both letters to the Speaker about the Lebanese developments couched the conditions of the deployments in terms of Section 4(a)(2), which applied when troops were equipped for combat but not in a hostile situation or where hostilities were imminent. In discussions reviewing various drafts of the eventual resolution, members struggled some over the term "hostilities," since there was no definition in the resolution or elsewhere, but in the opinion of many, given the Marines' deaths, an actual state of hostilities existed. Some disagreement remained with administration representatives over defining the situation in Lebanon as hostilities, but certainly the proviso "while equipped for combat" now seemed out of touch with reality. In a letter to the chair of the House Foreign Affairs Committee, the president seemed to accept all this and said that if it became necessary to retain the forces for more than eighteen months, he would "work together with the Congress with a view toward taking action on mutually acceptable terms." Yet after signing the resolution on Lebanon, President Reagan questioned the constitutionality of the eighteen-month time frame and indicated he felt no obligation to seek congressional authorization afterward.[75]

Since then the Congress has not exercised as strong an opportunity to invoke this key provision in the War Powers Resolution. Nevertheless, in the aftermath of the negotiations on the length of deployment, the president still stood by the claim that he held constitutional authority as commander-in-chief to deploy military force in such operations. Clearly President Reagan and his successors experienced much more success in determining how an administration will deal with the War Powers Resolution than any efforts by Congress.[76]

The first Gulf War illustrated as well as anything the extent of presidential dominance over the War Powers Resolution. Exactly one week after the Iraqi invasion of Kuwait on August 2, 1990, President George H.W. Bush wrote congressional leaders to tell them he had ordered a sizable forward deployment of U.S. military personnel into the region based on his power as commander-in-chief and "our inherent right of individual and collective self-defense." Nevertheless, the president assured Congress that he did not think hostilities were imminent.[77] As the number of troops increased during the next several days, the president wrote House Speaker Tom Foley (Washington) and the president pro tem of the Senate, Senator Robert Byrd (West Virginia). The only other visible consultation with Congress was with Senator Sam Nunn (Georgia), the chair of the Senate Armed Services Committee.[78] As important as Nunn was, this was hardly appropriate consultation with all key congressional leaders. Bush continued to stress his powers as commander-in-chief and the authority that he claimed originated from UN Security Council Resolution 678, approved on November 29, 1990. Bush emphatically claimed he did not need congressional authorization— at one point saying colorfully he did not need the approval of an "old goat" in Congress to act against Saddam Hussein. The Department of Justice argued there was a distinction between "war-making" and "offensive actions" giving the president sole authority to take the latter steps.[79] This incredible

assertion overlooked a fundamental theme in the Constitution and the debate surrounding it that authority for offensive uses of military force had to
come from congressional action, but it nonetheless reflected a growing belief in presidential power that revealed itself through the twentieth century.

The Gulf War was hardly representative of the forms of limited military
operations that became so characteristic of the late twentieth and early
twenty-first centuries, but the prelude before the actual authorization the
president requested was interesting. Several members in both chambers, especially Democrats, had misgivings about the fast movement toward a
likely war. Some argued that additional time was needed for diplomacy and
selected punitive measures, such as sanctions, to have their effect before resorting to armed force. The president's repeated assertions on executive authority also caused consternation, which generally showed itself along party
lines. In December 1990, the House Democratic Caucus voted 177–37 on
a resolution stipulating the president must seek congressional authorization
before acting.[80]

Some members tried another option—a solution from the federal courts.
Representative Ronald Dellums (California) and fifty-three other members
joined to seek a court action that would require the president to seek congressional authorization before using force. The federal district judge who
ruled on the case, Harold Greene, fully appreciated the congressional concerns and so indicated in his opinion, but added that the onus still rested
with Congress on this matter. In language that would echo in later court decisions on this matter during the Clinton administration, Judge Greene
wrote, "Unless the Congress as a whole, or by a majority, is heard from, the
controversy here cannot be deemed ripe; [it] is only if the majority of the
Congress seeks relief from an infringement on its constitutional war-decla-
ration power that it may be entitled to receive it."[81] The time was not ripe
because Congress had not acted through legislation to bring the entire question into the courts.

Bush's decision to seek an authorization originated clearly as much from
political need as from his interpretation of the Constitution. His own inner
circle of advisers was divided on the question.[82] Approval, even if divided
(the Senate voted 52–47, the House 250–183), would in a sense put the debate about war powers to rest. Bush's position would be stronger both domestically and internationally because of the approval.[83] An authorization
also arguably diminished Saddam Hussein's ability to try to benefit from a
divided American public and Congress. Finally, Bush knew that Congress
would have to shoulder some of the responsibility if Operation Desert

Storm turned out to be costly or, even worse, a stalemate or protracted defeat. However, the Gulf War swiftly concluded, as had an intervention in Panama against President Manuel Noriega nearly a year earlier, for which a House resolution had praised Bush. The presidential hand in using military force, large or small, was now stronger.[84]

When War Is Not War: The Continued Diminishment of the War Powers Resolution

The Cold War ended when the Soviet Union broke up in 1991. Understandably we could have expected that the same turn of events might slow or halt the concentration of power in presidential hands over military force and limited war. In fact, the trend of such concentration continued. None of Bill Clinton's actions, for example, ever received an explicit authorization from Congress before their execution.[85] Throughout his presidency, Clinton intentionally tried to maintain limits on the scale and duration of military operations for various reasons, including cost, fear of casualties and subsequent public and congressional criticism, personal unease with the U.S. military, and a desire to perfect a form of limited military operations that could be used for various foreign policy purposes.[86] He relied on the traditional claims about executive authority and the commander-in-chief provision, but what is especially significant about his arguments was the claim that some operations occurred on so small a scale no viable state or condition of war actually existed, so congressional authorization was unnecessary. Until now, presidential arguments relied on assertions of constitutionally permissible powers, but here was an arguably new dimension depending on the argument that low-scale or -intensity environments permitted the president much more authority in using military force.

This argument surfaced first in the Somalia intervention, which began in late 1992 because of a serious famine there caused largely by civil war. On December 3, the United Nations Security Council authorized the use of troops for purposes of humanitarian relief; the next day President Bush announced that the United States would contribute more than 20,000 troops to this multinational force. As this intervention was not a combat mission but one of humanitarian goodwill, it admittedly was debatable whether the president needed congressional authorization.[87]

The emergence of humanitarian missions involving U.S. forces was a fairly new development in the war powers issue. Senator George Mitchell

(Maine) believed that the president needed congressional authorization
even in these circumstances. Thus, in the first weeks of the Clinton administration, the Senate agreed on February 4, 1993 to a measure starting the
sixty-day clock in the War Powers Resolution if hostilities broke out. The
House did not vote on a measure until May 25; nonbinding, it partly reflected a more partisan debate arising earlier that month over the extent to
which U.S. troops should be under UN command. The two chambers never
reconciled their differences.[88]

Obviously, it was only a matter of time before deaths in the peacekeeping force occurred—in June twenty-three Pakistani peacekeepers were
killed, later three Italian soldiers, and then in August four U.S. soldiers died
after their vehicle hit a land mine. These events seemed to embody the type
of hostilities that should invoke the authority of the War Powers Resolution,
but in a response to the ranking minority members on the House Foreign
Affairs Committee, Representative Benjamin Gilman (New York) and Senate Foreign Relations Committee, Senator Jesse Helms (North Carolina),
Assistant Secretary of State for Legislative Affairs Wendy Sherman argued
that a state of hostilities did not exist. Sherman's response walked a very
fine line by stating the War Powers Resolution was intended for "sustained
hostilities," which did not describe the present situation. The letter characterized the incidents in Somalia as "intermittent military engagements" that
did not justify beginning the sixty-day clock or withdrawing U.S. troops.
Thus, the Clinton administration took advantage of undefined terminology
in the resolution to claim the characteristics or conditions on the ground did
not justify invoking it. In such cases, it believed presidential prerogative
should prevail.[89]

Ultimately, the mission shifted from humanitarian relief to peacekeeping,
making more and more members of Congress uncomfortable. This was more
a United Nations responsibility, and the military services, especially the
Army, did not want to find themselves pinned down in such operations. By
autumn 1993, Democrats had joined in drafting legislation to require the
withdrawal of U.S. troops. The deaths of eighteen U.S. soldiers, additionally
with the televised image of one of their bodies being dragged through the
streets, ended any politically sustainable argument for retaining U.S. forces
in Somalia for the long term. President Clinton agreed to a compromise that
cut off funds for any U.S. troops in Somalia after March 31, 1994.[90]

The White House made a similar argument about the characteristics of
the situation in Haiti to argue that the president did not need congressional
authorization for intervention there, either. After Clinton ordered 1,500 U.S.

troops to Haiti in September 1994, Congress passed resolutions supporting the troops and president but not giving formal authorization. As with Somalia, the president's dependence on a UN resolution to justify his deployment of U.S. forces stirred extensive criticism. To try to justify the president's action, Assistant Attorney General Walter Dellinger argued, as had Sherman, that the War Powers Resolution did permit the president to act with military force in a national emergency. Dellinger said the situation in Haiti was not definable as "war":

> We are not suggesting, however, that the United States cannot be said to engage in "war" whenever it deploys troops in a country at the invitation of that country's legitimate government. Rather, we believe that "war" does not exist where United States troops are deployed at the invitation of a fully legitimate government in circumstances in which the nature, scope, and duration of the deployment are such that the use of force involved does not rise to the level of "war."

War required greater duration and scope than this type of operation. Dellinger's interpretation even claimed that the resolution recognized such presidential authority in circumstances in which hostilities or imminent hostilities existed.[91]

Another elaboration on how the word "war" applied in relation to presidential and congressional control over using force occurred during the air operations against Serbia in the Kosovo crisis in 1999. On March 29, 1999, President Clinton reported his orders on U.S. air strikes to Congress using the standard "consistent with the War Powers Resolution" phrase. In testimony before the House International Relations Committee on April 21, Secretary of State Madeleine Albright told its members the United States was "not at war with Yugoslavia or its people." Any reference to war, of course, would have entailed activating the War Powers Resolution.[92] However, not everyone associated with U.S. policy spoke from the same script, as was evident a few weeks later when vice chair of the Joint Chiefs of Staff General Joseph Ralston described that situation as "a major war theater, as far as the air war is concerned."[93] Almost two hundred years ago, presidents, the Congress, and the courts agreed Congress had a role to play in deciding to use force in a limited or low-scale operation that was part of imperfect war, but now the proclaimed absence of conditions definable as war repeatedly were used as explicit reasons to exclude Congress from decisions to use military force.

Congress's reaction to these developments during the 1990s often was inconsistent and illustrated how partisan criticism, sometimes combined with a lack of intraparty unity, made an effective challenge to the president extremely difficult. This was especially true of the Republicans, as both the speaker of the House, Representative Dennis Hastert (Illinois), and the Senate majority leader, Senator Trent Lott (Mississippi), placed their party in a wait-and-see mode during the early spring of 1999, while Congress tried to determine what exactly to do after President Clinton announced air strikes.[94] The choices were to authorize, declare war, withdraw, or place limits on U.S. operations[95] The hesitancy was disturbing to watch for supporters of congressional authority, especially as the self-described "world's greatest deliberative body" procrastinated while some major parliaments, such as the British House of Commons or the German Bundestag, examined the reasons and uses for military force against Serbia more carefully.[96] The Rubicon that would probably have prompted congressional action was if the president decided to introduce ground troops. The House minority leader, Representative Richard Gephardt (Missouri), declared that air operations seemed to be pressuring the Serbian leader, Slobodan Milosevic, and that use of troops might be unnecessary. A key House Republican, Representative Douglas Bereuter (Nebraska), remarked that most members thought the use of ground troops as the point where Congress had to act.[97]

The actions that Congress took reinforced an image of inconsistency and hesitation. In April alone, the House voted against providing funds for ground troops in Yugoslavia unless Congress authorized their use. The House then defeated a concurrent resolution that would have required the president to remove U.S. forces from their existing position, rejected quite strongly (427–2) a declaration of war against Yugoslavia, and finally defeated by a 213–213 tie vote, a resolution supporting the air and missile strikes and other air operations against Yugoslavia the Senate passed nearly five weeks earlier. In May, the House rejected an amendment that would have denied authorized funds for ground forces in Yugoslavia except in circumstances of war. After supporting air strikes in late March, on May 4 the Senate tabled a resolution, by Senator John McCain (Arizona), that would have authorized the president "to use all necessary force and other means, in conjunction with the allies to establish NATO and U.S. objectives in Yugoslavia."[98] Altogether, these actions showed a Congress unable to muster the clarity of thought and resolve to pressure the president on the war powers issue.

The one attempt that tried to challenge the president on lack of authorization was a lawsuit filed by Representative Thomas Campbell (California) and twenty-five other members after the sixtieth day since the introduction of U.S. force through air strikes, which gave Campbell and his supporters grounds to argue the president had violated the War Powers Resolution. The federal district judge who ruled on the case, Paul Friedman, said that Campbell and the other plaintiffs did not have legal standing to bring this lawsuit, an opinion upheld by the federal court of appeals. The ruling stated that Congress had not done enough on its own to demonstrate its grievance, such as legislating a block on expending funds for military operations, which the president nonetheless had continued. Like the previous *Dellums* case, the court in essence said it could not do what the Congress must first attempt to do itself.[99]

It is not easy for Congress to challenge a president's policy in a way that undermines the office's authority, especially in the international arena. Yet Congress had fallen into a problem created by the very nature of the Balkan military operations, particularly in Kosovo. Using air power and avoiding ground intervention kept the hostilities on a scale that did not create very much grave concern or public alarm despite all the discussion in Congress about strategic objectives, time limits, and exit strategies. The Clinton administration tried to develop a format for military operations on such a limited scale that its representatives could argue the U.S was not in a state of war. Without the contexts of Cold War or a graphic act of aggression, such as Iraq's invasion of Kuwait, the administration believed it needed to find a way to use military force that would not encounter the type of political opposition during and after Vietnam or even after Somalia in 1993. Thus, the emphasis on definitions or conditions of war was very important, as was the claim that the War Powers Resolution gave the president the authority to initiate such actions where hostilities, not war, existed or were imminent.[100] The resolution's open-ended quality gave their argument credence.

What Congress tried to concentrate on during the Clinton administration to challenge this development was not irrelevant. Attempts by the president and others to argue that authority to use force without congressional approval could be derived from the UN—either from the self-defense clause of Article 51 or the authority of various UN Security Council resolutions—were a serious challenge to congressional authority.[101] In fact, the Contract with America, which the Republicans used as part of their successful strategy to regain control of both congressional chambers in 1994, criticized the administration for relying on UN authority and placing U.S. troops under UN command. The contract also promised to amend the War Powers Resolution to solve its problems.[102] Similar congressional concerns developed over the president's use of NATO obligations as a source of authority to use force in 1999 against Serbia. Even though Clinton's critics obviously pressed at times for political reasons, the downward spin of congressional authority over the use of military force did not reverse. Congress's role in war powers during the Clinton years probably slipped as much as it had in the early 1960s.

The next president, George W. Bush, built on Clinton's arguments for presidential control over military force even while disagreeing with the objectives of many of Clinton's actions. While Bush and other key Republicans campaigned in 2000 with promises that they would not commit U.S. forces to humanitarian or nation-building missions pursued by the Clinton administration, they had their own arguments and strategic justifications for seeking greater presidential freedom to use military force without Congress's consent. The Republicans did not wish to continue using the military as an instrument in "foreign policy as social work." The objective, instead, would be to wield armed force as needed against terrorists or hostile governments possessing weapons of mass destruction capable of hitting the United States.[103] As with the Clinton administration and others before, the disputes over power between the president and Congress originated from arguments over the desired uses and purposes of military force.

9/11 and Presidential Victory in War Powers

What had been an argument within the policy community about the appropriate role of military force in strategy took on more immediate ramifications after the terrorist attacks of September 11, 2001. The president may not have needed an authorization to use military force after 9/11. It was a clear attack made by non-state actors, Al-Qaeda, who operated primarily from Afghanistan, a country controlled by the Taliban, a very strict Islamist government that sympathized with them. By Article 51 of the United Nations Charter and the U.S. Constitution, the president was entitled to use force in the nation's self-defense. In such circumstances, U.S. legal and historical precedent showed that a president did not need congressional authorization to act in self-defense. However, a congressional authorization would show Al-Qaeda, the Taliban, any sympathetic governments, and the entire international community the extent of support the president had in a military response. A broadly written resolution also would provide the White House with additional authority to take certain measures both domestically and internationally to protect the United States and the American people. Although this work concentrates on military force, the authorization that Congress finally provided furnished the basis for U.S. policies on treating noncombatants and electronic monitoring of communications between selected foreign parties and people in the United States. The White House certainly wanted congressional authorization giving it greater flexibility in using force to pre-empt attacks against the United States. The wording in the draft resolution sent to Congress wanted the authority "to deter and pre-empt any future acts of terrorism or aggression against the United States."[104]

The controversy in those words was that the president seemed to seek an open-ended authority to use force not only against those directly linked to the 9/11 attacks but against countries and other possible actors who, it was thought, might be planning such action. This was very sweeping and potentially diverted attention from pursuing those most directly related to 9/11. Terrorism is not confined to Al-Qaeda or the Middle East, and the fact that no nation or combination of nations can ever fully eliminate it meant that this resolution could contain permanent authority. Relying on "pre-emption" invited actions that might be interpreted as offensive as much as defensive. Although both domestic law and some international lawyers argue that pre-emption is a defensive measure, this notion hardly enjoys unanimous support.[105] The chief counsel for the Democrats on the House Committee on International Relations later wrote that a consensus emerged to remove the problematic word "pre-empt" with "prevent."[106] While hardly itself a word with ironclad meaning—prevent might invite pre-emptive action—Congress ultimately gave the president the authority he sought by votes of 420–1 in the House and 98–0 in the Senate. The final version included as well the authorization "to use all necessary and appropriate force against those nations, organizations, or persons he determines planned, authorized, committed, or aided the terrorist attacks that occurred on September 11, 2001, or harbored such organizations or persons . . ."[107]

Unlike previous congressional authorizations, this one directed the use of force against another state and also "organizations" and "persons," which reflected the character of this conflict. Furthermore, as long as the president could determine such parties were linked to the September 11 attacks, he could use force against them. With the difficulties of determining who was in Al-Qaeda, which groups had ties with it, and the mobility of some in terrorist networks, this still could be very open-ended authority.[108] By giving the president the power to make these determinations, Congress authorized possible future operations. Vigorous congressional oversight would be necessary to ensure the accuracy of such determinations; whether Congress actually would provide it was unlikely. Finally, senators and representatives should have better anticipated that this language would become the foundation for future U.S. policies and actions about detainees and wiretapping.

It is hard to explain the resolution requesting authority to use force against Iraq without discussing the rationale behind the U.S.-led intervention there, but if the administration had been able to prove clearly that Saddam Hussein had assisted Al-Qaeda, it probably could have acted under the authority of the resolution passed after 9/11. However, it could not and never was able to prove Iraq "aided" the attack. Even without such proof, the Bush administration still argued it did not need an authorization. It cited the authorization for using force in the first Gulf War and suggested that the nonbinding resolution calling for removing Saddam Hussein from power in the Iraq Liberation Act of 1998 provided this authority.[109] Thus, accusations of Iraq's possession of weapons of mass destructions and ties with Al-Qaeda fallaciously justified defining the intervention in Iraq as a defensive act. Subsequent studies have shown that some claims also relied on distorted and manipulated evidence.[110]

The political and intellectual rationale behind the Bush administration's actions toward Iraq relied on arguments for preventive and pre-emptive measures advocated in September 2002 in the New National Security Strategy. Consequently, the U.S.-led operation against Iraq was a self-enunciated defensive war that hardly met the criteria set forth in international law. It resembled nothing more than the type of offensive action requiring clear congressional consent since the nation's founding. Bush also argued that his powers as commander-in-chief gave him the necessary authority to use force against Iraq, an argument a few key Republican senators, particularly Richard Lugar (Indiana) and Chuck Hagel (Nebraska), questioned. Given their prominence in the Senate—Lugar was then chair of the Senate Foreign Relations Committee and Hagel a committee member—the president probably recognized the need to turn to Congress.[111]

Also, it probably was important to the president to have a separate authorization to show to the American public, the international community, particularly the United Nations, and Saddam himself that he had Congress's support and was not just acting on his own. Given how much of the world's opinion regarded President Bush as little more than a gunslinger president, the backing of Congress would be critical. Finally, some of his advisers argued that the president would have political advantage in the upcoming

2002 mid-term elections if he could be seen as a "wartime president," particularly against candidates from a Democratic Party that still wrestled with its antiwar legacy from Vietnam, its perceived opposition to defense spending, and its misgivings and votes against the resolution in Congress just before actual operations in the first Gulf War. The Democrats might still emerge from the debate and vote looking weak on defense. The political backdrop in October 2002 is hard to quantify, but it certainly played a part in the preparation for the final vote authorizing military force.[112]

A White House draft of a resolution circulated among key Senate and House offices by mid-September. Rather than confining any operations to Iraq, the draft language sought authorization to use force to "restore international peace and security in the region."[113] Some members had strong misgivings about the draft. Senator Lugar and the ranking Democrat on the Foreign Relations Committee, Senator Joseph Biden (Delaware), wanted much stronger assurances the Bush administration would continue to explore diplomatic options and try to obtain support in the United Nations. In fact, they planned to introduce a draft version of the authorization saying so.[114] In his book about Congress's treatment of the Iraq resolution, Senator Robert C. Byrd of West Virginia wrote that when he showed the administration draft to Walter Dellinger, who prepared one of the major defenses of President Clinton's use of force, he told Byrd, "If Congress passes this, you can just hang out a sign that says 'Out of Business.'"[115]

In considering the bill, the Senate used the administration draft, introduced by the majority and minority leaders, Senators Thomas Daschle (South Dakota) and Trent Lott. However, in the House of Representatives, Speaker Hastert and House minority leader Richard Gephardt introduced a separate version. Gephardt was also preparing his campaign for the Democratic nomination in 2004. It is unclear how much his political ambition figured into his role in the House version, but he was certainly sensitive to Democrats' general vulnerability on national defense. He also was receptive to the arguments of former Clinton national security specialists, including Richard Holbrooke, Kenneth Pollack, and James Steinberg, who believed that the United States had to confront Saddam Hussein.[116] While the president was seeking authorization to use force in a way that contestably involved pre-emptive or preventive war, the House version supported the administration's goals more than the final legislation that might have emerged from the Senate.[117] The House International Relations Committee approved the resolution 31–11. The report language accompanying the resolution explained what many representatives and senators hoped—

namely, Saddam Hussein and some still reluctant allies finally would see the determination behind the U.S. position and would choose their respective positions with or against the United States.[118] While some who voted for the resolution hoped to avoid war, the president's most likely course in Iraq was pretty obvious.

In the Senate, Joseph Lieberman (Connecticut) introduced a slightly modified version of the House bill, which became the one considered for debate and voting. Even though the Senate defeated five amendments to the bill, floor deliberation on the Iraq Resolution was almost pro forma, with most senators reading prepared statements and then departing. The strategy of the administration's supporters seems to have been to get the Senate to vote just on the House-approved version without any amendments, since the latter would have required creating a House–Senate conference committee. In fact, a cloture vote eventually limited remaining debate to thirty hours, and not all of that time was used. On October 10, the Senate approved the resolution by a vote of 77–23.[119] The authorization gave the president the authority "as he determines to be necessary and appropriate in order to (1) defend the national security of the United States against the continuing threat posed by Iraq; and (2) enforce all relevant United Nations Security Council resolutions regarding Iraq."[120]

The Use of Force Against Iraq Resolution stated that it provided the president authority under Section 5(b) of the War Powers Resolution, which was Congress's effort to assert its authority over a decision that the president believed he controlled. Yet if Congress had failed to approve the resolution, President Bush undoubtedly would have asserted the same authority his father had said was his during the first Gulf War and continued with the military operation. Presidential requests for authority to use force no longer originated from a conviction that the Constitution required them. Dwight Eisenhower was probably the last president who arguably saw the issue that way. What always had been a decision with central constitutional concerns and domestic and international political considerations was now almost completely political. Presidents wanted maximum political support behind their actions. If they thought an authorizing resolution improved their standing and enhanced their ability to accomplish their policy objectives, they turned to Congress. If not, they bypassed it. Meanwhile, when Congress provided a president with such an authorization, it thought it met its constitutional requirements.

However, Congress had not met its obligations. By giving the president the authority to determine the necessary measures, Congress surrendered most of its ability to influence future events. After the mid-term election in November 2006, the Democratic-controlled Congress found itself trying to correct the course that the United States took since October 2002, thanks partly to the cooperation of some who then had voted with the president. Review of the administration's claims about Iraq's ties to Al-Qaeda was totally inadequate. Much was taken at face value because most members disliked Saddam Hussein as well. Congress's actions had been as deleterious as in 1964 with the Tonkin Gulf Resolution. Deciding to use force in an offensive operation, and Iraq was a war of choice, required both the president and Congress's deliberative judgment. Such deliberation did not happen. The fear that presidents could take the country into war on their own had materialized, regardless of Congress's approved authorizations. Congress's concern was more about whether to give the president the authority he requested rather than examining the cited assumptions and evidence and claims made about the prospects for success in postwar Iraq.

Again, arguments similar to those against the Gulf of Tonkin Resolution have been made about the use-of-force measure for Iraq. If, in 2002, Congress acted on false or misrepresented evidence, some claim that the war is unconstitutional. Yet reliance on contestable evidence is a weak foundation on which to make accusations against the president and his advisers. Congress could have delved much more into the veracity of the administration's claims and accusations. Many observers at home and abroad urged caution and closer review of the administration's justifications and estimates about the necessary level of military force to accomplish the mission. However, the weight of not wanting to oppose a president in a period of crisis, of not desiring to take a controversial position so close to mid-term elections, and of not being able or willing to take the necessary steps to reassert Congress's voice prevailed. By 2007, the monetary cost and loss of human lives—Iraqi, American, and other coalition members—had become increasingly difficult to bear.

Congressional Losses on Other Fronts

The controversy over war powers and executive and congressional collaboration is not the only area where Congress has lost influence or control over the use of military force. In recent years, a disturbing trend has emerged to circumvent or weaken congressional control over the expenditure of funds on selected military and foreign policy operations. Congress has used its authority to stop funding for military operations after specific dates, and is trying to do so as of this writing in 2007 to end most military operations in Iraq. Suspending money is tantamount to repealing an authorization, even if Congress did not pass one earlier, and it should effectively either block an operation or end it after a specific date. After all, the Constitution prohibits the spending of funds if not appropriated by Congress. If a president or government office does so, Congress has little other control over the use of force, particularly if it has not exercised its power through an authorization or tried to suspend operations through a joint resolution. At this point, Congress must take additional steps to stop a president from bypassing its control of the purse for government policy.

The Iran–Contra crisis was an example of an administration trying to continue a controversial operation even after Congress denied it funds. The Contras were insurgents opposed to the Sandinista government in Nicaragua. Beginning in 1982 and culminating in 1984, Congress began to block expending appropriated funds to support the Contras. Some initial efforts to stop the funding were not completely successful, but in late 1984 Representative Edward Boland (Massachusetts) won House support for an amendment to block spending funds for the Contras by the CIA, Department of Defense, or other government offices involved in intelligence matters. That provision appeared quite watertight, but a memo written by a legal counsel to the president's Intelligence Oversight Board argued that the Boland Amendment did not cover the NSC, a controversial, debatable claim. Also, no evidence showed that the president, as required by law, had determined to have the NSC coordinate an operation that should have been in the CIA's hands.[121] Nevertheless, armed with that memo, the Reagan administration found a rationale linking illegal arms sales to Iran to the use of some of that money, as well as money from other private sources, to support the Contras.

Here was a scheme that completely bypassed Congress's ability to set terms on expending funds and have a role in determining the use of military force. This operation was not reported to Congress as part of any presidential finding about a covert operation. The implication of the legal memo on the NSC was that it was not accountable to the elected representatives of the American people but only to the president. The best means of guaranteeing accountability, and not just the green-visor type that provides and tracks money, but accountability for decision and action, is by comprehensive congressional review. Defenders of such independent NSC action naturally argued that the administration had so acted out of its responsibility for the well-being and protection of the American people, and the election process would enable voters to render judgment about both the process and outcome—that is, if they ever learned the pertinent facts about the case. As Louis Fisher suggests, the argument that these private measures were constitutional because they were not appropriations as specified in the Boland Amendment misses the fundamental point in the Constitution about separation of the purse and sword.[122] Even if in the national interest, the Iran–Contra Affair was a serious violation of the Constitution. In 1989, after vetoing two earlier versions, President George H.W. Bush signed a bill prohibiting the transfer of appropriated funds to any foreign government or party, as well as U.S. citizens, to support operations forbidden by U.S. law.[123]

A different type of outside funding for the use of U.S. military forces occurred during the first Gulf War. To become a member of the coalition of nations against Iraq's invasion of Kuwait, a government had to promise that its funds would go directly to the Department of Defense for compensation for U.S. forces' military operations. On learning about this arrangement, Senator Robert Byrd, then the Senate majority leader, protested that this arrangement bypassed Congress's appropriations power. Based on that concern, the money ultimately went to the Department of Treasury instead, where it could be released to the Department of Defense only after Congress appropriated it.[124]

In recent years, Congress's practice of lump sum appropriations has strengthened the presidential hand. Such appropriations allow presidents to move funds from one program to another without much congressional input or approval, a practice almost the equivalent of giving the president an independent spending authority; for example, money can go to military expenditures without specific authorization or appropriation.[125] President George W. Bush repeatedly requested such lump sum arrangements after 9/11, at the beginning of the "global war on terrorism," and for military operations in Iraq. Spending such money requires no previous notice or report to Congress, although the White House must consult with the appropriations committees. So far Congress has largely insisted on appropriating money through traditional accounts and not just in lump sums left to presidential discretion. When consultation has occurred, it has not always met congressional expectations.[126]

The use of lump sum appropriations illustrates why it is unrealistic to rely solely on the appropriations power as the source of authorization for using military force. The magnitude of modern defense budgets goes beyond the wildest imagination of any delegate to the Constitutional Convention. Congress can certainly remove or adjust funds, but the complexity and size of defense appropriations bills for today's standing military, combined with the global scale of U.S. defense commitments, make it harder to link defense funding to specific future operations. In fact, since 2003 defense planning requirements have depended on projections for necessary capabilities rather than assessments of specific threats.[127] It was possible in 1787 to try to anticipate beforehand the specific location and scenario in which an authorized, funded weapons system would be used, but given the diverse nature of modern conflict today, it is very unrealistic, difficult, and possibly reckless. Thus, Pentagon program managers do not regularly prepare funding requests based on projections to use a particular weapons system in a specific theater of operations. The president takes initial action with the existing military and funding when committing military force, even if he or she must request additional funds to support the deployment. Once military forces are deployed, it is unlikely that Congress will pull them back by denying funding before shots are fired. With such a large standing military, Congress operates with serious disadvantages that it did not have 200 years ago.

A related pattern that has weakened Congress's control over defense spending is the use of requests for supplemental appropriation. Supplementals, as they are called, often do relate to the costs of specific operations that did not fall within the normal defense authorization and appropriations cycle. In 1965–66, President Johnson and Secretary of Defense McNamara repeatedly relied on such requests to fund the costs of increasing the American commitment in Vietnam. Estimating the costs of a war is not easy under most circumstances, but using supplemental requests enables a president and others to avoid providing Congress with estimates it can evaluate in the annual budget process. McNamara argued that supplementals were a way of controlling the military by not giving it more open-ended funding through the regular legislation. Congress did not like the practice, and later the White House backed away from resorting to such requests. However, President George W. Bush has recurrently submitted supplementals to Congress to fund wars in Iraq and Afghanistan. These bypass the authorization process and weaken Congress's ability to exercise effective control over defense spending and the overall budget. Congress justly argues that it should be possible to do a better job of estimating costs than can be included in the annual defense budget submitted for its review.[128]

If the Congress's role is diminished, so too is the status of accountability in the American system. Responsibility for decisions is not necessarily lost, but what should be a decision-making process involving as much interaction between Congress and president as possible increasingly has become the action of an individual—the president. Accountability remains, but after the fact, in the form of the next election. The American system, though, sought accountability in making a decision through congressional involvement. Consultation, review, deliberation, and authorization would ensure the citizenry that full consideration of known options had occurred. Through Congress's vote, presidential action would have both an endorsement and stronger assurance of public and congressional backing.

That mixture of assurance and accountability increasingly is missing in the United States. Ironically, this development is occurring when several democratic governments are trying to strengthen their accountability procedures related to using military force.[129] Why this is happening clearly depends on history, the content of their own constitutions, and their societies' values and characteristics. However, the mission and characteristics of the types of military force used also affect interpretations and judgments about one's own constitution and future developments. That is a lesson of the American experience. Using limited military force has always been an area where no completely satisfactory formula exists in the U.S. Constitution. But to understand why imperfect war poses such difficult constitutional challenges, it is also vital to move beyond the Constitution, presidents, courts, and Congress, and look at some of the features and history of imperfect or limited war in the United States. The very characteristics of limited war and how presidents have assessed the value and role of military force have significantly affected the outcome of constitutional and political struggles over the use of force.

Chapter 4

Keeping War Usable:
A Place for Imperfect War

As the twentieth century advanced, the conviction that limited war or other types of low-scale military operations fell under presidential prerogative to use as necessary grew. Whether the justification rested on the commander-in-chief clause, using military support to support foreign policy, humanitarian concerns, or arguments the operations were too limited in scale to qualify as war or hostilities, presidents' actions increasingly challenged the framework for legislative control over the use of force contained in the Constitution and subsequent law. This included effective control of both the uniformed military as well as other instruments of force involving the intelligence community or, as discussed later, contractors. The increase in presidential control over the military grew hand in hand with the increase of American power and responsibility on the global level.

Not surprisingly, as the military became a large, permanent, standing force after mid-century, opinions developed within it as to how presidents should use the military. An inherent tension began to emerge at times between military professionals who sometimes thought their civilian leadership did not understand the military instrument of power and presidents who believed that their commanders did not appreciate the political factors and strategic objectives the White House thought important to both its political stature and the national well-being. Such tension had occurred previously, but by the early 1950s the military, especially the Army, recurrently disagreed with presidents who wanted to use force in various limited or low-scale operations to accomplish foreign policy objectives that were not always clearly defined. This disagreement or difference of perspective significantly influenced how presidents used force. Not only did they have to weigh congressional and constitutional factors, they also had to consider the capabilities of the military and what it believed it could or could not do. A question emerged as to how presidents could use force, military or otherwise, in ways that could diminish both congressional and military resistance. A triangle of tension existed with both Congress and elements of the military sometimes disagreeing with presidents over the use of force.

Keeping war usable is a consideration that would have perplexed America's founders. They did not want the United States so immersed in the world's political problems that it would have to regularly turn to war to advance or defend its interests. The Constitution sought to make war difficult to commence, thanks to the separation of powers, the division of purse from sword, and the intentionally small size of the military itself. The limited types of engagements fought at the very end of the eighteenth and first decades of the nineteenth centuries were acceptable uses of military force aimed at defending American rights and property or advancing expansion. That was especially true of the former rather than the latter reason, since expansionism generated debate, such as that over the War of 1812 and more so the Mexican War, about justifying both the goal and means of offensive use of force. A "usable" war requires objectives that the majority of Americans and Congress can support.

Two destructive world wars and the atomic age raised different questions about keeping war usable. Thanks to technology and the mobilization of entire populations, war was now so costly, especially in human terms, it was harder to justify. By the last half of the twentieth century some thought war was obsolete, a suicidal instrument guaranteeing the destruction of its initiator as much as of the enemy. If any form of war could still be practiced, it had to occur at a reduced level of destruction and loss of human life. Ideally, those using war would find ways to calibrate and control it at lower levels at which it could not accelerate on its own momentum to unleash the fury of mass destruction. The United States pursued that course because even in the nuclear age it believed it had to find ways to retain war as a usable instrument of policy.

Limiting War to Make It a Better Political Instrument

To credit the revolutionary and constitutional generation with an appreciation of von Clausewitz's famous dictum, "War is nothing but the continuation of policy with other means," is not unrealistic or nationalistic.[1] Those Americans knew why they resorted to military force, whether against a foreign country seizing their ships on the high seas or Indians. America was one of the theaters of the constant eighteenth-century Anglo-French wars, even if the country escaped the violence of large mobilized wars occurring after the French Revolution through Napoleon—the wars that so affected von Clausewitz. When Alexander Hamilton told his readers in *The Federalist, No. 28,* that "the means to be employed must be proportioned to the extent of the mischief," he reminded them that war must not be allowed to spin out of control in either its objectives or conduct. In fact, "for a long time to come," Hamilton believed the United States would have to "recollect that the extent of the military force must at all events be regulated by the resources of the country."[2] Hamilton knew resources greatly determine the usability of war. He also knew that resources went beyond materiel such as weapons, industry, and food supply to include public spirit and conviction. But when an army was necessary, Hamilton knew the United States would have to fight wars on a limited scale and match its objectives to its means, including in almost any conflict against another state. Only in the arena of war against Native Americans might Hamilton's fellow citizens argue otherwise and pursue neither limited means nor limited objectives.

The concept of limited war has gone by many names among both soldiers and statesmen—small wars, *petit guerre, kleine Kriege,* brushfire wars, guerrilla warfare, insurgency and counterinsurgency, expeditions, proxy wars, low-scale and low-intensity operations, or military operations other than war.[3] Each term embodies its own subtle differences as well. An American military dictionary published right before the War of 1812 defined *petit guerre* as "a war of post, or that species of warfare used in carrying on military operations upon a small scale, and consist[ed] in surprising the enemy's posts, convoys and escorts, planting ambuscades, and taking every advantage of *ruses de guerre.*"[4] Writing in the early 1980s about American notions of limited war two hundred years earlier, Reginald Stuart stated, "'Limited war' refers to the restricted use of armed forces to achieve specific objectives short of prostrating the antagonist state."[5] In his recent study of American military culture, Adrian Lewis makes a critical point by noting that limited war is at the strategic or operations level. At the tactical level, "where the killing takes place, . . . [t]here is nothing limited about limited war."[6]

Only a few years ago, Max Boot sought to demonstrate that the United States had a long history of fighting limited wars overshadowed by public memory of major conflicts. Boot commented, "Most of these campaigns were fought by a relatively small number of professional soldiers pursuing limited objectives with limited means."[7] Reflecting the impact of military operations during the 1990s and 9/11, Boot intentionally studied only struggles "between American forces and those of less-developed countries."[8] However, to understand how the founders and the early republic's leaders understood limited war demands consideration of some conflicts that Boot excludes—the American Revolution, the Quasi-War, and campaigns against Native Americans.

Nearly all definitions illustrate how the meaning of limited war refers to the amount of resources and personnel used, scope of the conflict, or extent of the threat and the enemy's characteristics. Over-relying on any single factor in defining limited war can lead to confusion. If we focus on just the scale of resources committed, for example, we could argue that U.S. strategy during World War II was that of a limited war because the United States imposed limits on the number of people in uniform to avoid undermining industrial output. Yet calling that war "limited" is ludicrous. No single definition of limited war is perfect; circumstances and objectives greatly influence each.

The desire to place war under some recognized limits or control already existed a century before the American Revolution. The horrifying destructiveness of the Thirty Years War in Europe (1618–1648) produced a movement to try to develop laws to govern states and their conduct of war, which inspired Hugo Grotius's *Rights of War and Peace* (1625). If war became too destructive its utility as an instrument of state would become useless.[9] Human and financial costs increased to nearly unbearable levels during those thirty years. One German historian estimates that the percentage of troops killed in battle rose from 5.7% in the fifteenth century to 15.7% in the seventeenth, and that the Thirty Years War had killed one million out of thirteen million Germans. While more expensive than "hire-for-fire" mercenaries, one consequence was a move to professional armies to ensure that the state or sovereign had more control over the conduct of war. Simultaneously, because of the costliness of armies, governments became more anxious not to allow them to be destroyed in spasms of state-initiated violence. War and society should largely be separate; in Frederick the Great's opinion, an ideal war was one in which civilians were unaware of its existence.[10]

These objectives were admittedly concerned more with limitations on war than implementing limited war as understood today. However, much as the Enlightenment sought to find balance in the rules of nature and the universe, the eighteenth century witnessed an effort to achieve balance in war, and to establish and adhere to rules governing its conduct and objectives that would make war serve reason rather than passion.[11] Annihilating or to-tally defeating an enemy was not the customary objective; goals were tangible or quantifiable, such as possessing key pieces of land, recognizing a right of succession, or settling a disputed claim.[12]

The leaders of the American colonists who fought and won their independence from Great Britain shared Enlightenment ideals. As they tried to establish boundaries on the effects of public passion in politics in the Constitution, they also hoped to limit the degree of passion in conduct and outcome of the revolution itself. The American ministers in Paris assured the French they did not want their revolution to fuel passion in ways that would revisit the barbarities of the past. The message was one to reassure any member of the French court that the Americans' goal was not to undermine social and political order. Moreover, also consider advice by John Adams and Benjamin Franklin against mobilizing merchants, farmers, and fishermen to limit war's impact on society, the economy, and public emotion.[13] Like their European counterparts, they believed war should not become a total experience.

The conduct of the war showed not only conformity to Enlightenment standards of warfare but also the realization that new, unconventional types of warfare were necessary. Interestingly, the British had made a similar conclusion. One could conduct war by siege, maneuver, and set piece battles, which reflected the Enlightenment tradition, or resort to irregular forces, rangers, and Native American allies in raids that the British had learned alongside the American colonists, especially in the French and Indian War. Both sides turned to these options.[14] General George Washington had read some standard contemporary military works on fortification and sieges and tried to concentrate his forces to defeat the British in battles he hoped might be decisive, although that type of victory eluded him throughout most of the revolution. Washington also resorted to unconventional means to try to erode the British position, but his record in this endeavor became overshadowed by that of his trusted subordinate, General Nathaniel Greene, who often dispersed his small army and relied on partisan or irregular raiders to harass the British in the Carolinas.[15]

This form of warfare drew on a separate thread of American experience in war having little to do with the Enlightenment model. Early American leaders knew more of the latter from reading, but they often experienced the former personally or by proximity to the actual events. Even in Europe there had been a form of limited war that many would not regard as part of the European and later American military traditions so affected by von Clausewitz or Antoine Henri, Baron de Jomini. It was war against "rebels, infidels, and 'savages,'" and the English tended to regard the Irish as all three.[16] The same rules applied in North America to Native American tribes against whom the British colonists and their American successors demanded "extirpative" warfare. It was war unlimited in its goals, even though fought with limited numbers and resources. While the European model moved to avoid war against noncombatants, this form of war relied on it. Recently called the "first way of war" by John Grenier, its pattern was continued in many nineteenth-century campaigns against Native Americans and was evident in some Civil War operations, and left a legacy traceable to the present day.[17] Two interrelated lessons emerged from this experience. The first is that one person's limited war can be a war of survival for the enemy, compelling the latter to resort to all available unlimited means. The second is that limited means and measures in war sometimes can produce decisive results, particularly when waging war against an adversary lacking in technological resources or perhaps equal prowess.

Never declared and rarely authorized, as these wars occurred in American territory—claimed, already organized, or adjacent to it—they obviously were seen as an internal matter, not subject to the rules governing conflict among states. However, they were as much acts of policy as any use of limited military force against a foreign power. They were not pointless exercises, although certain acts of violence within them were. Justified by a sense of mission to expand the realm of liberty on the North American continent and differing concepts of property and use of land, many excused such wars by the very purpose of the conflict, not through any congressional action. This part of the American historical record created a pattern for using limited military force that often rationalized contemporary or subsequent actions against foreign governments or parties for the same reasons—a combination of special mission reinforced by a conviction of technological superiority.[18]

Yet as shown earlier, the first generation of American leaders demonstrated an appreciation of both the strategic role of using limited military force and the value of collaboration between Congress and the president in undeclared or imperfect wars against traditional states. The wars against republican France or the Barbary pirates were as clear examples of the calculated use of limited military force for a political objective as we could want. Of course, given its small size, the American navy had little other choice. Defeat, annihilation, or subjugation of any of these early adversaries was neither possible nor desired. The objective was to defend Americans' rights to engage in commerce on the high seas as a neutral or to conduct that same type of commerce without danger of acts of piracy or seizure of American property and citizens. This strategy worked well in those early conflicts.

However, the War of 1812 signaled a change in the rationale in American thinking that started to move the nation away from Enlightenment concepts of war and policy. Rising American nationalism paralleled a similar development in Europe, where the instigator was not Great Britain but Napoleonic France. Although it is fair to argue that the overall course of the War of 1812 remained within the older parameters of limited war, the clamor for territorial expansion and the rise of the trans-Appalachian West would become a factor in pressing the United States toward more offensive forms of war, such as that against Mexico. Popular passion and European nationalism similarly affected attitudes toward war that supported a trend some call "military romanticism."[19] This line of thought was a reaction to the mass mobilized armies of the early French Revolution, the rise of European nationalism, and clearly the model of Napoleon himself. True to the age's spirit, military romantics reversed the formulaic Enlightenment approach to war, stressing the role of individual creativity and force in warfare. Framing their arguments with examples from the Napoleonic Wars, the romantics sought the decisive battle that could turn both military and political tides to the victor's favor. With their acceptance of large armies and the role of battle, it seemed that limited war had little place.[20]

Today the most-read and -remembered military romantic is Carl von Clausewitz. Because of his later impact on American military thinking and the modern American strategic community, it is important to consider briefly what he said about limited war. Some, of course, would argue that he said very little, and thanks to his emphasis on battle was instead a high priest of mass mayhem on the battlefield. World War I often serves as the evidence for this interpretation.[21] Perhaps that view of Clausewitz ultimately depends more on the conclusions and applications that some readers draw from his writings than on what Clausewitz himself actually said. He saw a role for limited war or limits on its scale for both operational and strategic reasons. Operationally, limited operations already had an established place, illustrated by operations in the American Revolution. While the Americans drew their notions from their own experience and their shared knowledge with the British, Clausewitz was more familiar with the French experience. Several writers, French and German among others, had discussed *petit guerre*. Indeed, scholars estimate that by 1750 about 20 percent of the French army was devoted to such missions, mainly as light infantry to conduct raids, patrols, and reconnaissance.[22] Clausewitz delivered some lectures in 1810–1811 reviewing his thinking on these types of limited operations, which he probably saw as more of a sideline or complement to larger military operations than a completely separate alternative.[23]

However, Clausewitz endeavors to remind the reader that war must always serve political ends and not become the end itself, an argument that converged effectively with convictions of some Americans like Alexander Hamilton. Clausewitz's message states that the chosen means of a conflict must serve the desired political objective. To a modern reader, Clausewitz can sound contradictory on limited war, as noted by modern scholar Peter Paret, who refers to Clausewitz's 1804 distinction between wars to destroy an opponent and those intended just to weaken an adversary enough to get acceptable terms at the peace table. Yet, Clausewitz goes on to argue that an opponent's willpower must be broken, which, depending on the scale of destroyed willpower, is not always an objective of limited war.[24] By 1830, when Clausewitz indicated that he regarded Book One in his study as complete, he presented a somewhat more nuanced view of war that obviously reflected his ability to reflect on the entire subject while not immediately affected by wartime events.

> We can now see that in war many roads lead to success, and that they do not involve the opponent's outright defeat. They range from *the destruction of the enemy's forces, the conquest of his territory, to a temporary occupation or invasion, to projects with an immediate political purpose and finally to passively awaiting the enemy's attacks.* Any one of these may be used to overcome the enemy's will; the choice depends on circumstances.[25]

Here is a set of considerations anticipating the late 1950s and 1960s arguments for flexible response and the choices of capabilities to fight low-, medium-, and high-intensity operations in today's terminology. Clausewitz argued that circumstances must define the means used. He does not talk of total defeat, and overcoming "the enemy's will" does not inevitably mean breaking it but rather influencing it. The objective must be to guarantee that war and the use of force serve political ends. Force was not only a means used in matters of national survival but also an instrument of pressure or coercion to secure a major foreign policy objective.

American contemporaries did not know of Clausewitz, and of course

American control over the use of military force originated from a strong suspicion of the military and fear that a standing military could seize control of the country and its government. Clausewitz still wrote for a monarchy, not a German republic, but his emphasis on political control of military force clearly paralleled American convictions, even if he worried much more about war's momentum and its capacity to seize control of its direction without subservience to political ends. For war to be a usable, effective instrument for a state, it had to serve the political purposes of national strategy and not become the master of the state and its leadership.

Through the mid-nineteenth century, presidents used the military in various ways—an instrument of territorial expansionism against Mexico, an agent of commercial growth in the opening of Japan, a force for Indian removal and protecting settlers and overland routes, protecting American personal, property, and trade rights on high seas throughout the world, and, finally, as a mechanism to quash secession and the dissolution of the Union. Most of these involved using actual force at one time or another, except Commodore Perry's visits to Japan, where his ships symbolized a potential for the use of force if necessary. Clearly, presidents and Congress alike viewed the military as an instrument of foreign policy as well as defense and used it as such, sometimes at the cost of congressional influence but often with respect for Congress's role. Perhaps a factor was continued suspicion toward the military. For example, the Union quickly demobilized its army after its victory in 1865. Simultaneously Congress aggressively fought to regain powers it yielded or lost during the Civil War. Both before and after the War, Congress did not always give presidents the authority to use force.

American Military Culture and Imperfect War

While disputes between Congress and presidents over the control of military force occurred during the nineteenth century, other debates transpired in the military, and sometimes between the military and a president, over how the military should be used. Everyone who has studied the Mexican or Civil War briefly can identify examples of how generals and officers sometimes chafed under presidents' commands, the most noteworthy General George B. McClellan's struggle with President Lincoln, often portrayed in terms of the former's condescending contempt for the latter. Yet a recent study of McClellan shows that his disagreements with Lincoln rested greatly on professional and political judgments about the war's nature, conduct, and objectives.[26] Like any number of successors, McClellan lost to the president's constitutional position and authority. However, in the aftermath of the Civil War a growing clarity about the preferred use of the military started to emerge in some officers' writings and statements. A noticeable divergence developed at times between national political aspirations stated by civilian leadership and the perspectives of the services' emerging professional cultures.

How much the American military, particularly the Army, systematically studied and integrated lessons from its more limited operations during the nineteenth century is open to question. Professional Army education at West Point relied heavily on Napoleonic and military romantic models, which concentrated on, among other things, using large armies and conducting large battles with hoped-for decisive results.[27] The Civil War fulfilled those intellectual preconceptions and predilections in ways for the Army that were not available to the Navy. There was no Trafalgar in the Civil War. Afterward the Army's experiences revolved around frontier duty and missions resembling constabulary or police work—monitoring the movement of Native Americans and settlers, attempting to enforce the terms of peace treaties, pursuing and fighting bands of Native Americans and bandits, and exploration. In 1881 Brigadier General John Pope, Commander of the Department of Missouri, complained that campaigns against Native Americans were not "conducive to the proper discharge of military duty or the acquirement, either in theory or practice, by officers and soldiers of a professional knowledge or even of the ordinary tactics of a battalion."[28] In short, Pope preferred to avoid these operations. Nearly 120 years later some officers similarly complained that humanitarian or peacekeeping missions eroded military skills. Reflecting on parallels with the modern Army, in 2002 Lieutenant Colonel John Nagl wrote, "The Indian wars never reverberated in the collective consciousness of the American army."[29]

Starting in the 1870s, what did reverberate was the European, especially Prussian, legacy, and Clausewitz, whose work appeared in translation in 1873. Pressed by reforms led by Emory Upton and others, the Army oriented itself even more to conceptions and the experience of war drawn from European experience—especially from Napoleon through the wars of German unification. Thus, "the U.S. Army embraced the conventional Prussian military system as a paragon of professionalism at the same time that the American Army was engaged in a frontier war against the Indians—the most unorthodox of the U.S. Army's 19th century enemies."[30] An even older tradition arguably shaped both Prussian and American biases—"a presumption that battle under any guise other than a no-nonsense, head-to-head confrontation between sober enemies is or should be unpalatable"—which Victor Davis Hanson attributes to the ancient Greeks.[31] Yet as compelling as the Greek model might be to late nineteenth-century officers' intellect and emotions, it did not present frameworks for training, organization, and, as Upton particularly maintained, freedom from "excessive civilian control."[32]

The Army, in particular, seemed to position itself to fight the types of war it desired rather than the missions that the nation's leadership wanted it to fulfill. The conditions during and after the Spanish-American War, particularly with the Filipino Insurrection, confronted the United States with the fact it now needed an imperial army like Great Britain's. For the British army, colonial campaigning, often against capable adversaries equipped with less technology, was the norm during the nineteenth century. Put another way, small wars to the British were conflicts in which both sides did not fight with regular troops or very similar weapons and equipment. In contemporary military discourse, they were "asymmetrical"; one side used resources and capabilities quite different from the other. Such notions varied greatly from the prevalent American military mindset at the end of the nineteenth century.[33] To get American forces to operate in ways that they did not prefer required strong civilian leadership rather than any internal impulse for change. That began with Elihu Root's appointment as secretary of war in August 1899 and climaxed, one might say, when Theodore Roosevelt became president in 1901 after William McKinley was assassinated. Root found himself responsible for an army of 100,000, two-thirds of whom were deployed overseas—an unprecedented situation for an army that only a decade before was largely garrisoned on the closing American frontier.[34]

At the start of the twentieth century, most Army or Marine operations abroad relying on forces in limited or low-scale dimensions occurred by executive prerogative, without formal congressional consent. Nevertheless, a practice emerged of systematic review of field successes and failures and initial attempts to develop some doctrine related to small wars or low-intensity military operations. Going into the Philippines, the Army relied on "lessons" learned mostly from its occupying the American South during Reconstruction, with little structured knowledge to draw on for what today we might describe as a stabilization, peacemaking, and peacekeeping operation.[35] The Army also changed its conduct during some operations against Native Americans during the late nineteenth century, when it attempted somewhat to improve civil–military coordination, provide fairer governance through attention to grievances, economic needs, and efforts to avoid noncombatant casualties.[36] However, as yet there was no simultaneous effort to present these experiences in any systematic analysis that could then be presented in the form of a doctrine.[37] The Army itself was divided over the question of going into the Philippines. A Civil War veteran like General Nelson Miles thought the islands were too far away and that defeat of the rebels would be impossible; in fact, Miles wanted to return the Army to one of its old functions in the United States—building roads! Others, such as General Leonard Wood, governor of U.S.-occupied Cuba, shared the American Progressivism optimism about government-led reform, and argued the Army could bring stability, economic growth, and new infrastructure. Wood tried such programs in Cuba and Puerto Rico, and believed these policies applied to the Philippines.

Through its role in suppressing the Philippine insurrection and its response to domestic crises, such as the San Francisco earthquake, some in the Army began to consider moving it away from the late nineteenth-century, Prussian-inspired model, and into settings where it became more involved in civilian-related activities.[38] The Army tried to create a doctrine from its Philippine experiences and other limited engagements during the first years of the twentieth century. The 1905 *Field Service Regulations* discussed insurrections and the importance of protecting local populations while placing the burden of fighting on the insurgents themselves, but at the same time discouraged patrolling and offered little insight on how to obtain intelligence. Regulations for cavalry and infantry drill referred to "minor warfare," but said little about the importance of civil affairs, intelligence, or field operations.[39] However, the experience of World War I drew the Army back toward its earlier operational and intellectual comfort zone. It was the Marines who developed a much more elaborate formal doctrine on small wars.

As ocean-going soldiers, the Marines were obviously well placed for presidents to order them into several low-scale operations or small wars. While they studied the Army's Philippine experience, it was their own role in interventions in Haiti (1915–1934), the Dominican Republic (1919–1924), and Nicaragua (1927–1933) that pushed the Marines to discuss small wars in memos and their professional journals and then in 1935 compile much of this into a *Manual of Small Wars Operations,* which five years later the Marines decided to publish as the *Small Wars Manual.* Their definition of a small war is of obvious interest, but what is even more interesting is the source of political authority cited for such operations.

Operations undertaken under executive authority, wherein military force is combined with diplomatic pressure in the internal or external affairs of another state whose government is unstable, inadequate, or unsatisfactory for the preservation of life and such interests as are determined by the foreign policy of our nation.[40]

The immediate reference to executive authority indicates that the *Manual* assumed such conflicts were on a scale where congressional authorization was unnecessary. This did not reflect the Marines' calculated intent to deny a congressional role, but rather the historical pattern of such operations all the way back to most of their nineteenth-century missions involving protecting the rights of American citizens and property. The second key point is the explicit context of these operations within foreign policy. As they occur within a foreign policy framework, they also are within boundaries in which the president has a broader degree of authority than in defense and war-making. Thus, even before World War II the constitutional control of using force in small wars or the founders' imperfect war was now based, it seemed, on presidential authority. In 1940, as the United States turned its attention toward the wars in Asia and Europe probably no one in Congress ever would have noticed the concept outlined in the *Small Wars Manual,* and if they had, it is unclear what they might have done.

The Pendulum between Perfect and Imperfect War

The scale and nature of the military mission, not the constitutional framework, had become a significant determinant of whether a deployment or intervention occurred with or without congressional approval. Limited military operations provided a president stronger control over a decision. This practice had developed before the United States declared war on Japan after the Pearl Harbor attack. Now, after declaring war, the United States entered a world war witnessing many limited military operations that were components of far larger endeavors. The U.S. military learned much from allies' and adversaries' operations and from its own actions that provided invaluable lessons about the planning, role, and conduct of such operations. However, their context was a world war; they were not performed to coerce or influence another state in the foreign policy arena but were part of a global war aimed at defeating enemies and destroying their capabilities to wage war.

The magnitude of World War II and use of the atomic bomb toward its end in the Pacific created such an image of total war that the prospects for a strategic role for limited warfare seemed irrelevant. Future war assuredly would escalate into a global firestorm. Such convictions set into motion a pendulum about the utility of limited war that has swung back and forth ever since. Seyom Brown has noted that after 1945, "Military force could no longer be regarded as an integral part of diplomacy. . . . [G]oing to war could be justified only as a last resort—an indication of the failure of diplomacy." However, the pendulum reverted in the late 1950s and 1960s to advocating limited war and force as instruments of foreign policy. After Vietnam the pendulum swung back for very different reasons to a desire not to let the military be used for such ends. Then by the end of the twentieth century it reversed to an intellectual landscape not unlike the years before Vietnam.[41] What will emerge after the Afghanistan and Iraq conflicts is still unclear.

Still, even before the Soviets detonated their first nuclear device in 1949, two threads of argument emerged to argue that limited war had a future. In fact, it was the one realistic option to pursue against the likelihood of actual nuclear exchange. The first arose from military elements and civilian government leadership; the second developed from an emerging community of academic specialists. If a politician thought war was too important to be left to the generals, the central place of war and national security after 1945 now established an environment in parts of academia that believed it was too important to be left just to governments.[42]

One important source of the government discussion commenced with George F. Kennan's research and work at the National War College in 1946–1947. Although still with the State Department, Kennan found time during that year to question the wisdom of an American style of war seeking its adversary's complete defeat. Kennan thought that nuclear weapons should be used only for retaliation and urged creation of smaller forces for limited military operations.[43] Kennan's skepticism was not isolated. Even while the Department of Defense used its conclusions to justify increasing the U.S. nuclear program, a report prepared for the Secretary of Defense by Air Force Lieutenant General H.R. Harmon warned that initial nuclear attacks on the Soviet Union would probably not weaken its military capacity.[44] Finally, a key strategic document, NSC 68, approved just before the Korean War, contained a rationale for limited warfare even if its primary author, Paul Nitze, assigned more importance to military power than Kennan had. Citing the sentence from Alexander Hamilton's *Federalist, No. 28* discussed earlier in this chapter, NSC 68 contained the Clausewitzian observation,

"Our aim in applying force must be to compel the acceptance of terms consistent with our objectives, and our capabilities for the application of force should, therefore, within the limits of what we can sustain over the long pull, be congruent to the range of tasks which we may encounter."[45] Within months the first real application of trying to maintain limits on an actual conflict occurred in Korea—a military operation the president regarded as so limited he did not seek Congress's authorization to send troops there.

Academic intellectuals' contributions were instrumental to how this debate and its application evolved through the 1950s toward Vietnam. The economist Jacob Viner questioned the utility of nuclear weapons only months after Hiroshima and Nagasaki. In 1946, Bernard Brodie's *The Absolute Weapon* argued that nuclear weapons would serve as a deterrent rather than in a war-fighting role. War would be so horrible to contemplate that reasonable people would shun it.[46] As the 1950s progressed, social and physical scientists began to apply systems analysis to arguments related to strategy, whether conventional or nuclear. In their simplest forms, operations research and its related successor, systems analysis, used scientific means of measurement and analysis to quantify and improve the performance of weapons on the battlefield and their relationship to tactical and strategic considerations. Such analytical means combined with early computers lent the Cold War a new element in the interaction of technology and strategy, as one recent commentator has noted in his observation that we can best understand the Cold War "in terms of *discourses* that connect technology, strategy, and culture."[47] Such forms of research were also becoming instrumental in American corporations and the study of decision making. John F. Kennedy's selection of Robert S. McNamara to become secretary of defense brought to the helm of the Pentagon a leader who was confident in the abilities of these means to more accurately measure a particular policy's success or failure.[48]

The case for developing capabilities of limited war rested partly on systems analysts' claims, but their arguments that war's success could be represented in quantifiable terms could not have carried the day without a revived argument over the dependence of U.S. strategy on nuclear weapons. Not surprisingly, the Korean War generated among some military officers and politicians a determination the United States should never again allow itself to be pulled into a limited Asian land war. Writing several years after the Korean War ended, Morris Janowitz in his study, *The Professional Soldier,* observed two views that divided the post-Korea military—a faction who sought absolute victory to ensure the most likely achievement of political goals and a more pragmatic group who saw war as just one instrument in international relations.[49] The proponents of total victory were a "never again" school who held the nation's civilian leadership responsible for failure to pursue total victory. Adrian Lewis's *The American Culture of War* presents a recent variation of this view in which the "new approach to war, initiated in Korea, was culturally un-American. Strategically defensive wars of attrition would never be acceptable to the American people, particularly with a citizen-soldier Army." Lewis goes on to say in a setting with nuclear weapons and missiles, "*conscription* made little sense. . . . It was inexplicable to the American people to possess all this power and not use it."[50] The arguments immediately following Korea resembled those of Upton and others seventy years earlier who complained about civilian interference and the danger of conducting operations that could weaken the Army. Lewis's reflection on Korea is through the prism of the current conflict in Iraq and attests not only to a disagreement with civilian leadership but to a dislike of a form of war that began the breakdown of a "citizen-soldier Army, which depended on the support of the people" and "could not adapt to this new strategy and doctrine . . ."[51]

Yet the "never again" arguments ran up against a major debate in political, academic, and military circles over the reliance of U.S. strategy on massive retaliation during the 1950s. President Eisenhower's policies rested on assumptions about the inevitability of nuclear war as well as concerns about the distorting effect of military spending on the nation's economy and infrastructure. Better to spend less money on strategic and tactical nuclear capabilities than higher amounts for a more diversely structured military.[52] This drew criticism from several directions. Academic scholars such as Robert Osgood and Henry Kissinger decried the U.S. tendency to let war evolve to a total level rather than seeing it as a measured instrument of policy. Of course, the scale of limited war sometimes discussed in the 1950s exceeded the scale of some low-intensity operations discussed today. Kissinger, for example, wrote about the potential application of tactical nuclear weapons.[53] Not all the major civilian students on warfare shared this confidence about the value of limited war. Bernard Brodie doubted that the major powers could keep war limited, and therefore the notion of keeping combat at a level serviceable to national strategy was suspect.[54] From the military community, especially the Army, dissenting critiques of massive retaliation came from Generals Maxwell D. Taylor and James M. Gavin. Part of their disagreement originated from their concern as to what role this strategy left for the Army. Like their civilian counterparts, they regarded massive retaliation as a path with two choices—either nuclear response or essentially conceding to the enemy, with nothing in between. In 1958 as Army chief of staff, Taylor proposed a plan for fighting limited wars and a "strategy of flexible response." Taylor retired from the service and wrote his book *The Uncertain Trumpet* to express his disagreement. Gavin's book, *War and Peace in the Space Age,* which appeared just before Taylor's, decried the loss of capabilities to deal with conventional and limited conflicts and urged a commitment to air mobility.[55]

The purpose of this debate over U.S. strategy was to find a way to ensure that military force could be used as an instrument of policy without invoking inevitable escalation to all-out nuclear war. If that could not be done, war as a political instrument had little future. The dangers perceived because of the emergence of communist- or socialist-inspired liberation movements in much of the developing world were mounting in Africa, Southeast Asia, the Middle East, the Caribbean, and South and Central America. The United States needed the capacity to respond in kind or symmetrically in ways that would not prompt a nuclear conflict with the Soviet Union or a major war with the People's Republic of China's millions in uniform. On entering office in January 1961, the Kennedy administration first acted by creating a spectrum of options that it could use to address the challenges it saw—ranging from an invigorated government information program for overseas audiences through the creation of the Peace Corps to strengthening a neglected Army component, the Special Forces—to help local nationals oppose rebels involved in liberation movements and work alongside the local population in civil affairs.[56] Kennedy often receives credit for creating the Special Forces, but they traced their origins back to World War II and were reactivated in June 1952.[57]

All this occurred alongside a remarkable surge of confidence about the U.S. ability to use limited military force as an instrument within a much larger policy objective. During the late 1950s and into the Kennedy administration, theories of economic development promoted a conviction that the right combination of economic assistance, sometimes complemented by military advisors and other very low-scale counterinsurgency operations, not only would stem the tide of communist expansion but would also enable the U.S. to build new nations.[58] Equipped with systems analysis, a diverse menu of flexible response options, a renewed sense of national mission, and emerging technologies for the military and developing economies alike, "the national security managers of the 1960's," James Nathan insightfully writes, "believed they had stumbled upon an unparalleled opportunity to school Americans in the Clausewitzian imperative to measure force not by its emotional content, but by its service to policy."[59] Limited war definitely had a place in this strategy, and even though much of the Army's leadership remained skeptical about the Special Forces' ability to significantly affect the situation, the Department of Defense increased the U.S. commitment to them and other special operational forces.[60] The enabler of so much of this was the strong civilian control over the Department of Defense by Secretary McNamara and his senior level of appointees—a forceful assertion of civilian control many resented and that certainly showed itself prone to preferring its own internal counsel over that offered by their military colleagues.[61] This scenario reappeared some forty years later when U.S.-led forces entered Iraq.

The limited-war phase of the commitment to South Vietnam was a presidential-initiated action with little effective congressional oversight. Less than a year after the Gulf of Tonkin Resolution, the war turned into one of big units. The United States took or avoided certain measures to try to limit the war in Southeast Asia—the continued selection of targets for bombing and avoiding certain infrastructure targets or harbors until near the war's end, reliance on various Special Forces missions, or the Marines' Combined Action Program, which tried to destroy local Viet Cong capabilities by helping local leaders, protecting local infrastructure, and aiding in civic action.[62] Computers crunched numbers based on body count, bomb tonnage, numbers of patrols, or the number of pacified hamlets to measure the war's progress.[63] Night vision and infrared technologies monitored Viet Cong or North Vietnamese forces' movements, microphones and sensors also caught movement, and laser-guided munitions struck targets accurately. At the tactical and operations level, some of these systems saw noteworthy success yet none of them reversed the direction the war took for the United States and its allies. What began as a limited war, initiated and escalated by three presidents beginning with Eisenhower, ended in a congressionally sanctioned big war, even if not nuclear. The argument that limited war could not be kept easily limited seemed confirmed in the eyes of many, including a leading U.S. historian of war who ended his book, published in 1973 as the U.S. role in the ground war ended, with the observation, "Because the record of nonnuclear limited war in obtaining acceptable decisions at tolerable cost is also scarcely heartening, the history of usable combat may at last be reaching its end."[64]

After Vietnam the resurgence of a "never again" mindset determined to prevent another limited war that could grow into a leviathan nightmare was no surprise. As a foreign policy instrument, limited war was a contagion that needed to be under quarantine and used only in specific circumstances. Whether in Congress, the community of national security experts, or the military, arguments and actions followed to make the decision to use limited war a difficult one. They were one factor in Congress's approval of the War Powers Resolution, and an obvious factor in all the military services' determination to stress the importance of fighting wars decisively with a minimum of interference from political leadership.[65] The objective of military force was not to coerce an adversary but to destroy the latter's abilities to wage war.[66]

For the service most affected by the Vietnam War, the experience of the war itself, the disintegration of morale and cohesion, and the difficult postwar adjustment were almost tantamount to a "near-death experience." Not only did the Army and other services want to advocate strategic choices that they believed would best serve national interest, but they also wanted to pursue policies that would preserve their own organizations.[67] Ending conscription in 1973 presented a serious challenge to the Army, which envisioned itself as symbolic of a "nation in arms." Within two years military and civilian critics alike questioned whether an all-volunteer force gave the Army enough people of sufficient caliber needed to meet its responsibilities.[68] Furthermore, the Army still struggled with the legacies of President Lyndon Johnson's refusal to call up the National Guard and Reserves during the Vietnam War. Army planning depended on the expectation of available reserve units, and the president's decision seriously affected both the Army itself as well as the Reserves, which became a popular destination for men who wanted to avoid conscription and possible service in Vietnam. The solution to this was the "Total Force Concept," or Abrams Doctrine, named after U.S. Army Chief of Staff General Creighton Abrams, who implemented it. Besides keeping a place for the citizen-soldier, Abrams wanted to ensure that no president could again so easily take the United States to war without mobilizing the Reserves. The objective behind the Total Force Concept was to make some key support functions, such as transport, dependent on the Reserves. Indeed, several active Army divisions depended on mobilizing reserve "round-out" brigades to achieve full strength.[69]

Of course, this concept could have downsides. As Franklin Roosevelt's political adviser Harry Hopkins remarked, "Politicians thought that only ground troops had mothers." Since the infantry were often conscripts in Hopkins's day, would politicians care as much when the military was an all-volunteer force? As one observer wrote nearly thirty years after the start of the Total Force Concept, relying on a professional or all-volunteer force enables "Western societies [to] absolve themselves from some of the responsibility of placing soldiers in harm's way. . . . Using force does not involve risking society but those elements that have accepted such risks. . . ."[70] Reflecting on these events, Adrian Lewis wrote, "The citizen-soldier army went away, passed into history, effectively removing the American people from wars of the United States."[71]

Efforts to try to place boundaries or strict criteria over future uses of limited military force also served to steer the nation's leadership toward thinking of conflict and the services in more conventional settings. If there was going to be a war, the Army especially hoped it would be analogous to European land campaigns in 1944–1945, not to Vietnam. The latter, many hoped, was an "aberration." Much professional literature in the late 1970s concentrated on scenarios for larger-scale conflicts rather than Southeast Asia or in similar situations. The most read, publicly recognized of these works was *On Strategy: A Critical Analysis of the Vietnam War* by Colonel Harry G. Summers, Jr., whom the Army assigned to teach at the Army War College. Published in 1981, Summers's work reinforced the criticism many understandably had about decisions by the nation's political leadership during the war. It also repeated a message many were ready to hear—the Army mistakenly went after the Viet Cong in counterinsurgency operations when it should have relied on more conventional methods against the North Vietnamese. Preaching to a largely converted audience, Summers's book, lectures, and articles figured greatly in debates over the use of limited force right into the 1990s.[72] Of course, some argued otherwise. A critical commentary by Andrew F. Kripinevich, Jr., *The Army and Vietnam,* faulted the Army for over-relying on tactics from larger conventional wars. Likewise a 1980 report provided to the Army by BDM, an outside contractor, delivered a similar judgment.[73]

Naturally, wishing away the existence of limited war was impossible, especially during the Cold War, but what to do about it was a difficult question to answer. One preference was to try to have the host nation assume responsibility for counterinsurgency operations, a course discussed in the 1974 Army Field Manual, FM-100-20, *Field Service Regulations: Internal Defense and Development.*[74] Another, a solution from the 1980's, was the Army's focus on "AirLand Battle," a concept of conventional war depending on superior intelligence and communications as the preparatory phase to subsequent attacks that would disrupt the rear, so vital to its support, behind an enemy's line of attack. The revised Field Manual FM 100-5 spoke of "low-intensity," "mid-intensity," and "high-intensity" conflicts, but it was clear AirLand Battle would be fought in the latter two categories. Low-intensity conflict would require Special Forces, rapid deployment to the operational locale, and restraint in executing the operation.[75] Some even questioned whether such operations qualified as war. Field Circular 100-20, *Low-Intensity Conflict,* stated that such conflict "involves the actual or contemplated use of military capabilities up to, but not including, combat between regular forces."[76] It was a highly problematic definition because its writers, probably unintentionally, used a concept of low-intensity operations that would make it difficult for Congress to review and authorize such measures. The War Powers Resolution easily applied to regular forces, but the status of irregular forces, such as special operations, was murkier, particularly if such groups or units did not fall under the intelligence committees' authority. When considered together such concepts of limited operations potentially strengthened presidential control over use of this form of force.

Keeping Military Force an Instrument after Vietnam

However, the services' attempts to stress more conventional operations over various forms of limited or low-intensity operations conflicted with presidents' desire to use limited force for foreign policy and related national security purposes. That became evident as the services opposed the deployment of U.S. military units to Central America during the early 1980s to deal with destabilizing situations in El Salvador and Nicaragua. Still, simultaneously in 1982, President Ronald Reagan's advisers deliberated sending U.S. forces to Lebanon to try to stabilize a country torn apart by civil war, terrorists supported by Iran and Syria, Palestinian refugees, and incursions from Israel in retaliation for attacks from Lebanese soil. Inserting U.S. troops into the uncertainties of the Middle East for foreign policy purposes was something neither Secretary of Defense Caspar Weinberger nor the chairman of the Joint Chiefs, General John Vessey, were anxious to do.[77]

To get military support for using limited force for political purposes required overcoming the legacies and "lessons" of Vietnam. By the 1980s, the struggle to use military force for such purposes was also linked to a politically driven effort to erase the broader effects of the Vietnam War on the public at large. In his masterly study of the impact of national security policy on the United States, Michael Sherry wrote that the goal of American interventions was "to bolster how Americans (at least many of them) felt about themselves, rather than to shape the world." What Sherry labels "Gilbert-and-Sullivan wars," such as the invasion of Grenada in 1983 or the bombing of Libya in 1986, could entail true death, but the triumphant crescendo afterwards, which tried to match them to feats like Guadalcanal or Overlord, reinforces his point. Frederick W. Kagan writes, "These operations were not part of any coherent strategy except . . . to show American strength and resolve."[78] While these assessments may be a little too dismissive of the security concerns that the Reagan administration rightly or wrongly held, the judgment is still insightful. In the nineteenth century, Libya or Grenada would have seemed less spectacular to almost any president or the American public. In early 1991, Reagan's vice president, now President George H.W. Bush, believed that he finally had put Vietnam to rest in the war he led against Iraq. Regardless of their merit or need, these conflicts became means to regenerate the American spirit and sense of national purpose that Vietnam had so seriously undermined.[79] Getting the military beyond Vietnam was especially important, as then Secretary of Defense Dick Cheney believed, when he warned about the first Gulf War, "The military is finished in this society if we screw this up."[80]

It was not that easy, though, to achieve agreement on the wisdom of these types of operations. From the Reagan presidency's first term well into the Clinton administration, debate continued over the utility or place of limited military force in U.S. strategy and the circumstances in which military force could be properly used. Much of the initial debate occurred openly between Secretary of Defense Weinberger and Secretary of State George Shultz between 1984 and 1986. The instigating event was the bombing of U.S. Marine quarters in Beirut in October 1983, which killed 241 Marines and led to their complete withdrawal by February 1984 and Secretary Weinberger's subsequent opposition to the Grenada operation. Speaking before the Trilateral Commission in April 1984, Shultz called for a balanced understanding of the roles of power and diplomacy. He noted, "The hard reality is that diplomacy not backed by strength is ineffectual," and then commented on the American tendency to believe "power and diplomacy are two distinctive alternatives."[81] Shultz, writes Christopher Gacek, was really not trying to sell the nation on limited war but rather to stress that successful diplomacy sometimes needed the threat of or actual force behind it. Nonetheless, the speech was as explicit an attack on the "never again" syndrome as any senior cabinet official had made. Speaking to it directly, the secretary stated, "The need to avoid no-win situations cannot mean that we turn automatically away from hard-to-win situations that call for prudent involvement." Shultz followed with another speech in October 1984 before the Park Avenue Synagogue in New York City.[82]

On November 28, 1984, Weinberger finally responded in a speech to the National Press Club that soon became labeled as the Weinberger Doctrine. The secretary of defense laid out six criteria that must be met for the proper use of military force:

- The United States should use force only when its vital interests are at stake;
- Should the United States decide to commit its forces to combat, we must commit them in sufficient numbers and with sufficient support to win. If we are unwilling to commit the forces or resources necessary to achieve our objectives, or if the objective is not important enough so that we must achieve it, we should not commit our forces;
- If the U.S. commits forces to combat, it must have clearly defined political and military objectives. If these objectives cannot be formulated then military power should not be used;
- The relationship between objectives and means should be continually reassessed and adjusted as necessary;
- Before the United States commits combat forces abroad, the U.S. Government should have some reasonable assurance of the support of the American people and their elected representatives in Congress, and
- American forces for combat should be used as a last resort only after diplomatic, political, economic and other efforts have been made to protect our vital national interests.[83]

Here was a challenge that did not absolutely eliminate the use of limited military operations, but certainly required any planned prolonged deployment meet very stringent criteria. "Vital" was open-ended; it would have been a stretch to characterize Grenada as vital to U.S interests by most meanings of the word. By emphasizing "sufficient" numbers, Weinberger certainly raised a caution flag, since that could imply more than a limited operation might need. The "last resort" provision arguably ruled out using force as a diplomatic option until every other diplomatic means was explored. Obviously, the criteria would not encourage a display or use of military force at any earlier state. The reference to Congress also signaled an expectation that it should become more attentive and involved in decisions related to using armed force. While not going so far as to request an authorization for each situation, Weinberger's remarks implied a desire for congressional awareness and participation in some form.[84] Shultz had his final say in this debate in his 1993 memoirs; he wrote that the Weinberger Doctrine was "the Vietnam syndrome in spades, carried to an absurd level, and a complete abdication of the duties of leadership."[85]

Whether Congress will ever meet Weinberger Doctrine expectations would be an interesting test. Most in Congress were certainly averse to long, open-ended conflicts, but that did not mean that Congress would automatically take responsibility when it had the opportunity to authorize beforehand the use of military force. However, Weinberger's proposals enjoyed strong support among many in the military, most notably Colin Powell, who later amplified and elaborated on them during his tenure as chairman of the Joint Chiefs of Staff. Powell wanted Congress to assume its responsibility, and during preparations for the first Gulf War he pressed for congressional authorization of Operation Desert Storm, which undoubtedly was an important factor beyond those already mentioned in Chapter 3 in President Bush's decision to go to Congress.[86]

Even though limited or imperfect war and low-intensity operations were such difficult issues for Congress, several of its actions indicated that a majority of its members held a more flexible or tolerant position on the utility of such operations than the then secretary of defense. In November 1986, Congress approved an amendment to the Defense Reorganization Act sponsored by Senators Sam Nunn of (Georgia) and William Cohen (Maine) establishing a U.S. Special Operations Command and an Office of the Assistant Secretary of Defense for Special Operations and Low-Intensity Conflict. The Department of Defense in-house advocate for special operations was Noel Koch, who worked in the Office of the Secretary of Defense. Koch clearly disagreed with the direction that the Pentagon and services seemed to be headed on when and how to use force, and in late May 1986 he left the department, probably under encouragement. Koch's opinions and the work of several congressional staffers, most notably Jim Locher with the Senate Armed Services Committee, provided more intellectual substance to support the use of special operations. Locher would become the assistant secretary of defense for special operations and low-intensity conflict, and his office would play a major role in developing the case for "peacetime engagement," a series of phased low-intensity actions ranging from diplomatic and humanitarian measures to actual use of force. Special operations personnel derived from all the services—the Special Forces, Rangers, Delta

Force, SEALs, and other elite groups. The U.S. intervention in Panama became the first test of the combined capability. Thus, here Congress was instrumental in creating a better capability at the lower scale of military operations, but it had not clearly thought through where special operations fit into its responsibilities over the use of force.[87]

The First Gulf War definitely was how the military and the nation wanted to fight a conflict. In most ways, this war was testimony supporting the wisdom of the Weinberger Doctrine. The military power and force used were overwhelming. Although General Powell urged a longer period for use of sanctions, Congress's authorization initially secured public and congressional opinion, unless casualties proved very high. The victory against Iraqi forces confirmed the wisdom of the massive preparations. At the same time the success of air power and precision-guided munitions reinforced the prospect and hope that future military operations could rely more on air power and not risk large numbers of casualties. Some critics thought the military's caution against entering Baghdad, combined with political desires to maintain the coalition negotiated with European and regional allies, denied the United States complete victory. Furthermore, analysis of the war's outcome would have shown Weinberger's criteria had omitted the responsibilities following in the wake of a conflict. The focus was battlefield victory more than longer-term strategic victory possibly requiring an extended presence. Not surprisingly, though, the nation's leadership focused on the positive imagery of the swift operational victory against Saddam and did not dwell on remaining problematic questions. To some the small number of American and allied combat dead suggested that air power now provided a way to use limited military force without unacceptable danger or risk.[88] Claims that Operation Desert Storm's victory erased the legacy of Vietnam were greatly exaggerated. Bill Clinton's succeeding administration would quickly learn that lesson when it showed that it wanted to use limited military force in its foreign policy.

The end of the Cold War shifted political tectonics in ways that few had anticipated. "When the Red Army went away," writes a recent commentator, "the Pentagon lost its measuring stick."[89] Trying to gauge just what the new strategic landscape would be fueled military and civilian debate alike. The occurrence of several conflicts within the former Soviet Union and in the Balkans seemed to be a release of forces held in stasis by the Warsaw Pact, but problems beyond Europe and Central Asia demonstrated that the Cold War's end had largely unanticipated global consequences. During the Cold War, the antagonists defined parties and conflicts in terms of who was identified with the West or the communists, a practice often causing the major powers to underestimate or ignore the local origins of conflict. The "new" wars, as some called them, were often about preserving a distinct national, ethnic, or religious identity against the pressures of a globalized economy and outside culture. They were sometimes "wars of necessity," driven by despair and need for food and water. Groups uncontrolled by any state frequently fought them; they gave their loyalty to charismatic leaders rather than organizations. They were cheap wars, fought with a mixture of simple and modern technology (such as cell phones), and they could be of long duration. They also caused high numbers of civilian deaths; indeed, the distinction between combatant and noncombatant became harder to ascertain. A British general, Rupert Smith, describes this type of conflict as "war amongst the people." These "wars of a third kind" had no fronts, often no uniforms, and depended many times on crime and hostage-taking for monetary or political gains.[90] Terrorism became a visible instrument of some of these conflicts because of its ability to communicate messages of vulnerability to its targets and terrorists' ability to use minimal amounts of resources to press an adversary to their desired objective.[91]

Examining the recent historical record suggests that the United States was not intellectually well prepared to assess these conflicts realistically. Reluctance to intervene in them was understandable. They lacked characteristics or the perimeters with which much of the military and political leadership was comfortable. They were indeed Rudyard Kipling's "savage wars of peace."[92] Thomas Barnett, a trenchant critic of the Pentagon's actions, notes how the services fell back on the concepts of threats that would be fought most traditionally to thereby preserve the military—the fear of Soviet resurgence or strategic statements concentrating on being able to fight two simultaneous major regional conflicts.[93] Arguably, some of that view has survived to the present day in the argument over the strategic threat that mainland China poses. A different problem was that most analysts— civilian or military—had trouble grasping the fact "most wars do not involve state actors only, and . . . that many wars do not necessarily threaten national survival." The legacy of World War II overshadowed American thinking.[94] The First Gulf War strongly reinforced that inclination.

While still Joint Chiefs of Staff chairman, during the transition between Presidents Bush and Clinton, General Powell wrote an article in *Foreign Affairs* outlining his views on the use of military force. He reminded his readers that all wars are limited in one way or another, and added "peacekeeping and humanitarian missions are a given." However, he revealed his preferences when he wrote, "When the political objective is important, clearly defined and understood, when the risks are acceptable, and when the use of force can be effectively combined with diplomatic and economic policies, then clear and unambiguous objectives must be given to the armed forces."[95] With the new Clinton administration, some of his reactions were less restrained, particularly when it came to the opinions of Madeleine Albright, who was the U.S. ambassador to the United Nations and later secretary of state. In his memoirs, Powell wrote of nearly having an aneurysm after hearing Albright ask, "What's the point of having this superb military that you're always talking about, if we can't use it?"[96] During the 1993 debates over whether to commit U.S. forces in Bosnia, Powell remarked, "As soon as they tell me it is limited, it means they do not care whether you achieve a result or not."[97] What Powell understandably wanted was decisiveness; as he wrote, "Decisive means and results are always to be preferred, even if they are not always possible."[98] "Decisive" rang especially well when referring to the more traditional notions of using force, and remains in pivotal documents to the present day, whether the U.S. Army's Posture Statement for 2001 or *Joint Vision 2020.*[99] "Decisive" did not have to mean victory through overwhelming force. Limited means can provide decisive results, but much contemporary discussion in the press and elsewhere took the word to mean victory by overwhelming numbers.

The Clinton administration repeatedly used limited military force to advance its foreign policy, but it did not completely override the Weinberger Doctrine, which by now had Powell's name added to it. The Clinton White House tried to circumvent the challenge that Powell and others posed by resorting to forms of limited military force that promised limits on both casualties and negative publicity while serving foreign policy objectives—the use of air power and precision technologies. Committing ground forces sometimes became an uncrossed Rubicon, a point beyond which the administration was extremely reluctant to advance.

Since the new administration could not decide whether to send U.S. forces into Bosnia, it was the Somalia episode of October 1993 that confronted it with the problems of limited military force. The mission's shift from humanitarian relief to peacemaking and stabilization, Secretary of Defense Les Aspin's decision not to allow armored personnel carriers and tanks on a mission to capture General Mohammed Farrah Aidid and other faction leaders, and the subsequent death of 18 U.S. soldiers were powerful factors that confirmed to critics the danger and doubtful value of such limited missions.[100]

The legacy of Somalia shaped the administration's position on intervention during the next few years, even after it became more activist and willing to use force. Starting with a speech delivered by Anthony Lake, the president's national security adviser, in late September 1993 (just days before the actual events in Mogadishu), a speech by President Clinton only a week later, a subsequent statement of policy on multilateral operations and Presidential Decision Directive 25 in May 1994, and finally another speech by Lake in March 1996, the administration essentially restated the Weinberger–Powell Doctrine, but with one much-noticed addition—an emphasis on an exit strategy.[101] Assuring the public and Congress alike that there was a plan to get out, that there would no more Vietnams or Somalias, became, it seemed, as important as clarifying the missions' actual strategic objective.

A fundamental question facing the United States was whether military force could be used incrementally or deliberately to support foreign policy rather than through larger, more unlimited ways that sought defeat or total defeat. Alexander George, a leading academic who wrote extensively on the subject during the 1990s, called the U.S. policy "coercive diplomacy." This means, George wrote, "employs threats of force to persuade an opponent to call or undo its encroachment. . . ." It was an attractive option because it offered "the possibility of achieving one's objectives economically, with little if any bloodshed, and with fewer political and psychological costs than warfare. . . ."[102] Madeleine Albright also adopted the term.[103] By the middle of the 1990s the Clinton administration came to believe that U.S. leadership was critically needed in several settings, whether because of instability so close to the heart of Europe, the desire to strengthen the North Atlantic Treaty Organization, the continual problems with Saddam Hussein and Iraq, political turmoil in Haiti, and the development of various humanitarian and reform-minded justifications for intervention.[104] While it certainly wanted to avoid the term "flexible response," the administration definitely tried to develop a set of different types of responses it could use, depending on the nature of the challenge or threat perceived. The hope was to calibrate U.S. policy in ways to avoid an escalation to unacceptable numbers of casualties or serious domestic political controversy. As with Vietnam, military force was an instrument that could be used selectively to try to obtain political ends.

Furthermore, the new chairman of the Joint Chiefs of Staff, General John Shalikashvili, seemed more sympathetic to the president and his foreign policy advisers' wishes. In May 1995, probably after reflecting on the intervention in Haiti in September 1994, which some in the Pentagon had opposed, and the continuing debate over options in Bosnia, Shalikashvili remarked, "Some at least in my profession, would prefer that we put a sign outside the Pentagon that says 'We only do the big ones.' That is because we feel comfortable with yesterday. We understand terms like 'overwhelming force'. . . . But as strong as the temptation may be to do this, the fact is that we cannot."[105] Shalikashvili's sympathy with Clinton's objectives possibly originated from both an emotional link from his own childhood in wartime Poland as well as his concern about civil-military relations and the critical view many in the military held of Clinton. Although a Vietnam veteran, he appeared not to have drawn conclusions from it as absolute as many of his colleagues had.[106] Regarding relations between the military and the commander-in-chief, Shalikashvili possessed astute political antennae.

Some scholars have depicted the military's post-Vietnam stance, especially during the Clinton years, as equivalent to shirking, or literally avoiding what the nation's civilian leaders wanted, to protect the military and pressure the president and his advisers to fight wars the way the military wanted.[107] While this verdict may be somewhat unfair, since senior military leaders are duty-bound to give the president, his advisers, and Congress their professional assessment and even personal opinion if asked, their thoroughly understandable efforts to prevent another Vietnam became as much a crusade as a conviction based on analytical thought of what best served U.S. interests. Nevertheless, despite the misgivings many may have had, the Joint Chiefs revealed a noticeable philosophical shift under Shalikashvili in June 1995 in their *Joint Doctrine for Military Operations Other Than War,* which stressed that such operations "are more *sensitive to political considerations. . . .*" Furthermore, using "*military forces in peacetime helps keep the day-to-day tensions between nations below the threshold of armed conflict or war. . . .*" (emphasis in original).[108] Emphasizing "operations other than war" neatly agreed with the Clinton administration's legal arguments that certain types of operations did not cross that threshold and therefore did not require congressional authorization. The doctrine had emerged as well out of the Army's own reassessment of its missions directed by General Gordon Sullivan, its chief of staff, in 1993 that recognized the emerging practice of peacekeeping and humanitarian operations in its mission.[109]

Although U.S. ground forces joined the peacekeeping force in Bosnia after the Dayton Accords in 1995, some congressional and media criticism about the open-ended nature of the commitment and the fear of eventual casualties compelled the Clinton administration to always try to avoid controversial forms of limited military force. The "body-bag factor" became a much-debated aspect of the decision making about the Balkans, whether Bosnia or Kosovo in 1999. Conventional wisdom argued that the public would not tolerate sizable casualties, especially in a limited war lacking clear objectives and a strict time frame, although some observers argued the public might be more tolerant than credited.[110] Given Clinton and his inner circle's sensitivity about the president's image with the military, the administration also was concerned about how any presidential order would be perceived at a time of increased troop rotation due to more deployments and a popular belief that civilians without military experience were more prone to use military force than those who had served in uniform.[111] Air power adherents both inside and outside the administration saw in the Kosovo operation an opportunity to prove that a bombing campaign could compel a government to change its policies and behavior to the desired objective. They cited the bombing of Iraq in 1991 and air strikes in Bosnia as proof of their case for air power as an effective instrument of coercive diplomacy. Combined with precision-guided munitions and other information technologies and means providing immediate knowledge and intelligence about targets in Belgrade, Serbia's capital, and elsewhere, the Clinton administration supported a NATO air campaign without UN authorization to try to pressure Slobodan Milosevic's Serbian government to make concessions about the province of Kosovo.

The administration believed the 1999 air campaign, known as Operation Allied Force, was successful. It had not proved necessary to send in ground forces or even Army Apache helicopters, as General Wesley Clark, the Supreme Allied Commander for Europe and Commander of U.S. forces in Europe, had requested. Clark has written at length on this hesitation, much of which he argues emanated from military officers still wedded to the notion that armies fight wars to win, who thus remained unwilling to use limited force as an instrument of political pressure. The president for his own political reasons also was reluctant to commit ground forces.[112]

The instruments of limited war and low-intensity operations were returned to the fold, one might say, of effective options to use in foreign policy. The Clinton White House could argue that it used such force successfully against the Serbian government and ended the ethnic violence in Kosovo. Furthermore, the shadow of the Weinberger/Powell Doctrine was no longer as large as it had once been, although significant use of ground forces still seemed out of question. In the aftermath of Operation Allied Force, serious talk emerged about capabilities that now seemed certain to

enable using specific types of limited force without much risk. New technologies ensured fast, fairly casualty-free operations. Reflection on 1998
missile strikes against Afghani and Sudanese targets thought linked to
Osama bin Laden, then a fairly unknown terrorist believed to be behind the
bombing of U.S. embassies in Tanganyika and Kenya, should have raised
caution, as neither strike accomplished its purpose. However, Operation
Allied Force "lessons" overshadowed in many minds anything suggesting
otherwise. The prospect of a technologically dominated war that might
avoid most negative aspects of limited conflicts seemed at hand. Air power,
enthusiasts claimed, was completely successful against Serbia, as it could
be in future conflicts.[113] The complete erasure of the Weinberger/Powell
Doctrine now seemed attainable, but that would await the next administration of President George W. Bush.

The Clinton administration tried to intervene with a number of military
personnel calibrated to a level thought necessary to obtain the desired end.
During the 1990s, some advocates of intervention argued against such a
guarded approach; Richard Haass warned that the United States must not
follow the type of gradualism pursued in Vietnam or later in Lebanon. Echo-
ing some concerns of those who fought in Vietnam, Haass stated that it was
"better to err on the side of using more rather than less." A larger commitment at the start enhanced the likelihood of a shorter conflict as well as better prospects for public support.[114] However, the overall record of limited
force and coercive diplomacy proved mixed. Even if the United States and
its allies "triumphed" against Slobodan Milosevic in 1999, they did so only
after escalating coercive measures to an air war and a threatened ground
campaign. Other efforts at coercive diplomacy showed far less success, as
was the case with Saddam Hussein through the 1990s. One clear reason for
the clouded record of coercive diplomacy was that the United States con-
sciously used the number of troops and operational characteristics of each
deployment as a measure of just how important a specific mission was to
national interests. Washington often seemed more preoccupied with the
right force level than accomplishing the policy objective. Reflecting on the
U.S. intervention in Bosnia, Susan Woodward observed, "Without ground
troops, there [was] no compulsion to define a policy and particularly for the
president to articulate its purpose." Concentrating on means (military force)
rather than desired ends almost ensured misuse and unfulfilled expectations
about the use of force. The fixation on force, Woodward feared, would lead
to its overuse in interventions.[115]

Imperfect War, Technological Superiority, and Special Mission

In 1969 during the peak of the Vietnam War, the prominent British historian J.H. Plumb predicted that Americans soon would find less appeal in the historical metaphors, such as manifest destiny, that had guided their conduct. Writing over thirty years later, Christopher Coker, another British writer, noted, "The Vietnam War can lay claim to being the last modern war because it was the last war in which the United States sought—and failed—to impose its will on another power for a metaphysical end."[116] Those judgments were obviously very premature. While the U.S.-led operation in Afghanistan explicitly responded to the 9/11 attacks on the United States, Operation Iraqi Freedom, after all the confusion about Iraqi weapons of mass destruction and an imminent threat to the United States dissipated, revealed that the subsequent American hope of rebuilding nations and spreading democracy was far from dead. The "metaphysical" factors Plumb and Coker thought dead were very much alive and reinvigorated in an affirmation of special mission and Wilsonian vision.[117] In Operation Iraqi Freedom, the Bush administration succeeded in eliminating the last segments or restraints of the Weinberger/Powell Doctrine, even while Powell was secretary of state. While hardly a low-intensity operation, the U.S. portion of the war definitely was limited in scale, as much a foreign policy war with longer-term security issues in play as a war directly linked to defense of the United States. Military force served political goals. Yet the war's conduct revealed that a "clash of cultures" still remained. The first phase was fought to obtain a decisive battlefield victory against Saddam Hussein, reflecting traditional perspectives about the purpose of the military and force, but the military victory did not automatically produce the desired political objectives. Civilian leaders' capability of wielding military force as an effective instrument serving national policy remained elusive.

Two points are worth considering when examining the checkered record of this latest effort to use military force as a political instrument. The preparations for conflict in both Afghanistan and Iraq clearly reflected, as one defense analyst wrote, a lack of "systematic thinking about the processes and capabilities needed to translate military victory into strategic success." The Defense Department's "model acknowledges the importance of 'interagency constabulary forces,' for instance, but it does so *not* with the intent to achieve a better result in the end game, but with the goal of freeing up 'elite forces' for further combat operation."[118] By mid–2006 even administration officials acknowledged some of this, and several books and reports by participants and study groups stressed the same conclusions.[119]

The second point was the unrealistically high expectations of what technology can accomplish in war. Writing in 2000 about the "revolution in military affairs" (RMA), as it was still called, the prominent British military historian Jeremy Black cautioned:

[T]he RMA is a means to total victory, providing the opportunity for a universal warfighting doctrine that offers very little role for the Low Intensity Conflict that was the combat norm during the Cold War and has become even more so subsequently. In short, there is a danger that the RMA serves as an apparent substitute for a political willingness to commit troops, and also as a cover for the failure, first, to develop effective counter-insurgency doctrine and practice, second, to conceive of a strategy for successful long-term expeditionary expeditions, and, third, to work within the difficult context of alliance policy-making and strategic control.[120]

Special operations units had operated in and out of neighboring Pakistan since the early 1990s and played an instrumental role in early phases of both the Afghan and Iraqi conflicts. Nevertheless, civilian and military authorities used them more as predecessors or complements of larger deployments of U.S. forces.[121] The real thrust of Black's verdict was that the RMA was still oriented to the desire for absolute victory rather than the subservience to political missions implied in his reference to "long-term expeditionary expeditions." One could restructure services and forces in many ways, but Black implied that the real restructuring needed to occur in the professional cultures of the military and part of the national security community.

The Bush administration and Secretary of Defense Donald Rumsfeld substituted the label "transformation" for RMA, but essentially much of the new brand sought the same objectives—the ability to wage war by using advanced information technologies and rapid communication to obtain dominant knowledge and control over the battlefield and then to rely on highly mobile units backed as much as possible with precision-guided munitions (PGMs). The initial successes in Afghanistan seemed to confirm the wisdom of this approach.[122] Evidence from Afghanistan also suggested the contrary. March 2002 studies of Operation Anaconda involving elements of the 101st Airborne and 10th Mountain Divisions found that there was a lot of just plain hard fighting in areas that had survived attacks using PGMs.

Massive firepower, as Stephen Biddle observed in his commentary on the Afghan conflict, would not carry the day against fortified positions in terrain that sometimes was impenetrable to the most advanced electronic surveillance techniques. Soldiers still had to go in and fight it out in ways recognizable to their professional ancestors.[123] It also seemed that the first phase of Operation Iraqi Freedom against Saddam Hussein's regime validated the new form of warfare including the array of technologies at the call of the U.S.-led coalition. In terms of defeating the Iraqi army and Saddam's government, the battlefield victory was decisive, proving some of the old adages—such as the necessity to have a three-to-one advantage over the defender—did not apply against forces like Saddam's. A total of 137,000 U.S. ground troops participated in a noteworthy operational victory.[124]

This warfare overwhelmed the enemy not by numbers but by technology and concentrated firepower. It was relatively fast and not burdened with exceedingly high numbers of U.S. casualties. The fact that volunteer troops fought with technologies (such as unmanned aerial vehicles and PGMs, which minimized the number of required sorties to destroy a target from the air) that complemented and even reduced the number of soldiers required on the battlefield diffused the war's impact from most of the American public. Here was a way to conduct war *and* use ground forces that promised to attract little public alarm or congressional criticism. In fact, if no trouble had followed in Iraq after the announced end to organized resistance on May 21, 2003, the administration would have complied with the 60-plus–30-day formula of the War Powers Resolution.

Of course, political victory did not emerge then. The doubts and fears some had expressed since the 1990s about the unrealistic expectations that others held about technology or the military's continued focus on battlefield victory rather than strategic or political objectives were fully borne out. The technologies succeeded; extensive evidence proved their merit in planning as well as in actual operations. The fallacies rested rather with assumptions about Iraqi adversaries and the numbers of military personnel needed to stabilize the country. The planning resurrected a pattern common during the conflicts after the Cold War ended—a tendency to portray the enemy not "as the state, but as a regime or even an individual leader." Underneath these oppressors, the Americans hoped, waited a suffering people anxious for freedom.[125] As to the number of troops necessary, the administration could not pursue the intervention at the desired limited number if it had accepted Army Chief of Staff General Erik Shinseki's judgment that two hundred thousand personnel would be needed to stabilize postwar Iraq.[126] His advice deserved a much more sober reception than it received in either the Pentagon or Congress, where it should have created particular concern, but by refuting it so completely the administration largely defused its immediate effect.

A major quandary with limited war or small wars is that their public support often erodes if the war becomes long and less limited. While the Bush administration arguably asserted civilian control over the military to a degree not seen since the Kennedy administration, it was not totally successful in controlling public perception and reaction. President Bush's popularity dropped as U.S. casualties increased, but whether that reflected dislike of casualties or criticism of a mission that now seemed poorly defined and potentially indefinite was debatable.[127] John Mueller has concentrated on several factors that historically show Americans' dislike of such operations, such as an aversion to long-term policing operations, presidents' difficulty in winning political gain, or a bias against war and acts of aggression.[128] Nevertheless, as two scholars wrote nearly thirty years ago about intervention, the political use of military force often experienced more positive outcomes "when U.S. objectives were at least loosely consistent with prior U.S. policies."[129] The discrepancy that emerged between the focus on Iraq's alleged possession of weapons of mass destruction before and during the early part of the war and the later emphasis on transforming Iraq and the Middle East into democracies was a gap that much of the public found hard to cross, particularly since the administration could not show any such weapons. Likely, too, was the public unease after the release of photographs from Abu Ghraib prison in Baghdad and the controversy about whether the United States officially condoned or practiced torture. Obviously, any policy appearing to transgress U.S. or international law and contradicting Americans' cherished values created discrepancies between perceived deed and declared goals that many Americans could not accept. By fighting wars with volunteers and relying on technology and contractors, the administration arguably hoped that these wars would attract little controversy.[130] Limited or "imperfect war," that still-apt eighteenth-century description, is seldom supposed to be that visible in public attention or, worse yet, surrounded by controversy.

By the beginning of the twenty-first century, it seemed that presidents forgot the legacies of Vietnam and secured their control over the military in ways giving them almost unprecedented freedom to use military force as a political instrument. The Clinton administration argued that some scenarios did not merit being recognized as war, so there was no need for congressional or even public attention. The second Bush administration hoped that it had found a way to enable it to wage war with limited numbers of ground troops, avoiding public or congressional alarm—especially if it could declare victory fast. Whether the United States resorted to military force too often instead of other instruments was a critical question, but one beyond the scope of this work. Clearly, though, presidential use of limited military force was where the Congress needed to assert itself, since these uses of military force often were optional, not defensive. Each time that Congress did not or did so only belatedly, with excessive caution, it created a precedent for stronger presidential authority in the next occasion. That was the problem Congress faced in the first decade of this new century.

The extent to which all the services concurred with this convergence of military force with broader political policy, especially foreign policy, remained unclear. The 2006 Quadrennial Defense Review (QDR), which emphasized more mobility, smaller units, and continued reliance on technologies, implied as much. Definitely, the stress on special operations pointed in this direction. However, the QDR is a joint document, and does not fully represent each service's perspective. Under the British system, the military cannot play off the prime minister and cabinet against Parliament, since they all are members of Parliament. The American system does enable this. If some services are uncomfortable with the QDR's direction, Congress is one avenue of potential opposition that they can explore. In fact, some scholars argue that the British Army's willingness to be an imperial force reflects its willingness to accept the cabinet's direction and its inability to turn to another branch of government to support an alternative view. This situation also makes the British army more responsive to change.[131] However, before overworking this comparison, we should remember that the thrust of British foreign policy was to avoid involvement in major European wars unless necessary, thereby negating to a large degree the need for an army to fight in large land campaigns. If the U.S. military chooses to pursue such a course with Congress right now, it would do so when both Congress and the president seem relatively united in the major danger that the United States faces—namely, terrorism.

An irony exists about the intraservice debates regarding their preferred types of operations or disagreements with presidents and other administration officials over the use of the military. The more traditional operations advocated by critics who fear repeating Korea, Vietnam, and now possibly Iraq, were larger-scale operations more easily requiring congressional authorization before a president can act. This concern was visible in the Weinberger and Powell doctrines, which stressed the importance of strong domestic political support, including Congress's. The operations about which Powell and others held misgivings were often the same types in which presidents used force more arbitrarily and without previous congressional authorization. Whether in the Iraq war's aftermath public, congressional, and some military pressures converge to revise laws or develop new laws to ensure stronger congressional control over the use of force remains uncertain. Right now the president and Congress are more focused on whether to terminate the Iraq war than on how to handle executive–congressional relations in future conflicts. The challenge, though, is that despite any "Iraq legacy," the United States in future will conclude that it must use force in circumstances similar to those of during recent decades. Finding a solution that restores the congressional voice in this decision will not be easy because the several factors explored in the last two chapters greatly favor the presidential hand.

Chapter 5

Justifying Intervention and the Increase of Presidential Power

By the end of the 1990s, presidents embarked on a series of actions testing various concepts of limited military operations ranging from Somalia through Kosovo. These intentionally confined uses of force depended on and benefited from arguments that tried to make intervention easier and more justifiable. Meanwhile, technological developments and new capabilities in both the military and private sectors made such arguments more inviting to pursue. This chapter and Chapter 6 are focused on how these trends are increasing presidential power and why presidents could wield unprecedented resources to use limited force without effective congressional control.

Current critics of American policy argue that U.S. willingness to repeatedly use military force in the post–Cold War era is part of a unilateral turn in American policy—an abandonment of the commitments the United States made during and after World War II to multilateral institutions such as the United Nations and the role of international law. That the United States has been willing to initiate military operations without United Nations approval has opened Washington to charges that it is violating the prohibition of aggression in the UN Charter.

Indeed, much evidence in word and fact supports such an accusation. While working as an adviser to the campaign of George W. Bush in early 2000, the current secretary of state, Condoleezza Rice, wrote that a new Republican administration's foreign policy "will . . . proceed from the firm ground of the national interest, not from the interests of an illusory international community."[1] The word "illusory" suggested that the multilateral world America's critics preferred had no real foundation. The *National Security Strategy* released by the Bush administration in September 2002, with its emphasis on preemptive war and preventive measures, directly countered the views of many in the international community.[2] To many critics, Operation Iraqi Freedom, the detention policies at Guantanamo Bay, or the rendition of detainees to other countries reaffirmed this trend. However, to agree that the United States had turned away from its own values and contributions to international institutions requires us to ignore much evidence suggesting the more independent or unilateral path being taken was not that historically unique.[3] A subtler approach would have recognized the Bush administration's justifications drew on history even while there were also new, disturbing patterns.

Justifying Intervention

How presidents and Congress decide when, where, and in what form to use military force reflects not only external strategic concerns but also the cultural prisms through which national leaders understand both their nation and the outside world. To best understand why the United States is willing to act independently, it is imperative to examine several developments in American political thought, ethics, religion, and views on international law. In turn, presidents find support in Congress and the public for military force because these developments have created a disposition to think that force is the best way to proceed.

A powerful justification to use military force, if necessary, is found in the conviction that it is the responsibility of the United States to spread democracy as part of a mission inspired and endorsed by God. The belief in a special covenant between God and those who settled in North America and the conviction that the promised millennium could occur here originated from English Protestants, and especially the Puritans. The American hope of changing the world by rejecting the rivalry-ridden European state system and doing so through commerce and example, not war, was the vision of Thomas Jefferson and other Founders.[4] Both intellectual traditions desired separation from the Old World because of the latter's ability to contaminate the New, although Jefferson hoped that the American model would reform the outside. His war against the Barbary pirates also illustrated how he was willing to use force and bring the United States down from the hill where the Puritan forefathers might have wished it to remain. Two historians have recently argued that from the War of 1812 on, the United States used force to "liberate the oppressed and expand the sphere of freedom."[5] The growth of American nationalism made the United States more willing to rely on force to serve its goals and destiny.

Thus, the desire to change the world through American values and institutions long preceded Woodrow Wilson—the term "Wilsonianism" seems to embody all responsibility for this notion. The words of the prominent Unitarian minister William Ellery Channing in 1837 would sound familiar to American audiences today: "The more civilized must always exert a great power over the less civilized communities in their neighborhood. But it may and should be a power to enlighten and improve. . . ."[6] The modern reader would only need to replace "civilized" with "developed," and "power" with "duty" or "obligation." Speaking before religious broadcasters in 1991, President George H.W. Bush connected the United States with God by stating, "My fellow Americans, I firmly believe in my hearts of hearts that time will be soon on the side of peace because the world is overwhelmingly on the side of God." A decade later, in the aftermath of September 11, 2001 attacks, his son delivered speeches filled with religiously inspired imagery of fighting against evil and spreading liberty.[7]

Tying the potential power of religion to the use of force can subordinate a government's potential obligations to the international community to the convictions and values of religious belief. Adherents of a religious persuasion can easily become both executor and judge of actions inspired by its beliefs. In his study of ethics and conflict, Richard Miller observed that a religious impulse in national policy can enable Americans to see "themselves as obeying a higher law, inaccessible to outsiders or critics. This belief allows, among other things, Americans to reconcile opposite tendencies, leaving the contradiction in the eyes of the 'watching world.' Since they are unique, Americans need not heed conventional expectations of outsiders."[8] These notions of self-vindication and justification are recurrent in U.S. history, often creating domestic political comfort and security. At the same time, in a world where multilateral institutions have grown since 1945, a case for American exceptionalism and the right of exemption from standards other nations have agreed to respect can create much suspicion and criticism of the United States.

When dealing specifically with military force, several current arguments to justify its use are either new or amplify older views that supported independent action. The United States is openly willing to justify force in terms of what it believes just and right rather than what may be legal or permissible by multilateral processes, particularly that of the United Nations. In fact, some specifically stress how adhering to or respecting the process and content of international law or multilateralism may impair the ability to do what is "right" and "good."[9]

The increased selective use and reliance on "just war" theory in framing discussions on deciding when and how to use military force may partially explain this. Writing twenty-five years ago, William O'Brien distinguished between the traditions of "just" and limited war. "The just-war tradition," O'Brien noted, "looks for the moral justification of war as well as its limitation. The limited-war tradition looks for the political justification of war as well as its limitations."[10] O'Brien saw an overlap between the two. Both addressed the need for limits on the conduct of war and its objectives, but each offered different considerations for justifying it. In the post–Cold War era explanations and justifications for using limited force increasingly rely on moral persuasion, perhaps because the Cold War provided an easier, clearer line of argument for political justification that now was more difficult to find. Appeals to morality and values substituted for traditional arguments resting on reasons of state or political calculation.

One significant example of this trend toward self-justification to use force has been a revision of attitudes about the respective place of state sovereignty versus values, such as human rights, in segments of American and international opinion. The international multilateral system that emerged from World War II understandably newly emphasized both the right of protecting state sovereignty from foreign attack as well as defending citizens from both the types of mass slaughter totalitarian regimes practiced during the 1930s and the war itself. Different traditions of thought drew on that historical record among political leaders and intellectuals during the last half of the twentieth century. "Realists" stressed the supremacy of sovereignty and states' need to protect themselves from aggressors. What occurred within their boundaries was largely their own business, unless the behavior might point to potential aggression beyond their borders. "Idealists" argued sovereignty is conditional and factors such as human rights must rank higher than a state's rights.[11] The first Gulf War and George H.W. Bush's appeal for a New World Order, for example, depended on the realist approach, as that president seemingly wanted to ensure that the United Nations and supporting armed coalitions would preserve the sovereignty of states against foreign aggression.[12] Little was said or done about human rights except for a belated, half-baked effort to try to stir a Shiite revolt against Saddam Hussein's Sunni-dominated government.

Through the last decades of the twentieth century the United States slowly retreated from a credo it liked to believe about itself—namely, it would not initiate war or be perceived as the aggressor. As we have seen, this became easier as ways emerged to weaken, overcome, or bypass congressional approval of such actions. When the political scientist Robert W. Tucker wrote about just war in 1960, he added in a footnote, "In American doctrine the just war is also the lawful war. . . ." In his main text he commented, "The insistence that whatever its grievances a state cannot justify initiating war, that whatever its interests a state should not resort to war to preserve or protect these interests, stretches back through Roosevelt, Stimson, and Wilson and surges forward through Truman, Acheson, Eisenhower, and Dulles."[13] While reflecting on nineteenth-century wars against Mexico and Spain might give one pause, Tucker limited himself to the twentieth-century experience. Moreover, he defined war in a strategic sense, not as various low-intensity operations where the early twentieth-century historical record would not have been as supportive. In larger-scale wars, we could argue the United States tended to wait and let the other side strike first to provide clear justification.[14]

The recent contentious debate over preemptive war or preventive measures that can include war did not originate in President George W. Bush's administration. Rather, the development of strategic nuclear weapons forty years before that opened the debate over the arguable necessity for preemptive or preventive actions.[15] No longer could a president easily argue, as had Franklin D. Roosevelt on the morning of December 7 after seeing diplomatic cables suggesting an imminent Japanese attack, that the United States as a peace-loving country could not attack Japan but would have to await an attack.[16] The existence and proliferation of weapons of mass destruction (WMD) raised serious questions about the potential value of preemptive and preventive measures.[17]

The second Bush administration adopted these Cold War arguments and transferred them to the situation involving Iraq, a state allegedly developing WMD and by the end of the 1990s unwilling to comply with the inspections regime the international community demanded. Actual Iraqi possession of WMD capabilities still would not have persuaded some that attacking Iraq was a legitimate or legal defensive response—at least without a UN Security Council Resolution authorizing it. Of course, the fact that none were found tended to validate such caution. As discussed below, accepting U.S. arguments also depended on one's definitions of critical terms such as "self-defense," "imminent threat," or "acts of aggression," and, ultimately, whether one thought international law covered or applied to U.S. actions.

Throughout the 1990s Republican and Democratic presidents used military force to influence the behavior of organized states, individual groups, non-state actors, and even individual leaders. Some perceived successes, such as the First Gulf War and the course of events in Bosnia and later Serbia and Kosovo, showed that limited force could bring desired results at minimal cost and probably faster than relying on additional diplomatic endeavors or measures such as economic sanctions. After the second Bush administration entered office, trust and confidence in military force, due in part to the 9/11 attacks, accelerated.

Just why many in this new administration, particularly those labeled "neo-conservatives," seemed willing to turn to military force so often requires additional study. Some, such as Paul Wolfowitz, were students of Bernard Brodie, Albert Wohlstetter, and other key post–World War II U.S. figures who developed strategic studies focusing particularly on the two superpowers' military rivalry and capabilities. Thus, one intellectual prism tended to concentrate on military factors and options. In his study of Bush's inner circle, James Mann notes how different they were from their predecessors during the early and middle part of the Cold War because of their relative inexperience in business, international law, and diplomacy, although that was not universally true. Certainly, unlike many Americans immediately after the Vietnam War, the second Bush administration had little concern about the shortcomings of military power or the necessity of placing congressional limits on its use to avoid another situation like Vietnam, to which Secretary of State Colin Powell would have been the one noticeable exception.[18]

Some have charged that the neo-conservatives proclivity to use military force reflected their personal inexperience with it—in its most cynical form, the "chicken hawk" syndrome, referring to the lack of military service by some of Bush's advisers, including the vice president, during the Vietnam war. Certainly, at times many of the civilians with no wartime experience appeared fascinated with military force and purposely wanted to overcome post-Vietnam intellectual perspectives and reservations. The confidence, trust, and attention to military themes resembled elements of early to mid–nineteenth-century romanticism, whether in the writings of Wordsworth, Johann Gottlieb Fichte, or Sir Walter Scott. Magazines and newspapers supporting the president's policy paid renewed attention to the value of action and honor acquired through combat.[19]

The various 1990s arguments and justifications justifying intervention and the use of military force worked very much in favor of increased presidential power. The president, much more than Congress, can articulate the reasons for such actions. The office's ability to speak with a single voice is extremely important. Furthermore, if the justifications rested on themes of special mission, images of religious and ethical validation, and threats of imminent danger, the cumulative effect was to strengthen and encourage the president's hand, which would have been so with any president. Combined with all this was the desire to use military force in ways that did not equate with war but were instead carefully weighed and considered actions that would move other parties toward behavior or concessions the United States sought. The convergence of such arguments with recently developed concepts of limited military operations and the capabilities of new technologies invited a much more optimistic attitude toward the use of limited military force than had existed ten or twenty years after Vietnam. In fact, intervention could now occur in various ways individually tailored to each situation.

Defining Intervention

Since the end of the Cold War, American leaders have defined and applied intervention inconsistently. Most probably would agree intervention means forms of coercion falling short of actual war. In the 1980s most would have characterized intervention as involving "the use or threat of force, whether in the internal or external affairs of another state. It may be invited or not and it may involve a desire to change or to preserve the existing distribution of power."[20] This view of intervention left open the possibility of other, not necessarily military, forms, a perspective that had become much more acute by the 1990s, when terms like "diplomatic coercion" and "humanitarian intervention" had become part of the daily discourse. In 1994, as the United States moved closer to direct intervention in the Balkans, James Roche and George Pickett suggested a more elaborate definition:

> Intervention can be defined as the deliberate intrusion of U.S. military, economic, and/or diplomatic activities into a sovereign nation, group of nations, or transnational group. Interventions are for the most part episodic actions, often in the nature of a crisis. Combat is the most destructive form, but other examples include trade sanctions, foreign aid, military assistance, and political pressure from alliances.[21]

By the beginning of the new century, the term became cloudier with the prospect of information intervention, which one expert defined as the "use of technological, informational, and psychological warfare techniques against incendiary media outlets (public or private) located in a target state." This form of intervention opened new questions because among other things it was unclear whether international law would ever regard it as use of force. If information measures reached that threshold, their use arguably would violate international law unless the United Nations Security Council had authorized them under the UN Charter's Article 42. Others would argue that measures such as "most technological, psychological, and information warfare techniques" would not violate norms or policies against intervention.[22]

Through its first 150 years, the United States intervened with military force to protect citizens' and property rights, advance or protect the flow of commerce, promote territorial expansion, or prevent or preempt attacks by or remove Indians. However, intervention in a state to correct a government's abuses against its own people was out of the question. Part of the discussions during the Washington administration that led to a declaration of neutrality in the war between republican France and Great Britain revolved around this very point. All feared that foreign intervention in the United States would destroy its ideals or political system—perhaps even its very existence.[23]

In the Monroe Doctrine, the United States repeated its position on non-intervention—both in its promise not to intervene in European matters and in its quest to deny the right of foreign intervention in the Western Hemisphere. Through this doctrine, the United States tried to set itself apart from the regions covered by the Holy and Quadruple Alliances negotiated at the end of the Napoleonic wars. These agreements justified the major powers, especially Austria and Russia, later France itself in the early 1820s, in intervening with force in areas of unrest and instability in Europe or European possessions overseas.[24] Theodore Roosevelt's famous corollary to the Monroe Doctrine justified U.S. intervention in the Americas to protect American property and investment and prevent new European intrusion or dominance of regional governments to collect debts.[25] Ultimately, in 1907, Secretary of State Elihu Root pushed through the Hague Conference a compromise proposal to stop all such interventions for debt collection by referring the disputes to an arbitration settlement.[26] However, the United States intervened in the Caribbean and Central America to protect property and citizens. The global expansion of the Cold War guaranteed that the United States would assess any revolutionary movement and threatened or actual coup in terms of a potential victory or loss in the struggle against Moscow,

Beijing, and later Havana, thus leading to covert intervention in Guatemala, Iran, the Congo, and the Bay of Pigs, for example, or military commitment in Lebanon in 1958, Vietnam, or Grenada in 1983. During the Cold War, the humanitarian factors that became so prominent in the 1990s were distant secondary considerations when matched against governments' or opposition movements' political leanings.

Humanitarian Intervention versus the Right of Sovereignty

The case for humanitarian intervention, however, actually has a long history, going as far back as the writings of St. Ambrose during the fourth century. In the early seventeenth century, the great jurist Hugo Grotius argued that in some instances it is justifiable to wage war on behalf of other people, especially in cases in which people sought outside assistance from other states against their oppressors.[27] Martha Fennimore has pointed out that most nineteenth-century humanitarian intervention involved European governments' actions to protect Christians against the Ottoman Empire's policies. This legacy involving an Islamic power, a fact we need to remember more often today, was evident from the intervention in the Greek war for independence in 1821–1827 to the "Balkan Atrocities" of 1876–1878 and then the outcry following the Armenian massacres between 1894 and 1917.[28] In her strongly argued study to urge an active, firm international and American punishment of genocide, Samantha Power begins with the Armenian massacres, which stirred some American consciences, although not enough to insist that the rights of people surpassed the right of governments to control what occurs within their boundaries.[29] To its proponents, humanitarian intervention is the model of the Good Samaritan practiced through war and statecraft.

After the Cold War a disagreement arose between those who defended the rights of sovereignty and others who argued that sovereignty, even in international law, is not a shield allowing crimes against humanity. The emphasis on protecting the rights of national sovereignty and states against "threat or use of force" in the UN Charter, Article 2(4), probably conflicted with the 1946 Judgment of the International Military Tribunal at Nuremberg and 1948 United Nations Convention on the Prevention and Punishment of the Crime of Genocide.[30] Humanitarian crises during the 1970s in Pakistan, Cambodia, Central Africa, and Uganda fueled arguments for a more assertive interpretation of the right of humanitarian intervention within or outside of the UN Charter's powers. Articles 39, 41, and 42 provided general frameworks and procedures for the UN to authorize the use of military force. Some scholars argued in favor of interpreting Article 2(4) to allow some types of humanitarian intervention. To claim that this article excludes all uses of force, regardless of the nobility of the cause, seems a pernicious interpretation of the Charter.[31] In 1991, the then UN secretary-general, Javier Perez de Cuellar, stated in the annual report, "The principle of non-interference within the domestic jurisdiction of states cannot be regarded as a protective barrier behind which human rights could be massively or systematically violated with impunity."[32] His successors Boutros Boutros-Ghali and Kofi Annan expressed similar views.[33]

The debate over what exactly encompasses national security and how to measure or assess it complicated this debate over criteria for intervening and, even more, the place of humanitarian intervention. In her 2003 study, Karen Feste observed how national security "gradually" became "enlarged and remodeled into a social, public good, reflecting both individual levels of human security and a collective international security. . . . American national security is embedded in, and derives from, both global development and global contentment. . . ." Thus, the United States increasingly depended on "two justifications for intervention to encompass these expanded levels: (1) an offensive security goal: alleviate immediate suffering and help build civil society foundations within countries experiencing violent domestic conflict . . . and (2) a defensive security goal: eradicate international terrorism. . . ."[34] While the latter fell within more traditional terms of understanding national security—protecting the territorial United States—the former and any use of armed force accompanying it rested in the arena of foreign policy. Furthermore, if military force were deployed in either, it would be in limited forms short of war.

Resolving the tension between states' and individuals' rights was central to humanitarian intervention, as Michael Ignatieff explained in an exchange of letters with Robert Skidelsky: "[S]tates have rights and immunities but so do individuals." Describing himself as an "internationalist," Ignatieff disagreed with those who regard states as "the only relevant actors in the international system. . . . When persecuted individuals or national groups have exhausted all remedies and stand defenseless before aggression their home state, they have the right to appeal and to receive humanitarian and even military assistance."[35] Ignatieff, a proponent of such intervention, captured the critical part of the interventionist agenda during the 1990s and even today.[36]

At least until George W. Bush's presidency, one could arguably claim that humanitarian intervention, the rights of humanitarian claims over those of sovereignty, had been the prevalent rationale behind recent interventions. In Iraq, the Bush administration initially relied on claims about the threat to the United States from alleged weapons of mass destruction on Iraqi soil—a realist argument—and only later emphasized democratic reform rather than humanitarian relief, which the new administration wanted to avoid for peacekeeping or nation-building purposes. In fact, if the Bush administration had tried to prove charges of genocide against Saddam Hussein's regime to justify intervention because of his actions against the Kurds and won UN agreement (admittedly unlikely), punishment by the international community based on the 1948 Convention's definitions would have been mandatory.[37]

Some specialists argue that there is a legal right, derived from customary international law separate from the UN Charter, to intervene unilaterally or with others in a humanitarian crisis. If a large share of the international community has regarded as acceptable a pattern of intervention, we can claim that this pattern establishes customary law for such actions. This argument followed several such interventions that occurred during the 1970s. The supporting evidence for a claim for customary law was not strong. The UN discussed but officially condemned only a few of these cases, and close scrutiny of the reasons cited for intervention finds that not all intervening parties even relied on grounds of humanitarian intervention. Many legal scholars argue that the pattern here was too inconsistent to establish customary international law. A different case for unilateral intervention prominent in American thinking about the United Nations is that the United States or any nation (or nations) must act when it is evident the United Nations is unable to maintain a functioning world order. In fact, if the UN fails, this perspective insists, individual states are obligated to intervene.[38]

Through the 1990s the United Nations authorized several operations, often as peacekeeping measures or with broader enforcement goals against acts of aggression, such as Operations Desert Shield and Desert Storm in 1990–1991 against Iraq, and in Somalia, Rwanda, Haiti, Bosnia and Herzegovina, Kosovo, and East Timor.[39] The effectiveness of some of these operations, such as Somalia, was debatable, and that doubt became an issue for those who still argued that it was justifiable, if necessary, for the United States to act on its own or through negotiated coalitions, so-called coalitions of the willing, without UN authorization. To some, Somalia proved the dangers of acting with the United Nations, a negative "lesson" that fed anti-UN sentiments as much as frustration over the UN's inability to act in other instances. To its critics, inaction because of lack of UN consensus was unacceptable; ineffective action because of UN command and operational limitations was unforgivable.

When we pour American military capabilities, resources, and 1990s superpower status into its historical sense of special mission, the conviction that the United States is "the indispensable nation," in Secretary of State Madeleine Albright's phrase, was no surprise. Whether in Somalia or later in the Balkans, the conviction that only the United States was in a position to do something was widespread. As one unnamed official observed before the intervention in Somalia, "If you really wanted to deliver the goods on time, you go with the U.S. military."[40] President Clinton referred to the Balkans as a political tinderbox that had caused World War I and now endangered the stability of Europe and the integrity and effectiveness of the North Atlantic Treaty Organization (NATO). However, alongside these arguments was a determination to do the just, right thing. The televised images of Serbs killing ethnic Albanians in Kosovo were, in Albright's words, "an outrage we cannot accept." Her own parents had fled Nazi Europe, and it was no surprise to find the secretary of state arguing that defeating such forms of ethnic nationalism was similar to fighting fascism. Even some on the political right in the United States agreed with her.[41] Yet as the 1994 genocide in Rwanda showed, U.S. policy contained no universally consistent formula. The distinction arguably might have been that the Balkans were much closer to vital national interests than Rwanda. Unable to explain clearly how the national interest was at stake in the Balkans, the Clinton administration relied on moral arguments of ethnic cleansing and the fundamental wrongness of doing nothing.[42]

In Operation Allied Force, the bombing campaign against Serbia, the United States demonstrated that it was prepared to act without UN authorization, although the operation had a NATO umbrella over it. The absence of a UN authorization troubled British officials in the Foreign Office. When Foreign Secretary Robyn Cook told Secretary Albright that he was having some trouble with the ministry's lawyers, she offered plain advice: "Get new lawyers."[43] Legal interpretation can become subservient to state interests, and no matter whether international law permitted such action, the objectives were to resist violent nationalism, prevent the destabilization of southeastern Europe, and fulfill a strong desire to do what was just and right through humanitarian action.

Intervention after 9/11: Where Strategic Concerns Intersect with Divine Destiny

Regardless of the incoming Bush administration's determination not to engage in the humanitarian or peacekeeping missions that its predecessor had, much of the world probably had moved closer to adding humanitarian intervention to intervention by right of treaty, invitation by a sovereign state, and protection of citizens and other aliens as justifiable causes.[44] Also, arguably, the new administration did not reject humanitarian operations as much as it claimed. Administration representatives such as Richard Haass, director of the State Department Policy Planning Staff, spoke of the need to use all means—diplomatic, economic, financial, military, and other—to integrate more states into a peaceful international order. As part of that framework, Haass did not rule out using armed intervention to protect people within another state's borders. This concept of sovereignty stressed its responsibilities as much as its rights.[45]

However, the new administration wanted to add one more reason for intervention, under discussion well before it arrived in the White House—the possession of weapons of mass destruction by "rogue" states or states that both threatened their neighbors and U.S. security and refused to comply with international inspection regimes. Much of the national security strategy document released in September 2002 focused on these states and WMD, as did the follow-up document released in early 2006.[46] To act for this reason, the United States would have to challenge both the international political and legal communities and, if necessary, work outside or against many of the previous fifty years' multilateral institutions and processes.

Before considering those factors that made the United States more willing to argue for changes in international law to deal with WMD or act alone in the absence of that change, we cannot dismiss the scarring effects of the 9/11 attacks. No matter our opinion on the concepts of preemptive and preventive war, it is undeniable that the attacks brought to a wider audience compelling arguments about how to counter the proliferation of WMD that before were confined mainly to specialized policy journals and strategic conferences. The preemptive use of force now became an option to consider if non-state actors, much less states, could obtain control over weapons of mass destruction and threaten to use them. It was thus no surprise in the wake of 9/11 that many emphatically pressed for close study and review of preemptive and preventive actions and the sovereign right to use force, even if they apparently conflicted with international law.

Thanks to television and other electronic media, the shared experience of terrorist attacks on the United States made it and much of the world willing to pursue and defeat those responsible for such attacks. The morning of September 11, 2001 was the defining moment for President George W. Bush; most of what he subsequently did in defense and foreign policy occurred in the shadows of that day. Bush found a nation shocked and horrified, but more united than in decades and ready to respond. The president could turn not only to the various arguments on national security, instability in the Middle East and southwest Asia, the rise of terrorism, and a determination to show national resolve and a firm response, but also to currents of thought and emotion within American society itself. Within days of the attacks, the president tried to warn against viewing the conflict in terms of a clash between Islam and Judeo-Christianity, yet underlying developments within some segments of American Christianity provided him with a stronger foundation to justify and expect public support for measures of war. It is important to understand the impact of these factors on American thinking before completing the discussion on why the United States after 9/11 became more willing to use preemptive force in the face of much international criticism.

Religion and the Use of Force

The entire subject of religion's influence and role in the shaping of U.S. foreign policy and influencing actual decisions needs serious study. While many strategic commentators on U.S. foreign policy and strategy acknowledge it, they tend only to pay lip service to it. The subject, its vocabulary, and its motivations are quite removed from most security studies' themes and topics. The role of radical Islamic movements has awakened an interest and attention to religion, but because most security experts are not comfortable with the subject, they have trouble dealing with it on its own terms. Yet, a religious worldview may be as or more decisive in shaping individual, group, or national actions than poverty, wealth, weaponry, or political institutions.

How a debate over reasons to justify foreign intervention with military force relates to the "Fourth Great Awakening" in U.S. history is a complex question. These recurring movements in American religion, tracing back to the early to mid-eighteenth century, focus not only on individuals' salvation but also their relationship with their church, each other, their community, and the state. The current religious awakening was evident by the 1970s, when many U.S. Christian conservatives came to believe that the country's secular leadership essentially had abandoned the American covenant with God, jettisoning laws and values tied to Christianity. Some conservative leaders determined to return the United States to its Christian foundations. Vietnam also shook the providential view of America's role in the world; the status of the United States in its relationship with God became uncertain. A war most Americans supported because of their anti-communist convictions gradually pushed more churches and Americans into opposing the U.S. role in it.[47]

These developments bore implications for American attitudes on force and intervention because some members of this emerging conservative movement saw current and future armed conflict as part of God's plan. Why they believed this depended greatly on the conclusions believers drew from various traditions in Protestant Christianity on the millennium, the thousand years of peace and righteousness. Early in the republic, religious Americans believed that they were trying to build a godly nation that actually was the beginning of the millennium, after which they believed Christ would return. However, the last half of the twentieth century witnessed the emergence of a premillennial perspective arguing that Christ's last judgment would occur before the thousand years of peace. Adherents of both traditions thought that the United States must have a pivotal role in the millennium and humanity's spiritual fate. Some students of religion in the United States point out the earlier postmillennial perspective paid more attention to the betterment of each person and mankind at large. It lent itself to optimism and a belief in progress, although it did not necessarily exclude using force to advance the divine plan.[48]

Premillennial followers focused much more on signs drawn from the Bible that might tell when the Second Coming and the Rapture, the meeting of dead believers with those living in heaven, would occur. With the ultimate crisis in world history appearing so near, the climate was conducive to the Moral Majority, a coalition begun by the late Reverend Jerry Falwell in 1978, to bring to this movement conservatives from several mainstream denominations. The premillennial view favored candidates who were ready for Armageddon. Falwell, the Reverend Pat Robertson, and others urged followers to support increased defense spending, new weapons, unqualified support for Israel, and an unyielding position on moral issues. Since all were living near or at the end of time, there was no need for money or programs for social betterment. Violence and war could not be stopped until Christ returned. Other phenomena, such as globalization, also were instrumental steps in fulfilling Biblical prophecies.[49]

This community of Christian conservatives supported George W. Bush and many Republican candidates in both the 2000 and 2004 elections. However, it is hard to claim that these believers voted for him mainly because of the Republican Party stance on defense and use of force. In a 2001 study of voting and religion, Geoffrey Layman cautioned that among evangelical Protestants the determinant depended much more on conservatism and social welfare values than warfare. Evangelical Protestantism focuses much more on the individual and his or her salvation than improving society; evangelical Protestants tend to favor "economic individualism."[50] Nevertheless, as Charles Marsh, an evangelical who teaches at the University of Virginia, observes, many evangelicals from the premillennial tradition definitely backed the Iraq war. One poll taken after Operation Iraqi Freedom began showed 87 percent of the white evangelical Christians polled supported it. A 2005 poll showed a decrease to 68 percent, certainly higher than the general public's support, which had dropped to less than half of those polled. From his study of sermons about the war, Marsh concluded that their prevalent theme was the president was a "brother in Christ, and because he has discerned that God's will is for our nation to be at war against Iraq, we shall gloriously comply."[51] Whether the difficult turn of events in Iraq would cause these voters to turn away from the president remained unclear due to the importance they assigned to values and morality in domestic issues.

The strong conviction that some conservative Christians held about Iraq and the use of force also partly influenced disagreements between the United States and several European allies over both the operation itself and the U.S. decision to proceed without UN authorization. The desire to be separate from European evils is a long-standing one in some threads of American religion; it certainly was evident in Puritanism.[52] Some arguments were a form of Europe-bashing with little direct relationship with religion. In some conservative circles, an image of effeminate European males who lacked virility became popular. Christina Hoff Sommers wrote in *The American Enterprise* that Europeans just could not grasp why "fighting enemies and protecting the nation are overwhelmingly male projects." Other writers found deeper reasons related to religion and argued that the cautious European response, particularly of France and Germany, showed what one could expect from overly secular European societies that had pushed religion and a sense of right and wrong out of their lives.[53]

From arguments driven by religious conviction about national responsibility, it would not be difficult to conclude that the United States had no obligation to adhere to international law or multilateral institutions' deliberations and decisions (or indecisions). America's responsibility was not only to its national interests but also to the standards or frameworks enabling it to act as necessary to serve those interests. However, it would be very unfair to suggest that Christian conservatism's stance on foreign and security policy focused completely on the right of intervention and the use of military force. The movement was not a bloc. Some preferred to work alongside more mainstream denominations to promote economic development, alleviate poverty in the developing world, and protect human rights, especially those of Christians who were being persecuted.[54]

The Use or Abuse of Just War Theory

A recurring factor in many discussions about the religious or moral correctness of intervention relied on the language and concepts of just war theory. Disagreement over the very notion of just war and its application in interventions during the 1990s and early twenty-first century appeared in U.S. religious, philosophical, and security discussions. In more secular European countries, such as Germany, the theory came under heavy criticism because it was seen as justifying and validating actions that violate international law.[55] In fact, two inviting subjects for future scholars are to analyze why just war theory enjoys more support in the United States than abroad, and also how various U.S. denominations view it.[56] Just war theory has particularly strong links with Catholicism. An early 1990s study noted that modern Catholicism tends to treat pacifism and just war convictions equally. As Catholicism believes "it is the duty of the state to protect its citizens," a teaching based on St. Augustine that to the present has "require[d] the use of force to defend the community." A 1993 statement from the National Conference of Catholic Bishops, "The Harvest of Justice Is Sown in Peace," amplified this view through the bishops' support for humanitarian intervention, which, the statement added, was an obligation designated by Pope John Paul II "where the survival of populations and entire ethnic groups is seriously compromised." Thus, in May 1993 the bishops' International Policy Committee urged U.S. intervention in Bosnia. However, the bishops' statement reaffirmed pacifism or nonviolence as a fully viable option for those who so believed.[57]

In contrast, contemporary American Protestantism stresses "the sovereignty of God," and thereby diminishes "the importance of pacifism or just-war tenets by stressing the belief in God's sovereign rule over all human actions."[58] For some conservative Protestants, this supremacy of God and His judgment over all human conduct obviously reinforces accepting war as part of a worldly order before Christ's return. That said, as a criterion for political support, Christian conservatives' political affinity for recent Republican policies seems more dependent, as observed earlier, on the priority that these Christians give select domestic policies and issues than to how a president uses military power, since it is the domestic arena where these same individuals fear that God's place has been most seriously threatened. The leeway that some Christian conservatives may give a president in decisions about military force is more of a secondary benefit. This applies to Congress, too, where those who share these same convictions would likely allow a president additional discretion in using force.

Clear connections exist among trends in changing criteria for intervention to religion, the renewed interest in just war theory, and increased criticism of international law and multilateral process. Just war theory is where many of these considerations converge the most. Yet it is critical to understand here the intention of just war theory is not to make it easier to turn to war. Its questions and standards are demanding, and if applied objectively, create a high threshold to justify the use of force. Taken from this context, though, just war theory can be used and cited to justify actions for political purposes.[59] If scholars need to examine its appeal among various denominations and within diverse cultures and states, they also need to seriously study its influence on American policy on military force and imperfect war. So far, most evidence is more indirect or anecdotal than the result of serious analysis. For example, the names for the U.S. intervention in Panama under the first President Bush, Operation Just Cause, and the initial name for the U.S.-led response in Afghanistan after 9/11, Operation Infinite Justice, superficially illustrate both an American determination to claim and seek justice and some level of influence of just war thinking on decision makers. The short discussion here only poses several tentative notions and thoughts on its role in influencing American policy on the use of force.

In its simplest form, just war theory sets forth criteria to use both in deciding to go to war and then how to fight it. More recently, some have proposed criteria for how a victor should conduct policies afterward.[60] The discussion here concentrates on the first two. The first criteria, *jus ad bellum*, deal with the actual decision to use force. These standards examine the justness of the cause and the "proper authority" in making the decision, ascertain right intentions, ensure that war comes as the last resort, and try to guarantee that the decision to use war is in proportion as an instrument of policy to those factors causing or contributing to it. Additional criteria, *jus in bello,* require discrimination, particularly in terms of noncombatants, and proportionality of means used.[61] Just war theory brings a set of considerations that governments must address before they choose to turn to war or military force and revisit throughout the conduct of the operation.

There is no intent here to question the legitimacy of just war theory or its applicability. If used properly without inherent bias, just war theory requires a very rigorous review of considerations before a government or any other actor decides to intervene or act with armed force. It is also critical to appreciate that just war theory is also a part of the history of international law, especially the law on armed conflict. Today, there is irony in that relationship, since some seek to use the theory to challenge international law rather than reinforce it.

Recent attention to just war theory originates from at least three directions. One is the increasingly destructive nature of warfare over the twentieth century. The Allies' strategic bombing campaigns in World War II and the development of nuclear weapons presented questions about destroying both the innocent and guilty on such a great magnitude that philosophical and moral questions were inevitable. Added to that was the experience of Vietnam, a conflict that began as a limited, small war, but whose violence, high number of civilian casualties, and corrosive effect on the morality and morale of both the United States and many who fought demanded efforts to prevent such a political and moral breakdown from happening again. The Vietnam experience was a critical factor in Michael Walzer's decision to write what remains the most important U.S. book on this subject, *Just and Unjust Wars: A Moral Argument with Historical Illustrations,* first published in 1977.[62]

The first factor leads to a second one—namely the belief following World War II and the creation of the UN Charter that states lost the right to go to war, which was something they had taken for granted in previous centuries. If so, then what reasons could exist to argue that war in certain instances was still necessary and just? The postwar climate created very high expectations about the United Nations and the hope that states would not have as strong a voice in international matters. However, events during subsequent decades revealed the UN's and other multilateral organs' limitations and demonstrated that war still had a place in the international system. Guidelines for war were still necessary. Proponents of just war theory argue it never tried to provide an ethical or moral rationale to bypass the UN Charter's ban on aggression. In fact, many scholars, policy practitioners, and military officers have issued failing grades and deemed a war unjust based on their evaluation of the conflict and just war theory. The framework of just war theory provides questions that enable a person to examine those circumstances that condone or justify using force or war.[63] However, it does not guarantee an affirmative verdict.

A third reason for a new emphasis on just war theory emerged from the growing criticism of the traditions and concept of "realism" in statecraft, a philosophy that runs from Thucydides through Machiavelli, E.H. Carr, Hans Morgenthau, Henry Kissinger, and modern variations, such as the work of John Mearsheimer or Stephen Walt. Michael Walzer's own explanation depicts this development. As a graduate student in the late 1950s and early 1960s Walzer found realism to be the prevalent approach in the study of international relations. Realism concentrated on national interest, not on matters of justice, as its dominant criterion.[64] Religion, morality, and legality were not, some realists argued, viable reasons to resort to war. In fact, if they were factors, they could contribute to an escalation of the war's conduct and scale to more destructive levels. In that sense realism could provide compelling arguments not to use force or go to war, and in its simplest form, tended to see self-defense as the best reason for going to war. However, self-defense could embrace actions based on imminent danger and might include further steps, such as preemptive or preventive war.[65] If one were both a realist and strict adherent of international law, motives for self-defense, such as imminent threat or preemption, would be very problematic because they arguably fell outside the permissible boundaries of international law.

In hindsight, it is clear that waging limited warfare became particularly dependent on the ability to claim and prove the justice underlying one's use of force and intentions. Such forms of war often lacked the clarity of purpose of declared wars or defensive wars. Again, Walzer notes how modern warfare must often depend on public support, both foreign and domestic. Adversaries often must draw their support and strength from the same pool of people among whom they operate. Defeating the enemy also means convincing the surrounding population of the justness of one's actions and purpose. At the same time, the government needs to assure the domestic population that using armed force is for just purposes and that the operation itself is being conducted justly.[66] In his study of the contemporary revival of the romantic conception of war, George Fletcher argues that the term "justice" rather than "war" is perhaps a way of conciliating those who found the latter term too bellicose. Yet Fletcher adds "to think of war as justice by other means runs the risk of imitating the holy mission of the enemy."[67] Walzer thinks that both Bush presidents, while appreciating aspects of just war, such as proportionality to limit casualties, essentially succumbed to the danger that Fletcher mentions—confusing just war with crusade.[68]

The word "crusade" naturally raises more questions about the extent to which just war theory and religion are interlinked—not an irrelevant question when the United States is engaged in conflicts in the Muslim world and anxiously tries to argue that its actions are not religiously inspired or targeted toward another religion. Certainly, the American understanding of the theory embodies a visible component of Christian tradition. The story of the Good Samaritan reminds Christians of the obligation to assist others, especially if they can do so with little inconvenience to themselves.[69] In a religion so often identified with pacifism, just war theory argues that religiously grounded reasons exist to act or intervene on behalf of others. In the fourth century, St. Augustine wrote that military action could be an act of love for a neighbor. Writing nearly nine hundred years later, Thomas Aquinas placed just war in the context of charity: "[I]n the context of war we find in its sharpest and most paradoxical from the thought that love can sometimes smite, and even slay."[70]

It is a serious error to think that "just war" is a Christian concept only. Various historical cultures and religions have provided advice on the necessity of limiting the scale or destructiveness of war, including the writings of Sun Tzu, the ancient Egyptians, Babylonians, classical Greeks, and Romans. Hinduism, Judaism, and Islam also have criteria for just war, both in going to war and standards for its conduct.[71] Also, a more secular concept of just war parallel to the early development of international law slowly emerged. The early Christian writers through Thomas Aquinas concentrated particularly on the reasons or just causes of war; for Augustine it was a Roman Empire increasingly swayed by Christianity against barbarians, for Thomas Aquinas it was the world of Christendom. The Catholic Church's loss of authority during the Reformation significantly shook the concept of just war, which largely had confined itself to what Christians could do to each other but not what they might do against nonbelievers. During the mid-sixteenth century, Francisco de Vitoria concentrated on the brutal Spanish treatment of native people in the New World and advocated a minimum standard of conduct that must govern the treatment of all peoples. Later, the unbelievably brutal Thirty Years Wars (1618–1648), in which Christian fought Christian, occurred without any guidelines. What emerged from this bloodshed intermingling religion and state ambition was a tradition of international law and just war focusing less on the cause of war than on regulating its conduct.[72]

Is There a Tension between Just War Theory and International Law?

Amid and after the Thirty Years War, the great legal scholar Hugo Grotius tried to place war in the state sphere. In his writings, the state now received recognition as a sovereign entity, and after the Treaty of Westphalia in 1648 all states were essentially equals. He did not recognize a right of intervention based on religion. Grotius's work established a tenet of international law applicable to the present day—namely, war was legal only when undertaken in self-defense. James Turner Johnson, a leading scholar of the just war tradition, stresses Grotius's emphasis on the law of nature as the foundation for the right to war states had held. What Grotius could not anticipate was the writing and events of one to two centuries later that argued the rights of man also rested on nature. The American and French revolutions at the end of the eighteenth century counteracted state tyranny based on the rights of man, and furthermore claimed an inherent right to spread their message and the blessings of human rights to other people.[73] These revolutions set in motion a tension that has played so large a role in the continuing critique of international law—the rights of people versus the rights of states—and underlaid the assertion of the right of independent action that might be contrary to international law.

The nineteenth-century notion of going to war as "the paramount attribute of sovereignty" fell into question during and after the horrible experience of World War I. The League of Nations, which the United States chose not to join, gave the League Council the power to make recommendations to countries considering going to war, but the Council lacked any enforcement authority, and if its members did not agree, states could proceed as their interests demanded.[74] As the Versailles Treaty was hardly an ironclad guarantee against another war in Europe, the Kellogg-Briand Pact of 1928 "condemn[ed] recourse to war for the solution of international controversies, and renounce[d] it as an instrument of national policy in their relations with one another." However, this agreement, which one cynic characterized as "an international kiss," lacked a means of enforcement and was as closely tied to the dynamics of the Versailles Treaty and a French quest for security as it was to postwar ambitions of the international legal movement.[75] Thus, it was not until the United Nations Charter and subsequent measures and other acts built on it that the international community had a body of law on aggression with enforcement mechanisms that, while visibly flawed, were nonetheless in place. "[T]he inherent right of individual or collective self-defense" in case "of an armed attack" was the one right to turn to war the Charter recognized, in Article 51.[76]

Just war theory was a key foundation for the law of armed conflict. But a divergence between that portion of international law and just war theory emerged during the last half of the twentieth century. International law had evolved from depending mainly on natural law to a tradition of "legal positivism," a conviction that law consists of written text of the practices of states. Natural law, critics argued, gave national leaders too much freedom in determining and justifying their decisions to go to war. To counter that charge, others argued that the absence of an effective international final authority that recognized power to override sovereign states' legal interpretations and actions proved both the need to preserve the rights of national sovereignty and the realism of a natural law perspective. A contemporary writer on just war has stressed how "international law, like all law, needs to be developed in relation to cases; but lacking the courts to develop it, it can too easily become locked into an abstractly doctrinaire posture." The place and role of international law are undermined "if it is held to prohibit actions which people in general are inclined to think not only justifiable, but even morally obligatory."[77]

During the 1960s the need to place moral obligation above law found an especially vocal advocate in the work of Paul Ramsey, a United Methodist, who, unlike later writers such as Walzer, depended greatly on religious arguments. In 1965 Ramsey wrote, "The use of political power by a nation-state should not always stick by the legal boundaries, else the erosion or the order of power and of realized justice may make worse befall than a violation of the legalities." In short, a greater wrong or injustice could occur as a result of adherence to law. Ramsey does not condemn law or respect for it, but he cautions that it should not be held as the highest or ultimate standard. Sometimes it was necessary to commit illegal actions or even a "lesser evil" for the sake of preventing a greater one. "In fact, not to do so and allow a greater evil to prevail would be gravely wrong."[78] Writing at the peak of the Vietnam War and also during the age of strategic nuclear deterrence, Ramsey's arguments nonetheless resemble those thirty to forty years later in their desire to find ways to enable war to be usable in particular instances.[79]

If international law restricted a state to defensive war only, just war, some argued, could condone certain forms of offensive war. Constitutionally, such forms of war are difficult because they should have congressional consent; in the arena of international law offensive actions can be synonymous with aggression, but where law might not give the desired answer, as was the case with Iraq, some conservatives argued just war theory justified invading that country. Both George Weigel, a prominent conservative Catholic intellectual, and Richard J. Neuhaus, a Catholic priest who had worked with President Bush's campaign in 2000 and also edited *First Things,* a conservative journal, argued as much, and praised the Bush administration for its understanding of just war theory.[80]

A different argument to justify intervention occurred earlier with the operations in the Balkans, where "the rescuing forces are the invaders" and "are the ones who, in the strict sense of international law, begin the war."[81] Yet the Clinton administration's concern about a just outcome in this region showed its susceptibility to just war thinking as well. For an offensive measure to be legal under international law, it would most likely be an "enforcement action" authorized by the United Nations Security Council. In turn, if a state operates under the claim of "legitimate authority" of just war theory and not on UN authority, it relies on a key distinction from international law, even though many modern just war advocates recognize that the UN is a principal source from which to obtain "legitimate" authority. Not all advocates would, however. In the actual conduct of an operation both just war theory and international law would emphasize the importance of discrimination and proportionality, but the former could permit independent state or government action while the latter expected cooperation with "regional authorities and organizations." In the area of war aims, the distinctions arguably would be greater. International law seeks to "(re)establish peace and security" while just war theory seeks "redress for wrongs, including punishment," although not permitting acts of vengeance or territorial aggrandizement. Retaliatory air strikes, such as those the United States undertook against targets in the Sudan and Afghanistan in 1998 after terrorist bombings of U.S. embassies in Kenya and Tanzania, could be a justifiable act under just war theory but not easily permissible under international law.[82] The broad point to remember is the case for "offensive" war based on such interpretations of just war theory could enable a government, such as the United States, to argue that it had the right to intervene in Iraq as a rescuer to topple Saddam Hussein's regime and bring greater political and personal freedom to millions of Iraqis. Two successive presidents from different parties used their respective justifications to regard themselves as rescuers in the international system. They also believed they could use force without congressional approval.

Just War Theory and War Itself

While this explanation concentrates on how just war theory has affected the debate over intervention and contributed to arguments that override international law, a few words must be said about some of its other criteria affecting decisions on when and how force will be used. Limited military operations present some significant challenges to the applicability of these criteria. For example, consider the requirement that war should be a last resort only. The problem here is the same one that has challenged the United States since the Constitution was completed. What does "war" mean? In an environment where armed force is seen as an instrument of foreign policy, which has characterized many operations during the last sixty years, it is clear that the use of force has not always been a last resort. It has occurred because presidents and others have hoped it would bring faster, clearer, less costly results. Determining whether all other options have been reasonably explored requires some subjective judgment. In both 1991 and early 2003, for example, some in and outside the United States thought that diplomacy and other measures vis-à-vis Iraq deserved more time.

The prospect for reasonable chances for success seems a clear criterion to require in any decision to use force. Few countries would resort to military force or war just to "give it a whirl." They usually assume that the war, conflict, or operation is winnable.[83] Perhaps only in cases of attack, when a nation believes that it must fight even in the face of overwhelming odds, would a decision acknowledging the likelihood of defeat be made, and just war theory would urge that government to ask whether it would be better to surrender. Yet self-delusion about prospects for victory is not only the practice of mad kings and megalomaniacal dictators, it also can be the fallacy of democracies. When a democratic government ponders its intention to use force, it should do so as extensively as possible, which must include its parliament's or congress's involvement and deliberations. In doing so it may enter that conflict better appreciating the sacrifices and costs it will incur initially and later. As Chapter 3 suggests, that did not happen in 2002 and

2003 before intervention in Iraq through the fault of both the president and Congress.

As to the requirement for proper authority in just war theory, we must return to the first chapters of this book. Depending on how a person interprets the Constitution and historical record, the argument can fall either way as to whether the United States has entered war or used military force with proper authority. This book argues in favor of the power of congressional authorization, but recognizes Congress itself, tacitly by its action, inaction, and behavior, has often enabled a president to assume more authority in this area. Since the designation of proper authority between the congressional and presidential camps is so controversial, it probably is fair to argue that most engagements entered through presidential authority represent proper authority. However, it is a weakened authority that works without the full involvement of the legislative branch of government. A clear exception, though, where proper authority would have been questionable, was the Iran-Contra affair, which, while not a war, arranged a use of force that intentionally concealed U.S. responsibility. Even covert operations conducted with U.S. funds do not function in this manner when reviewed by the intelligence committees. The outside world may not know the U.S. role, but Congress should. Iran-Contra was unconstitutional, and by any application of just war theory, if one thinks it applicable, it was unjust.

Historically, just war theory required a public declaration of war, but many of its advocates regard this as irrelevant in the modern era. This provision is a vestige of the Roman contribution to just war theory.[84] Some believe that it remains a valid requirement, as a public declaration is a signal to the international community and the adversary, particularly citizens living within the latter's territory, of the other party's willingness to use force.[85] However, in the twenty-first century it is hard to imagine that such public declarations will always be possible. War can occur in a matter of seconds, so the expectation of a public declaration is unrealistic. Also, explicit warnings about the likelihood of war unless a country or state meets another state's or coalition's expectations can be almost tantamount to a declaration. It would be hard to claim that Saddam Hussein did not know about the prospect of war, given the many warnings in presidential speeches in 1990–1991 and 2002–2003. While not a formal, legal declaration, the warnings to him, the Iraqi people, and the international community were clear. If one believes that a declaration is necessary, it seems "to be trivially satisfied whenever the nation under attack sees or hears the enemy coming before suffering its first blow."[86] A future challenge to any declaration will occur when states rely on different, nontraditional technologies such as information means in actions construable as a surprise attack. Such operations can conceal the origin of the attack and may defy traditional meaning of an armed attack.[87]

Proportionality in both justifying an action and its later conduct, especially in terms of discrimination, are two just war factors figuring significantly in modern decisions to intervene. The American approach to war strongly desires decency, but how to achieve it can depend on two different approaches: either "a multilateralist, humanitarian approach with all due attention paid to minimizing harm in every day of every battle; or wage war with overwhelming force, to make the process brutal, decisive, and brief, so that peace may be achieved sooner, even if on bloodier wings."[88] In reality, this argument simply states in ethical language the same arguments over the political utility of limited versus overwhelming force. However, today military commanders and civilians in the national security community work in an environment that expects fewer casualties on all sides. In 1990, the planner for air operations against Iraq, Brigadier General Buster Glosson, observed that the American people "would never stand for another Dresden."[89] Even advocates of "shock and awe," the use of selected technologies or weapons to establish "rapid dominance" over the course of battle and, more importantly, the adversary's willpower and decisions, perceive this form of warfare in humanitarian terms. War cannot be kept immaculate; "brutal levels of power and force" may be necessary to "frighten, scare, intimidate and disarm." Yet, "there are surely humanitarian considerations that cannot or should not be ignored."[90] This strategy, symbolically attempted in the early phase of the 2003 war against Iraq, was not an attempt at mass destruction.

Preemptive Intervention and International Law

One consequence of new technologies, particularly precision-guided munitions, on the content of existing law in modern warfare may be to make intervention more feasible or inviting. Chapter 6 will further examine this implication. Here, a few comments on law, proportionality, and intervention are necessary. The emergence of the lawyer on the battlefield is a positive development in efforts to ensure proportionality, discrimination, and accountability. The more than 200 Army attorneys in the field in the first Gulf War formed the basis for the Pentagon's characterization of it as "a legal war."[91] Simultaneously, because precision-guided munitions and less-lethal weapons may ensure better proportionality and limit the scale of destruction, death, and discrimination—and thus reduce collateral damage and civilian casualties—some commentators argue that war has become easier to consider and execute. The convergence of advanced battlefield technology with law has made the law of war less concerned about going to war than with the procedures of war to maintain its proportionality and scale of destruction. The law of armed conflict has worked to humanize war in various ways and therefore to make it more usable and accessible.[92]

American confidence about technological capability has induced its leaders to intervene and use force in limited or select ways. New weapons technologies reinforce the conclusion that military force is a justifiable foreign policy instrument because improved capabilities enable these weapons to be used in ways that demonstrate the intention to adhere to the criteria of just war theory, such as proportionality and avoiding large numbers of civilian casualties. When conducted on a limited scale, the application of war is less likely to be seen as disproportionate to the causes of the problem or the desired goals. More accurate weapons may indeed reduce destruction and loss of life. In fact, a pivotal question is whether increased use of such weapons will legally obligate states to use precision-guided munitions if they have them.[93] A more problematic implication is that assumptions about what such technologies can accomplish may be inflated and cause a state to turn to military force without examining other options and different outcomes more completely. The decision on how to use force initially in Iraq in 2003 and then the later difficult turn of events strongly suggest that such assumptions guided U.S. thinking.[94]

While the United States asserts that preemptive and even preventive uses of force are acceptable within international law and reserves the right to act beyond such limits, it does so partly from a confidence that such new capabilities can illustrate and even justify its argument. Potentially, successfully using such forms of advanced military force could even diminish the controversy created by initial actions. Would the international community criticize the United States and others so much if it realized the extent to which Americans tried to insulate the general public from such operations and greatly reduce casualties and damage? What, in fact, would have been the international reaction if the United States had prevented the difficult spiral in Iraq that has caused so many civilian, noninsurgent deaths? Admittedly, in hindsight this was unlikely. Yet it would have been harder to condemn such interventions when the means that Americans chose showed such commitment to avoiding harm to all.

While much of the international legal community disagrees with the American assertion of the right to use preemptive military force or conduct a preventive military operation, not all evidence supports that position. Article 51 assumes that states would be the aggressors, not terrorists or other non-state actors. The UN Charter reflects the impact of aggressive attacks by imperial Japan, Nazi Germany, and Mussolini's Italy, which sometimes carried a legal pretext of preventive justifications, as Nazi Germany claimed about Poland. Moreover, non-state actors' potential possession of WMD changed circumstances by presenting a type of threat not easily envisaged in 1945. Whether preventive or preemptive measures are the best way to deal with terrorists' possession of such capabilities is a fair question for debate. Nevertheless, while other factors might constrain terrorists from using such weapons, invoking their respect for international law will not. In its 2006 restatement of the right to use such measures, the Bush administration spoke of the "duty that obligates the government to anticipate and counter threats. . . . To forestall or prevent such hostile acts by our adversaries, the United States will, if necessary, act preemptively in exercising our inherent right of self-defense."[95] "Inherent" refers one not only to the right of sovereignty being reserved, but also the concept of natural law as well as law written in code and treaty that can be the base for government action.[96]

Two problems coexist here. The broader one is the degree to which the United States is required to adhere to international law. The UN Charter's Article 51 recognizes the "inherent" right of self-defense in case of "an armed attack." A state's sovereign or "inherent" right of defense may seem obvious. Adding the qualifying words "an armed attack" is what raises the bar. What does "armed attack" mean? Can a state act beforehand to preempt or prevent it? In the next chapter that will be discussed further in terms of information warfare, but here the question centers on whether those words can justify preemptive or preventive measures. Some scholars, such as Michael Byers, argue that such an attack does not. Others, such as Alan Dershowitz, leave that right open but note the difference between reserving that right in very select circumstances and announcing it as a matter of strategic policy, as the Bush administration did.[97] The first is a legal question; the latter is definitely both a political and strategic choice.

The United States' relationship to international law demonstrates a range of opinion. Article VI of the Constitution states that treaties entered into "shall

be the supreme law of the land." But Congress repeatedly has passed trade
legislation that contradicts and arguably violates the multilateral trade agreements to which the United States has belonged for over half a century. If Congress chooses, it can subsequently create laws after a treaty that, if signed,
would negate one or more of its provisions. In effect, the latest law is the law
of the land.[98] Nevertheless, as the constitutional scholar Louis Henkin claims,
"International law is law for the United States." While he concedes nation-
states have "the power . . . to violate international law and obligation," they
also must contend with the consequences, as the United States sometimes
must in unfavorable World Trade Organization decisions.[99] At the opposite
end of the spectrum, John Yoo, who teaches at the University of California,
Berkeley, and was a deputy assistant attorney general in the Bush administration in 2001–2003, argues, "[P]residents are not constitutionally or legally
bound by international law." In relation to presidential war powers, Yoo
claims that allowing "international law and treaties to interfere" with these
powers "would expand the federal judiciary's authority into areas where it
has little competence, where the Constitution does not textually call for its intervention, and where it risks defiance by the political branches."[100] Perhaps
John Murphy has most constructively portrayed the two sides of this argument on international law when he notes that one system considers "international law and national law as parts of single legal system." Furthermore, this
view "often see[s] national law as deriving its validity from international
law." The opposite perspective regards them "as two separate legal systems."
Here, international law must be "incorporated into national law," and even in
this case "is subject to constitutional limitations applicable to national law,
and may be repealed or superseded by legislative action for purposes of national law."[101] Contemporary Germany would lean very much toward the
former camp, while the United States seems distinctly to fall into the latter.

   The United States has tried to argue its view of preemptive use of force,
in particular, rests within the boundaries of international law and the "inherent" right of self-defense granted in the UN Charter. First, does some
flexibility within the UN Charter and subsequent international law permit
forms of anticipatory self-defense, such as preemptive use of military force?
Part of the answer depends on the definition of aggression or an armed attack. For example, UN General Assembly Resolution 3314, which the Assembly approved without a vote in December 1974, implied certain
preparatory or anticipatory actions before the actual use of armed force in
an attack would not violate Article 51. The resolution stated, "The First use
of armed force by a State in contravention of the Charter shall constitute

prima facie evidence of an act of aggression. . . ." The Security Council could decide whether what occurred before the actual first use was actual aggression.[102] Hypothetically, based on this, it would seem a state could position troops before an attack but could not assume that these actions would necessarily justify a response in self-defense.

Twelve years later in the *Nicaragua* case, the International Court of Justice restricted the right of self-defense when it relied on a scale assessing the magnitude of an attack to claim that it did not "consider . . . the provision of arms to the opposition in another State" as constituting "an armed attack on that State." The United States based its case for assisting the Contras in Nicaragua on the claim the latter state's provision of arms to anti-government guerrillas in El Salvador amounted to an armed attack on that country. Nicaragua filed suit against the United States; with five judges dissenting, the International Court agreed with Nicaragua's argument that U.S. actions violated the UN Charter and were unjustified on grounds of El Salvador's self-defense. Displeased with the Court's ruling, the United States withdrew from the case and then a year later announced that it no longer accepted the jurisdiction of the International Court of Justice.[103]

All these factors largely diminish or significantly restrict any use of preemptive force. The strongest argument in favor of preemptive action is based on "imminent" threat, although this certainly is not a unanimous view. The concept of "imminent" is a temporal one, meaning an immediate threat. Advocates of the imminent threat argument for preemptive action repeatedly turn to an incident of nearly 170 years ago involving the *Caroline,* an American ship on the Niagara River that was supplying guns to Canadians rebelling against British rule in 1837. Not surprisingly, British and Canadian forces crossed to the American side of the river, attacked the vessel, and set it afire; the ensuing controversy was not fully resolved until 1842. Secretary of State Daniel Webster set forth criteria for justifiable preemptive measures. Such attacks were acceptable in cases "in which the necessity of that self-defense is instant, overwhelming, and leaving no choice of means and no moment for deliberation." No time would exist for negotiation. Webster also stressed the importance of proportionality in such actions. They must do "nothing unreasonable or excessive; since the act, justified by the necessity of self-defense, must be limited by that necessity, and kept clearly within it."[104] These were clearly restrictive guidelines not intended to allow easy resort to such action.

In some ways, the *Caroline* affair is a slender reed on which to rest such a major argument. Even an advocate of preemptive measures, such as Abraham Sofaer, has cautioned against sweeping claims based on a rule that "was meant to apply to situations in which the state on whose territory preemptive action is contemplated is not responsible for the threat involved."[105] Other scholars have stressed that the right of self-defense must come down to the evidence of the attack itself or anticipatory self-defense, when a state after an initial attack can show that it has viable reasons to anticipate later attacks.[106] Just war theory provides more flexibility on the right of preemptive measures, but has very strong reservations about preventive war. Michael Walzer finds the Webster formula fairly unworkable for the modern era because it is too restrictive by leaving one with little more choice "than to respond to an attack *once we had seen it coming* but before we had felt its impact." However, preventive war is a much more difficult act because it "presupposes some standard against which danger is to be measured," but, as Walzer notes, "that standard does not exist."[107]

In its two national security strategies and many other statements, the Bush administration has tried to establish a standard for preventive use of military force—namely, possession of weapons of mass destruction by terrorists, rogue states, or other non-state actors who stand outside the boundaries of legal and moral accountability. Some scholars argue the Bush administration also tried to move the concept of imminent threat away from criteria related to time to those of intention and possession of WMD. If the accused party could not prove it did not possess WMD, it was then an imminent threat.[108] Of course, the fact that the United States was unable to find weapons of mass destruction in Iraq significantly weakened those efforts to justify preventive use of force through any interpretation of "imminent." Much of the international community shares U.S. concerns and alarm about the growing proliferation of WMD capabilities, but remains unconvinced that military force is the best means of dealing with it. To be fair, the Bush administration repeatedly has emphasized its own belief that other preventive measures, not military force, are preferable. Yet, distrust and concern about American policy remain because the United States explicitly continues to state its right of independent action and use of military force without UN authority—a right that many elsewhere believe the United States agreed to yield after World War II.

In response to international developments and new threats that have emerged or will emerge in future, it is fair to ask whether international law can operate and even remain relevant to both states' and peoples' security needs. That is one of the underlying questions driving calls for new criteria for intervention or reinforcing the appeal of just war arguments. The formula many seek would give international bodies and states the ability to deal more directly and quickly with new threats. For example, some have proposed new definitions of imminent threat by considering less a temporal dimension and more the extent of potential damage and the likelihood of attack. Other legal frameworks, such as those analyzing cases involving battered women who killed or attacked their aggressors when in "imminent danger," offer different criteria for measurement.[109] American arguments about WMD have been harmed by their absence in Iraq, miscalculations and misjudgments in Iraq itself, and subsequent misdeeds, such as the horrible imagery of Abu Ghraib prison. Nevertheless, the value of prodding the international community to reexamine international law and its frameworks for using military force in response to threats posed by WMD remains legitimate. These dangers await the address of the next administrations, American allies, and the United Nations. If they do not do so, not only does the physical danger to all increase, but the ability of international law to avoid a return to the self-started wars of the first half of the twentieth century will be ever weaker.

The decision to use military force increasingly has become a presidential one, and changes in both the domestic and international intellectual and cultural landscape have made both Republican and Democratic presidents more willing to use force and intervene independently of international opinion. Congress's open or tacit acceptance of nearly all this reflects the simple observation that all members similarly experience and share these same perspectives and convictions. The historical record repeatedly demonstrates that pattern. Congress does not live in a separate universe untouched and unaffected by developments and arguments that influence presidents. While the influence of the "neo-cons" during the second Bush administration may be the latest proof of how a fairly small number of actors can determine policy, they, like the "best and brightest" during the Kennedy and early Johnson years, benefited from the fact that many in Congress shared some if not most of their national security concerns. As a body that is better in reacting to developments than anticipating them and is divided by party and chamber, it would be very hard for Congress to pose a strategic alternative. Nevertheless, full or partial intellectual and political concurrence cannot excuse Congress's surrender or inattention to its constitutional responsibility. While the press can promote rigorous inquiry and oversight, only the legislative branch can do both and then either accept shared accountability with the president for White House decisions or try to pose a constructive alternative.

Presidents' use of military force will not disappear because of the outcome in Iraq or Afghanistan. Continuing developments in technology, the future of special operations, and the phenomenon of private military firms could significantly enhance presidential ability to use military force without much, if any, congressional involvement. If Congress and others do not address these issues, they could take American use of military power, especially in limited or low-scale operations, in very problematic directions in terms of accountability to Congress, the public, and the international community at large. The future possibly presents greater challenges to the constitutional process and accountability than anything encountered in the past or present.

Chapter 6

Why Challenges to Accountability
Will Grow

Nearly two hundred and twenty years after the delegates gathered in Philadelphia, defining war and warfare remains as elusive as ever. If those delegates understood that some wars would be undeclared or imperfect, they would not find this 1995 statement surprising: "Warfare does not require a declaration of war, nor does it require existence of a condition widely recognized as 'state of war.'" Like John Adams in the quasi-war against France, warfare is conducted "merely to subdue the enemy," not to kill him. A subdued enemy "behaves in ways that are coincident with the ways in which we—the aggressor or the defender—intend for him to behave."[1] However, that the United States might be an aggressor or would use offensive force without clear congressional consent would make the delegates and leaders of the early American Republic extremely uncomfortable.

The permanent standing military of the last sixty years would surprise, even depress, most of the founders. What some call the "postmodern military" possibly would seem astonishing. Such militaries exist in what sociologist Martin Shaw describes as postmilitary societies—those that have replaced the large mass armies of the mid-twentieth century with smaller professional forces dependent on technology, which enable most in that society to never experience the military. Postmodern militaries also mix civilian and military functions and cultures in ways that raise questions about who really conducts or fights the war. Some scholars foresaw the influx of civilian skills and outlooks into the modern military, but this had nothing to do with civilian control or oversight over the military; instead it suggested a convergence of outlook and method in culture and operations. That would have frightened many of the founders, for they feared that a large standing military would become an instrument of an ambitious executive branch and would spread military values throughout society.[2]

The mission and characteristics of some modern operations that were no longer "military in the traditional sense," such as those during the 1990s, reflected changed notions of military force, and definitely created new challenges to the existing constitutional process to provide congressional authorization or consent.[3] The early twenty-first–century strategic climate will further develop existing concepts of unorthodox missions and present new ones as well, whether in special operations, the expanded role of civilian contractors and private security or military firms, or the infusion of concepts of information and less lethal warfare. The latter, in particular, demands reexamination of the meaning of terms like weapons, armed force, or combatants, among others.

Special Operations and Covert Operations: Who Should Control What?

Special operations are a major theme in current thinking about the use of force.[4] The development of expanded capabilities in special operations alongside those of covert operations has created a constitutionally and legally vague area in terms of accountability and Congress. Chapter 3 briefly examined the system of congressional review and oversight of covert actions undertaken by the Central Intelligence Agency, but the two intelligence committees' jurisdiction did not include special operations, handled by the Department of Defense. Arguably, the latter should fall under the purview of the War Powers Resolution, but covert actions definitely have not. Public congressional action based on the War Powers Resolution obviously would compromise the purpose and nature of many special operations. Further, in 1973 Congress was only beginning to try to determine what reforms were necessary to control presidential use of armed force and intervention. Serious thinking about covert operations had not evolved to the point where Congress knew what it wanted to do.[5]

There is noticeable disagreement over the effectiveness of the process to review the intelligence community. In comparing intelligence legislation with the War Powers Resolution, Lori Fisler Damrosch argues that the latter provides a stronger framework, as the Resolution contains a forty-eight–hour reporting requirement and limits the armed forces to defensive measures except when Congress has indicated otherwise. The 1980 Intelligence Oversight Act and provisions in the 1991 Intelligence Authorization Act offer no guidance on what forms of military force the Constitution permits, since the military, as such, is not the focus of these laws. Congress does not give prior authorization to covert actions, but does receive a presidential finding (the determination and explanation of the action to be taken) that must be delivered before the operation except in "extraordinary circumstances." Still, no sixty- to ninety-day time frame, like that in the War Powers Resolution, exists for covert operations that would require cessation of an action absent congressional authorization.[6]

Turning to the actual operation of the Senate and House intelligence communities, Loch Johnson, a former CIA officer who now teaches at the University of Georgia, argues that the system operates rather poorly and has not established full accountability. Senators and House committee members do not regularly participate in committee hearings, the absence of television cameras discourages vigorous oversight, and, furthermore, members are susceptible to "clientitis," or an overly sympathetic view of the agency. In fact, several committee staff people have taken jobs in the CIA or elsewhere, which could imply that the relationship between overseer and those overseen is too close.[7] The author's discussions with committee staff suggest a more varied, sometimes surprising picture, with a large number of briefings held by the CIA for members and staff to inform or update them on the progress of a particular covert program. Yet, these same staff members have worried about increased partisanship in the committees. William Daughtery, another former intelligence official now in academia, stresses the importance of Congress's direct involvement, since it must appropriate money for covert programs. The money, he notes, is "fenced" off, which means that it can be spent only on the program designated by Congress.[8] Evaluating the intelligence committees in the wake of the 2001 terrorist attacks, the 9/11 Commission found congressional oversight of intelligence to be "dysfunctional."[9]

One of the many consequences of the Afghani and Iraqi operations has been to blur the distinction between covert operations and special operations. For example, in Afghanistan in late 2001 both CIA operatives and special operations forces on the ground jointly engaged in extensive improvised activity. However, regardless of operational distinctions, significant differences exist between the legal steps that must be taken for both types of operations to be accountable. For example, as Iraq and Afghanistan are described as theaters of war already requiring traditional military activities, some officials have argued that the CIA's special covert operations there do not have to be justified in a presidential finding or reported to Congress for prior approval.[10]

Whether special operations do not have to be reported to Congress, as asserted above, is murky. The United States conducts these operations under the authority of Title 10 of the U.S. Code, which states that the purpose of the Armed Forces is to "[s]upport and defend the Constitution of the United States against all enemies, foreign and domestic; ensure, by timely and effective military action, the security of the United States, its possessions, and areas vital to its interests; and uphold and advance the national policies and interests of the United States."[11] Title 10 also requires the Department of Defense to report to Congress "deployment orders," Joint Chiefs of Staff instructions on positioning of U.S. forces around the world for combat. Through the appropriations process and its control over the Uniform Code of Military Justice, the U.S. military legal code, Congress possesses means of accountability over military activities.[12] The Department of Defense, however, has challenged this reporting requirement on at least two grounds: (1) a claim that special operations forces can conduct certain secret human intelligence missions before a notice, and (2) the view that the global war on terrorism is both continuing and indefinite, thereby negating the secretary of defense's ability to judge when troops are about to be placed into imminent combat.[13]

The National Commission on Terrorist Attacks Upon the United States, more commonly known as the 9/11 Commission, recommended the "lead responsibility for directing and executing paramilitary operations, whether clandestine or covert, should shift to the Defense Department." Of course, "paramilitary" does not include all covert operations, but the Commission stressed that CIA capabilities were weaker in paramilitary operations, so it often relied on proxies who lacked proper military training.[14] The recommendation certainly complements and reinforces former Secretary of Defense Donald Rumsfeld's desire to increase special operations capabilities at the Central Intelligence Agency's expense and operate in a more flexible, independent arena than existing intelligence oversight law permits. Given Congress's hesitation to assert its own powers forcefully, in spite of detractors, the War Powers Resolution in practice is less restrictive and confining than the process to oversee covert operations. The Resolution's weakness and limits become more evident if the Secretary of Defense or other officials claim covert operations are part of "traditional military activity." Congress can try to control such activity through the War Powers Resolution or appropriations, but it is fighting uphill against justification that rests on the support of continuing military operations.[15]

Besides strengthening the executive's hand in using force without congressional authorization, Department of Defense control over all such operations would present other difficult challenges. Covert operations often operate under a construct of plausible deniability. A future president might have to abandon military personnel compromised or caught in the field and deny knowledge of their actions, essentially sacrificing them—an action that would have both civilian and military repercussions. It is also unclear whether using military force in special operations could be an act of war because of U.S. military personnel activities on another state's sovereign territory. The Department of Defense and U.S. military personnel are bound to international law or provisions in the Law of Armed Conflict, to which the United States is a signatory. In covert actions operating under plausible denial, U.S. military personnel could lose their claim to combatant status. Since the CIA is not explicitly bound by international law, if its personnel are caught, the arguably vague but potentially important argument exists that its actions, unlike those of military personnel, are not legally an act of war or aggression.[16]

If Congress is to regain effective control over such measures and guarantee accountability, it will have to either revise the War Powers Resolution in light of the characteristics of special operations missions, especially if they embrace "traditional military activity," or reverse the present shift of such capabilities away from the CIA. To enable the United States to have recourse to such capabilities, Congress also would need to increase CIA funding for these types of activities. None of these are attractive or easy alternatives. Revising the War Powers Resolution along these lines could present a whole new array of problems in enforcing it and its impact on actual operations, since the resolution was not intended to address secret or covert activities. Simultaneously expanding CIA capabilities in such operations could divert resources and energy from other forms of intelligence work critical to national security.

Private Military Firms and Accountability in War

Of course, if a solution is unavailable within government itself, another option is relying on means neither funded nor employed by the U.S. government—in short, private agents. The legal restraints established after the Iran-Contra affair seemingly would preclude this course today, since that scenario involved arrangements to privately fund a resistance movement opposed to the then-government of Nicaragua. However, the question of what roles private citizens and companies may play in national defense or security increasingly confronts the United States and the world at large.

The notion that a state can rely on private actors rather than its own military to conduct or support battlefield operations is an old one. Many Italian Renaissance principalities relied on *condottiere,* military contractors who basically offered their services to the highest bidder.[17] The author remembers a story from his freshman Western civilization course about how seventeenth-century Spanish monarchs relied on contractors who provided artillery and charged the government each time they moved their guns, the result being that the artillery was seldom fired but was always on the move. (Who says overcharging a government is a modern practice?) Great trading companies like the British East India Company had their own military separate from the monarch's. After the Thirty Years War in Europe, states began to place more military functions under their direct control and depend less on contractors or mercenaries.[18]

"Mercenary" creates a distorted, overly dramatic image of what occurs today with private military companies. These are not camouflaged soldiers of fortune parachuting out of a hired C–130 to take over some sun-soaked, rain-drenched country, although vestiges of that type of mercenary behavior remain today. Geneva Protocol I, an addition to the Geneva Convention of 1949, which the United States has signed but not ratified, strictly defines mercenaries' legal status.[19] They do "not have the right to be a combatant or a prisoner of war." The Protocol then provides six definitions for "mercenary" as a person who:

(a) is specifically recruited locally or abroad in order to fight in an armed conflict;

(b) does, in fact, take a direct part in the hostilities;

(c) is motivated to take part in the hostilities essentially by the desire for private gain and, in fact, is promised, by or on behalf of a party to the conflict, material compensation substantially in excess of that promised or paid to combatants of similar ranks and functions in the armed forces of that party;

(d) is neither a national of a Party to the conflict nor a resident of territory controlled by a Party to the conflict;

(e) is not a member of the armed forces of a party to the conflict; and

(f) has not been sent by a State which is not a Party to the conflict on official duty as a member of its armed forces.[20]

The international community has taken additional steps to eliminate or restrict what a mercenary is allowed to do. Parts of Africa have suffered heavily from mercenaries, and in 1977 the Organization of African Unity approved the Convention for the Elimination of Mercenarism in Africa, which described using mercenaries as "a crime against peace and security in Africa."[21] In 1989, the UN General Assembly approved the UN Convention against the Recruitment, Use, Financing and Training of Mercenaries, but this document has several problems, including the fact that at least three of its signatories have used mercenaries themselves.[22] Neither the United States nor several of its major allies have ratified it.

One key factor above all distinguishes private military firms from the mercenaries addressed in these resolutions or as depicted in airport bookstore thrillers and motion pictures. That factor is accountability to a government. Mercenaries work only for money. Nothing in the Geneva Protocol I recognizes or even implies they are legally accountable to a state or government. Private military firms or companies also work for money, but do so as a contractor; the very word contract expresses a legal agreement. These firms are organized as legal entities subject to the laws of the state, if based in the United States, in which they are incorporated and to any federal laws affecting their business or sale of services. Private military firms, unlike mercenaries, are also interested in long-term relations with a national government, since they want to be seen as reliable, trustworthy suppliers. The international community has generally treated mercenaries as operating outside the "constraints built into the nation-state system."[23] However, as will be seen, it is debatable how effectively some existing laws and processes regulate private military firms.

Whether they are called private security companies or private military companies or firms, the companies now serving the U.S. military, Department of Defense, and many allies' militaries and defense ministries offer a wide range of services ranging from logistical support (supplies, transportation, food, etc.) through consultation and training to combat support operations and, in select instances, actual operations.[24] Some are well-known, especially because of the role and fate of contractors in Iraq, such as Kellogg, Brown, Root, a division of Halliburton, or Military Professional Resources International, part of L–3 Communications. Others may be very small and specialized with just a handful of staff.

The reasons for the growing importance of these firms in U.S. security and defense policy originate from both domestic and international factors. Scholars including P.W. Singer and Deborah Avant stress the impact of large reductions in the size of the military in the United States and elsewhere after the Cold War ended. Many highly skilled and educated men and women now sought new jobs to continue their career. The Cold War's end also left an abundance of equipment available for them to use. In some cases, military units actually transformed themselves into private companies, as was the case with the South African 32d Reconnaissance Battalion or the Soviet Alpha special forces unit.[25] However, unless their services are in demand, a large pool of talent does not automatically lead to creation of such firms. The strategic environment following the Cold War presented some different, almost unfamiliar, strategic challenges requiring people with appropriate skills. At the same time, state control over instruments of power, including military ones, eroded. New concepts of security and threats— terrorists, drug cartels, and religious sects, to name a few—emerged, requiring new instruments or new ways of using existing ones. Private military or security firms could supply the people to deal with these problems or train other personnel to do so.[26]

The situation was particularly serious for poor countries or those in the developing world who sometimes had depended on U.S. or Soviet support, and lacked the resources and government infrastructure to develop and maintain effective militaries or police forces. For them, private military companies offered an attractive alternative, whether in training or actually providing the necessary service.[27]

Warfare and military forces have also undergone significant changes during recent decades, thanks to the immense impact of new technologies and subsequent dependence on them. These new capabilities increasingly have come into the hands of less developed states as well as non-state actors, multiplying the number of potential threats. The technology with arguably the greatest impact on militaries may be information technologies, which reduce the number of personnel needed on the battlefield due to improved abilities in command, control, and communications between commanders and individual soldiers as well as enhanced accuracy and lethality. Behind these new capabilities stands a vast array of high-tech support demanding the attention and time of many people, a needed expertise that contractors and security companies can provide.[28]

Increased reliance on private military firms is part of a trend that has narrowed the gap between the military and commercial worlds. New technologies have created new organization, management, and operational requirements in downsized military forces worldwide. The U.S. and other militaries' dependence on commercial technologies and civilian organizations has required the uniformed world to learn more from its commercial counterparts. Especially since the end of the Cold War, the military has intentionally borrowed business concepts to try to make itself more efficient, less costly, and more capable on the battlefield. Whether by buying commercial parts for weapons, developing and using leaner inventories of weapons and munitions for combat, and maximizing the individual soldier's capabilities, militaries employing these technologies hope to reduce costs—a significant objective for military services during the 1990s and afterward.[29] A 1996 Department of Defense report, "Improving the Combat Edge Through Outsourcing," stressed potential savings in six different areas, such as materiel management, commercial activities on military bases, depot maintenance, accounting and finance operations, education and training, and data center operations.[30] Some private military firms offer their customers these skills, while other such firms support more traditional military duties or combat operations.

The case for cost savings is not clear-cut. The examples of contractors' reported abuse in Iraq may not be the best examples from which to draw lasting conclusions. The Department of Defense claims that savings of 20 to 30 percent occur, based on estimates of savings at the initial bidding stage. The Government Accountability Office (GAO), however, has questioned some of these savings claims.[31] While the debate over cost-saving continues, the momentum in the Department of Defense and military services remains directed toward privatization and using various security firms. If the services know that they will not obtain substantial increases in personnel, one way that they can maintain the number of combatants for actual armed operations is to put more support functions in private hands. In fact, in some theaters of operation, such as Bosnia or Iraq, contractors do not count towards the troop ceilings that Congress or the president establish to limit the scale of U.S. military involvement. At the peak of the Vietnam War, the United States had 80,000 contractors not counted as troop strength in the theater; in Bosnia the United States was able to surpass the congressional limit of 20,000 troops by more than 2,000, thanks to contractor personnel. The estimated figure in Iraq in July 2007 was 182,000 contractors employed by the Departments of Defense and State as well as other government offices—a number that surpassed that for U.S. military personnel in the country .[32]

Using contractors to enhance military capability while limiting the number of actual uniformed personnel in the operation entails a vital question. Can contractors make it easy for governments to use military force? P.W. Singer has noted one benefit of using military contractors is that not only do they make it easier to resort to military force, but in some instances depending on private military firms may be the only way intervention occurs. The 2003 Iraq intervention excepted, Singer notes that major powers generally are more reluctant to intervene with military force, the lesson from Somalia in 1993 and possibly in future likely drawn from Iraq. Given concerns about casualties and public disillusionment, relying on private firms may be one way to preserve an independent ability to use force. More than one officer has told the author that the United States hypothetically could remove its troops from Iraq and replace them with contractors. Ironically, the same dependence on private firms may prove true for the United Nations too, Singer argues, given the relative ineffectiveness of its interventions due to many members' limited resources and lack of military skills. As to regional security organizations, NATO's capabilities are an exception. Perhaps more typical may be the troubled Organization of African Unity joint mission in the Darfur region in western Sudan.[33] Such regional organizations could find private military companies a better instrument than any of their respective militaries.

That assessment about such firms' appeal becomes more sobering considering that use of contractors already has become one way the United States tries to limit public opposition to certain policies or interventions and bypass congressional authority, as has occurred in both military and covert actions. Iraq is one setting where, sadly for those involved and their families, public attention to contractors' deaths seems noticeably less than that for troops, so the government is not as accountable to the public and Congress.[34]

The United States also sometimes relies on private military firms to do tasks that other countries handle with military personnel, such as using DynCorp personnel as verification monitors in Kosovo. However, other nations may not have access to as many private contractors or their laws may specifically require the military to handle such a task.[35] In the "war on drugs" in Colombia, Congress restricted the types of activities that U.S. military personnel could do, so the Clinton administration turned to contractors to handle out-of-bounds functions; some incidents involved combat with Colombian rebels. These actions occurred without any congressional authorization to use force, and it is debatable whether Congress would so authorize a private force. In authorizing and appropriating money to pay contractors, Congress can prohibit expending money to prevent use of contractors instead of military personnel in those parts of operations where force actually is used, but distinctions between combat and support operations sometimes can be artificial. Also, since the government is not required to disclose information about contactors' deaths, it is easier for the government to distance itself from the policy and even exercise plausible denial. Contractors potentially make congressional accountability and responsibility in using force more difficult.[36]

Within the constitutional arena of war powers, it is unclear how much authority Congress has to control or authorize the use of force when private military firms are involved. Some argue that the Constitution's letters of marque and reprisal clause from Article 1, Section 8 provides the necessary framework for congressional control. Yet, are private military firms modern-day counterparts to the privateers the American colonies and later the early Republic relied on to supplement a small navy? One important distinction is that the privateers were self-supporting; they paid their own costs. Contractors or private military companies depend on government money, although questions admittedly remain about whether a company could use its own capital to bypass congressional or legal restrictions.[37] But if the parallel between privateers and private military firms does not withstand close scrutiny, one key point in favor of congressional power remains implied in the letter of marque and reprisal provision. Namely, the power given to Congress suggests that the Constitution's authors wanted to prevent a president from relying on privately funded military resources to circumvent congressional authority.[38] This point is not easy to circumvent because the founders clearly wanted to ensure that all means of force were under national government control to diminish the likelihood of war with foreign powers. If Congress addresses this question in the future — and it better be prepared to do so given contractors' increased role—it should not rely on the specific application of the letters of marque and reprisal clause but rather insist that contractors' role is a war powers issue requiring inclusion in a rewritten War Powers Resolution or in separate legislation. Of course, if it wishes, Congress actually could resuscitate practices much closer to actual privateering by licensing people who would seize goods and property for compensation or offering funded bounties.[39] Many in the international community probably would raise their eyebrows and argue that this violates international law, specifically the 1856

Paris Declaration Respecting Maritime Law, which abolished privateering and nominally remains effective today, even though it seems to apply only in maritime settings.[40]

Other legislative approaches to this question are questionable or somewhat ineffective. One argument is that existing neutrality laws prohibit U.S. citizens from being hired in their own country to fight in conflicts with nations or parties with which the United States is at peace. However, a pivotal point involving contractors is that the U.S. government actually hires them; thus, if doing so violates any neutrality law, the government would have to bring charges against itself.[41]

Current U.S. law treats the business of private military firms as an export. The governing law is the Arms Export Control Act of 1976, which states the president "is authorized to control the import and the export of defense articles and defense services and to provide foreign policy guidance to persons of the United States involved in the export and import of such articles and services."[42] Through its Office of Defense Trade Controls, the Department of State is primarily responsible for deciding whether the International Traffic in Arms Regulations (ITAR) governs export items. Those regulations contain the United States Munitions Lists, which include not only weapons and technologies but many of the services private military firms offer. Companies wishing to provide services on the market must register with this office. If a sale involves a transfer of major defense equipment valued at over $14 million based on original acquisition cost, or defense articles, training, or services at $50 million or more, the administration must file a report with Congress. Congress can override the decision to grant a license through a joint resolution, but the president can implement a transfer immediately in case of an emergency important to U.S. national security.[43]

The Arms Export Control Act is not as toothless as some claim. Administrations have modified either the timing of the arms sale or the proposed materiel to less sophisticated versions of a weapon because of congressional concerns. Yet the $50 million threshold is a fairly sizable loophole, depending on the nature or purpose of the contract. Moreover, it is possible to divide much larger projects into separate, smaller amounts to remain under this figure and avoid the required report to Congress.[44] It is clearly worth asking whether this law is now the appropriate framework to control private military firms' function or place as they assume a larger role in using military force. The most ideal way that Congress can assert its authority would be to increase the number of military personnel, fund them, and "renationalize" some functions that contractors perform that arguably are combat operations or closely support them. This would produce a stronger line of accountability and authority over use of military force. Any president likely would oppose such measures on grounds of cost and infringing on presidential freedom of action, and renationalizing functions would require Congress to revisit issues that it would prefer to avoid, such as conscription, in increasing total U.S. force strength. Without examining the broader implications of depending on contractors, the best thing that Congress can do is strengthen its oversight. If Congress retains the Arms Export Control Act, it needs to reexamine the reporting language, including reducing the $50 million military limit. Congress also should establish more vigorous reporting requirements from the companies about their activities in the field to the Department of Defense and then to Congress. Besides costs, Congress should review contracts by category of activity to better understand the contractors' role in military operations initiated by presidential command.[45]

A particularly important legal point is contractors' position within the chain of command. For a long time, U.S. military commanders had no "command and control" authority over private military firms. Significantly, commanders could require contractors to adhere to instructions or orders applicable to all military personnel and Department of Defense civilians, but commanders could not "command" contractors. Allegations of an unjustified shooting of Iraqi civilians by Blackwater USA, a contractor providing security for the Department of State in Iraq, raised serious questions about their accountability, and in relation to contractors working for the Department of Defense, the deputy secretary of defense, Gordon England, released a memorandum on September 25, 2007 that held commanders "responsible for establishing lines of command responsibility within their Area of Responsibility (AOR) for oversight and management of DOD contractors."[46] The Department of Defense or government also have other options if a contractor disobeys orders or acts detrimentally to broader U.S. interests. Firms can be fired, denied future business, or even prosecuted for felony illegal activities.

The problem is that the laws governing all of the above are still not very clear. The major law subjecting contractors to legal accountability is the Military Extraterritorial Jurisdiction Act of 2000. Before this law, the United States did not have very effective means to prosecute civilians who accompanied military units and personnel overseas. Thus, this law governs criminal activity, rather than addressing the larger question of the contactors' appropriate role in situations involving the use of force. The original version of the law applied only to civilians contracted by the Department of

Defense to support its missions. The Abu Ghraib prison scandal in spring 2004 revealed a serious loophole in the law because Titan, one of the contractors involved, was not paid by the Department of Defense but instead by the Department of the Interior. As a result, Congress amended the law to cover any other departments' or agencies' contract employees supporting a Department of Defense mission. Yet, a loophole still remained, since contractors employed by the CIA or State Department supported those agencies rather than Department of Defense missions. Thus far, the Military Extraterritorial Jurisdiction Act has been toothless; individual contractors have remained unpunished, although some companies have lost contracts, while military personnel have gone to trial for actions at Abu Ghraib and elsewhere. However, as of October 2007 the controversy surrounding the practices of Blackwater seemed to be moving Congress closer to closing this loophole.[47]

The other possible legal framework is the Uniform Code of Military Justice, the U.S. military legal code, enacted in 1950. The Code's Article 2(10) states, "In times of war persons serving with or accompanying the armed forces in the field are subject to court-martial and military law." The Manual for Court Martial defines a "time of war" to mean one when Congress has declared war or made a determination to that effect.[48] Since that rarely occurs, a problem of accountability remains. In 2006, Senator Lindsey Graham (South Carolina) tried to correct this shortcoming by inserting into the 2007 defense funding bill five words adding "contingency operations" to the coverage of the Uniform Code of Military Justice for contractors. This significant change immediately raised new questions. Can civilians really be put on trial in a military court? Does the Military Extraterritorial Jurisdiction Act instead cover such situations? Defense contractors and legal watchdog groups, such as the American Civil Liberties Union, expressed strong concerns about this provision.[49] Subsequent legislation introduced in both the House and Senate tried to clarify this by putting the jurisdiction issue and the role of contingency operations in law back under the Military Extraterritorial Jurisdiction Act, and on October 4, 2007, the House voted by 389–30 to place all U.S. contractors in the Iraq war zone under this Act's jurisdiction. In the case of Blackwater, uncertainty remained, since it might be argued that its duties were not part of the war operations in Iraq.[50]

Regardless of the legal status of contract personnel, the military commander is responsible for their protection.[51] Congress can change this relationship between the commander (representing government authority) and contractor, but as noted, must do so very carefully in light of a private company's legal rights and due process of law; altering this relationship should require legislation, not just an executive order. Such changes in the command relationship could give contractors "combatant" status, which would improve their legal rights if taken prisoner, for example, but simultaneously make them more accountable to the laws of armed conflict. At present the law of armed conflict treats supply contractors and other services supporting military forces' welfare as noncombatants.[52]

Still grounded in dated notions about mercenaries, international law is not terribly helpful in settling issues involving private military firms and accountability.[53] This is a serious problem, because both the international community and individual governments, including the United States, may find it more convenient to use contractors rather than government-controlled militaries to intervene in selected trouble spots. During the late 1990s advocates of humanitarian interventions, such as Michael O'Hanlon at the Brookings Institution, argued that the ability to use private firms rather than militaries could circumvent the honored adage in democratic political cultures that military force should be a last resort. Adherents to this view argue some horrible atrocities of the 1990s, such as Rwanda, could have been prevented if governments had used their own or a private force earlier.[54]

While conceding the point that earlier intervention might have prevented a tragedy like Rwanda, this argument contains disturbing implications. Governments may avoid using military forces not only due to political repercussions at home, but because public sensitivity about casualties discourages their use. However, does this inference imply that such sensitivity diminishes if a private military firm is involved? Although individuals employed by a company may receive higher salaries than their military equivalents, their lives seem more expendable. Enough evidence now suggests that these companies' employees are engaging in actual combat operations or in support roles so intimately connected to combat that their status as noncombatants is questionable. As noted earlier, if captured they will not enjoy combatants' rights under the Geneva Conventions. It is unclear how well the captors of contractors in Iraq understand any of the Geneva process, but the brutal treatment and death of several contractors there illustrates their vulnerability and lack of recourse under international law.

Thus, it is perhaps time to consider reforming both U.S. and international law to enable contract personnel to have the rights of lawful combatants,[55] which also would make them more accountable to international law than they currently are, and in so doing, would reinforce measures to keep them accountable to national laws. However, accountability is a two-way street for government and citizen alike. While a government seeks to ensure accountability of those in its employment and service, citizens equally can expect their government to take the necessary measures to protect personal welfare and individual rights. At present, military or security firms' employees operating overseas function in a legal twilight zone that compromises their rights. Just how well some of them understand this situation is unclear. Nevertheless, any argument claiming that they knowingly signed up for dangerous missions and therefore must accept risks without clear legal rights or recourse is ethically untenable. Accountability must travel in both directions. A government using private sector services should seek to assure those hired of maximum protection in both national and international law.

In the short run, though, legislation at the national level is the best, fastest way to deal with this issue, even if individual national attempts to regulate private military companies may fall short.[56] Some of these suggestions may be difficult and perhaps unrealistic, but if nothing occurs, the United States and Congress will lose a major opportunity to assert more responsible control over a growing dimension in using military force, especially over low-intensity, "contingency" operations that depend on many of the skills and services that private military firms can provide. The likelihood of low public support for such operations may well encourage governments to turn to private means with or without government funding. No one should ever interpret the Constitution's vagueness in the area of limited war to imply that its authors would have advocated using private military forces without effective review and authorization powers. Doing so compromises accountability traceable to both the act of approving the use of force and the power of the purse.

Information Technologies and the
Quest for Low-Casualty War

While considering the appropriate degree of control over private companies, Congress must weigh one additional dimension to how these firms operate. Not only do they function in a legally ambiguous zone when undertaking combat, but to a sizable extent their work also relies on technologies that challenge the traditional concepts of weapons and war. In the case of a civilian employee involved in computer support of an armed operation against an adversary, what is his or her legal status? Is the computer itself a weapon? Can technical support make the employee a combatant? Was the operation itself an act of aggression or war?[57] None of these questions have simple answers, and they all become complicated when computers and information technology are involved.

The development of the computer and the diverse application of battle-field information technologies are the latest effort to place war "safely under the aegis of science," here meaning a combination of technology, rigorous analysis, and systematic planning that can make war serviceable and usable, since the other option is to let war evolve on its own momentum to where it can destroy its own initiators and managers.[58] At least twice during the last century, the place of science in war confronted strategists, national leaders, and lawmakers with very difficult choices. The nuclear age and threat of mass destruction made war almost unthinkable. To ensure a usable form of war remained, as discussed in Chapter 4, many in the U.S. strategic community argued for "flexible response" capabilities that could operate at all levels of conflict.[59] Otherwise, it seemed that the world was left at the mercy of the "mad" science that contributed to the nuclear weapons race and mutual assured destruction (MAD). However, from experiences drawn from Vietnam, as well as conflicts such as the 1973 Arab–Israeli war, the possibility of war again operating under scientific frameworks and constraints seemed real. This theme was implicit in much of the 1990s discussion about the revolution in military affairs, relabeled in the 2000s as "transformation." Both terms were part of postmilitary societies' efforts to find ways of conducting war that would accomplish strategic objectives without high human cost.

The determination to avoid large losses, particularly on one's own side, became greater after the major world wars and development of postmilitary societies with different values. Vietnam added its special imprint on American resolve to avoid high casualties in the future. For many Western countries, the solutions came from two frequently used directions—relying on "foreigners as private soldiers" or "automated warfare."[60] U.S. reliance on funding foreign groups or soldiers to fight wars advancing its national interests was a recurring strategy from the Cold War to the present. Using surrogates in warfare is an old practice; in the Cold War examples abounded in U.S. policy, such as the Vietnamese Montagnards or Afghani *mujahed-din*.[61] One advantage of surrogates or proxies is that their deaths do not reverberate that much within the United States, but controlling these forces is not always easy and they may be unable or unwilling to stop fighting once their foreign supporters have stopped backing them.

"Automated warfare" has an obvious simple appeal because it relies on technology, not people. The hope of battlefield and political victory due to technology rather than human blood is a long-standing trend in warfare. The introduction of computers during World War II and their development in the 1950s opened new possibilities in the conduct of war. What was characteristic of both the revolution in military affairs in the late twentieth century and the recent emphasis on transformation was the central role of information technology. This latest version of "automated warfare" required adopting elaborate information technologies. The relationship that transformation would create between information technology and the individual soldier showed that it was not just a road map for using new weapons, organization, and tactics, but actually a "profound shift in the complex of social, economic and deep technological forces that shape the way in which a society wages war," particularly evident when contrasting these new concepts with the nature of mass mobilized or industrial warfare so prevalent in the first half of the twentieth century.[62]

Today it is unclear how the Iraq war will affect opinions about the realism of seeking an ever more science- and information-dependent form of war promising reduced casualties. The confidence about waging low-casualty war that arose after the 1991 Gulf War and the 1999 conclusion of Operation Allied Force and the Kosovo crisis now seems deluded given the sad numbers of combat dead and injured from Iraq and Afghanistan. Yet if future presidents believe they must retain military force, especially in limited forms, as a viable instrument for national policy, the characteristics and values of a postmilitary society like the United States leave little choice but to continue on the path of replacing human personnel with technology. As one commentator wrote only a few years ago, the greatest change that may result from continuing efforts at military transformation is "in the realm of . . . broader social and political contexts." This revolution or transformation will "enable war politically by conferring moral approbation," perhaps unlikely in 2007 as public disillusionment with armed force increases. Continued development and perfection of precision-guided weaponry, thanks to the role of information technologies, will continue to offer a promise of fewer casualties to all sides.[63] Will it be possible to anticipate a lower barrier for using military force, when the projected costs seem so slight?[64] Only public opinion, professional military judgment, and presidential and congressional political judgment would serve as restraints. When the prospects of human losses are low, presidents have found it easier to use force through their prerogative as commander-in-chief. "The future of 'warfare'" in the

Why Challenges to Accountability Will Grow

United States thus "lies predominantly in technology" where one can hope "to reap the economic and technical benefits of a strong defence programme while avoiding the political costs of its own casualties."[65]

Michael Ignatieff calls this form of conflict "virtual war"[66]; James Der Derian speaks of "virtuous war." In this type of conflict the United States would rely on just war doctrine—Der Derian even argued the willingness to resort to holy war; yet, "[a]t the heart as well the muscle of this transformation is the *technical capability* and *ethical imperative* to threaten and, if necessary, actualize violence from a distance—but again, with minimal casualties when possible."[67] Even though the hard lessons of Iraq and Afghanistan demonstrate the limits of these hopes in real warfare, continued developments in information operations (including information warfare) and non- or less-lethal weapons ensure the perpetuation of these trends in warfare.[68]

The role of information in warfare is as old as conflict itself. There are different definitions and applications of information on the battlefield. Militaries have or obtain knowledge about an enemy ("intelligence"). Furthermore, they use information to influence an adversary's behavior ("propaganda," "misinformation," and/or "disinformation"). Governments provide information to their own population to maintain its support for a military action (part of mobilizing national will). Within a military campaign itself, a commander relays information to a unit or an individual soldier; in turn, a reverse flow goes from the latter to the former about the battlefield situation. Simultaneously, information ought to flow among individuals and units on the battlefield. Lastly, information technology may constitute an actual weapon, used through various means as a computer virus, a "worm," or some other means that actually could damage or destroy targets as a bomb would. Nearly all these applications of information have existed and functioned for centuries, but the notion of information actually having the characteristics of a physical weapon is quite recent.

What has empowered the role of information in national security policy is the impact of electronics. Over a century ago the telegraph made it possible to relay instructions or orders within minutes, thus perhaps better centralizing the chain of command in business, diplomacy, and military services.[69] During World War II computers began to play a role in analyzing information for battlefield application. Field telephones, radios, and so on, added to the ability to communicate simultaneously. The real change came later, after miniaturization of all the electronic components and many of the information products, such as computers. Imagine a soldier stumbling across a battlefield carrying a mainframe computer, and the image is perversely tragic and funny at the same time. Imagine that same soldier with a small hand-held or mounted device with communications and computing capabilities surpassing almost any mainframe ever built. This man or woman can communicate simultaneously with everyone in the unit and the command. Satellites support this type of communication and moreover enable a single fighter on a chaotic battlefield to locate him- or her-self through contact with a global positioning system like that found in many automobiles. The soldier ideally should be able to communicate with air support and other units from his or her own and other services.[70] Soldiers in the fray of battle on the ground or attacking from the air or sea can fight with precision-guided munitions containing electronics that receive information guiding the bomb, rocket, even the bullet, right to the target. Additional capabilities exist, and not everything always functions as smoothly as intimated here. Nonetheless, this battlefield occurs with virtual simultaneity in decision and event.

The anticipated benefits from all this were and remain very attractive to civilian policymakers, military leaders, and those in the field. A segment of that desire to submit warfare to scientific means and rigors has always wanted to reduce the human element in it, not only to reduce casualties but to ensure greater certainty of outcome. Frederick the Great probably would have used such technology to eliminate the variable factor of human will as he saw the requirements of eighteenth-century warfare.[71] However, contemporary advocates view such technology as a means of empowering the battlefield soldier rather than drone-like reaction. Having such immediate information may enable personal initiative based on what the soldier knows is occurring in the area. This is a battlefield network of soldiers, commanders, systems, etc., in which information flows in all directions, not primarily from the top down. It also produces results with near simultaneity. The linear notion of planning from the time of actual decision to the later action diminishes significantly. In the 1991 first Gulf War commanders selected about 20 percent of the targets after the planes were airborne. A decade later in Afghanistan that figure increased to 80 percent.[72] Against militaries not similarly "networked" or connected, such as the Iraqi Army and Republican Guard units in spring 2003, the results could be overwhelmingly favorable.[73] In operations against insurgents in Iraq or Al-Qaeda and Taliban contingents in Afghanistan, the record was more mixed.[74]

In the years immediately before Afghanistan and Iraq, there was much discussion about battlefield information dominance. Knowing more and acting on it would provide both the advantage of knowledge and operational control of what was happening.[75] Some have stressed the applicability of "knowledge war" as an inclusive way to consider all the options and elements in play.[76] Many of the same proponents stressed that these technologies would help achieve actual "jointness" and full coordination among all the military services, for which the United States has striven for decades.[77] Also, although the military resources, scale, and objective of the military operation might be limited, their backers were strongly convinced that these technologies would produce decisive results. The interest in "rapid decisive operations" that emerged in 2001 sought to create an ability to use a "full-spectrum joint force operating in an interagency context to defeat a regional power."[78] Using information-dependent technologies, such as precision-guided munitions in what was called "precision engagement" would assist these operations; although the Army in particular did not always define what it meant by "decisive" operations, the assumption was that they were accomplished rapidly and with few casualties.[79]

All along these arguments drew skeptics. Like a lot of conjectural literature, there was an obvious tendency to make assertions that could not be easily grounded in current experience. The unnamed enemy in some of the literature seemed almost comatose, as if on an operating table. One officer remarked some of the discussions reminded him of the Queen in *Alice in Wonderland* who announces, "first the verdict, then the trial." Writing in 2001, military historians MacGregor Knox and Williamson Murray described these proponents as "technological utopians" who operate "from the deeply and quaintly American belief that all human problems have engineered solutions" and the "profoundly un-American . . . post-Vietnam search for technological silver bullets that will permit U.S. forces to wage war without suffering—or perhaps even inflicting—casualties."[80] When Murray paired with retired General Robert Scales to write an early history of the current Iraq war, the two observed the retirement of the generation of officers who had served in Vietnam caused the loss of individuals who understood technology's limitations, while many of their successors and the nation's civilian leadership did not. Reflecting on the stabilization phase of the war after the spring 2003 campaign, they warned, "Machines alone will never be decisive in this new phase of the war."[81] For such skeptics, technology has always held a tenuous place in conducting war, even while others have so vigorously pursued its advantages. Whether they doubt its promised effectiveness on the battlefield, or harbor long-standing concerns as to how technology might compromise the masculine model of battle and conduct that has shaped so much Western thinking about war and society, technology has never enjoyed an unconditional embrace by some closest to the actual battlefield.[82]

Information Warfare's Challenge to Accountability

Besides the application of information technologies in various aspects of war—weapons, command, and coordination on the battlefield—during the last two decades there has been great interest in what is popularly called information warfare. Currently this evolving concept of warfare still seems to entail more questions than answers. What exactly does information warfare mean, what are its legal implications, and why could it pose significant questions about accountability and presidential or congressional control over the use of military force? Defining information war with traditional words and concepts is difficult because it does not match popular understanding of the word "war." Some of its forms envision no bombs, bullets, planes, or guns. This form of war can be waged "in a silent but nonetheless effective mode." Thus, it can occur in its own silence or alongside more physical, traditional warfare.[83]

In the mid 1990s, Martin Libicki, one of the most prolific students of the subject, identified seven different forms of information warfare:

(1) command and control,
(2) intelligence-based,
(3) electronic,
(4) psychological,
(5) "hacker" warfare
(6) economic information, and
(7) cyber warfare.[84]

Not everyone would agree with these seven categories; some would use a few interchangeably. John Arquilla, another prolific writer on information warfare, has tried to distill many of its concepts to a few key characteristics by stressing that this form of warfare usually aims at "communication nodes and infrastructures." Thus, some measures would try to attack the means by which a president or senior military commanders send commands to others or also damage the systems enabling them to coordinate actions. Infrastructure can mean various elements, including financial networks, a nation's energy grid, air traffic control, or the broader telecommunications network, among others. Obviously, some of these targets are interdependent. The weapons could be computer viruses, worms, imperfections built into computer chips, and other measures that can affect the information technology operations on which so much of the developed world depends.[85]

The implications of all of this on warfare are immense. For example, both the attacker and targets can be remarkably dispersed. Simple reflection on the havoc that antisocial sixteen-year-olds in their bedrooms have wreaked on computer network systems worldwide should invite a pause, especially if they collaborate with others across the globe. Tracing the origin of such actions can be difficult, and assessing the intent is just as difficult. Is it a malicious prank with criminal intent at most, or is the behavior more serious, the harbinger of an armed attack or an actual attack using new technologies? The very characteristics of an information "attack" and uncertainty about origins and intent are new factors for political and military leaders who only twenty years ago thought of attacks in terms of air raids on specific targets or armies crossing a frontier or border.[86]

If a nationwide attack on an energy grid or financial network is an operational advantage of information warfare, another quite opposite benefit is how precise information attacks can be. The advantages of precision-guided munitions in U.S. strategy already point in the direction of increasingly exploring technologies that can be both precise and destructive. Even while the military continuously studies these systems' performance in Afghanistan and Iraq, it still seeks greater capabilities in precision weaponry, particularly when delivered from a distance. Public expectations about war, U.S. strategy objectives, and the types of preferred military operations drive this trend. In the present and future strategic environment, the United States may want to avoid seizing and occupying territory and try instead to target particular locations or individuals.[87] The obvious hope behind some of this is to reduce casualties. Advanced technology surveillance systems, such as satellite or unmanned aerial vehicles, combined with precision weaponry offer the prospect of using special operations units more sparingly or judiciously. Commanders need not employ them for information or battlefield gains technology can provide.[88] This might prove especially critical in limited or low-scale operations where as much as 70 percent of "all close combat engagements" result from efforts to find the enemy and learn more about the composition of his force.[89]

Not everyone is a total convert to precision. Precision-guided munitions are only as accurate as the information provided to those controlling them and sometimes mistakenly can kill friendly forces or civilians, as happened in Kabul with two strikes on International Red Cross facilities.[90] Others argue that depending on precision weapons at a "stand-off" distance "is a dead-end road to attrition warfare. . . . [F]ighting a cunning and resolute enemy with purely technological means induces the adaptive enemy to move down the spectrum of conflict to mitigate the effects of superior technology." In settings where the enemy comes from the local population and tries to conceal its members among the populace, it is necessary to have troops on the ground to make accurate judgments—a lesson that revealed itself in Afghanistan by 2003.[91] As General Scales writes, "The mountains of metal, consisting of expensive yet often second-rate air, sea, and ground machines of war that today serve as potentially lucrative targets in a conflict against the United States are rapidly disappearing. . . . The need to survive and remain effective against the threat of overwhelming American killing power" is causing dispersion and elimination of "vulnerable logistics, transportation, and communications facilities."[92] One must locate these targets by either technology or human reconnaissance.

Electronics and information technologies make possible such diverse types of weapons in such profusion that it is hard to do them justice in only a few pages. Pilotless aircraft already play key roles, and the disappearance of the pilot from combat operations will continue. Imagine *hand*-launched unmanned aerial vehicles that can conduct surveillance or environmental surveys.[93] Robotics, used already in some reconnaissance missions, for example, can also detect mines, release smoke or fog, designate targets, and evacuate casualties, among other applications.[94] One can place electronic agents that look for certain types of information or collections of words in computers, their network systems, or on the digital highway, a very sophisticated application of current "data-miners" that often transfer a computer's confidential information to an outsider.[95] The scenarios seem almost boundless, and sometimes one must concede that the best place to get an advance peek at some future weapons concepts is to read and watch the better science fiction endeavors.

If the development and existence of such technologies make it easier to consider and use the option of armed force because they promise reduced casualties, they also raise the old question of whether technology will dehumanize warfare.[96] Blood and death are not the only requirements for the human experience of war; the larger question is what the implications are when the architects of war find ways to use military force with as little human participation as possible. The crossbow, artillery, rifles, bombers, and missiles—all generated earlier versions of this argument. Bloodless war seems highly unlikely, but what will be the implications for national leaders when or if they believe a relatively cost-free war in human terms is within reach? Even while recent experience in Iraq may suggest otherwise, the question remains because of determined efforts to find such means. The questions trouble ethicists, lawyers, students of warfare, and military leaders, but they should also disturb U.S. and foreign national leaders and lawmakers. What would be the fate of accountability in such an environment? Such wars, Robert Kaplan claims, will reflect an environment that could greatly diminish Congress's and the public's voice. Meanwhile, military and civilian experts will become increasingly interdependent, and the president's authority will greatly expand. The role and stature of international law will erode, and, if there is justice in the war, it often will come from the moral fiber of the military commanders themselves, not from efforts to maintain national and international standards.[97]

Rather than Kaplan's solution of moral fiber, the United States needs constitutional and legislative restraints, but he rightly stresses the importance of values or moral fiber in settings where warfare may become both less human and maybe less humane. Consider a now all-too-possible scenario in which humans participate in battle, but through significant alterations to their mental and physical features. Embedding chips in the human body to improve certain sensory or analytical functions is no longer a remote, speculative idea. Combined with exoskeletal attachments (similar to some insects' anatomical structure) or uniforms that can increase body strength or defend against weapons, troops so equipped would in a sense become cyborg soldiers, the posthuman warrior needed for the postmilitary society seeking to avoid casualties.[98] Genetic research also presents future possibilities. Can scientists identify, reproduce, or alter the genes involved in aggressive character in combat in ways to change behavior or create a class of professional warriors?[99] Continuing research in robotics has not yet produced a robotic warrior, but the concept is under discussion and exploration.[100] What will be the effect of such changes on the language of war, when today experts can already speak of "servicing" the target, whether a soldier or a headquarters, instead of bombing or shelling it? Will it be easier to dehumanize the enemy, even if that adversary fights at a more human, less technological level?[101] Will a comparative ranking system in the value of human life emerge?

It is hard to draw serious attention to such questions in any government when so many more immediate problems abound. Some scenarios described here are distant, but it is likely that in the life span of those born in

2007 none are out of reach. While none would automatically eliminate the place of accountability in using force, they present serious challenges to it. They defy traditional understanding of almost every existing legal term, because generations have believed weapons are under direct human control, even if used from a distance. Some, such as a cyber attack using electronic means, defy the customary meaning of a weapon. What if civilians rather than military personnel control such systems? What is the status of the civilian in U.S. and international law? Using contractors already has provided scenarios in which a president or head of government can bypass constitutional controls. The capabilities examined here greatly magnify that potential.

Answering these questions requires a short review of key legal issues to understand just how nebulous the status of information warfare is in both national and international law. In 1997 a report prepared for the President's Commission on Critical Infrastructure Protection closely looked at existing U.S. legal foundations to deal with information warfare. The answers were not reassuring. The War Powers Resolution did "not contemplate an information-based attack within its parameters. . . . Its language clearly anticipates warfare as a physical attack." Looking closer at the Resolution, the Commission was troubled also by the ambiguity of some terms in it. Commenting on the Resolution's concession to the president to send forces into "hostilities" without Congress's approval in case of an emergency caused by an attack, the study's authors could not answer whether "hostilities" or an "attack on the United States" included a cyber attack. Turning to international law, the situation was equally uncertain. The United Nations had made no effort to address the question of whether the articles dealing with the use of force in its Charter include information warfare. Arguably, even if the UN classified an information attack as an "armed attack," international law requires proportionality in response. Could the United States or any country use conventional forces, for example, to respond to an attack falling within the realm of information operations and warfare, or could it respond only electronically?[102]

Of course, a precision-guided munition with the most advanced information-based system in it would qualify as a weapon for armed attack; it is a traditional weapon simply assisted by an information technology application. Yet when has a computer been described as a weapon, unless a court case has involved someone throwing one or hitting a person with it? (Apparently, the actor Russell Crowe contributed to establishing the cell phone as a weapon when he assaulted a hotel worker with one.) For the precision weapon, information technology provides the means, but information is now increasingly a target itself because of its central role in so many military operations. In deciding whether to launch cyber or information operations against Serbia during the Kosovo crisis, military planners had to obtain legal guidance on whether computers could be a legitimate target. The ultimate answer was "yes," but the very fact the question had to be asked illustrates the uncertainty and legal ambiguity in aspects of information warfare.[103]

In May 1999, the Defense Department's Office of General Counsel prepared a long study on the legal implications of information warfare. It asked, "Is a computer network attack an *act of war?*" [emphasis in original] The answer was that the term "act of war" is "obsolete" because it is a measure "so egregious that the victim would be justified in declaring war." Declarations of war hardly occur these days; thus, the overall concept no longer applies in "the modern international legal system." Others second this opinion for other reasons. Because conflict is often "a process of escalation," it can be difficult to determine when the line is crossed to label something "an act of war." Instead we see a "continuum where unfriendly acts become increasingly hostile."[104]

Returning to the language in the UN Charter, the key terms are "use of force," "breach of the peace," and "acts of aggression." Interestingly, very little discussion of information warfare has asked whether it is a "breach of the peace"—a status between "threats to the peace" and "acts of aggression."[105] Rather, the arguments have tried to resolve where information warfare stands in relation to kinetic warfare relying on physical objects such as bullets and bombs. If the Charter provides no clear guidance on this, it also does not resolve the earlier question of whether a computer actually is a weapon.

Although the United States traditionally does not regard most resolutions the United Nations General Assembly has approved as international law but rather as recommendations, it has respected the 1974 UN effort to define aggression. The definition stressed "aggression is the use of armed force by a State against the sovereignty, territorial integrity or political independence of another State. . . ." Interestingly, Article 2 of this resolution stated the UN Security Council retains the right to determine whether "the first use of armed force" would involve "acts" and "consequences . . . of sufficient gravity" to allow them to be judged as an "act of aggression." Here we can foresee the possibility that the Security Council, at least in principle, might not judge an information attack as meeting this standard. Given the permanent members' veto authority, reaching such an agreement could be quite difficult. Most actions listed in the resolution as acts of aggression involve using physical force, such as troop movements, bombardment, blockading ports or the coastline, and relying on "armed bands, groups, irregulars or mercenaries, which carry out acts of armed force" with "such gravity as to amount to the acts listed above."[106] The latter could apply to special operations missions, but the 1974 resolution contained nothing on including information operations.

One way to assess whether an information operation taking the form of cyber or electronic warfare is an armed attack is to measure the extent of damage, bypassing the question of whether the means used were weapons and concentrating on the operational results. However, this does not mean physical destruction is automatic proof of an "armed attack." Since international law contains no standard definition of armed attack, we must work with some common assumptions involving a certain degree of physical destruction and some violation of sovereign rights or intrusion into another's territory.[107] Certainly, if people are killed or an information attack produces results "indistinguishable from conventional kinetic weapons," a strong case for designating the attack as armed would exist.[108]

How to respond to an information attack likewise poses some difficult questions. Any retaliation within customary international legal restraints must seek to halt the initial attack or prevent further ones, and "must be proportional to the attack to which it is a response."[109] What is proportionate to an information attack? If an attack has damaged a national or even regional power grid, thus causing civilian deaths in hospitals and elsewhere, is the attacked state justified in responding the same way? Is it justified in resorting to more traditional weapons, such as air strikes, to accomplish a similar magnitude of destruction? Some argue that such a response, if calibrated to accomplish a similar destructive extent, would be justifiable, even if the form and consequences of an information attack were not accomplished through violent means.[110] However, willingly killing civilians just to match the level of death and destruction already committed would violate international law. Depending on the nature of an information attack, it may not be quickly evident whether it is an armed attack. Until the perpetrator and intentions actually are known, it is important to proceed under the guidance of criminal laws because several U.S. and state laws do apply to computer attacks. The attacker's intent, nature, and identity will help determine whether the response should be through arrest and the courts or retaliation.[111] If retaliation is correct, an additional complication arises because the retaliating nation then should report to the United Nations Security Council its exercise of self-defense, as stated in UN Charter Article 51.[112] Most states conceivably would declare self-defense, but scenarios could exist in which it might be operationally advantageous to try to withhold the declaration until later.

Part of defining "armed attack" also revolves around defining a weapon or weapons system. Traditionally, definitions have relied on a weapon's physical characteristics, but we also can define an instrument or object based on its intended use. A single computer sitting in a house or office would not easily meet the criteria of being a weapon, but what if the computer is used to launch a cyber attack or is part of a networked system that supports and manages the attack? Is it now a weapon? The answers have varied even among the military services. For example, a 1994 Air Force Instruction specifically states that "electronic warfare devices" are not weapons. Yet, according to Joint Chiefs of Staff Instruction 3210, the "capabilities of many information warfare systems make them weapons systems that may be used during armed conflict."[113] Like a rock used by a murderer, an object's intended use, rather than its characteristics, increasingly may become the criterion by which "weapon" is defined in information operations.

The implications of these problems for governments and multilateral organizations seeking to regulate both the process of commencing war and its conduct are serious. The strength of law and the ability of any democratic system to maintain accountability face major hurdles because agreement is lacking on key words or terms that define aggression or war. Accountability relies significantly on clarity of government process *and* words. It also depends on an assumption that all parties use the same vocabulary with the same meanings. Neither clarity in process nor meanings of words exist here. Whether an information operation is an act a president should report to Congress under War Powers Resolution provisions is unclear. The Resolution is grounded in earlier concepts of warfare. Without a clearer, better understanding of the meaning of its own terms, the Resolution is completely unsuited for dealing with information warfare, especially since international law itself provides so little guidance. The increased number of civilians who support information operations makes the situation even more complex. Are they combatants? How well can a government ensure that its actions are accountable within the particular procedures in place to govern the decision to use military force?

Non- and Less-Lethal Weapons

Similar questions arise with a closely related category of weapons—non-lethal or less lethal weapons. These weapons and systems range widely, from acoustic weapons at unbearable pitches, nausea bombs, beanbags and nets fired by handheld or truck-mounted devices, foam, and retractable spike barriers to various forms of information warfare, to name just a few.[114] The lethality of a weapon is not a new subject for argument in strategy, law, or ethics. For example, the World War II debate between area and pinpoint bombing held a strong element of this discussion; however, the purpose of those weapons and the scale of destruction and human loss acceptable then are radically different from what is sought with less lethal weapons. Although the term "non-lethal weapon" traces to the 1960s, the importance of these weapons did not become apparent until the 1990s and the emergence of peacekeeping or peace support operations. While there is a strong concern about dehumanizing warfare in relation to the many potential electronics applications, new advanced materials, and genetics, the objective here is to make war more human.[115] An influential example showing the value of such weapons was Operation United Shield to evacuate UN forces from Somalia in 1994. U.S. Marine Corps Lieutenant General Anthony Zinni, who commanded the operation, later remarked that the limited non-lethal weapons he used were so valuable he would not enter a similar operation without them.[116]

Advocates of these weapons need to be cautious about both their promised and potential consequences. First, some specialists are uncomfortable with the very term because it implies that there will be no fatalities. That is not always true. Non-lethal weapons sometimes kill, even if that is not their intended use. Consequently, experts have substituted the terms "less lethal," "less than lethal," or "sublethal."[117] It is the character of the weapon's intended use rather than its consequences that determines its status and category. Many discussions about non-lethal weapons envision their use in stabilization and peacekeeping missions where militaries have to assume police as well as combat duties. The struggle to win and control the population's "hearts and minds" is part of the context of their application. Nonetheless, non-lethal weapons also can be used in actual combat, such as in measures that would temporarily incapacitate enemy soldiers so that their positions could be captured.[118]

Information warfare and non-lethal weapons carry their own risks with a significant bearing on accountability and the control of military force. As with information weapons, the War Powers Resolution apparently would not cover missions using less lethal weapons. If providing them to troops defines the mission's objective or purpose, a president conceivably could argue the deployment is below the standard meant by terms such as "war," "hostilities," or "imminent hostilities"—an argument similar to the Clinton administration's in cases of humanitarian intervention. Yet, the mission's intention does not guarantee that others will see it the same. The goal of operations using less lethal systems is to keep missions symmetric and proportionate to the previous or anticipated danger. There is absolutely no assurance that a second party will not decide to respond with lethal force. At that point, hostilities have occurred, without any legislative authorization.

Non-lethal weapons also raise the recurring concern that using force will become more accessible and attractive for governments, thus undermining the international legal community's efforts to make the use of force more difficult to justify and pursue. At the same time, using such means in both humanitarian intervention and anticipatory self-defense may make these instruments of force more acceptable to the international community.[119] Clearly, reliance on non- or less-lethal weapons could increase the tendency to use force. Conceding the likelihood that their use will cause fewer casualties and less damage does not erase the necessity of examining them closely in the context of national and international law.

The Feasibility of International Agreements on Information Warfare and Non-Lethal Weapons

International arms control agreements regulate or prohibit some non-lethal weapons. The 1980 UN Conventional Weapons Convention and four protocols added later forbid several weapons in this category, including those that "injure by fragments which in the human body escape detection by X-rays," mines, booby traps, incendiary weapons used against civilian targets, and laser weapons causing blindness.[120] The United States has ratified the Convention and two protocols covering weapons using undetectable fragments and land mines, booby traps, and similar devices.[121] When the Senate provided its advice and consent in ratifying the treaties, it is important to note that it added its conviction the term "incapacitating" would not prevent or limit non-lethal technologies that might be temporarily disabling.[122]

Several international agreements could also limit or forbid some information warfare operations. The Outer Space Treaty prohibits putting nuclear and other weapons of mass destruction into orbit. At least two questions arise here—the specific role of computers and other information systems in supporting, initiating, or managing such an attack and the potential magnitude of an information attack that could produce destruction on a scale comparable to a weapons of mass destruction (WMD) attack. Another agreement, as yet unratified by the United States, the Agreement Governing the Activities of States on the Moon and Other Celestial Bodies (the "Moon Treaty"), prohibits making the moon a "military asset." International telecommunications agreements, such as the International Telecommunications Satellite Organization Agreement (INTELSAT), the Convention on the International Maritime Satellite Organization (INMARSAT), and the International Telecommunications Convention of Malaga-Torremolinos, seek to ensure peaceful use of international telecommunications but contain language allowing military uses of satellites, radio systems, and other information services.[123]

Could frameworks similar to those in arms control or nonproliferation treaties govern the development of technology and use of information operations in warfare? Germany actively tries to preserve and demonstrate the continued value of such international frameworks, which the Germans believe has eroded in the United States. Some in Germany argue that an agreement could be made to prohibit offensive information operations that are "attacks on the physical and nonphysical information structure of an enemy."[124] Conferences have explored this prospect, but the challenges to implementing it are insurmountable. First, the argument for such agreements is hindered by the fact that international law is unable to clearly answer whether a digital attack on networks and information technology is an act of force. Furthermore, while it could be feasible to try to negotiate such an agreement among states, would non-state actors adhere to it? Certainly, there is no guarantee of their compliance, whether terrorists or irate teenagers. The frequent problem with such technology is its universal availability. Unlike most weapons technologies developed specifically as weapons, information technology depends on the commercial sector. Many of its latest features or capabilities surpass the military's. Any process to limit and verify technological development, including software applications, seems impossible, simply because it is too widespread.[125]

This is not to argue that the international community should not try to negotiate an agreement on information warfare and other operations. However, basing it on characteristics or features of a technology or application is unrealistic in the long run. Efforts to prevent the export or diversion of specific technologies, applications, or categories of knowledge might win a short-term respite, but the worldwide spread of talent, technology, and research is too extensive to prevent eventual development and production. Future criteria in an agreement should focus on specific uses or intentions that international law would identify as unacceptable. However, before doing so it will be necessary to address the elusive issue of whether an information attack is tantamount to an armed attack and aggression. Absent that, any advance in designating specific actions as illegal will be fruitless. Also, the supporters of any international agreement must acknowledge that adhering to and enforcing it will be more difficult than with other arms control or nonproliferation regimes due to the vast availability of much of the technology and knowledge. Thus, any agreement will be porous and only partly successful at best.

This is why individual governments' action is critical. Whether in statutes dealing with the criminal code, counter- or anti-terrorism measures, or in the war powers arena, Congress must examine and address more directly the constitutional and legal questions posed by information operations. Such action may require Congress to establish legal definitions of terms that become more difficult as we move away from criminal to aggressive, armed acts requiring congressional authority for presidential use of military force. Congress will have to try to clearly define accountability and military force in a gray zone where meanings of words and operational concepts related to force will be vaguer and subject to differing interpretation. For example, Congress could define information warfare technologies as applicable only if used at "the operational level of warfare."[126] Below that level, military use of such technology would not require congressional approval. Yet "operational" is a term subject to different interpretation. Congress must allow some flexibility in whatever it might legislate because no strictly or narrowly written law can include all the possible conditions in which use of force will come into question. Congress also might prohibit using such systems against foreign noncombatants or domestic groups.[127] However, legislating such restrictions or guidelines means Congress also should find the resolve to try to enforce them. Any president likely would refuse to sign such legislation, and, if signed, he or she inevitably would then work covertly against those statutory limits if the president believed that it was in the national interest to do so. As with the War Powers Resolution itself, the efficacy of any change or new law is only as effective as the extent of presidential acceptance and congressional determination to enforce it.

Conclusion

The Dilemma of Limited Military Force and the Constitution

Discussing presidential use of military force combined with military, intellectual, and technological developments explains how presidential control over the use of force may expand. Correcting the constitutional imbalance must come through the framework of law, Congress's willpower and deliberations, and future presidents' judgment. Without the right laws, institutions, and procedures, we will have no assurance against arbitrary use of military force—a scenario the founders so strongly feared in 1787. No one can realistically expect that a country with a constitution over two centuries old can handle the decision to use military force in the exact same way as it did during the first decades of the early republic. After all, the international standing of the United States is radically different, the immediate nature of threats is more real, and the characteristics and missions of military forces are more complex. Finding the right legal measures, legislating them, and obtaining presidential approval will be difficult. The contemporary imbalance that so strongly favors a president's ability to initiate using force and reflects important long-term historical realities presents substantial barriers.

Today's American system so concentrates power in presidential hands that it would astonish, even frighten, many who gathered in Philadelphia during that warm summer so many years ago. Some might fear the modern presidency is now like an old monarchy—an office dominated by unchecked ambition. Yet "presidential machismo" does not explain very well what has happened in the record of American wars; presidents have not been so fascinated with their position that they have used the military instrument just to maximize power for their own gain and little else.[1] A threat, misjudged or accurately seen, or an opportunity, mistakenly or wisely taken, is almost always part of the story. Admittedly, maximizing power has sometimes been a result, particularly since the end of World War II, but presidents also have wished to fulfill national missions or accomplish international objectives, whether in 1846, 1964, or 2002.

This book blames a deferential, timid Congress, as much as opportunistic, ambitious presidents. Congress's action or inaction has often reflected its assessment and agreement with a president's justification of using force, as it did in October 2002 in Iraq. No one should ever underestimate the importance of political considerations in what Congress sometimes decides in matters of force and war. Challenging a president during a time of danger or national emergency is a genuine political gamble, and confronting a president from one's own party can be political suicide, which becomes even more evident in an election year, such as 1964 or 2002. No senator or representative has an unlimited reservoir of political disagreements that he or she can initiate with a president. As generals choose their military battles, legislators must choose their political battles and decide when and how to resist a president or the party leadership while retaining effectiveness in other key areas of policy and legislation.

The international stature of the United States and the contemporary role of military force in American policy would likely astound the founders. No doubt they would find satisfaction and even elation in the fact that the American Republic has survived and expanded to its current size. The sense of national mission and the universal message in American political values have endured. However, global military deployments, memberships in formal alliances, negotiated coalitions, and other security relationships would probably distress those who hoped that the United States would be a successful commercial power with minimal political entanglement with the outside world. Military force was not the means through which the founding generation hoped to influence the world. Of course, as the Quasi-War against France or the Barbary Wars showed, they understood that military force might be used in undeclared wars, but importantly, with congressional consent when Presidents Adams and Jefferson wanted authority to order actions that were not just defensive. If commercial rights on the high seas were at stake, the United States was ready to use its small navy to try to rectify the problem. If the nation's leaders avoided entanglement in foreign political crises, they hoped large armies would prove unnecessary, would arise only when called on to address a crisis and then would demobilize and go home. That model served the United States well for the first 130 years of nationhood, but it became increasingly impractical and finally impossible after World War II.

From this change it is tempting to conclude that the solution to the disagreement over presidential and congressional control of military force would be for the United States to retreat from its position and role in the modern world. It would seem better to save the republic's ideals than to destroy them through the nation's immersion in the dangers of global politics. Looking at today's world, the founders would have acknowledged that military force was an instrument of national security *and* foreign policy during the early Republic, but they probably would be alarmed that modern American leaders have made it *the* most visible instrument of power.

The road to such a situation was gradual. While the nineteenth century saw arbitrary uses of military force, most notably the Mexican War, most of that century's historical record showed that presidents were uncomfortable in launching offensive measures without Congress's consent. Polk's actions produced a public and congressional backlash in what became an increasingly unpopular war. Abraham Lincoln wielded presidential power on an unprecedented scale in April 1861 to raise troops and order a blockade, but he also chose to turn to Congress in retrospect to approve those actions involving the military and military force against states that had seceded. The Supreme Court upheld his actions in *The Prize Cases* decision, but added that presidents must seek congressional approval when using force offensively. In 1898, President William McKinley gradually yielded to congressional pressure to seek war against Spain.

Almost every study of presidential power and military force argues that the pattern of presidential activism and military force began with the Cold War. That is only partly correct. It is true that from President Truman on, presidents repeatedly relied on the Constitution's commander-in-chief clause to justify acting without congressional concurrence. The fact that the military was now a large, permanently standing one, not one significantly expanded for each crisis, made it much easier to use this key clause as necessary. Furthermore, the extensive length of the Cold War, its many crises, and then those following in the unstable world after it ended, created a security environment resembling a prolonged emergency with occasional intermissions of peace. Congresses and presidents shared similar assessments of this world and largely agreed on how to deal with the threats and challenges they saw emerging from it.

Yet the real foundation for expanded presidential use of military force occurred at the beginning of the twentieth century. It corresponded to a global expansion of U.S. interests and the rise of a conviction that the United States could use military force to improve the world as well as to protect and serve its interests. The gap between Theodore Roosevelt's world policeman and George W. Bush's desire to transform and stabilize the Middle East is not very wide, especially when the bridge is a Wilsonian idealism that believes in the universal appeal of American political ideals and values. When presidents used military force for these purposes, it was not for reasons of traditional defense. The objectives were stability or creating order to enable reforms that would bring stability, objectives that were more a goal of American foreign policy than national defense. Interventions in locations as varied as the Philippines, the Caribbean, and Central America established the precedent for several Cold War uses of military and covert force. Marines and soldiers who tried to draw lessons from these operations before World War II knew that presidents directed these actions to advance the goals of American foreign policy.

Of course, the Cold War diversified these types of operations and the options available to implement them. Strategists and political leaders wanted to use force in ways so that limited hostilities would not escalate to nuclear war. Sometimes foreign surrogates were used, as occurred in the Bay of Pigs, the early part of the Vietnam conflict, or later in Central America and Angola, but if they failed and the strategic stakes were high enough, U.S. forces increasingly took over, as in Vietnam. Presidents also desired to limit the use of force to avoid inflicting high domestic social or economic costs and the political controversy that could inevitably break out with Congress. During the Cold War, Congress repeatedly consented beforehand to presidentially initiated uses of force, accepted them retrospectively, and asserted itself only if the strategy began to fail. While the Vietnam War was winding down, Congress passed the War Powers Resolution in 1973 to try to prevent open-ended deployments of military forces that had occurred up to then. In one sense, the Resolution influenced presidents' decisions by making them more aware of the potential political damage that could ensue from missions that seemed to be operational and strategic failures, but the Resolution failed to curtail presidential use of force or compel presidents to seek previous congressional consent.

Through the end of the century, various presidents tried to use force in limited ways to keep casualties light and the duration of the actual operation short, thereby defusing the prospects of any serious congressional criticism. Grenada, air strikes against Libya, the first Gulf War, and U.S. intervention in Bosnia and later against Serbia over Kosovo were success stories. The *Mayaguez*, the failed rescue mission of U.S. hostages in Iran, Lebanon, and Somalia demonstrated the potential dangers. Throughout the rest of the

Cold War, the United States used surrogates or proxies when it could—the Contras in Nicaragua or the *mujaheddin* in Afghanistan. When Congress tried to quash the Nicaraguan operation, the White House sought to continue illicitly funding it by equally illicit arms sales.

During much of the Cold War and up to the present Iraq and Afghanistan conflicts, Congress actually found itself at times in the crossfire between various presidents and some military components. After Korea and again after Vietnam, influential voices in the Army vowed that they would "never again" accept using troops in limited scale conflicts with open-ended objectives and timelines. Furthermore, these critics, ultimately embodied by the Joint Chiefs of Staff Chairman General Colin Powell, wanted assurance that presidents would deploy forces only after obtaining congressional and public support. However, as many operations during the 1980s and 1990s demonstrated, presidents did not want to have to satisfy that requirement before acting. They did not want Congress, the Army, or any collective military voice to set criteria or standards for using force, because these would violate the powers that they believe they hold as commander-in-chief to use the military for national defense or as an instrument to advance strategic interests. By 2002 and 2003, President Bush and his inner circle of advisers believed that air power and a transformed army employing new technologies would secure victory quickly enough to overcome potential Capitol Hill or Pentagon critics. For both Afghanistan and Iraq, Bush obtained congressional authorization after inadequate consideration and review of the administration's claims and evidence in both the House and Senate. Congress, the military and their families, many Iraqis, and ultimately the American taxpayer would pay greatly for those decisions.

While the Constitution's authors would rightly view the current U.S. situation with dismay, they would be honored by the fact that their concerns about military power and the need for strong constitutional control over its use became a framework for many constitutions that followed. In fact, the historical development of the American system toward stronger control over military force by the president contrasts sharply with a pattern in several democracies during the closing decades of the twentieth century to establish stronger constitutional control over the military by giving more authority to an elected legislature.[2] Furthermore, in parts of Europe and elsewhere, a desire to try to rid the world of major conflicts resulting from the competitive state system has attempted to base states' actions less on their own constitutions and more on the tenets of international law.[3] The United States shared in this movement, which produced the United Nations and strengthened international law after the World War II, but it never conceded the superiority of international law over the Constitution. Disaffection with the UN and aspects of international law became stronger during the last decades of the twentieth century. The implications of this increased concentration of presidential power and collision with the reach of international law are significant. Increased presidential power over the use of military force reinforces a tendency to more independent decisions that challenge the limits of both national and international law. How a government decides to use military force can also have a major bearing on how it then deploys and uses it.[4]

Certainly, not all democracies reflect this trend. In fact, two of the oldest in Europe, France and Great Britain, have systems leaving more discretion and power to the French president or the British prime minister and War Cabinet than the American president holds.[5] Yet if the trend toward more parliamentary control and submitting decisions to use military force to international law continues, the U.S. practice of strong executive prerogative may cause it to disagree repeatedly with allies and find it more difficult to obtain their commitment to joint operations elsewhere in the world, already a significant problem with the international stabilization force in Afghanistan, where some North Atlantic Treaty Organization members restrict their participating forces to noncombat roles.

Congress certainly understands this last factor, but if Congress is determined to restore a better balance in presidential and congressional control over using force, senators and representatives must realize that failure to do so could further divide the United States from some international allies and friendly states. Much of that community is watching the 2007–8 debates to ascertain whether Congress will reject assertive presidential claims and reestablish a better balance in the process by which the United States decides to use military force. They see such steps as correcting independent, impulsive features of U.S. decision making. Admittedly, some American observers believe that such distance may be inevitable, even desirable, particularly if other governments are more concerned with how the United States adheres to international law when it makes decisions rather than the intent and outcome that Americans may see as justifying their actions. Fairly or not, a sizable sector of informed opinion in allied capitals judges the United States not only for its policies but also for inattention, even disregard, of its own constitution in both war and peace.

Currently, amid debates over the status of U.S. forces in Iraq, it is unclear whether Congress is willing to take steps to correct the long-term imbalance between itself and the president. The November 2006 mid-term elections clearly signaled the electorate's discontent with the course of U.S. policy in Iraq and the prospect of an open-ended commitment costing more American and Iraqi lives. Both the House and Senate responded more tactically, by either passing a nonbinding resolution disapproving a "surge" of 21,000 troops to assist the Iraqi government or attempting to establish various deadlines by which U.S. forces must start to withdraw or halt funding. No major effort has occurred to repeal the October 2002 resolution to authorize using force against Saddam Hussein's Iraq, as Congress did with the Tonkin Gulf Resolution, although Senators Hillary Clinton (New York) and Robert Byrd (West Virginia) have urged such action. Terminating funding, as Congress did in 1973 with ground operations in Southeast Asia, presents a very difficult strategic, political choice. The likelihood of chaos in Iraq after U.S. forces withdraw is all too possible, as is the prospect that Iran could benefit from this decision. Whether the United States might use force against Iran has admittedly intensified congressional determination to defend its constitutional powers. The president should seek congressional authorization to do so, but if Iranian support for Lebanese and Palestinian terrorists and Iraqi insurgents is a major factor, some may argue that the broad powers in the authorization passed after 9/11 may be enough. Meanwhile, Democrats fear that their party could again be labeled as the vessel for defeat and dishonor, especially if scenes reminiscent of the 1975 fall of Saigon occur. The November 2008 presidential and congressional election overshadows every word and action taken over war powers and the struggle between the White House and Capitol Hill.

If a lasting "Iraq syndrome" arises, one inviting not only reexamining events since 2002 but also a reversal of concentrated presidential power from previous decades, it will confront very strong opposing currents. The prevalent conclusion from twentieth-century experience is strong executive power is essential for the national interest and for practicing and extending U.S. power worldwide. Today, even as critics charge the president with misusing military power in Iraq, others discuss the possibility of sending U.S. forces into other crises, such as the famine-stricken, violent Darfur region in western Sudan. Neither the Democratic nor Republican 2008 candidate will likely pursue a comprehensive reassessment of the role of the military in U.S. national security policy.

I have not tried to answer whether the U.S. military's current role is appropriate in the present or future global environment, although a reader can infer that I am deeply troubled by this trend. Over-reliance on such an instrument not only has serious consequences for the position of the United States and its effectiveness internationally; as many have feared or argued since the nation's beginning, it also significantly affects the political system domestically. Conservatives often criticize the rise of "big" government, and sometimes identify America's global role and the strong presidency it entailed as a cause; liberals distrust concentrated presidential power when it diverts resources to international ambition rather than domestic need or commits U.S. forces to an unpopular foreign war.

Since the Cold War ended, executive–congressional relations have evolved in a way that makes resorting to military force easier, often without serious congressional scrutiny. Government operations and even trends in public thinking and culture have seemed to move toward backing military force.[6] The absence of serious review and debate, which goes far beyond congressional duty to review budget figures and approve program funding, has caused questionable applications of U.S. military power when other measures, such as diplomacy and aid, might have dealt more effectively with the causes than with the consequences or when the extent of military force used proved inadequate. The congressional approach to war powers has been *pro forma* too frequently—checking the box without the attention the situation actually demands. Such treatment of war powers contributes to an erosion of accountability that has slowly worked its way down to both military services' and civilian departments' operational levels. If lawmakers do not fulfill their responsibility by demanding full justification of policies and subsequent conduct, it is hard to expect that others will feel a higher obligation to try to do the same. If many in Congress believe that the United States struggles in Iraq due to inadequate numbers of troops and other personnel, they cannot just blame George W. Bush's administration. Congress had ample opportunity to inquire and discuss other options, but did little of what it actually should have.

To be realistic and honest, there is little reason to think that Congress will take the necessary steps to assert its role in decisions on war, conflict, and low-scale military force. One reason is Congress's correct role in such operations has been difficult to find for over two hundred years. Its right to be consulted and involved in deciding to use such force did not originate from explicit constitutional guidance but evolved during the republic's early decades. Even before World War II, the status of limited or low-intensity operations took on that of an executive action. Using military force as a foreign policy instrument, the impact of five decades of Cold War, and efforts to develop specific strategies to use limited force rather than nuclear or larger conventional systems increased the president's powers. Given the current global role of the United States, how could Congress reverse these developments? As much as any president, it has accepted the reality and function of limited military force as an instrument of policy controlled by the president. Shaken by the 9/11 attacks and anxious to respond, Congress took a fully understandable route: it deferred to presidential power. Afghanistan may have offered little choice, but Congress should have undertaken deliberative review and examination before the Iraqi intervention or in its aftermath in March 2003. Congress did not do so until four years later.

The change in both the House and Senate majority certainly was a major factor in reexamining U.S. policy in Iraq. It is a mistake, though, to think the opposing party's control of Congress will guarantee a check on the president. After the Republicans took control of Congress with their 1994 midterm election victory, they did not aggressively assert congressional power over the interventions President Clinton ordered. In fact, the greatest challenge to expanding presidential authority between World War II and the current Iraq conflict occurred between President Lyndon Johnson and a Democratic-controlled Congress that later struggled against the actions of Johnson's Republican successor, Richard M. Nixon.

If Congress were to act to restore balance to the process controlling the authorization and deployment of armed force in limited operations, what could it do? Complicated answers take the War Powers Resolution apart line by line, or rely on emphasizing several suggestions that might work better or, at least, stir further discussion and study. Even though this discussion proposes some changes in the War Powers Resolution, it leans much more toward a different solution: a separate committee to deal with authorizing the use of force.

At different times key senators or representatives have called for establishing a joint consultative group that would work with the president and staff on matters of using armed force.[7] In truth, given the nature of modern military operations and frequent use of limited operations, Congress needs a special joint committee on the use of armed and military force. Future operations may rely on types of force outside the military—contractors or potentially individuals employed by other government agencies involved in areas where law enforcement and force may mingle in a legally ambiguous zone. The variations and dimensions of armed force are much greater than envisioned over two hundred or even sixty years ago. The magnitude of all the questions and issues involved arguably is beyond the capability of any existing House or Senate committee responsible for the War Powers Resolution, currently the House and Senate Armed Services Committees, Senate Foreign Relations Committee, and House Foreign Affairs Committee. If Congress is to establish a closer balance through resolve and greater oversight, it will need better means to do so, which will require both institutional and legal changes.

Composed of members selected by the majority and minority leadership in both chambers, committee members would come at a minimum from the committees responsible for armed services, foreign affairs, appropriations, intelligence, homeland security, and possibly judiciary and government operations. Absent a special committee, the current division of tasks among committees will probably never support a strong congressional presence or role. The armed services committees are too preoccupied with program funding and management and personnel issues. The foreign affairs committees should have the best expertise to assess the value and objectives of using limited force as a foreign policy instrument, but their influence has waned in recent years due partly to problems with the current War Powers Resolution and overuse of foreign assistance and State Department funding bills as magnets for domestic political issues, such as birth control and abortion. The intelligence committees could oversee military operations in the context of continuing intelligence actions, and because this new joint committee would deal with special operations, intelligence committee members would more inclusively view all U.S. actions overseas. Appropriators would enable these committees to have early cost estimates. Having homeland security members confronts the obvious fact that domestic security operations, regardless of their scale, may lead to a foreign reaction that significantly affects the nation's physical security.

This committee, not any appropriations committee, would have the initial congressional vote explicitly authorizing military force. The argument that the authorization to use force is within the appropriations power perhaps made sense during the first decades of U.S. history when ground forces were mobilized for specific purposes and subsequently funded, but not today with immense defense spending bills covering myriad programs. After the joint committee's vote, the provision would go to both chambers for further consideration.

A primary objective of any reform must be to strengthen Congress's ability to be informed beforehand as much as possible. To strengthen Congress's voice in consultation, its lawmakers should consider legislating a reporting requirement on projected uses of force that combines the concepts of advance notice used for armed sales and for the intelligence committees. As much as possible, except when time and emergency factors make it difficult for Congress to act or for reasons of the strictest operational necessity, the president should make a finding that military force will be used and deliver it to the special joint committee beforehand. The time frame for this notice must allow some flexibility. Given the variety of situations that can promote using force, a thirty-day advance notice for all reports may be impractical, but any legislation must make the reporting standard as rigorous as possible to encourage advance presidential notice. The role of congressional oversight is critical here, because recurring congressional attention and review of developments would enable committee members to examine whether an administration was considering the use of force and remind its representatives of the requirement to report to Congress. The White House seriously deliberated using force long before both the Gulf of Tonkin Resolution and October 2002 Iraq Resolution. These were not developments impervious and inaccessible to congressional oversight.

Existing committees would receive some of these presidential reports. For example, the armed services committees would oversee rotating personnel and units, placing personnel in military exchange agreements, and assigning soldiers to standing or permanent alliance or multinational operations. The same would apply to U.S. troops being sent to train or supply existing U.S. personnel already in place, or to repair their equipment. However, reports to the joint subcommittee should include missions for rescue or humanitarian aid and relief, which would include situations in which troops are equipped for combat even if the president anticipates that they would use their weapons only for self-defense. Such reports also must address the nature, size, and mission of deployments of U.S. and other contracted personnel; relying on contractors is a growing phenomenon that Congress must follow much more closely than it has until now. If a president acts without reporting to Congress, the existing War Powers Resolution deadline of a presidential report within forty-eight hours can probably remain. However, the president must still seek congressional authorization, except in cases of attack. The committee would reaffirm the decision and improve accountability between both the president and Congress. At any time both the House and Senate could pass by majority vote a resolution repealing the authorization approved earlier or requiring a recall of U.S. forces sent by the president. Such measures obviously must be subject to a veto. If overridden, a president might try to continue military operations, as did Richard Nixon in Vietnam, but Congress has the recourse of terminating funding to end all operations.[8] In doing so, Congress should stipulate that a president cannot turn to foreign or private sources of money to continue operations by U.S. personnel or contractors.

One problem with the War Powers Resolution has been its lack of definitions, but definitions can create new problems as well. Whether speaking of "hostilities," "imminent hostilities," "combat," or "equipped for combat," we still address warfare and war in terms of objects and physical force. Information warfare and some forms of non-lethal or less lethal weapons defy any classification in this area. Rather than falling back on definitions of operational art or weapons, it is best that reports about use of force, including information operations and non and less lethal weapons, rely on the planned uses of the personnel and equipment involved and the mission's desired objective and consequences, addressed not only in terms of the policy the use of force supports, but also possible economic, infrastructure, and human consequences. What are both the United States' and the targeted adversary's projected (not possible) loss of human life? Will infrastructure be physically destroyed? What economic costs must the United States and others absorb? While exact figures are difficult to provide, the report must contain estimates, because in limited and low-intensity operations these factors contribute to deciding whether any measure is an act of force. Congress should not accept the descriptions of military operations that the Clinton administration presented to circumvent requesting authorization from Congress.

Finally, Congress should reconsider how it writes language in authorizations to use military force. For example, the Afghanistan and Iraq resolutions say "all necessary means," an open-ended expression creating a great deal of controversy. It is difficult to imagine many members who voted for those resolutions thought that their vote could become one of the bases cited for controversial policies on detainees, interrogation methods, and monitoring domestic phone calls. These measures may or may not be necessary in the current struggle against terrorism, but some, such as wiretapping, are clearly unrelated to using military force in intervening or conducting operations. Congress needs to restrict the language to authorizing military force (physical or information) and compel the president to find other legal justifications or seek necessary congressional authority to engage in activities entailed in a state or condition of war but not under military control. A 2005 report of The Constitution Project noted that there were nearly 200 "standby statutory authorities" that Congress triggers when it declares war or authorizes force. Many involve domestic powers and need updating.[9] Otherwise, Congress should specifically stipulate the other powers and accompanying limitations that it is giving the president with such an authorization.

Creating a committee on the use of force does not guarantee a restored balance in executive–congressional relations. To a large degree the committee would work as effectively as Congress wants. The intelligence committees have not been as successful as some had hoped, due to increased partisan differences. This should not be surprising. Congress, after all, is a partisan institution. Exercising Congress's constitutional obligations sometimes conflicts with party loyalty and a desire not to challenge the president. For these purposes, whether Congress creates a separate committee or a subcommittee within an existing committee, or chooses to retain the existing oversight and committee structure, partisan differences will remain. However, a new committee will devote more resources to the issues of using force and protecting Congress's constitutional role than currently exist. As troubled as the work of the intelligence committees may be at times, nonetheless, Congress is better informed about this critical policy area than it was in any era before their creation.

If Congress passes a law even partly similar to the one proposed here, any president would veto it on the grounds that it infringed on the office's constitutional powers. Perhaps the law would in fact do so, and that point would likely take the entire controversy about war powers ultimately to the Supreme Court. The federal courts repeatedly have told plaintiffs, who are often members of Congress, that there is no basis on which to accept and rule on the matter of war powers. The courts have agreed that constitutional questions are at issue, but they have in various ways told Congress that it must assert its own position more clearly and vigorously to provide the grounds for a ruling.[10] Until that occurs, Congress and other interested parties can expect little change. If Congress maintains the *status quo,* it only reaffirms the criticism that Congress essentially accepts the expanding extent of presidential control over military force under way for decades.

That would be unfortunate for the American people. U.S. presidents may have used military power recklessly but not thoughtlessly with no concern for human costs. One appreciates that on examining the record of various twentieth-century authoritarian and totalitarian regimes, to which human life was so easily expendable. Nevertheless, a democratic system owes its people, particularly those it sends in harm's way, the most comprehensive process that it can undertake within a reasonable time frame in deciding whether to use military force. This expectation demands accountability. The citizen, whether at home, in uniform, or in other government agencies' service, deserves the right to believe that the president and Congress have examined to their best abilities the options they face and the outcomes that may emerge. No president, general, or cabinet secretary can foresee all that will happen once an operation, large or small, has started. Hardship and resistance occur where little were expected, victory may be swift and easy when high casualties were expected. The projected time may be shorter or longer. Military victory may be obtained, while political victory in accomplishing the strategic objective remains elusive. However, the legislative branch's full, complete engagement with the president, and Congress's serious respect for its responsibilities, may reduce uncertainties and loss of life. A government in the person of the president must be able to assure those who may die or become gravely injured and their families that it tried the best it could to consider every option and outcome before sending citizens into combat and war. If it does not, it invites justified criticism and, worse, inevitable cynicism. And that is a terrible condition for the future of the United States and a world that still looks to it for leadership.

Notes

Introduction

1. See Michael Traenor, "Fame, the Founding, and the Power to Declare War," *Cornell Law Review,* 85 (May 1997), 699, available at http://www.law.berkeley.edu/faculty/yooj/courses/forrel/reserve/treanor. Also see Douglass Adair, "Fame and the Founding Fathers," in Trevor Colbourn, ed., *Fame and the Founding Fathers: Essays of Douglass Adair* (Indianapolis: Liberty Fund Inc., 1991), 3–36.

2. Richard H. Kohn, "How Democracies Control the Military," *Journal of Democracy,* 8 (1997), 146. Electronic edition available at http://muse.jhu.edu/journals/journal_of_democracy/v008/8.4kohn.html.

3. Ibid., 141.

4. This point is partially drawn from Jules Lobel, "War and Responsibility: A Symposium on Congress, the President, and the Authority to Initiate Hostilities: 'Little Wars' and the Constitution," *University of Miami Law Review,* 61 (October 1995), 64. Electronic edition available at http://web.lexis-nexis.com/universe/.

1 Where Is Limited War in the Constitution?

1. Louis Henkin, *Foreign Affairs and the U.S. Constitution,* 2nd ed. (Oxford: The Clarendon Press of Oxford University Press, 1996), 28.

2. A point made by James Madison; see David C. Hendrickson, *Peace Pact: The Lost World of the American Founding* (Lawrence: The University Press of Kansas, 2003), 45.

3. John Jay, *The Federalist, No. 4,* in *The Federalist Papers,* introduction and commentary by Garry Wills (New York: Bantam, 1982), 17.

4. Jay, *The Federalist, No. 3,* in *The Federalist Papers,* 13.

5. See the discussion in Jack N. Rakove, *Original Meanings: Politics and Ideas in the Making of the Constitution* (New York: Alfred A. Knopf, 1996), 161–202, and Akhil Reed Amar, *America's Constitution: A Biography* (New York: Random House, 2005), 45–47.

6. Karl-Friedrich Walling, *Republican Empire: Alexander Hamilton on War and Free Government* (Lawrence: University Press of Kansas, 1999), 50–51. Hamilton expressed his concerns in *The Continentalist No. III,* August 9, 1781, reprinted in Joanne B. Freeman, ed., *Alexander Hamilton: Writings* (New York: The Library of America, 2001), 101–106. Also see Gilbert L. Lycan, *Alexander Hamilton and American Foreign Policy: A Design for Greatness* (Norman: University of Oklahoma Press, 1970), 20–24; Forrest McDonald, *Alexander Hamilton; A Biography* (New York: W.W. Norton & Co., 1979), 38–43, and John Lamberton Harper, *American Machiavelli: Alexander Hamilton and the Origins of U.S. Foreign Policy* (Cambridge and New York: Cambridge University Press, 2004), 30–32.

7. Jay, *The Federalist, No. 4,* in *The Federalist Papers,* 20.

8. This theme is examined in David A. Bell, *The First Total War: Napoleon's Europe and the Birth of Warfare as We Know It* (Boston: Houghton Mifflin, 2007), 68–75.

9. Jay, *The Federalist, No. 4,* in *The Federalist Papers,* 17–18. A valuable discussion of this relationship between commerce and order is found in Peter Onuf and Nicholas Onuf, *Federal Union, Modern World: The Law of Nations in an Age of Revolutions, 1776–1814* (Madison, WI: Madison House, 1993), 93–94, 105–107.

10. Monroe's views are discussed in Hendrickson, *Peace Pact,* 12.

11. Hamilton, *The Federalist, No. 6* and *No. 7,* in *The Federalist Papers,* 25–38.

12. Scott A. Silverstone, *Divided Union: The Politics of War in the Early American Republic* (Ithaca, NY: Cornell University Press, 2004), 19–20.

13. Walter Stahr, *John Jay: Founding Father* (New York: Hambledon & Continuum, 2005), 218–21.

14. Ibid., 219–20.

15. Thomas Jefferson, *Notes on the State of Virginia,* in Merrill D. Peterson, ed., *Thomas Jefferson: Writings* (New York: The Library of America, 1984), 300–302. Also see the discussion in Robert W. Tucker and David C. Hendrickson, *Empire of Liberty: The Statecraft of Thomas Jefferson* (Oxford and New York: Oxford University Press, 1984), 40.

16. Hamilton, *The Continentalist, No. VI,* in Freeman, ed., *Hamilton,* 114–15; Walling, *Republican Empire,* 69.

17. Tucker and Hendrickson, *Empire of Liberty,* 40–41.

18. This discussion draws on Richard H. Kohn, *Eagle and Sword: The Beginnings of the Military Establishment in America* (New York: Free Press, 1975), 42–46.

19. Garry Wills, *James Madison* (New York: Times Books, Henry Holt and Co., 2002), 21–23.

20. Kohn, *Eagle and Sword,* 74–75; Walling, *Republican Empire,* 118–19.

21. Hamilton, *The Federalist, No. 25,* in *The Federalist Papers,* 143–48; Walling, *Republican Empire,* 118–19.

22. Hamilton, *The Federalist, No. 8,* in *The Federalist Papers,* 42–43.

23. James Madison, "Fourth Letter of Helvidius," Letters of Helvidus, Nos. 1–4, August 24 1793–September 14 1793, electronic edition, http://press-pubs.uchicago.edu/founders/document/a2_2_2–3s15.html; Brien Hallett, *The Lost Art of Declaring War* (Urbana: University of Illinois Press, 1998), 32–33.

24. Kohn, *Eagle and Sword,* 171.

25. Henry is discussed in ibid., 82–83.

26. See Hamilton, *The Federalist, No. 23,* in *The Federalist Papers,* 134–37; Walling, *Republican Empire,* 119–20.

27. James Wilson, Pennsylvania Ratifying Convention, December 11, 1987, electronic edition, http://press-pubs.uchicago.edu/founders/document/ulch7s17.html; Frances D. Wormuth and Edwin B. Firmage, *To Chain the Dog of War: The War Power of Congress in History and Law,* 2nd ed. (Urbana: University of Illinois Press, 1989), 30.

28. Richard H. Kohn, "How Democracies Control the Military," *Journal of Democracy* 8 (1997), 145.

29. James Madison, remarks made in the Virginia Convention, June 6, 1788, in *The Documentary History of the Ratification of the Constitution,* vol. 9, *Ratification of the Constitution by the States, Virginia,* edited by Richard Leffler and Charles H. Schoenleber (Madison: State Historical Society of Wisconsin, 1990), 993.

30. Aristides, "Remarks on the Proposed Plan of a Federal Government," January 31–March 27, 1788, *The Documentary History of the Ratification of the Constitution,* vol. 3 of 15 vols., *Commentaries on the Constitution: Public and Private,* edited by John P. Kaminski, Gaspare J. Saladino, and Richard Leffler (Madison: State Historical Society of Wisconsin, 1984), 532.

31. Marcus IV, *Norfolk and Portsmouth Journal,* March 12, 1788, *Documentary History of Ratification,* vol. 4 of 16 vols., *Commentaries on the Constitution,* 385.

32. The one possible exception to this might be the War of 1812, and this assertion depends on how one interprets the motives and intentions of President James Madison. See Chapter 2 for a discussion on this war.

33. See Chapter 2.

34. See Chapter 3.

35. Edward Keynes, *Undeclared War: Twilight Zone of Constitutional Power* (University Park: Pennsylvania State University Press, 1982).

36. Bell, *The First Total War,* 5, 46–47.

37. Michael D. Ramsey, "Textualism and War Powers," *The University of Chicago Law Review,* 69 (Fall 2002), 1610.

38. Hugo Grotius, *The Law of War and Peace* (1625), electronic edition, http://lawmart.com/pubs/grotiussam.pdf and Hallett, *The Lost Art of Declaring War,* 74.

39. Both are quotes used by Ramsey in "Textualism and War Powers," 1610–11.

40. Carl von Clausewitz, *On War,* edited and translated by Michael Howard and Peter Paret (Princeton, NJ: Princeton University Press, 1976), 75. *On War* (original title *Vom Kriege*) was first published in 1832.

41. J.J. Burlamaqui, *The Principles of Political Law,* trans. Thomas Nugent, 5th ed., corrected (Boston: University Press, W. Hilliard, 1807). Available at http://www.constitution.org/burla/burla_2.

42. Ibid., 1 (electronic edition).

43. Ibid., 2, 5 (electronic edition).

44. William R. Casto, *The Supreme Court in the Early Republic: The Chief Justiceships of John Jay and Oliver Ellsworth* (Columbia: University of South Carolina Press, 1995), 120–21.

45. David Gray Adler, "The Constitution and Presidential Warmaking," and Dan Alfange, Jr., "The Quasi-War and Presidential War-Making" in David Gray Adler and Larry N. George, eds., *The Constitution and the Conduct of American Foreign Policy* (Lawrence: University Press of Kansas, 1996), 188, 274. Also see Albert Hall Bowman, *The Struggle for Neutrality: Franco-American Diplomacy during the Federalist Era* (Knoxville: University of Tennessee Press, 1974).

46. Casto, *The Supreme Court in the Early Republic,* 121.

47. The quotes are from the text of *Bas v. Tingy,* 4 Dall. 37 (1800), http://press-pubs.uchicago.edu/founders/. Chase is quoted in Casto, *The Supreme Court of the Early Republic,* 121. See also Adler, "The Constitution and Presidential War-Making," 209–11.

48. John Yoo, *The Powers of War and Peace: The Constitution and Foreign Affairs after 9/11* (Chicago: University of Chicago Press, 2005), 22; Yoo, "The Continuation of Politics by Other Means: The Original Understanding of War Powers," *California Law Review,* 84 (March 1996), 295.

49. As quoted in Wormuth and Firmage, *To Chain the Dog of War,* 18.

50. Almost every history of the American Revolution and the Articles of Confederation despairs about this situation. The significance of the debate over the Congress's proposed ability to wage war figures into all of the works on war powers cited in this book. For a recent example, see *Deciding to Use Force Abroad: War Powers in a System of Checks and Balances* (Washington, DC: The Constitution Project, 2005), 10–11. The Constitution Project is an initiative of former lawmakers and academics, mainly in Washington, D.C., to strengthen the Congress's role. See http://www.constitution project.org/.

51. James Madison, *Notes of Debates in the Federal Convention,* introduction by Adrienne Koch (New York: W.W. Norton and Co., [1966] 1987), 475–76; Adler, "The Constitution and Presidential War-Making," 185, and Wormuth and Firmage, *To Chain the Dog of War,* 18.

52. Wormuth and Firmage, *To Chain the Dog of War,* 18.

53. Adler, "The Constitution and Presidential Warmaking," 186.

54. Peter Irons, *War Powers: How the Imperial Presidency Hijacked the Constitution* (New York: Metropolitan Books, Henry Holt and Company, 2005), 20–27.

55. Ibid., 21; Adler, "The Constitution and Presidential Warmaking," 187.

56. Hamilton, *The Federalist, No. 69,* in *The Federalist Papers,* 420–21. Blackstone's influence on Hamilton is discussed in McDonald, *Hamilton,* 57–62.

57. William Blackstone, *Commentaries on the Laws of England: A Facsimile of the First Edition of 1765–1769,* vol. I (Chicago: University of Chicago Press, 1979), 249–51, electronic edition, http:// press-pubs.uchicago.edu/founders/documents/a1_8lls/html; Yoo, "The Continuation of Politics by Other Means," 205.

58. Yoo, "The Continuation of Politics by Other Means," 205. Much of the same argument, including the quotations, can be found in Yoo, *The Powers of War and Peace,* 41–42; see fn. 20.

59. See fn. 26 and Hamilton, *The Federalist, No. 69,* in *The Federalist Papers,* 420. Louis Fisher stresses the rejection of Blackstone in "Lost Constitutional Moorings: Recovering the War Power," *Indiana Law Journal,* vol. 81, no. 4 (Fall 2006), 1202.

60. James Kent, "Lecture III, Of the Declaration and Other Ably Measures of a State of War," in *Commentaries on American Law* (New York: O. Halstead, 1826), 15th ed., electronic edition, http://www.constitution.org/jk/jk_ooo.html; Yoo, "The Continuation of Politics by Other Means," 244–45.

61. Jay, *The Federalist, No. 4,* in *The Federalist Papers,* 17.

62. Joseph Story, *Commentaries on the Constitution of the United States,* book 3 (Boston: Hilliard, Gray and Company, 1833), paragraph 1166, electronic edition, http:// www.tulsa.edu/law/classes/rice/Constitutional/Story. The importance of Story's position is discussed in Fisher, "Lost Constitutional Moorings," 1205–206.

63. For the case, see R. Kent Newmyer, *Supreme Court Justice Joseph Story: Statesman of the Old Republic* (Chapel Hill: University of North Carolina Press, 1985), 94,

and Jean Edward Smith, *John Marshall: Definer of a Nation* (New York: Henry Holt and Company, 1996), 417–19.

64. Story, *Commentaries,* book 3, paragraphs 1172 and 1169, electronic edition.

65. Ibid., paragraph 1169.

66. Yoo, "The Continuation of Politics by Other Means," 214–16.

67. Alexander Hamilton, *The Federalist No. 25,* in *The Federalist Papers,* 16; see fn. 5. As is obvious in the previous quote of William Blackstone, "denunciation" meant something very similar to declaration, a very far cry from how a current reader would define it.

68. It is helpful to read *The Federalist No. 23* and *The Federalist No. 24* to appreciate this point.

69. See Ramsey, "Textualism and War Powers," 1591–92.

70. Walling, *Republican Empire,* 125–27.

71. Ramsey, "Textualism and War Powers," 1598.

72. See Louis Fisher, *Presidential War Power,* 2nd ed. (Lawrence: University Press of Kansas, 2004), 52.

73. Hallett, *The Lost Art of Declaring War,* 96–141; see fn. 3.

74. This point draws in part from Matthew S. Weingast, "The Strategic Necessity Perspective: A New Approach to Solving Old Constitutional War Powers Questions," *Journal of Legal Studies,* 8 (1997–1998), 1–7. The journal appears to be only online at www.usafa.af/mil/df/dfl/documents/constwar.doc.

75. David Gray Adler, "The Constitution and Presidential Warmaking: The Enduring Debate," *Political Science Quarterly,* vol. 103, no. 1 (Spring 1988), 8; Fisher, *Presidential War Power,* 24–25.

76. Louis Fisher, *Congressional Abdication on War and Spending* (College Station: Texas A&M University Press, 2000), 11.

77. Hallett, *The Lost Art of Declaring War,* 27.

78. Jules Lobel, "War and Responsibility: A Symposium on Congress, the President, and the Authority to Initiate Hostilities," *University of Miami Law Review,* vol. 50 (October 1995), 69–70, http://web.lexis-nexis.com/universe/.

79. Both are as quoted in ibid., 68. Also see Blackstone, *Commentaries,* I, 150, electronic edition; see fn. 57 for electronic citation.

80. Madison, *Notes of Debates in the Federal Convention,* 478; Lobel, "War and Responsibility," 68.

81. Jefferson as quoted in Lobel, "War and Responsibility," 68, from Letter from President Jefferson to Mr. Lincoln (November 13, 1808), from Albert E. Bergh, ed., *The Writings of Thomas Jefferson,* vol. 12 (1907), 195. The Bergh edition is available at http://www.constitution.org/tj/jeff.htm.

82. Story, *Commentaries,* book 3, paragraph 1171. Electronic edition. See fn. 62.

83. See C. Kevin Marshall, "Putting Privateers in Their Place: The Applicability of the Marque and Reprisal Clause to Undeclared War," *University of Chicago Law Review,* vol. 64 (Summer 1997), 958–63, http://web.lexis-nexis.com/universe/. Also see Yoo, *The Powers of War and Peace,* 147–48. The relationship between privateering and naval power is examined in Gary M. Anderson and Adam Gifford Jr., "Privateering and the Private Production of Naval Power," *CATO Journal,* vol. 11 (Spring/Summer 1991), electronic edition at http://web27.epnet.com/citation.asptb=1&_ug=sid+85EB 8BF9%2DA5E5%2D46F6%2D.

84. Marshall, "Putting Privateers in Their Place," 964–74. A similar judgment can be found in Matthew J. Gaul, "Regulating the New Privateers: Private Military Service

Contracting and the Modern Marque and Reprisal Clause," *Loyola of Los Angeles Law Review,* vol. 31 (June 1998), 1501–504, http://web.lexis-nexis.com/universe.

85. These issues will be examined more thoroughly in Chapter 4.

86. A point made by Yoo as well in *The Powers of War and Peace,* 148.

87. Wendy McElroy, "Is the Constitution Antiquated?" *The Independent Institute,* November 1999, http://www.independent.org/tii/news/991100McElroy.

88. One example of private actors who made money through their own initiative in land combat was scalp hunting. States retained the authority to issue bounties for scalps, and scalp hunters could take scalps during periods of hostilities as well as peace. They acted against Native Americans, whereas letters of marque and reprisal applied to the vessels and property of citizens of foreign powers. There may be an interesting distinction here in categories of limited war, with the Constitution only concerned with those that would affect U.S. relations with foreign powers.

89. The link to war power issues for this clause and that related to ambassadors is discussed in the section titled, "The President and War."

90. Yoo, *The Powers of War and Peace,* 104–105, and "The Continuation of Politics by Other Means," 208–13.

91. In all fairness, Yoo illustrates the reversal of priorities between the British and American systems by the latter's allotment of the power of declaring war to the Congress. Even today, the House of Commons has no "war power" equivalent to that of the Congress. It does not authorize military force, but it does have its appropriations powers to counter or support the recommendation of the prime minister.

92. The modern-day Congress works with both authorization and appropriations committees. For example, the Senate and House Armed Services Committees are authorizing committees. They decide which programs from the president's request to authorize, which literally means to create or to continue. These committees also often set maximum and minimum levels of spending for a program. They may also specify a certain amount. However, it is the appropriations committees that decide how much money will actually be spent. In recent decades, the appropriations committees have become stronger—they even act before the authorizers are finished with their work, and they sometimes appropriate money that the authorizers did not support. On the other hand, programs occasionally are authorized but then do not get any money.

93. There are cases where Congress actually authorizes an action but does not provide money to implement it. See the Congressional Research Service Report by Mary T. Tyszkiewicz and Stephen Daggett, *A Defense Budget Primer,* RL 30002 (Washington, DC: Congressional Research Service, Library of Congress, 1998), 34–40, electronic edition at http://digital.library.untedu/govdocs/crs//dafa/1998/uptmeta-crs606/RL30002_1998 Dec09.pdf. Supplemental requests are particularly problematic because they circumvent part of the process of congressional oversight—namely the input of the House and Senate Armed Services Committees. See Charles A. Stevenson, *Congress at War: The Politics of Conflict Since 1789* (Washington, DC: National Defense University Press and Potomac Books, 2007), 46.

94. James Madison, *The Federalist, No. 42,* in *The Federalist Papers,* 254–55.

95. Alexander Hamilton, *The Federalist, No. 69,* in *The Federalist Papers,* 420.

96. See fn. 67.

97. Most notably, Brien Hallett in *The Lost Art of Declaring War,* 39. Hallett argues that the Congress should declare war, and he is not satisfied with congressional authorizations to use military force.

98. John Locke, *The Second Treatise of Civil Government* (1690), Sections 147–48,

160, electronic edition, http://www.constitution.org/jl./2ndtreat.htm. All the quotes, including those from Locke, are also in Donald L. Robinson, "Presidential Prerogative and the Spirit of American Constitutionalism," in Adler and George, eds., *The Constitution and the Conduct of American Foreign Policy,* 115.

99. Ibid., 115.

100. Clinton Rossiter, *The Supreme Court and the Commander in Chief,* exp. ed., with an introduction and additional text by Richard P. Lonaker (Ithaca, NY: Cornell University Press, 1976), 68–73; Daniel Farber, *Lincoln's Constitution* (Chicago: University of Chicago Press, 2005), 115–43; Phillip Shaw Paludan, *The Presidency of Abraham Lincoln* (Lawrence: University Press of Kansas, 1994), 71–82.

101. Maeva Marcus, *Truman and the Steel Seizure Case: The Limits of Presidential Power* (New York: Columbia University Press, 1977), 58–86; Alonzo L. Hamby, *Man of the People: A Life of Harry S. Truman* (New York: Oxford University Press, 1995), 593–97.

102. See the discussion in Henkin, *Foreign Affairs and the U.S. Constitution,* 35–45.

103. Thomas Jefferson, "Opinion on Powers of the Senate Respecting Diplomatic Appointments," April 24, 1790, electronic edition, http://press.pubs.uchicago.edu/foundres/documents/a2_2_23s48.html; Fisher, *Presidential War Powers,* 21.

104. Fisher, *Presidential War Powers,* 21–22.

105. John Marshall, *Annals of Congress,* vol. 10, 613, electronic edition, http://memory.loc.gov/cg-bin/ampage; Henkin, *Foreign Affairs and the U.S. Constitution,* 41.

106. U.S. House of Representatives Select Committee to Investigate Covert Arms Transactions with Iran and U.S. Senate Select Committee on Secret Military Assistance to Iran and the Nicaraguan Opposition, *Report of the Congressional Committees Investigating the Iran-Contra Affair,* 100th Cong., 1st sess., H. Rept. No. 100–433, and S. Rept. No. 100–216, 389–90. William Shendow, "An Analysis of Foreign Affairs Powers: A Perspective for the Public Administrator Based on the Iran-Contra Affair," *Public Administration Quarterly,* vol. 15, no. 2 (Summer 1991), 182–83; Louis Fisher, The Law: Presidential Inherent Power: The "Sole Organ" Doctrine," *Presidential Studies Quarterly,* vol. 37, no. 1 (March 2007), 140–43.

107. Robinson makes this point in his essay, "Presidential Prerogative and Constitutionalism," in Adler and George, *The Constitution and the Conduct of American Foreign Policy,* 117.

108. Abraham D. Sofaer, *War, Foreign Affairs and Constitutional Power: The Origins* (Cambridge, MA: Ballinger Publishing Company, 1976), 117.

109. Ibid., 117–18.

110. It is probably worth remembering the immense trust that the great majority of the Congress had in President George Washington, particularly so early in his first term.

111. Variant Texts of the Plan Presented by Alexander Hamilton to the Federal Convention, June 18, 1787, *Debates in the Federal Convention of 1787,* reported by James Madison, edited by Gaillard Hunt and James B. Scott (New York: Oxford University Press, 1920), 118–20, electronic edition at http://yale.edu/lawweb/avalon/const/hamtexta.htm. Also see the discussion, including the quotation from Madison's notes, in Wormuth and Firmage, *To Chain the Dog of War,* 107–11.

2 Imperfect War and the Fragile Balance

1. Alexander Hamilton, *Pacificus No. 1,* in Joanne B. Freeman, ed., *Alexander Hamilton: Writings* (New York: The Library of America, 2001), 807–808.

2. Stanley Elkins and Eric McKitrick, *The Age of Federalism: The Early American Republic, 1788–1800* (New York and Oxford: Oxford University Press, 1993), 336–41; Ralph Ketcham, *James Madison: A Biography* (Charlottesville: University of Virginia Press, 1971, 1990), 340–48; John Lamberton Harper, *American Machiavelli: Alexander Hamilton and the Origins of U.S. Foreign Policy* (New York and Cambridge: Cambridge University Press, 2004), 105–24.

3. Hamilton, *Pacificus No. 1,* 806–808. This argument relies on Scott A. Silverstone, *Divided Union: The Politics of War in the Early American Republic* (Ithaca, NY: Cornell University Press, 2004), 196–97. Also see Karl-Friedrich Walling, *Republican Empire: Alexander Hamilton on War and Free Government* (Lawrence: University Press of Kansas, 1999), 145–52.

4. Richard H. Kohn, *Eagle and Sword: The Beginnings of the Military Establishment in America* (New York: Free Press, 1975), 97–103; Abraham D. Sofaer, *War, Foreign Affairs, and Constitutional Power: The Origins* (Cambridge, MA: Ballinger Publishing Company, 1976), 119–24.

5. Gilbert L. Lycan, *Alexander Hamilton and American Foreign Policy: A Design for Greatness* (Norman: University of Oklahoma Press, 1970), 216–22, 251.

6. The classic account of this undeclared war with France remains Alexander DeConde, *The Quasi-War: The Politics and Diplomacy of the Undeclared War with France, 1797–1801* (New York: Charles Scribner's Sons, 1966). From a legal perspective, see Gregory E. Fehings, "America's First Limited War," *Naval War College Review* (Summer 2000), electronic edition at http://www.nwc.navy.mil/press?Review/2000/summer/art4-Su0.htm. Also see Felix Gilbert, *To the Farewell Address* (Princeton, NJ: Princeton University Press, 1961), for an invaluable assessment of the impact of the early part of this crisis on American foreign policy and how the Americans hoped to interact with the outside world. For the number of American vessels seized by the French, see Frank N. Lambert, *The Barbary Wars: American Independence in the Atlantic World* (New York: Hill & Wang, 2005), 95.

7. This paragraph draws from DeConde, *The Quasi-War,* 64–65; Elkins and McKitrick, *The Age of Federalism,* 596–97; Lycan, *Alexander Hamilton and American Foreign Policy,* 304, 312–13; and Walling, *Republican Empire,* 228.

8. Forrest McDonald, *Alexander Hamilton: A Biography* (New York: W.W. Norton and Co., 1979), 338; Elkins and McKitrick, *The Age of Federalism,* 597–98, 612–18; DeConde, *The Quasi-War,* 103–107, 328.

9. The qualification about Adams's total deference to Congress comes from Dean Alfange, Jr., "The Quasi-War and Presidential War-Making," in David Gray Adler and Larry N. George, eds., *The Constitution and the Conduct of American Foreign Policy* (Lawrence: University Press of Kansas, 1996), 276. A more detailed account comes from Sofaer, *War, Foreign Affairs, and Constitutional Power,* 139–41.

10. DeConde, *The Quasi-War,* 106; Frances D. Wormuth and Edwin B. Firmage, *To Chain the Dog of War: The War Power of Congress in History and Law,* 2nd ed. (Urbana: University of Illinois Press, 1989), 60.

11. *Talbot v. Seeman,* 5 U.S. 1 (1801), 17, electronic edition from LexisNexis Academic.

12. Lambert, *The Barbary Wars;* Robert J. Allison, *The Crescent Obscured: The United States and the Muslim World, 1776–1815* (New York: Oxford University Press, 1995), 107–206.

13. Wormuth and Firmage, *To Chain the Dog of War,* 59.

14. Robert W. Tucker and David C. Hendrickson, *Empire of Liberty: The Statecraft of Thomas Jefferson* (Oxford and New York: Oxford University Press, 1990), 294–95; Sofaer, *War, Foreign Affairs, and Constitutional Power,* 208–209.

15. Jennifer K. Elsea and Richard F. Grimmett, *Declarations of War and Authorizations for the Use of Military Force: Historical Background and Legal Implications* (Washington, DC: Congressional Research Service, August 11, 2006), 7–8; Louis Fisher, *Presidential War Powers,* 2nd ed. (Lawrence: University Press of Kansas, 2004), 35–36.

16. Gallatin's argument and Jefferson's comments about Congress are from Thomas Jefferson to James Madison, February 19, 1812, in Paul Ford, ed., *The Works of Thomas Jefferson* (London: G.P. Putnam Sons, 1904–1905), XI, electronic edition at http://oll.libertyfund.org.Texts/Jefferson 0136/works/Vol11/0054–11_Pt06_1812.html; and Alexander DeConde, *Presidential Machismo: Executive Authority, Military Intervention, and Foreign Relations* (Boston: Northeastern University Press, 2000), 22. Also see James R. Sofka, "The Jeffersonian Idea of National Security," *Diplomatic History,* vol. 21 (Fall 1997), 37–38.

17. The question of whether the orders were also "offensive" in character is explored by Sofaer in *War, Foreign Affairs, and Constitutional Power,* 212–13, including the note at the bottom of both pages. Hamilton's reaction can be found in Alexander Hamilton, "The Examination," No. 1, December 17, 1801, electronic edition at http://press.pubs.uchicago.edufounders/documents/A1_8_11s_11.html, and quoted in Fisher, *Presidential War Powers,* 34–35, who quotes from John C. Hamilton, ed., vol. 7, *The Works of Alexander Hamilton* (1851), 745–47.

18. This is certainly the tone of DeConde's interpretation in *Presidential Machismo,* 22–24. Senator Jacob Javits argued the same in his book that supported the War Powers Resolution. See Jacob K. Javits with Don Kellerman, *Who Makes War: The President Versus Congress* (New York: William Morrow & Co., 1973), 49.

19. See Fisher's *Presidential War Power,* 32–37, or his essay, "The Barbary Wars: Legal Precedent for Invading Haiti?" in Adler and George, *The Constitution and the Conduct of American Foreign Policy,* 313–19.

20. John Adams, as quoted in Garry Wills, *James Madison* (New York: Times Books, 2002), 157.

21. Scott A. Silverstone, *Divided Union: The Politics of War in the Early American Republic* (Ithaca, NY: Cornell University Press, 2004), 78–79.

22. Different interpretations exist over the causes and goals of the War of 1812. See Donald R. Hickey, *The War of 1812: A Forgotten Conflict* (Urbana: University of Illinois Press, 1989), 29–51; Bradford Perkins, *Prologue to War, 1805–1812: England and the United States* (Berkeley: University of California Press, 1961, 1968), 342–437, and Reginald Horsman, *The Causes of the War of 1812* (New York: A.S. Barnes and Co., 1962).

23. This discussion draws from J.C.A. Stagg, *Mr. Madison's War: Politics, Diplomacy, and Warfare in the Early American Republic, 1783–1830* (Princeton, NJ: Princeton University Press, 1983), 79; Roger H. Brown, *The Republic in Peril: 1812* (New York: W.W. Norton and Company, [1964] 1971), 88–89, and Wills, *Madison,* 61–62. It is Wills who draws the analogy to later presidents.

24. Ronald L. Harzenbuehler and Robert L. Ivie, *Congress Declares War: Rhetoric, Leadership, and Partisanship in the Early Republic* (Kent, OH: Kent State University Press, 1983), 20–21.

25. The discussion draws from Skaggs, *Mr. Madison's War,* 111–15, and Sofaer, *War, Foreign Affairs and Constitutional Power,* 268–70.

26. Ibid., 292.

27. Ibid., 292–98.

28. Ibid., 298–326.

29. Ibid., 326–33.

30. Edward S. Corwin, *The President: Office and Powers, 1787–1984,* 5th ed., revised by Randall W. Bland, Theodore T. Hindson, and Jack W. Peltason (New York: New York University Press, 1984), 228. Emphasis by Corwin.

31. Ibid., 22; also see Wormuth and Firmage, *To Chain the Dog of War,* 153–55. The historical details of the *Caroline* incident are reviewed in Howard Jones, *To the Webster-Ashburton Treaty: A Study in Anglo–American Relations, 1783–1843* (Chapel Hill: University of North Carolina Press, 1977), 20–32, 152–54.

32. Wormuth and Firmage, *To Chain the Dog of War,* 153.

33. Corwin, *The President: Office and Powers,* 228; Fisher, *Presidential War Power,* 58.

34. Elsea and Grimmett, *Declarations of War,* 8–9; James Kent, *Commentaries on American Law,* vol. 1, 15th ed., edited by Jon Roland (New York: O. Halsted, 1826), 184, electronic edition, http://www.constitution.org/ik/ik.

35. Wormuth and Firmage, *To Chain the Dog of War,* 155–60.

36. The point about the impact of the telegram is best made by David F. Long in *Gold Braid and Foreign Relations: Diplomatic Activities of U.S. Naval Officers, 1798–1883* (Annapolis, MD: Naval Institute Press, 1988), 11–14. Long's book is a detailed account of these types of activities and actions. See Wormuth and Firmage, *To Chain the Dog of War,* 160–61, for the implications of greater presidential control.

37. Wormuth and Firmage, *To Chain the Dog of War,* 37; Sofaer, *War, Foreign Affairs and Constitutional Power,* 155. Also see Chapter 1, this volume.

38. Wormuth and Firmage, *To Chain the Dog of War,* 37.

39. Long, *Gold Braid and Foreign Relations,* 121–27. Cornelius Vanderbilt was a New York businessman who made a fortune establishing a shipping company to get prospectors faster to California via a transit of Nicaragua rather than going all the way around Cape Horn. See Leonard L. Richards, *The California Gold Rush and the Coming of the Civil War* (New York: Alfred A. Knopf, 2007), 135–38.

40. See Wormuth and Firmage, *To Chain the Dog of War,* 39–40, including the quotation by Pierce. Also see Corwin, *The President: Office and Powers,* 228–29.

41. Wormuth and Firmage, *To Chain the Dog of War,* 41.

42. Ibid., 42.

43. See Louis Henkin, *Foreign Affairs and the U.S. Constitution,* 2nd ed. (Oxford: The Clarendon Press of Oxford University Press, 1996), 98–99, for this point.

44. See the text of Polk's message in Russell D. Buhite, ed., *Calls to Arms: Presidential Speeches, Messages, and Declarations of War* (Wilmington, DL: Scholarly Resources Inc., 2003), 35–41.

45. See Thomas R. Hietala, *Manifest Design: Anxious Aggrandizement in Late Jacksonian America* (Ithaca, NY: Cornell University Press, 1985), 207–208; Thomas M. Leonard, *James K. Polk: A Clear and Unquestionable Destiny* (Wilmington, DL: Scholarly Resources, Inc., 2001), 43–45; and Silverstone, *Divided Union,* 172–73.

46. Leonard, *James K. Polk,* 79; Silverstone, *Divided Union,* 158; Sam W. Hayes, *James K. Polk and the Expansionist Impulse,* 2nd ed. (New York: Addison Wesley Longman, 2002), 121.

47. Ibid., 136–37.

48. Ibid., 136. Polk learned of Slidell's failure on April 7, 1846. See Allan Nevins, ed., *Polk: The Diary of a President: 1845–1849* (New York: Capricorn Books, 1968), 70.

49. Ibid., 81; Leonard, *James K. Polk,* 158.

50. Nevins, *Polk: The Diary of a President,* 87. For surveys of these events, also see K. Jack Bauer, *The Mexican War, 1846–1848* (New York: Macmillan Publishing Co., 1974), 1–78; and David M. Pletcher, *The Diplomacy of Annexation: Texas, Oregon, and the Mexican War* (Columbia: University of Missouri Press, 1973), 172–207, 258–65, 273–91, and 352–92; these provide a good account of the diplomacy and events leading up to Polk's announcement. Fisher, *Presidential War Power,* 39–44, and Wormuth and Firmage, *To Chain the Dog of War,* 56–57, examine this episode from the perspective of war powers.

51. Pletcher, *The Diplomacy of Annexation,* 386–90 (Clayton is quoted on 387); Seymour V. Connor and Odie B. Faulk, *North America Divided: War with Mexico, 1846–1848* (New York and Oxford: Oxford University Press, 1971), 134–135; Leonard, *James K. Polk,* 160–63. The quote by Lewis Cass is from Corwin, *The President: Office and Power,* 230.

52. For the political climate and the issues of expansionism and slavery, see David Potter, *The Impending Crisis, 1848–1861* (New York: Harper Colophon Books, 1976). For Calhoun's opinion, see Glenn W. Price, *Origins of the War with Mexico: The Polk-Stockton Intrigue* (Austin: University of Texas Press, 1967), 32. For Lincoln, see David Herbert Donald, *Lincoln* (New York: Simon and Schuster, 1995), 123–24. The story of the amendment and its language comes from Wormuth and Firmage, *To Chain the Dog of War,* 57.

53. Henry Bartholomew Cox, *War, Foreign Affairs, and Constitutional Power: 1829–1901* (Cambridge, MA: Ballinger Publishing Co., 1984), 78–79; DeConde, *Presidential Machismo,* 45–46; Arthur Schlesinger, Jr., *The Imperial Presidency* (Boston: Houghton Mifflin Co., [1973] 1989), 39–40.

54. *The Brig Amy Warwick; The Schooner Crenshaw; The Barque Hiawatha; The Schooner Brillante,* cited as *The Prize Cases,* 67 U.S. 635 (1863), 14, 20, electronic edition at LexisNexis Academic. See Philip Shaw Paludan, *The Presidency of Abraham Lincoln* (Lawrence: University Press of Kansas, 1994), 70–82; James F. Simon, *Lincoln and Chief Justice Taney: Slavery, Secession, and the President's War Powers* (New York: Simon and Schuster, 2006), 181–230; Harold M. Hyman, *A More Perfect Union: The Impact of the Civil War and Reconstruction on the Constitution* (Boston: Houghton Mifflin Company, 1975), 139–40; Daniel Farber, *Lincoln's Constitution* (Chicago: University of Chicago Press, 2003), 114–42; Clinton Rossiter, *The Supreme Court and the Commander in Chief,* exp. ed. with an introductory note and additional text by Richard P. Longaker (Ithaca, NY: Cornell University Press, 1976), 68–73; Louis Fisher, "Judicial Review of the War Power," *Presidential Studies Quarterly,* vol. 35, no. 3 (September 2005), 476–77.

55. Cox, *War, Foreign Affairs, and Constitutional Power,* 2.

56. Schlesinger, *The Imperial Presidency,* 68–81.

57. Wormuth and Firmage, *To Chain the Dog of War,* 81.

58. Silverstone, *Divided Union,* 247.

59. Ibid., 58–59.

60. Lewis L. Gould, *The Presidency of William McKinley* (Lawrence: University Press of Kansas, 1980), 69. McKinley's request on April 11 is quoted on page 85. Also see H. Wayne Morgan, *William McKinley and His America,* rev. ed. (Kent, OH: Kent State University Press, 2003), 260.

61. Morgan, *William McKinley,* 280–81, 286–87; Gould, *Presidency of William McKinley,* 86–88.

62. A point made by Kevin Phillips in *William McKinley* (New York: Times Books, 2003), 92.

63. Contrasting interpretations of McKinley abound. Just in the War Powers literature, compare Schlesinger, *The Imperial Presidency,* 82–83, with DeConde, *Presidential Machismo,* 78–82. Also see Fareed Zakaria, *From Wealth to Power: The Unusual Origins of America's World Role* (Princeton, NJ: Princeton University Press, 1998), 154–61; Ernest R. May, *Imperial Democracy: The Emergence of America as a Great Power* (New York: Harper and Row, 1961), 112–59; Walter LaFeber, *The New Empire: An Interpretation of American Expansion, 1860–1898* (Ithaca, NY: Cornell University Press, 1963), 326–406; and Lester D. Langley, *The Cuban Policy of the United States* (New York: John Wiley and Sons, 1968), 83–113.

64. The uses of that force are examined in Chapter 4.

65. See especially Zakaria, *From Wealth to Power,* and LaFeber, *The New Empire.* Also see Milton Plesur, *America's Outward Thrust: Approaches to Foreign Affairs, 1865–1890* (DeKalb: Northern Illinois University Press, 1971).

66. For a brief discussion of the origins of the humanitarian tradition in foreign policy, see W. R. Smyser, *The Humanitarian Conscience: Caring for Others in the Age of Terror* (New York: Palgrave Macmillan, 2003), 5–32. The role of British policy against the slave trade is examined in David Brion Davis, *The Problem of Slavery in the Age of Revolution, 1770–1823* (Ithaca, NY: Cornell University Press, 1975), 343–468.

67. See Richard D. Challener, *Admirals, Generals, and American Foreign Policy* (Princeton, NJ: Princeton University Press, 1973), 12–16; and Philip A. Crowl, "Alfred Thayer Mahan: The Naval Historian," in Peter Paret, ed., *Makers of Modern Strategy from Machiavelli to the Nuclear Age* (Princeton, NJ: Princeton University Press, 1986), 444–77.

68. Theodore Roosevelt, *An Autobiography,* introduction by Elting Morison (New York: Da Capo Press, 1913), 371–72; Harold Hongju Koh, *The National Security Constitution: Sharing Power after the Iran-Contra Affair* (New Haven, CT: Yale University Press, 1990), 89.

69. James R. Holmes, *Theodore Roosevelt and World Order* (Washington, DC: Potomac Books, 2006), 20, 41, 101, 230–31. The quote is on page 118.

70. Fisher, *Presidential War Powers,* 58–59; DeConde, *Presidential Machismo,* 89. Also see James Holmes, "Police Power: Theodore Roosevelt, American Diplomacy and World Order," *The Fletcher Forum of World Affairs,* vol. 27 (Winter/Spring 2003), 126. The full text of the Roosevelt Corollary is at http://historicaldocuments.com/TheodoreRoosevelt corollary to the Monroe Doctrine.htm.

71. Memorandum of the Solicitor for the Department of State, October 5, 1912, *Right to Protect Citizens in Foreign Countries by Landing Forces,* 3rd rev. ed. (Washington, DC: Government Printing Office, 1934), 25, 33, 38–45, 48. Also see Schlesinger, *The Imperial Presidency,* 89–90.

72. William Howard Taft, *Our Chief Magistrate and His Powers* (New York: Columbia University Press, 1916), 94–95; Schlesinger, *The Imperial Presidency,* 91.

73. Ibid., 90–91. The quotes of Root are by Schlesinger from Elihu Root, *The Military and Colonial Policies of the United States* (Cambridge, MA: Harvard University Press, 1916), 157–58.

74. Schlesinger, *The Imperial Presidency,* 91.

75. See fn. 41.

76. DeConde, *Presidential Machismo,* 100–101. Also see P. Edward Haley, *Revolution and Intervention: The Diplomacy of Taft and Wilson with Mexico, 1910–1917* (Cambridge, MA: MIT Press, 1970), 83–223.

77. A point made, although critically, by Wormuth and Firmage in *To Chain the Dog of War,* 132–33.

78. Louis Fisher, "*The Law:* Presidential Inherent Power: The 'Sole Organ' Doctrine," *Presidential Studies Quarterly,* vol. 37, no. 1 (March 2007), 143–44; Schlesinger, *The Imperial Presidency,* 100–101.

79. See Michael J. Glennon, *Constitutional Diplomacy* (Princeton, NJ: Princeton University Press, 1990), 18. The cases were *Panama Refining Company v. Ryan* and *Schechter Corp. v. United States.* The questions about domestic versus international authority is paraphrased from Fisher, "*The Law:* Presidential Inherent Power," 144.

80. A point made by Fisher in *Presidential War Powers,* 69.

81. See Henkin, *Foreign Affairs and the U.S. Constitution,* 14–15; and Fisher, "*The Law:* Presidential Inherent Power," 145.

82. Schlesinger, *The Imperial Presidency,* 101.

83. This discussion and the quote from Sutherland's opinion for the Court come from Henkin, *Foreign Affairs and the U.S. Constitution,* 17–18, and Fisher, "*The Law:* Presidential Inherent Power," 146–49. See *United States v. Curtiss-Wright Export Corporation,* 299, U.S. 304 (1936), 11, electronic edition at LexisNexis Academic.

84. *United States v. Curtiss-Wright Export Corporation,* 12.

85. Fisher, "*The Law:* Presidential Inherent Power," 147.

86. Ibid., 140–43.

87. Ibid., 139.

3   The Rise of Imperfect War and Presidential Power

1. To appreciate the demands on President Roosevelt, see Eric Larrabee, *Commander in Chief: Franklin Delano Roosevelt, His Lieutenants, and Their War* (New York: Harper and Row, 1987).

2. For the question of Soviet and mainland Chinese roles in the North Korean invasion of South Korea, see Sergei N. Goncharov, John W. Lewis, and Xue Litai, *Uncertain Partners: Stalin, Mao, and the Korean War* (Stanford, CA: Stanford University Press, 1993); William Stueck, *Rethinking the Korean War: A New Diplomatic and Strategic History* (Princeton, NJ: Princeton University Press, 2002), 61–83; and Vladislav Zubok and Constantine Pleshakov, *Inside the Kremlin's Cold War: From Stalin to Khrushchev* (Cambridge, MA: Harvard University Press, 1996), 54–72.

3. John Milton Cooper, Jr., *Breaking the Heart of the World: Woodrow Wilson and the Fight for the League of Nations* (Cambridge: Cambridge University Press, 2001), 109–375; Ralph A. Stone, *The Irreconcilables: The Fight Against the League of Nations* (New York: W.W. Norton and Co., 1970).

4. Gordon Silverstein, *Imbalance of Powers: Constitutional Interpretation and the Making of American Foreign Policy* (New York: Oxford University Press, 1997), 67, 83. Silverstein sees the beginning of this more with Lyndon Johnson rather than Kennedy.

5. Ibid., 8–9. Of course this is also the interpretation of Arthur Schlesinger, Jr., *The*

Imperial Presidency (Boston: Houghton Mifflin, [1973] 1989), or Peter Irons, *War Powers: How the Imperial Presidency Hijacked the Constitution* (New York: Metropolitan Books, Henry Holt and Company, 2005), especially 157–79.

6. Louis Fisher, *Presidential War Powers,* 2nd ed. (Lawrence: University Press of Kansas, 2004), 87, 91.

7. Schlesinger, *The Imperial Presidency,* 119–23; Fisher, *Presidential War Powers,* 88–94.

8. Fisher, *Presidential War Powers,* 86–87.

9. Irons, *War Powers,* 165.

10. Fisher, *Presidential War Powers,* 95. This is Section 7 of the UN Participation Act.

11. Ibid., 97–99. For Senator Connally's advice, see Gary R. Hess, *Presidential Decisions for War: Korea, Vietnam, and the Persian Gulf* (Baltimore: Johns Hopkins University Press, 2001), 34.

12. Ibid., 97–99. The author's father, who was wounded several months later, embodied the public cynicism about the term "police action," by often observing repeatedly in subsequent years, such as the early years of Vietnam, that one should not worry because it was only a "police action."

13. Douglas's remarks are quoted at length in Christopher H. Pyle and Richard M. Pious, *The President, Congress, and the Constitution* (New York: Free Press, 1984), 321–21.

14. Schlesinger, *The Imperial Presidency,* 132–33.

15. Fisher, *Presidential War Powers,* 169–70. Fisher stresses the desire to avoid appearing unilateral.

16. Thomas M, Franck, "Declare War? Congress Can't," *New York Times,* December 11, 1990, p. A27.

17. Fisher, *Presidential War Powers,* 180–82; Henkin, *Foreign Affairs and the U.S. Constitution,* 258; John Yoo, *The Powers of War and Peace: The Constitution and Foreign Affairs after 9/11* (Chicago: University of Chicago Press, 2005), 165.

18. Richard J. Harknett and Norman C. Thomas, "The Precedence of Power: Determining Who Should Authorize Military Force," *Congress and the Presidency,* vol. 25 (Spring 1998), 7.

19. For Eisenhower, Congress, and bipartisanship, see Chester J. Pach and Elmo Richardson, *The Presidency of Dwight D. Eisenhower,* rev. ed. (Lawrence: University Press of Kansas, 1991), 49–73; James T. Patterson, *Grand Expectations: The United States, 1945–1974* (New York: Oxford University Press, 1996), 262–310; and Robert Dallek, *Lone Star Rising: Lyndon Johnson and His Times, 1908–1960* (New York: Oxford University Press, 1991), 432–64.

20. Fisher, *Presidential War Power,* 118–25.

21. Ibid., 28–29.

22. Marshall Silverberg, "The Separation of Powers and Control of the CIA's Covert Operations," *Texas Law Review,* vol. 68 (February 1990), 576–90. Good overviews of the Congress and the intelligence community are available in Loch K. Johnson, "Covert Action and Accountability: Decision-making for America's Secret Foreign Policy," in Loch K. Johnson and James J. Wirtz, eds., *Strategic Intelligence: Windows Into a Secret World* (Los Angeles: Roxbury Publishing Co., 2004), 370–89; Johnson, "Accountability and America's Secret Foreign Policy: Keeping a Legislative Eye on the Central Intelligence Agency," *Foreign Policy Analysis,* vol. 1 (March 2005), 99–120; and Frank

Smist, Jr., *Congress Oversees the United States Intelligence Community,* 2nd ed. (Knoxville: University of Tennessee Press, 1994).

23. The quotation and the remarks about Congress's intention are from Harold Hongju Koh, *The National Security Constitution: Sharing Power after the Iran-Contra Affair* (New Haven, CT: Yale University Press, 1990), 103. Emphasis in quotation is by Koh. See Section 123 50 USC 403-3(c)(8), electronic edition, http: //www.intelligence .gov/o/security_1947.shtml. Short reviews of the operations in Iran and Guatemala are from Philip J. Cooper, *By Order of the President: The Use and Abuse of Executive Direct Action* (Lawrence: University Press of Kansas, 2002), 177–79; and Odd Arne Westad, *The Global Cold War: Third World Interventions and the Making of Our Times* (Cambridge: Cambridge University Press, 2005), 120–23, 146–48.

24. The quotation from the Central Intelligence Act is from Fisher, *Presidential War Powers,* 242.

25. See U.S. House of Representatives Select Committee to Investigate Covert Transactions with Iran and U.S. Select Committee on Select Military Assistance to Iran and the Nicaraguan Opposition, *Report of the Congressional Committees Investigating the Iran-Contra Affair,* with Supplemental, Minority and Additional Views, 100th Congress, 1st sess., H. Rept. No. 100-433 and S. Rept. 100-216 (Washington, DC: Government Printing Office, 1987), 376. Hereafter cited as the *Iran-Contra Report.*

26. William J. Daugherty, *Executive Secrets: Covert Action and the Presidency* (Lexington: University Press of Kentucky, 2004), 134–36.

27. Fisher, *Presidential War Powers,* 243, makes this point, and it will be revisited later in this chapter and in the closing chapter.

28. National Security Council Directive, NSC 10/2, quoted in the *Iran-Contra Report,* 375–76.

29. Daugherty, *Executive Secrets,* 13.

30. Ibid., 14. Also see Alfred Cumming, memorandum, "Statutory Procedures Under Which Congress Is To Be Informed of U.S. Intelligence Activities, Including Covert Action," January 18, 2006 (Washington, DC: Library of Congress, Congressional Research Service), electronic edition, http://www.findlaw.com.

31. See Westad, *The Global Cold War,* and John Lewis Gaddis, *Strategies of Containment: A Critical Appraisal of Postwar American National Security Policy* (New York: Oxford University Press, 1982), 175–82.

32. See discussion in Chapter 4, this volume.

33. Daugherty, *Executive Secrets,* 154–55.

34. See John Hart Ely, *War and Responsibility: Constitutional Lessons of Vietnam and Its Aftermath* (Princeton, NJ: Princeton University Press, 1993), 68–88. Of course the use of such "volunteers" was not new. The United States had sent such personnel to serve in China against Japan in 1940–1941. See Jack Samson, *Chennault* (New York: Doubleday, 1987), 60–95.

35. Ely, *War and Responsibility,* 70.

36. As quoted in ibid., 107.

37. Daugherty, *Executive Secrets,* 93–94.

38. A point made by Daugherty in *Executive Secrets,* 30.

39. See Ronald H. Spector, *Advise and Support: The Early Years, 1941–1960, United States Army in Vietnam* (Washington, DC: Center of Military History, 1983); and Neil Sheehan, *A Bright Shining Lie: John Paul Vann and America in Vietnam* (New York: Random House, 1988), 173–383.

40. Schlesinger, *The Imperial Presidency,* 200–205; Fisher, *Presidential War Powers,* 135–37.

41. Schlesinger, *The Imperial Presidency,* 202. For Schlesinger's pro-presidential views, see Fisher, *Presidential War Powers,* 102–104, and Fisher, "Scholarly Support for Presidential Wars," *Presidential Studies Quarterly,* vol. 35 (September 2005), 590.

42. This is drawn from Michael Beschloss, ed., *Taking Charge: The Johnson White House Tapes, 1963–1964* (New York: Simon and Schuster, 1997), 492–500; Hess, *Presidential Decisions for War,* 85–87; and Robert J. Hanyok, "Skunks, Bogies, Silent Hounds, and the Flying Fish: The Gulf of Tonkin Mystery, 2–4 August 1964," *Cryptologic Quarterly* (Winter 2005), 1–55, as well as Louis F. Giles, "The Gulf of Tonkin Mystery: The SIGINT Hounds Were Howling," December 5, 2005, released by National Security Agency on January 3, 2006. Both documents are on the NSA website at http://www.nsa.gov/vietnam/viet00005. An older account of the incident still worth reading for context is Edwin E. Moise, *Tonkin Gulf and the Escalation of the Vietnam War* (Chapel Hill: University of North Carolina Press, 1996).

43. Dallek, *Lone Star Rising,* 432–64; Randall Bennett Woods, *Fulbright: A Biography* (Cambridge: Cambridge University Press, 1995), 345–48.

44. Gary R. Hess, "Authorizing War: Congressional Resolutions and Presidential Leadership, 1955–2002," in Donald R. Kelley, ed., *Divided Power: The Presidency, Congress, and the Formation of American Foreign Policy* (Fayetteville: University of Arkansas Press, 2005), 52–53; Beschloss, *Taking Charge,* 494; Robert Dallek, *Flawed Giant: Lyndon Johnson and His Times* (New York: Oxford University Press, 1998), 147–56; H.W. Brands, *The Wages of Globalism: Lyndon Johnson and the Limits of American Power* (New York: Oxford University Press, 1995), 225–30; Fisher, *Presidential War Powers,* 129–30; and Silverstein, *Imbalance of Powers,* 86. As Dallek and Brands stress, Johnson was making his decision in the middle of a presidential campaign against Barry Goldwater, the conservative Arizona Republican, and did not want to appear weak on defense and foreign policy.

45. Gulf of Tonkin Resolution, The Avalon Project at Yale Law School, http://www.yale.edu/lawweb/avalon/tonkin-g.htm.

46. See Ely, *War and Responsibility,* 17–19, for a short review of the discussion and debate. Also see Woods, *Fulbright,* 354–59.

47. Schlesinger, *The Imperial Presidency,* 181, from Lyndon B. Johnson, *The Vantage Point* (New York: Holt, Rinehart and Winston, 1971), 116.

48. Ely, *War and Responsibility,* 12.

49. See fn. 42.

50. Pyle and Pious, *President, Congress, and the Constitution,* 360; Ely, *War and Responsibility,* 32–41.

51. The literature on the Vietnam War is immense, but two surveys that show the changes in objectives and means very effectively are Stanley Karnow, *Vietnam: A History* (New York: Viking Press, 1983); and Robert D. Schulzinger, *A Time for War: The United States and Vietnam, 1941–1975* (New York: Oxford University Press, 1997).

52. Fisher, *Presidential War Powers,* 145–47; Schlesinger, *The Imperial Presidency,* 301–302.

53. Schlesinger, *The Imperial Presidency,* 305; Fisher, *Presidential War Powers,* 147.

54. U.S. Congress, House Subcommittee on International Security, International Organizations and Human Rights of the House Committee on Foreign Affairs, *The War Powers Resolution: Relevant Documents, Reports, Correspondence* (May 1994), 1.

55. The point about treaties is noted in The Constitution Project, *Deciding to Use Force Abroad: War Powers in a System of Checks and Balances* (Washington, DC: The Constitution Project, 2005), 34, electronic edition at http://www.constitution project .org/pdf/War_Powers_Deciding_To_Use_Force_Abroad.pdf.

56. House Subcommittee on International Security, *The War Powers Resolution,* 1.

57. Ibid., 28–29. Report language or legislative history is very important because it is here where officials can turn to try to understand the intent of the legislation. While not enjoying the status of legal language, neglect of it can be the cause of serious congressional criticism.

58. Ibid., 29.

59. Koh, *The National Security Constitution,* 125.

60. House Subcommittee on International Security, *The War Powers Resolution,* 2.

61. Koh, *The National Security Constitution,* 50–51.

62. Ibid., 127; Fisher, *Presidential War* Powers, 149–50; Michael J. Glennon, *Constitutional Diplomacy* (Princeton, NJ: Princeton University Press, 1990), 103.

63. Louis Fisher, *Constitutional Abdication on War and Spending* (College Station: Texas A&M University Press, 2000), 62–63.

64. House Subcommittee on International Security, *The War Powers Resolution,* 4, 35.

65. See discussion in "When War Is Not War" section in chapter 3.

66. Richard F. Grimmett, *War Powers Resolution: Presidential Compliance,* CRS Issue Brief for Congress (Washington, DC: Congressional Research Service, Library of Congress, updated April 5, 2006), 1.

67. House Subcommittee on International Security, *The War Powers Resolution,* 53–54, 91. Cambodia had seized a U.S. container ship, the *Mayaguez,* after which President Ford ordered U.S. Marines to retake the vessel and to raid a prison camp where the administration mistakenly believed Cambodia had taken the crew as prisoners. See Douglas Brinkley, *Gerald L. Ford* (New York: Times Books, 2007), 100–105.

68. Ibid., 55; Grimmett, *War Powers Resolution,* 11.

69. Assistant Secretary of State Richard Fairbanks to Representative Clement Zablocki, letter dated April 6, 1981, reproduced in House Subcommittee on International Security, *The War Powers Resolution,* 61.

70. Ibid., 113–14. Also see Lee H. Hamilton with Jordan Tama, *A Creative Tension: The Foreign Policy Roles of the President and Congress* (Washington, DC: Wilson Center Press, 2002), 75.

71. A few years later the author learned from an acquaintance that Soviet television had initially shown a map of Spain to indicate a U.S. invasion of Granada. From Moscow's perspective, invasion of an ally would not have seemed that inexplicable.

72. See President Ronald Reagan to the Honorable Tip O'Neill, Speaker of the House of Representatives, letter dated March 26, 1986, in House Subcommittee on International Security, *The War Powers Resolution,* 116–17.

73. Fisher, *Presidential War Powers,* 161–64.

74. Ibid., 160; Letter from President Ronald Reagan to the Speaker of the House of Representatives, August 24, 1982 and Letter from President Ronald Reagan to the Speaker of the House of Representatives, Tip O'Neill, September 29, 1982, House International Security Subcommittee, *The War Powers Resolution,* 73–74 and 78–79.

75. Ibid., 83, Letter of President Ronald Reagan to the Chairman of the House Committee on Foreign Affairs, Clement L. Zablocki, September 2, 1983; Fisher, *Presidential War Powers,* 161.

76. A point made by Victoria A. Farrar-Myers in "Transference of Authority: The Institutional Struggle Over the Control of the War Power," *Congress and the Presidency,* vol. 25 (Autumn 1998), 3, electronic version, http://proquest.umi.com/pqdweb?indes= 17&sid=2&srchmode=1&vinst=PROD&fmt.

77. President George H.W. Bush to the Speaker of the House of Representatives, Thomas S. Foley, August 9, 1990 in House Subcommittee on International Security, *The War Powers Resolution,* 147–48.

78. Edward Keynes, "The War Powers Resolution and the Persian Gulf War," in David Gray Adler and Larry N. George, eds., *The Constitution and the Conduct of American Foreign Policy* (Lawrence: University Press of Kansas, 1996), 242; Jean Edward Smith, *George Bush's War* (New York: Henry Holt and Co., 1992), 106.

79. George H.W. Bush, Remarks at the Texas State Republican Convention in Dallas, Texas, June 20, 1992, *Public Papers of the Presidents, 1992,* vol. 1, 995. The Justice Department's position is discussed in Andrew Rudalevige, *The New Imperial Presidency: Renewing Presidential Power after Watergate* (Ann Arbor: University of Michigan Press, 2006), 193.

80. Fisher, *Presidential War Power,* 171.

81. *Dellums v. Bush,* 752 F. Supp. 1141 (D.D.C. 1990), electronic edition at http:// law.enotes.com/american-court-cases/dellums-v-bush. Also see David Gray Adler, "Court, Constitution, and Foreign Affairs," in Adler and George, eds., *The Constitution and the Conduct of American Foreign Policy,* 41–43.

82. Smith, *George Bush's War,* 238–43.

83. This is a variation of Justice Robert Jackson's concurring opinion in *Youngstown Sheet and Tube v. Sawyer* that the president's power is at its maximum when he or she acts with a congressional authorization. See Donald Robinson, "Presidential Prerogative and Constitutionalism," in Adler and George, eds., *The Constitution and the Conduct of American Foreign Policy,* 122.

84. For Panama, see Fisher, *Presidential War Powers,* 165–69.

85. Karl K. Schonberg, "Global Security and Legal Restraint: Reconsidering War Powers after September 11," *Political Science Quarterly,* vol. 119, (2004), 123.

86. See Chapter 4, this volume, for an examination of this point in much more detail.

87. See the discussion in Fisher, *Presidential War Powers,* 177–78.

88. Ibid., 178; Ryan C. Hendrickson, *The Clinton Wars: The Constitution, Congress, and War Powers* (Nashville, TN: Vanderbilt University Press, 2002), 25–31.

89. Assistant Secretary of State for Legislative Affairs Wendy R. Sherman to Representative Benjamin A. Gilman, July 21, 1993, reproduced in *Congressional Record* (August 4, 1993), E 1984–1985. Also see Hendrickson, *The Clinton Wars,* 33–34.

90. Fisher, *Presidential War Powers,* 179.

91. The quotation is from Assistant Attorney General Walter Dellinger to Senators Robert Dole, Alan K. Simpson, Strom Thurmond, and William S. Cohen, September 27, 1994; electronic edition at http://www.usdoj.gov/olc/haiti.htm. See David Gray Adler, "Clinton, the Constitution, and the War Power," in David Gray Adler and Michael A. Genovese, eds., *The Presidency and the Law: The Clinton Legacy* (Lawrence: University Press of Kansas, 2002), 3–38; Hendrickson, *The Clinton Wars,* 62, 64–65; William Michael Treanor, "The War Powers Outside the Court," in Mark Tushnet, ed., *The Constitution in Wartime: Beyond Alarmism and Complacency* (Durham, NC: Duke University Press, 2005), 148–49; and Walter Dellinger, "After the Cold War: Presidential Powers and the Use of Military Force," *University of Miami Law Review,* vol. 50 (1995), 107.

92. Hendrickson, *The Clinton Wars,* 130. See also U.S. House of Representatives, Committee on International Relations, "Situation in Kosovo" (April 21, 1999), 30.

93. Ralston, as quoted by Adler, "Clinton, the Constitution, and the War Power," 42, taken from a transcript of *Meet the Press,* May 2, 1999, as quoted in Plaintiff's Memorandum in Opposition to Defendant's Motion to Dismiss, in *Campbell v. Clinton,* 52 F. Supp. 2d. 34 (D.D.C. 1999), also at http://jurist.law.pitt.edu/ratner1.htm.

94. David Baumann and Richard E. Cohen, "Going Slow on Kosovo," *National Journal,* vol. 3 (April 17, 1999), p. 1055, electronic edition at http://pqdweb?TS=98389 4089&Did=000000040875540&Mtd.

95. Timothy S. Boylan and Glenn A. Phelps, "The War Powers Resolution: A Rationale for Congressional Inaction," *Parameters,* vol. 31 (Spring 2001), 117.

96. Jamie Dettmer, "Little Ado about Something Big," *Insight on the News,* vol. 15 (May 10, 1999), electronic edition at http:///pqdweb?TS=983892922&Did=ooooooo 41065023&mtd.

97. For Gephardt, see Dettmer, "Little Ado about Something Big," and for Bereuter, see Baumann and Cohen, "Going Slow on Kosovo," 1056.

98. Grimmett, "War Powers Resolution," 5.

99. Ibid., 5–6; Fisher, *Presidential War Power,* 201.

100. The strategic and operations aspects of this point are examined more in Chapter 4.

101. The Clinton administration cited UN Security Council Resolution 678, which authorized UN members to use force against Iraq, as one of the sources of its authority to conduct intermittent bombing missions against Iraq throughout the remainder of the decade.

102. Hendrickson, *The Clinton Wars,* 79–80.

103. The reasons for this are discussed in greater depth in Chapters 4 and 5, this volume.

104. 147 *Congressional Record* (daily ed., October 1, 2001), S9950–51; David Abramowitz, "The President, the Congress, and Use of Force: Legal and Political Considerations in Authorizing Use of Force against International Terrorism," *Harvard International Law Journal,* vol. 43 (Winter 2002), 73.

105. The role of preemption in U.S. strategy will receive closer attention in Chapter 5. Much of the argument supporting this claim depended on interpretations of Secretary of State Daniel Webster's observations in the *Caroline* case of 1837.

106. Abramowitz, "The President, the Congress, and the Use of Force," 74–75.

107. 147 *Congressional Record* (daily ed., October 1, 2001), S9950–51.

108. Richard F. Grimmett, *The War Powers Resolution: After Thirty Years,* CRS Report for Congress (Washington, DC: Library of Congress, Congressional Research Service, March 11, 2004), 46.

109. Fisher, *Presidential War Powers,* 215–16; Rudalevige, *New Imperial Presidency,* 219.

110. The literature on this is endless. Thomas E. Ricks, *Fiasco: The American Military Adventure in Iraq* (New York: Penguin Press, 2006), 49–56, 90–95; Karen De-Young, *Soldier: The Life of Colin Powell* (New York: Alfred A. Knopf, 2006), 480–82, 487–93; Michael Isikoff and David Corn, *Hubris: The Inside Story of Spin, Scandal, and the Selling of the Iraq War* (New York: Crown Publishers, 2006); and Craig R. Whitney, ed., *The WMD Mirage: Iraq's Decade of Deception and America's False Premise for War* (New York: Public Affairs, 2005). The entire last book contains documentation on this subject. An internal Department of Defense Study confirmed the lack of coopera-

tion between Al-Qaeda and Saddam Hussein. See R. Jeffrey Smith, "Hussein's Prewar Ties to Al-Qaeda Discounted," *The Washington Post,* April 6, 2007, A1, A4.

111. See Ryan C. Hendrickson, "Clinton, Bush, Congress, and War Powers: A Comparative Analysis of the Military Strikes on Iraq and Bin Laden" (paper presented at the Woodrow Wilson International Center for Scholars on May 17, 2004), electronic edition at http://www.wilsoncenter.org/events/docs/hendrickson.pdf.

112. DeYoung, *Soldier,* 409; Ricks, *Fiasco,* 62–63; Isikoff and Corn, *Hubris,* 125–29; and Rudalevige, *New Imperial Presidency,* 219–22.

113. Quoted in Winslow T. Wheeler, *The Wastrels of Defense: How Congress Sabotages U.S. Security* (Annapolis, MD: Naval Institute Press, 2004), 212.

114. Dianne E. Rennack, *Authorization of Use of U.S. Armed Forces Against Iraq: Side-by-Side Comparison of Selected Legislative Proposals,* CRS Report for Congress (Washington, DC: Library of Congress, Congressional Research Service, October 16, 2002), 5.

115. Robert C. Byrd, *Losing America: Confronting a Reckless and Arrogant Presidency* (New York: W.W. Norton & Co., 2004), 165.

116. Isikoff and Corn, *Hubris,* 127–28. So did this author, to be honest, although he remained unconvinced that there was a direct link between Saddam Hussein and Al-Qaeda.

117. Fisher, *Presidential War Power,* 225–26.

118. Ibid., 226–27.

119. Wheeler, *Wastrels of Defense,* 214–26; Rennack, *Authorization of Use of U.S. Armed Forces Against Iraq,* 1–3.

120. P.L. 107–243; Grimmett, *War Powers Resolution,* 15.

121. Fisher, *Presidential War Powers,* 250–55.

122. Ibid., 256–57. Also see *Iran-Contra Report,* 3–22.

123. Fisher, *Presidential War Powers,* 257.

124. Ibid., 169.

125. William C. Banks and Jeffrey D. Straussman, "A New Imperial Presidency? Insights from U.S. Involvement in Bosnia," *Political Science Quarterly* 114 (Summer 1999), 209, 212.

126. Byrd, *Losing America,* 63–64; Nancy Kassop, "The War Power and Its Limits," *Presidential Studies Quarterly,* vol. 33 (September 2003), 514.

127. Stephen Howard Chadwick, *Defense Acquisition: Overview, Issues, and Options for Congress,* CRS Report for Congress (Washington, DC: Library of Congress, Congressional Research Service, June 20, 2007), 4.

128. Robert D. Hormats, *The Price of Liberty: Paying for America's Wars* (New York: Times Books, Henry Holt and Company, 2007), 212–14 and 266–67; Mary T. Tyskiewicz and Stephen Daggett, *A Defense Budget Primer,* CRS Report for Congress (Washington, DC: Library of Congress, Congressional Research Service, December 9, 1998), 42–44.

129. The trend is discussed in Lori Fisler Damrosch, "The Interface of National Constitutional Systems with International Law and Institutions on Using Military Forces: Changing Trends in Executive and Legislative Powers," in Charlotte Ku and Harold K. Jacobson, *Democratic Accountability and the Use of Force in International Law* (Cambridge: Cambridge University Press, [2002] 2003), 39–60. Kenneth B. Moss, "Constitutions, Military Force, and Implications for German–American Relations," *SWP Comments,* vol. 56 (December 2005), compares systems of accountability and military

force between these two countries (electronic edition at http://www.swp-berlin.org/en/common/get_document.php?id=1518).

4 Keeping War Usable: A Place for Imperfect War

1. Carl von Clausewitz, *On War,* edited and translated by Michael Howard and Peter Paret (Princeton, NJ: Princeton University Press, 1976), 69.

2. Alexander Hamilton, *The Federalist, No. 28,* in *The Federalist Papers,* with an introduction by Garry Wills (New York: Bantam Dell, 1982), 159–64.

3. Most of these names are similarly listed by Roger Beaumont in "Small Wars: Definitions and Dimensions," *Annals of the American Academy of Political and Social Science,* vol. 541 (September 1995), 22–23.

4. Ibid., 21, quoted from E. Hoyt, ed., *A New Military Dictionary . . . ,* reprint ed. (Westport, CT: Greenwood Press, [1811] 1971), 449.

5. Reginald C. Stuart, *War and American Thought: From the Revolution to the Monroe Doctrine* (Kent, OH: Kent State University Press, 1982), xv.

6. Adrian R. Lewis, *The American Culture of War: The History of U.S. Military Force from World War II to Operation Iraqi Freedom* (New York: Routledge, 2007), xviii.

7. Max Boot, *The Savage Wars of Peace: Small Wars and the Rise of American Power* (New York: Basic Books, 2002), xiv.

8. Ibid., xvi.

9. Richard A. Preston, Alex Roland, and Sydney F. Wise, *Men in Arms: A History of Warfare and Its Interrelationships with Western Society,* 5th ed. (Fort Worth, TX: Harcourt Brace Jovanovich College Publishers, 1991), 116–18. For emergence of laws governing conflict, see Geoffrey Parker, "Early Modern Europe," in Michael Howard, George J. Andreopoulos, and Mark Shulman, eds., *The Laws of Warfare: Constraints on Warfare in the Western World* (New Haven, CT: Yale University Press, 1994), 40–58.

10. Herfried Münkler, *The New Wars,* translated by Patrick Camiller (Cambridge: Polity Press, 2005), 35, 47, published in Germany as *Die Neuen Kriege* (Reinbek bei Hamburg: Rowohlt Verlag GmbH, 2002). Also see K.J. Holsti, *The State, War, and the State of War* (Cambridge: Cambridge University Press, 1996), 29–31. Holsti refers to these developments in war as "institutionalized war."

11. John A. Lynn, *Battle: A History of Combat and Culture* (Boulder, CO: Westview Press, 2003), 192–93.

12. Preston, Roland, and Wise, *Men in Arms,* 120.

13. Stuart, *War and American Thought,* 27.

14. Ira D. Gruber, "The Anglo-American Military Tradition and the War for American Independence," in Kenneth J. Hagan and William R. Roberts, eds., *Against All Enemies: Interpretations of American Military History from Colonial Times to the Present* (New York: Greenwood Press, 1986), 26–27, and Stephen Brumwell, *Redcoats: The British Soldier and War in the Americas, 1775–1753* (Cambridge: Cambridge University Press, 2002).

15. Gruber, "The Anglo-American Military Tradition," 28; Russell F. Weigley, *The American Way of War: A History of United States Military Strategy and Policy* (New York: Macmillan Publishing Co., 1973), 19–39.

16. Michael Howard, "Constraints on Warfare," and Harold E. Seleskey, "Colonial America," in Howard, Andreopoulos, and Shulman, eds., *The Laws of Warfare,* 5, 60.

17. John Grenier, *The First Way of War: American War Making on the Frontier* (Cambridge: Cambridge University Press, 2005), 1, 3, 10, 21, 89–93, 223–25.

18. Fred Anderson and Andrew Cayton, *The Dominion of War: Empire and Liberty in North America, 1500–2000* (New York: Viking, 2005), xx. The concept of property in expansion is discussed in Albert K. Weinberg, *Manifest Destiny: A Study of Nationalist Expansionism in American History* (Chicago: Quadrangle Books, [1935] 1963), 72–99; and Anders Stephanson, *Manifest Destiny: American Expansion and the Empire of Right* (New York: Hill & Wang, 1995), 6–12.

19. Stuart, *War and American Thought,* 121–22. For more on Clay and American nationalism, see Merrill D. Peterson, *The Great Triumvirate: Webster, Clay, and Calhoun* (New York: Oxford University Press, 1987), 47–84; and Robert V. Remini, *Henry Clay: Statesman for the Union* (New York: W.W. Norton & Co., 1991), 57–122, 154–78, 296–310. The discussion of military romanticism is drawn from Lynn, *Battle,* 192–93.

20. Lynn, *Battle,* 190–200.

21. Samuel P. Huntington, *The Soldier and the State: The Theory and Politics of Civil–Military Relations* (New York: Vintage Books, 1957), 56–57.

22. Beatrice Heuser, "Clausewitz und der Kleine Krieg," in *Clausewitz-Information,* edited by Lennart Souchon (Hamburg: Fuehrungsakademie der Bundewehr), vol. 1 (2005), 37–40, and Stuart Kinross, "Clausewitz and Low-Intensity Conflict," *The Journal of Strategic Studies,* vol. 27 (March 2004), 37.

23. Ibid., 37. The observation about limited operations being more of a sideline comes from Juergen Frese, "Im Ruecken des Regulaeren," in *Clausewitz-Information,* vol. 1 (2005), 15–16.

24. Peter Paret, "The Genesis of *On War,*" in Clausewitz, *On War,* edited by Howard and Paret, 21.

25. Ibid., 94. The emphasis in the text is Clausewitz's.

26. See the fine study by Ethan S. Rafuse, *McClellan's War: The Failure of Moderation in the Struggle for the Union* (Bloomington: Indiana University Press, 2005).

27. Weigley, *The American Way of War,* 81.

28. As quoted by Perry D. Jamieson, *Crossing the Deadly Ground: United States Army Tactics, 1865–1899* (Tuscaloosa: University of Alabama Press, 1994), 120–21.

29. John A. Nagl, *Learning to Eat Soup with a Knife: Counterinsurgency Lessons from Malaya to Vietnam* (Chicago: University of Chicago Press, [2002] 2005), 44.

30. The quote and the discussion come from Robert M. Cassidy, "Prophets or Praetorians? The Utopian Paradox and the Powell Corollary," *Parameters* (Autumn 2003), 132–34.

31. Victor Davis Hanson, *The Western Way of War: Infantry Battle in Classical Greece* (Oxford: Oxford University Press, [1989] 1990), xv.

32. Upton as quoted in Cassidy, "Prophets or Praetorians," 133.

33. J. Paul de B. Taillon, *The Evolution of Special Forces in Counter-Terrorism: The British and American Experiences* (Westport, CT: Praeger Publishers, 2001), 4, 64; Avi Kober, "Low-Intensity Conflicts: Why the Gap Between Theory and Practice?" *Defense and Security Analysis,* vol. 18 (March 2002), 18–19.

34. Thomas S. Langston, *Uneasy Balance: Civil–Military Relations in Peacetime America Since 1783* (Baltimore: Johns Hopkins University Press, 2003), 43–44.

35. Frank N. Schubert, "The American Military Tradition and Post-Cold War Operations," in Conrad C. Crane, ed., *Transforming Defense* (Carlisle, PA: Strategic Studies Institute, U.S. Army War College, 2001), 34.

36. Robert M. Cassidy, "Back to the Street without Joy: Counterinsurgency Lessons from Vietnam and Other Small Wars," *Parameters* (Summer 2004), 74–75. Of course, the record was not that consistent, as demonstrated by the attack at Wounded Knee Creek in 1890.

37. Keith B. Bickel, *Mars Learning: The Marine Corps Development of Small Wars Doctrine, 1915–1940* (Boulder, CO: Westview Press, 2001), 48.

38. Langston, *Uneasy Balance,* 48–51. For more on the Philippines, see Brian McAllister Linn, *The Philippine War, 1899–1902* (Lawrence: University Press of Kansas, 2000); Stuart C. Miller, *"Benevolent Assimilation": The American Conquest of the Philippines, 1899–1903* (New Haven, CT: Yale University Press, 1982).

39. James R. Holmes, *Theodore Roosevelt and World Order: Police Power in International Relations* (Washington, DC: Potomac Books, 2006), 210–11.

40. As quoted in Bickel, *Small Wars,* xi, 1. The *Small Wars Manual* is available online at http://www.smallwars.quantico.usmc.mil/swm/1215.pdf.

41. Seyom Brown, *The Illusion of Control: Force and Foreign Policy in the Twenty-First Century* (Washington, DC: Brookings Institution Press, 2003), 17–18.

42. See the brief but insightful discussion in Weigley, *The American Way of War,* 406–407.

43. George F. Kennan, *Memoirs, Vol. I: 1925–1950,* pbk. ed. (New York: Bantam Books, 1967), 325–29. Also see Giles D. Harlow and George C. Maerz, eds., *Measures Short of War: The George F. Kennan Lectures at the National War College, 1946–47* (Washington, DC: National Defense University Press, 1991).

44. See Christopher M. Gacek, *The Logic of Force: The Dilemma of Limited War in American Foreign Policy* (New York: Columbia University Press, 1994), 40–41.

45. See NSC 68, which is printed in full in S. Nelson Drew, ed., *NSC-68: Forging the Strategy of Containment* (Washington, DC: National Defense University Press, 1994), 46. Also see John Lewis Gaddis, *Strategies of Containment: A Critical Appraisal of Postwar American National Security Policy* (New York: Oxford University Press, 1982), 89–109; Samuel F. Wells, Jr., "Sounding the Tocsin: NSC 68 and the Soviet Threat," *International Security,* IV (Fall 1979), 116–38, and Gacek, *The Logic of Force,* 45–47.

46. Ibid., 36–37. Also see Bruce Kuklick, *Blind Oracles: Intellectuals and War from Kennan to Kissinger* (Princeton, NJ: Princeton University Press, 2006), 59–60.

47. Weigley, *The American Way of War,* 407–409; Kuklick, *Blind Oracles,* 19–48; Paul N. Edwards, *The Closed World: Computers and the Politics of Discourse in Cold War America* (Cambridge, MA: MIT Press, 1996), 120.

48. Edwards, *The Closed World,* 125–34; Kuklick, *Blind Oracles,* 97–101.

49. Morris Janowitz, *The Professional Soldier: A Social and Political Portrait* (New York: Free Press of Glencoe, 1960), 264.

50. Gacek, *The Logic of Force,* 87–90; Lewis, *The American Culture of War,* 85.

51. Lewis, *The American Culture of War,* 85.

52. See Gaddis, *Strategies of Containment,* 127–63.

53. See Robert E. Osgood, *Limited War: The Challenge to American Strategy* (Chicago: University of Chicago Press, 1957); and Henry A. Kissinger, *Nuclear Weapons and Foreign Policy* (New York: Harper, 1957). For a short discussion of their writings, see Weigley, *The American Way of War,* 410–17. Also see Gacek, *The Logic of Force,* 134–35.

54. Weigley, *The American Way of War,* 434. See Bernard Brodie, *Strategy in the Missile Age* (Princeton, NJ: Princeton University Press, 1959), 35–57.

55. Maxwell D. Taylor, *The Uncertain Trumpet* (New York: Harper, 1960); James M. Gavin, *War and Peace in the Space Age* (New York: Harper, 1958). Also see Weigley, *The American Way of War,* 420–24; and Lewis, *The American Culture of War,* 203–10.

56. Gaddis, *Strategies of Containment,* 198–236.

57. Susan L. Marquis, *Unconventional Warfare: Rebuilding U.S. Special Operations Forces* (Washington, DC: Brookings Institution Press, 1997), 10–12.

58. See Richard Slotkin, *Gunfighter Nation: The Myth of the Frontier in Twentieth-Century America* (New York: Harper Collins, 1992), 445. Its title may cause students of U.S. strategy to overlook it, but the book's last half presents a very insightful analysis of U.S. strategy through the first Gulf War. Also see fn. 59.

59. For the quotation see James Nathan, "The New Strategy: Force and Diplomacy in American Foreign Policy," *Defense Analysis,* vol. 11 (August 1995), 122. For the trust in technology in both economic development and the battlefield, see Michael Adas, *Dominance by Design: Technological Imperatives and America's Civilizing Mission* (Cambridge, MA: Belknap Press of Harvard University Press, 2006), 261–336.

60. Marquis, *Unconventional Warfare,* 14–33; David E. Johnson, *Modern U.S. Civil–Military Relations: Wielding the Terrible Swift Sword* (Washington, DC: National Defense University Press, 1997), 26–28.

61. Michael S. Sherry, *In the Shadow of War: The United States since the 1930's* (New Haven, CT: Yale University Press, 1995), 243. For a good, short overview of a very complex subject, see Dale R. Herspring, *The Pentagon and the Presidency: Civil–Military Relations from FDR to George W. Bush* (Lawrence: University Press of Kansas, 2005), 118–23, 140–49.

62. Much of this is drawn from Cassidy, "Back to the Street Without Joy," 76–78.

63. James William Gibson, *The Perfect War: The War We Couldn't Lose and How We Did* (New York: Vintage Books, [1986] 1988), 78–82, 97–129, 155–64; Edwards, *The Closed World,* 139–40.

64. Weigley, *The American Way of War,* 477.

65. Gacek, *The Logic of Force,* 224–49.

66. John J. Weltman, *World Politics and the Evolution of War* (Baltimore: Johns Hopkins University Press, 1995), 184.

67. Kenneth J. Campbell, "Once Burned, Twice Cautious: Explaining the Weinberger-Powell Doctrine," *Armed Forces & Society,* vol. 24 (Spring 1998), 358.

68. Richard Lock-Pullan, " 'An Inward Looking Time': The United States Army, 1973–1976," *The Journal of Military History,* 67 (April 2003), 484, 491; Frederick W. Kagan, *Finding the Target: The Transformation of American Military Policy* (New York: Encounter Books, 2006), 17.

69. Andrew J. Bacevich, *The New American Militarism: How Americans Are Seduced by War* (Oxford: Oxford University Press, 2005), 39; Langston, *Uneasy Balance,* 87; Charles Moskos, "Toward a New Conception of the Citizen Soldier," E-Notes, Foreign Policy Research Institute (April 7, 2005), http://www.fpri.org/enotes/20050407.military.moskos.nowconceptioncitizensoldier; James Jay Carafano, "The Army Reserves and the Abrams Doctrine: Unfulfilled Promise, Uncertain Future," *Heritage Lectures,* no. 869 (Washington, DC: Heritage Foundation, April 18, 2005); Lewis Sorley, "Reserve Components: Looking Back to Look Ahead," *Joint Force Quarterly* (December 2004), electronic edition, http://64.241.242.253?p/articles?mi_mOKNN/is_36/ai_n13807580/print. Also see Kagan, *Finding the Target,* 17–18.

70. For the quote of Hopkins, see Andrew Huelfer, *The "Casualty Issue" in Amer-*

ican Military Practice: The Impact of World War I (Westport, CT: Praeger Publishers, 2003), xiii. Also see Colin McInnes, *Spectator-Sport War: The West and Contemporary Conflict* (Boulder, CO: Lynne Rienner Publishers, 2002), 69.

71. Lewis, *The American Culture of War,* xix.

72. See Harry G. Summers, Jr., *On Strategy: A Critical Analysis of the Vietnam War* (Washington, DC: Government Printing Office, 1981; Novato, CA: Presidio Books, 1982). Helpful critical discussions of Summers's influence are in Gacek, *The Logic of Force,* 224–29, and Cassidy, "Prophets or Praetorians?" 138–39; see fn. 30.

73. Andrew Kripinevich, Jr., *The Army and Vietnam* (Baltimore: Johns Hopkins University Press, 1986), 4–5. Also discussed in Gacek, *The Logic of Force,* 221–23, and BDM Corporation, *A Study of the Strategic Lessons in Vietnam, Volume III, Results of the War* (Washington, DC: Defense Technical Information Center, 1981), 4-3–4-14, 4-22; and Cassidy, "Prophets or Praetorians," 138.

74. This is discussed in Kinross, "Clausewitz and Low-Intensity Conflict," 50.

75. See discussion in Gacek, *The Logic of Force,* 234–36; and Lock-Pullan, "An Inward Looking Time," 505–509.

76. Quoted by Richard M. Swain, "Square Pegs from Round Holes: Low-Intensity Conflict in Army Doctrine," *Military Review,* vol. 69 (December 1987), 2–15. Also see Gacek, *The Logic of Force,* 236–37.

77. Ibid., 251–59.

78. Sherry, *In the Shadow of War,* 339; Kagan, *Finding the Target,* 95.

79. Slotkin, *Gunfighter Nation,* 651–52.

80. As quoted by Kenneth Campbell in "Once Burned, Twice Cautious," 366. Campbell draws the quotation from Robert Woodward, *The Commanders* (New York: Simon and Schuster, 1991), 324.

81. George Shultz, address before the Trilateral Commission, April 3, 1984, *Department of State Bulletin* (May 1984), 12. Also see Gacek, *The Logic of Force,* 263; and Barry M. Blechman and Tamara Cofman Wittes, "Defining Moment: The Thread and Use of Force in American Foreign Policy," *Political Science Quarterly* (Spring 1999), 1–3.

82. Gacek, *The Logic of Force,* 264–65.

83. Ibid., 265–66. The text is quoted from Gacek, including his quotes from the speech, which Weinberger iterated again in "U.S. Defense Strategy," *Foreign Affairs,* vol. 64 (Spring 1986), 675–97, especially 686–87.

84. Gacek, *The Logic of Force,* 266, mainly for the point on vital interests.

85. George P. Shultz, *Turmoil and Triumph: My Years as Secretary of State* (New York: Charles Scribner's Sons, 193), 650. Also see Jeffrey Record, "Weinberger-Powell Doctrine Doesn't Cut It," *United States Naval Institute Proceedings* (October 2000), electronic edition, pqdweb?TS=97412281&Did=000000062318539&Mtd=1&Fmt=4&Sid=3&Idx=1&Deli.

86. David Jablonsky, "Army Transformation: A Tale of Two Doctrines," in Crane, ed., *Transforming Defense,* 55. See section titled, "Who Respects the War Powers Resolution?," Chapter 3 of this volume.

87. Marquis, *Unconventional Warfare,* 80–86, 132–34, 136–46, 183–87, 187–201.

88. For the Gulf War, see Michael R. Gordon and Bernard F. Trainor, *The Generals' War: The Inside Story of the Conflict in the Gulf* (Boston: Little Brown and Co., 1995). Different views of air power in the Gulf War are in General Buster Glosson, USAF (ret), *War with Iraq* (Charlotte, NC: Glosson Family Foundation, 2003); General Chuck Horner (ret) with Tom Clancy, *Every Man a Tiger* (New York: G.P. Putnam and Sons,

1999), and Thomas A. Keaney and Eliot A. Cohen, *Revolution in Warfare: Air Power in the Persian Gulf* (Annapolis, MD: Naval Institute Press, 1995).

89. Thomas P.M. Bartlett, *The Pentagon's New Map: War and Peace in the Twenty-First Century* (New York: Berkley Books, 2004), 60.

90. The literature on this is immense. Right here, I have drawn from the following: Mary Kaldor, *New and Old Wars: Organized Violence in a Global Era* (Stanford, CA: Stanford University Press, 1999), 1–12; Münkler, *The New Wars,* 5–31, 75–81; Philippe Delmas, *The Rosy Future of War* (New York: Free Press, 1995), 149–53, first published in France as *Le Bel Avenir de la Guerre* by Editions Gallimard; Martin van Creveld, *The Transformation of War* (New York: Free Press, 1991), 197–98; Sam C. Sarkesian, "Special Operations, Low-Intensity Conflict (Unconventional Conflicts), and the Clinton Defense Strategy," in Stephen J. Cimbala, *Clinton and Post–Cold War Defense* (Westport, CT: Praeger Publishers, 1996), 104–105; Edward Rice, *Wars of the Third Kind: Conflict in Underdeveloped Countries* (Berkeley: University of California Press, 1988); General Rupert Smith, *The Utility of Force: The Art of War in the Modern World* (New York: Alfred A. Knopf, 2007), 5–6; Holsti, *The State, War, and the State of War,* 36–37; and Thomas X. Hammes, *The Sling and the Stone: On War in the 21st Century* (St. Paul, MN: Zenith Press, 2004), 2–4, 20–23.

91. See Münkler, *The New Wars,* 100.

92. The description is used by Max Boot for the title of his study of the United States in small wars.

93. Barnett, *The Pentagon's New Map,* 60–61.

94. M.L.R. Smith, "Guerrillas in the Mist: Reassessing Strategy and Low Intensity Warfare," *Review of International Studies,* vol. 29 (January 2003), 30–31.

95. Colin L. Powell, "U.S. Forces, Challenges Ahead," *Foreign Affairs,* vol. 71 (Winter 1992–1993), reprinted in Richard N. Haass, *Intervention: The Use of American Military Force in the Post–Cold War World* (Washington, DC: Brookings Institution Press, 1999), 216–17, 219.

96. Colin L. Powell, with Joseph E. Persico, *My American Journey* (New York: Random House, 1995), 576.

97. Powell quoted in Lawrence F. Kaplan, "Yesterday's Man: Colin Powell's Out-of-Date Foreign Policy," *The New Republic* (January 1, 2001), 5, electronic edition, http://www.tnr.com/01010/kaplan010101.

98. Powell, "U.S. Forces, Challenges Ahead," 220.

99. See John Stone, "Politics, Technology and the Revolution in Military Affairs," *The Journal of Strategic Studies,* vol. 27 (September 2004), 417–18.

100. David W. Lutz, "The Ethics of American Military Policy in Africa," 3–5, available on the website of the Joint Service Committee on Professional Ethics, http://www.usafa.af.mil/jscope/JSCOPE00/lutz00.

101. See Donald M. Snow, "Peacekeeping, Peace Enforcement, and Clinton Defense Policy," in Stephen Cimbala, ed., *Clinton and Post–Cold War Defense,* 97–99; and Haass, *Intervention,* 229–58, which reproduces most of the items in the text.

102. Alexander L. George, "Foreword," in Robert J. Art and Patrick M. Cronin, *The United States and Coercive Diplomacy* (Washington, DC: United States Institute of Peace Press, 2003), vii. Also see George, "The Role of Force in Diplomacy: A Continuing Dilemma for U.S. Foreign Policy," in H.W. Brands, ed., *The Use of Force after the Cold War* (College Station: Texas A&M University Press, 2000), 59–92.

103. Dana Priest, *The Mission: Waging War and Keeping Peace with America's Mil-*

itary (New York: W.W. Norton & Co., 2003), 52. For additional discussion of this coercive diplomacy see Daniel Byman and Matthew Waxman, *The Dynamics of Coercion: American Foreign Policy and the Limits of Military Might* (Cambridge: Cambridge University Press, 2002), 3.

104. The new criteria for intervention will be discussed in Chapter 5, this volume.

105. As quoted in Lyle J. Goldstein, "General John Shalikashvili and the Civil–Military Relations of Peacekeeping," *Armed Forces & Society,* vol. 26 (Spring 2000), 399–400, and David Halberstam, *War in a Time of Peace: Bush, Clinton, and the Generals* (New York: Charles Scribner, 2001), 278–79.

106. Halberstam, *War in a Time of Peace,* 279, 319–23; Goldstein, "General John Shalikashvili and Civil–Military Relations," 404.

107. See Peter D. Feaver, *Armed Servants: Agency, Oversight, and Civil–Military Relations* (Cambridge, MA: Harvard University Press, 2003), 65–67.

108. See *Joint Doctrine for Military Operations Other Than War,* June 16, 1995, Joint Pub 3-07 (Washington, DC: Department of Defense, 1995), vii-viii, and as discussed in Goldstein, "General John Shalikashvili and Civil Military Operations," 400.

109. Kagan, *Finding the Target,* 160, 167–70.

110. See Richard A. Lacqument, Jr., "The Casualty Aversion Myth," *Naval War College Review,* vol. 57 (Winter 2004), 39–57; Peter D. Feaver and Christopher Gelpi, *Choosing Your Battles: American Civil–Military Relations and the Use of Force* (Princeton, NJ: Princeton University Press, 2004), 94–148; Steven Kull and I.M. Destler, *Misreading the Public: The Myth of a New Isolationism* (Washington, DC: Brookings Institution Press, 1999), 81–112. For a recent alternative view, see John Mueller, "The Iraq Syndrome," *Foreign Affairs,* vol. 84 (November/December 2005), 44–54.

111. Concern about a widening civil–military gap that went beyond the matter of use of force was the subject of a large study released by Peter D. Feaver and Richard H. Kohn, eds., *Soldiers and Civilians: The Civil–Military Gap and American National Security* (Cambridge, MA: MIT Press, 2001). Feaver largely confirmed this view about civilian proclivity to support the use of force in *Choosing Your Battles,* 21–63. Thus, the belief had some basis. A slightly different interpretation by Benjamin O. Fordham, "A Very Sharp Sword: The Influence of Military Capabilities on American Decisions to Use Force," *Journal of Conflict Resolution,* vol. 58 (October 2004), 632–56, argues that decision makers are more inclined to use force when they know they have greater amounts of capability. This is less dependent on professional background of the person making the decision.

112. Wesley K. Clark, *Waging Modern War* (New York: Public Affairs, 2001), xxviii, but throughout the book at many points Clark criticizes the political restraints imposed from Washington. Also see Jeffrey Record, "Operation Allied Force Yet Another Wake-up Call for the Army?" *Parameters,* vol. 29 (Winter 1999/2000), 2.

113. The role of technology, especially information technology and its implications for strategy and Congress, is examined in greater depth in Chapter 6, this volume. For cautionary pieces at the time, see Stephen Blank, "The Illusion of a Short War," *SAIS Review,* vol. 20 (2000), 133–51; Max Boot, "Envisioning a Future of Casualty-Free Pushbutton Wars? Get Over It," *The American Enterprise* (October/November 2001), 28–31; and Boot, *War Made New: Technology, Warfare, and the Course of History, 1500 to Today* (New York: Gotham Books, 2006), 350. Also see Lewis, *The American Culture of War,* 378; and Kagan, *Finding the Target,* 194–98.

114. Richard N. Haass, *Intervention,* rev. ed. (Washington, DC: Brookings Institution Press, 1999), 93–94.

115. See Robert J. Art, "Coercive Diplomacy: What Do We Know?" in Robert J. Art and Patrick M. Cronin, eds., *The United States and Coercive Diplomacy* (Washington, DC: United States Institute of Peace Press, 2003), 361–70; and Susan L. Woodward, "Upside-Down Policy: The U.S. Debate on the Use of Force and the Case of Bosnia," in H.W. Brands, ed., *The Use of Force after the Cold War* (College Station: Texas A&M University Press, 2000), 123, 130.

116. J.H. Plumb, *The Death of the Past* (London: Penguin, 1969), 67; Christopher Coker, "The United States and the Ethics of Post-Modern War," in Karen E. Smith and Margot Light, eds., *Ethics and Foreign Policy* (Cambridge: Cambridge University Press, 2001), 155.

117. See Chapter 5, this volume, for an elaboration of this argument.

118. Antulio J. Echevarria II, *Toward an American Way of War* (Carlisle, PA: Strategic Studies Institute, U.S. Army War College, March 2004), 10.

119. For examples, see Thomas E. Ricks, *Fiasco: The American Military Adventure in Iraq* (New York: Penguin Press, 2006), still possibly the best overall view of the short-term aspects of political and military planning; Kagan, *Finding the Target,* 323–59; Larry Diamond, *Squandered Victory: The American Occupation and the Bungled Effort to Bring Democracy to Iraq* (New York: Times Books, 2005). The literature on American difficulties in Iraq continues to grow daily.

120. Jeremy Black, *War: Past, Present & Future* (New York: St. Martin's Press, 2000), 286–87.

121. For Pakistan, see Priest, *The Mission,* 110–11. Priest adds here the important factor that Congress in 1991 through the behest of the Special Operations Command permitted such units "to train in most foreign countries if the Pentagon certified that the training mainly benefited U.S. forces." Given the potential use of special operations, it was hardly the most vigorous congressional oversight.

122. James Kitfield, *War and Destiny: How the Bush Revolution in Foreign and Military Affairs Redefined American Power* (Washington, DC: Potomac Books, 2005), 140; Kagan, *Finding the Target,* 310–20.

123. Stephen Biddle, "Afghanistan and the Future of Warfare," *Foreign Affairs,* vol. 82 (March/April 2003), 31–46. The best account of Operation Anaconda is Sean Naylor, *Not a Good Day to Die: The Untold Story of Operation Anaconda* (New York: Berkley Books, 2005), 135–36, for one example of the problems mentioned by Biddle.

124. Parts of this are drawn from Kitfield, *War and Destiny,* 141. Although concerned about the challenge of long-term stabilization of Iraq, the success of the initial military campaign is described in Williamson Murray and Major General Robert H. Scales, Jr., *The Iraq War: A Military History* (Cambridge, MA: Belknap Press of Harvard University Press, 2003). John Keegan in *The Iraq War* (New York: Alfred A. Knopf, 2004) presents a fairly positive analysis, while Michael R. Gordon and Bernard E. Trainor, *Cobra II: The Inside Story of the Invasion and Occupation of Iraq* (New York: Pantheon Books, 2006) are more critical as is Ricks, *Fiasco.*

125. Colin McInnes, "A Different Kind of War? September 11 and the United States' Afghan War," *Review of International Studies,* vol. 29 (April 2003), 167. Even though this article is about Afghanistan, its point applies equally well to Iraq.

126. Kitfield, *War and Destiny,* 271.

127. John Mueller, "The Iraq Syndrome, *Foreign Affairs,* vol. 84 (November/ December 2005), 44–54.

128. John Mueller, *The Remnants of War* (Ithaca, NY: Cornell University Press, 2004), 141–51.

129. Barry M. Blechman and Stephen S. Kaplan, *Force Without War: U.S. Armed Forces as a Political Instrument* (Washington, DC: Brookings Institution, 1978), 525.

130. This is a central point in Lewis, *The American Culture of War.* The causes and implications of this are examined more closely in Chapter 6, this volume.

131. See, in particular, Deborah Avant, *Political Institutions and Military Change: Lessons from Imperial Wars* (Ithaca, NY: Cornell University Press, 1994), 130–39; and Nagl, *Learning to Eat Soup with a Knife,* 206–207.

5   Justifying Intervention and the Increase of Presidential Power

1. Condoleezza Rice, "Promoting the National Interest," *Foreign Affairs,* vol. 79 (January/February 2000), 62. Also see the discussion of this speech in Michael Byers, "Introduction; The Complexities of Foundational Change," in Michael Byers and Georg Nolte, *United States Hegemony and the Foundations of International Law* (Cambridge: Cambridge University Press, 2003), 45.

2. White House, *The National Security Strategy of the United States of America,* September 17, 2002, http://www.whitehouse.gov/nsc/nss.html.

3. The degree to which the Bush administration policies provided discontinuity or continuity with the historical record of U.S. foreign policy has generated a staggering amount of literature. Here, the author is thinking especially of John Lewis Gaddis, "A Grand Strategy of Transformation," *Foreign Policy* (November/December 2002), 56, and the same author's *Surprise, Security, and the American Experience* (Cambridge, MA: Harvard University Press, 2004). Also see Ivo H. Daalder and James M. Lindsay, *America Unbound: The Bush Revolution in Foreign Policy* (Washington, DC: Brookings Institution Press, 2003), and Walter Russell Mead, *Power, Terror, Peace, and War: America's Grand Strategy in a World at Risk* (New York: Alfred A. Knopf, 2004). Recently, see Tony Smith, *A Pact with the Devil: Washington's Bid for World Supremacy and the Betrayal of the American Promise* (New York: Routledge, 2007), especially 53–82. This writer discussed the question in Kenneth B. Moss, "Reasserting American Exceptionalism—Confronting the World: The National Security Strategy of the Bush Administration," *Internationale Politik und Gesellschaft,* vol. 3 (2003), 135–55.

4. See Anders Stephanson, *Manifest Destiny: American Expansionism and the Empire of Right* (New York: Hill & Wang, 1995), 7–15; and Robert W. Tucker and David C. Hendrickson, *Empire of Liberty: The Statecraft of Thomas Jefferson* (New York: Oxford University Press, 1990), ix, 11–21.

5. Fred Anderson and Andrew Cayton, *The Dominion of War: Empire and Liberty in North America, 1500–2000* (New York: Viking, 2005), xviii. Also see Robert A. Divine, *Perpetual War for Perpetual Peace* (College Station: Texas A&M University Press, 2000), 36; and Anthony F. Lang, *Agency and Ethics: The Politics of Military Intervention* (Albany: State University of New York Press, 2002), 36–37 and 50–51. A recent defense of this American tradition is in Michael Ignatieff, "Who Are the Americans to Think that Freedom Is Theirs to Spread?" *The New York Times Magazine,* June 26, 2005, pp. 42–47.

6. As quoted by Michael Northcott, *An Angel Directs the Storm: Apocalyptic Religion and American Empire* (London: I.B. Tauris & Co., Ltd., 2004), 22.

7. As quoted in Robert Jewett and John Shelton Lawrence, *Captain America and the Crusade Against Evil: The Dilemma of Zealous Nationalism* (Grand Rapids, MI: W.B. Eerdmans, 2003), 4, 126. Also see Stephen H. Webb, *American Providence: A Nation with a Mission* (New York: Continuum, 2004), 12.

8. Richard B. Miller, *Interpretations to Conflict: Ethics, Pacifism, and the Just-War Tradition* (Chicago: University of Chicago Press, 1991), 209.

9. An opinion forcefully argued by Robert H. Bork in "The Limits of 'International Law,'" *The National Interest,* no. 18 (Winter 1989–1990), 3–10.

10. William V. O'Brien, *The Conduct of Just and Limited War* (New York: Praeger Publishers, 1981), 3.

11. The distinctions are drawn by Mary Kaldor in "American Power: From Compellance to Cosmopolitanism?" *International Affairs,* vol. 79 (January 2003), 9.

12. Edward Luttwak, "Kofi's Rule: Humanitarian Intervention and Neocolonialism," *The National Interest,* no. 58 (Winter 1999/2000), 59.

13. Robert W. Tucker, *The Just War: A Study in Contemporary American Doctrine* (Baltimore: Johns Hopkins University Press, 1960), 11–12.

14. An argument made by Robert Divine in *Perpetual War for Perpetual Peace,* 18–19.

15. Bernard Brodie, *Strategy in the Missile Age* (Princeton, NJ: Princeton University Press, [1959] 1965), 241–57.

16. Robert E. Sherwood, *Roosevelt and Hopkins: An Intimate History,* rev. ed. (New York: Harper Brothers, 1948, 1952), 426–28.

17. See Alan M. Dershowitz, *Preemption: A Knife That Cuts Both Ways* (New York: W.W. Norton & Co., 2006), 19. Concern about WMD underlies much of this book. Alex J. Bellamy, *Just Wars: From Cicero to Iraq* (Cambridge: Polity Press, 2006), 164–65. Robert S. Litwak examines the claims about WMD in relation to other justifications for the invasion of Iraq in his *Regime Change: U.S. Strategy through the Prism of 9/11* (Washington, DC: Wilson Center Press, published by Johns Hopkins University Press, 2007), 125–68.

18. James Mann, *Rise of the Vulcans: The History of Bush's War Cabinet* (New York: Viking, 2004), xvi, 52; Stefan Halper and Jonathan Clarke, *America Alone: The Neo-Conservatives and the Global Order* (Cambridge: Cambridge University Press, 2004), 60–64, 92.

19. George P. Fletcher, *Romantics at War: Glory and Guilt in the Age of Terrorism* (Princeton, NJ: Princeton University Press, 2002), 15–16. Fletcher's book states a case for this form of romanticism.

20. J.E. Hare and Carey B. Joynt, *Ethics and International Affairs* (London: Macmillan, 1982), 151, as excerpted in Lawrence Freedman, ed., *War* (Oxford: Oxford University Press, 1994), 182.

21. James G. Roche and George E. Pickett, Jr., "Organizing the Government to Provide the Tools for Intervention," in Arnold Kanter and Linton F. Brooks, eds., *U.S. Intervention Policy for the Post–Cold War World: New Challenges and New Responses* (New York: W.W. Norton and Co., 1994), 196.

22. Monroe E. Price and Mark Thompson, "Introduction," and Eric Blinderman, "International Law and Information Intervention," in Price and Thompson, *Forging Peace: Intervention, Human Rights and the Management of Media Space* (Bloomington: Indiana University Press, 2002), 12, 106, 125. The quote is from Blinderman, 106.

23. Tucker and Hendrickson, *Empire of Liberty,* 50–52.

24. Ernest R. May, *The Making of the Monroe Doctrine* (Cambridge, MA: Belknap Press of Harvard University Press, 1975).

25. See section titled "Global Ambition, the Power, and the Presidency," Chapter 2, this volume.

26. Martha Finnemore, *The Purpose of Intervention: Changing Beliefs About the Use of Force* (Ithaca, NY: Cornell University Press, 2003), 31–38.

27. Simon Chesterman, *Just War or Just Peace? Humanitarian Intervention and International Law* (Oxford: Oxford University Press, 2001), 8–16; Bellamy, *Just Wars,* 203–204; Danish Institute of International Affairs, *Humanitarian Intervention: Legal and Political Aspects* (Copenhagen: Danish Institute of International Affairs, 1999), 11.

28. Martha Fennimore, *The Purpose of Intervention: Changing Beliefs about the Use of Force* (Ithaca, NY: Cornell University Press, 2003), 58–66; Hans Koehler, *Global Justice or Global Revenge/International Criminal Justice at the Crossroads* (Vienna: Springer-Verlag, 2003), 271–73.

29. Samantha Power, *A Problem from Hell: America and the Age of Genocide* (New York: Perennial, [2002] 2003), 1–16.

30. See Article 2 of the UN Charter in W. Michael Reisman and Chris T. Antoniu, eds., *The Laws of War: A Comprehensive Collection of Primary Documents on International Laws of Governing Armed Conflict* (New York: Vintage Books, 1994), 5; and for the Nuremberg Tribunal and Genocide Convention, see Adam Roberts and Richard Guelff, *Documents on the Laws of War,* 3rd ed. (Oxford: Oxford University Press, 2004), 175–84. The U.S. Senate finally ratified the Genocide Convention in 1980; see Susan E. Rice and Andrew J. Loomis, "The Evolution of Humanitarian Intervention and the Responsibility to Protect," in Ivo H. Daalder, ed., *Beyond Preemption: Force and Legitimacy in a Changing World* (Washington, DC: Brookings Institution Press, 2007), 60.

31. Reisman and Antoniu, eds., *The Laws of War,* 6–7. This and other more technical arguments are summed up very well by Chesterman in *Just War or Just Peace?,* 48–53.

32. As quoted in Danish Institute of International Affairs, *Humanitarian Intervention,* 14.

33. See Simon Reich, "The Curious Case of Kofi Annan, George W. Bush, and the 'Preemptive' Military Force Doctrine," in William W. Keller and Gordon Mitchell, eds., *Hitting First: Preventive Force in U.S. Security Strategy* (Pittsburgh, PA: University of Pittsburgh Press, 2006), 54–60; Ove Bring, "Should NATO Take the Lead in Formulating a Doctrine on Humanitarian Intervention?" *NATO Review,* vol. 47 (Autumn 1999), 2–3, electronic edition,pqdweb?TS=974132208&Did+000000046430829&Mtd=1&Fmt=4& Sid=1&Idx=20&Deli; and Kofi Annan, "Courage to Fulfill Our Responsibilities," *The Economist,* December 4, 2004, 25.

34. Karen A. Feste, *Intervention: Shaping the Global Order* (Westport, CT: Praeger, 2003), xvii.

35. Letter of Michael Ignatieff to Robert Skidelsky, May 97, 1999, reproduced in Michael Ignatieff, *Virtual War: Kosovo and Beyond* (New York: Metropolitan Books, 2000), 82.

36. The characterization of realist and liberal advocates of intervention come from Michael W. Doyle, *Ways of War and Peace* (New York: W.W. Norton & Co., 1997), 390–92, 396–402. See Ignatieff citation in fn. 5.

37. The trend is noted by Fennimore, *The Purpose of Intervention,* 79, but without mentioning Bush. See the text of the 1948 United Nations Convention in Roberts and Guelff, *Documents on the Laws of War,* 281–84.

38. Michael Reisman is the leading proponent of this particular argument. See W. Michael Reisman, "Coercion and Self-Determination: Construing Charter Art 2(4),"

vol. 78, *American Journal of International Law,* 642. A good overview is in Chesterman, *Just War or Just Peace?,* 55–56.

39. Ibid., 123–24.

40. Quoted in Anthony F. Lang, *Agency and Ethics: The Politics of Military Intervention* (Albany: State University of New York Press, 2002), 176.

41. Adam Wolfson, "Humanitarian Hawks? Why Kosovo but Not Kuwait," *Policy Review,* vol. 98 (December 1999/January 2000), 5–6, electronic edition, . . . /pqdweb? TS=974141257&Did=000000046824188&Mtd=1&Fmt=3&Sid=2&Idx=18&Deli. Also see Michael Dobbs, *Madeleine Albright: A Twentieth-Century Odyssey* (New York: Henry Holt and Co., [1999] 2000), 358, 403.

42. Dobbs, *Madeleine Albright,* 403.

43. Marcelo G. Kohen, "The Use of Force by the United States after the End of the Cold War, and its Impact on International Law," in Byers and Nolte, *United States Hegemony and the Foundations of International Law,* 229–30.

44. William V. O'Brien, "The Rule of Law in Small Wars," *Annals of the American Academy of Political and Social Science,* vol. 451 (September 1995), 41. O'Brien already gives humanitarian intervention that status.

45. This is an argument drawn from Reich, "The Curious Case of Kofi Annan," 61–64.

46. Robert S. Litwak, *Rogue States and U.S. Foreign Policy* (Washington, DC: Wilson Center Press, published by Johns Hopkins University Press, 2000); Litwak, "The New Calculus of Preemption," *Survival,* vol. 44, no. 4 (Winter 2002–2003), 53–80. See *The National Security Strategy of the United States of America,* September 17, 2002, http://www.whitehouse.gov/nsc/nss.html; and *The National Security Strategy of the United States,* March 16, 2006, http://www.whitehouse.gov/nsc/nss/2006/nss2006.pdf.

47. Gaines M. Foster, "A Christian Nation: Signs of a Covenant," in John Bodnar, ed., *Bonds of Affection: Americans Define Their Patriotism* (Princeton, NJ: Princeton University Press, 1996), 138; Webb, *American Providence,* 25, and Patrick Allitt, *Religion in America Since 1945: A History* (New York: Columbia University Press, 2003), 100–107.

48. Paul Boyer, *When Time Shall Be No More: Prophecy Belief in Modern American Culture* (Cambridge, MA: Belknap Press of Harvard University Press, 1994); Northcott, *An Angel Directs the Storm,* 15–17.

49. Jewett and Lawrence, *Captain America and the Crusade Against Evil,* 138–41; Anne C. Loveland, *American Evangelicals and the U.S. Military, 1941–1993* (Baton Rouge: Louisiana State University Press, 1996), 163; Warren L. Vinz, *Pulpit Politics: Faces of American Protestant Nationalism in the Twentieth Century* (Albany: State University of New York Press, 1997), 11–12; Northcott, *An Angel Directs the Storm,* 35–36, 44. Falwell and Robertson came under heavy criticism after 9/11 when they characterized the attacks as part of God's retribution against the United States because of homosexuality, abortion, and other issues; see Allitt, *Religion in America,* 253–54.

50. Geoffrey Layman, *The Great Divide: Religious and Cultural Conflict in American Party Politics* (New York: Columbia University Press, 2001), 264.

51. This discussion, including the polls, is from Charles Marsh, "Wayward Christian Soldiers," *The New York Times,* January 20, 2006, p. A19.

52. See the classic by Perry Miller, *Errand into the Wilderness* (Cambridge, MA: Belknap Press of Harvard University Press, 1956); Stephanson, *Manifest Destiny,* 10–12, and Miller, *Interpretations of Conflict,* 212.

53. Christina Hoff Sommers, "Men—It's in Their Nature," *The American Enter-*

prise, September 2003, p. 5, as quoted in Mary Nolan, "Anti-Americanism and Anti-Europeanism," in Lloyd C. Gardner and Marilyn B. Young, eds., *The New American Empire: A 21st Century Teach-in on U.S. Foreign Policy* (New York: New Press, 2005), 122. Also see George Weigel, *The Cube and the Cathedral: Europe, America, and Politics Without God* (New York: Basic Books, 2005).

54. See Joshua Green, "God's Foreign Policy," *The Washington Monthly* (November 2001), 26–33.

55. See Hans-Richard Reuter, "Die Militaerintervention gegen den Irak und die neuere Debatte ueber den 'gerechten Krieg,'" electronic edition at www.uni-muenster .de/Ethik/Reuter-Irakkrieg; and Lothar Brock, "Frieden durch Recht: Zur Verteidigung einer Idee gegen 'die harten Tatsachen' der internationalen Politik," in *Standpunkte,* Hessiche Stiftung Friedens-und Konfliktforschung, vol. 3 (2004), 6.

56. See the essays in Charles Reed and David Ryall, eds., *The Price of Peace: Just War in the Twenty-First Century* (Cambridge, MA: Cambridge University Press, 2007). Of particular value are George Weigel, "The Development of Just War Thinking in the Post–Cold War World: An American Perspective, 19–36; William Wallace, "Is There a European Approach to War?" 37–54; Nigel Biggar, "Between Development and Doubt: The Recent Career of Just War Doctrine in British Churches," 55–75; and James Turner Johnson, "Just War Thinking in Recent American Religious Debate Over Military Force," in Johnson, *Morality and Contemporary Warfare* (New Haven, CT: Yale University Press, 2001), 76–97.

57. Miller, *Interpretations of Conflict,* 35; Johnson, "The Question of Intervention," in *Morality and Contemporary Warfare,* 91–95.

58. Miller, *Interpretations of Conflict,* 27.

59. James Turner Johnson expresses this concern in his chapter, "Just War Thinking in Recent U.S. Religious Debate," in Reed and Ryall, eds., *The Price of Peace,* 93.

60. Bellamy, *Just Wars,* 121. Also, in Reed and Ryall, eds., *The Price of Peace,* see John Langan, "Justice after War and the Common Good," 219–35; Gwyn Prins, "Conditions for *Jus in Pace* in the Face of the Future," 236–54; and Mary Kaldor, "From Just War to Just Peace," 255–73.

61. This description borrows from J. Bryan Hehir, in "The Moral Dimension in the Use of Force," in Brand, ed., *The Use of Force After the Cold War,* 13.

62. Michael Walzer, *Just and Unjust Wars: A Moral Argument with Historical Illustrations,* 3rd ed. (New York: Basic Books, [1977, 1992] 2000).

63. The discussion draws from Nicholas Rengger, "On the Just War Tradition in the Twenty-First Century," *International Affairs,* vol. 78 (April 2002), 358–59; and Weigel, "Just War Thinking in the Post Cold War World," in Reed and Ryall, eds., *The Price of Peace,* 21–22.

64. Michael Walzer, "The Triumph of Just War Theory (and the Dangers of Success)," in Michael Walzer, *Arguing About War* (New Haven, CT: Yale University Press, 2004), 5–6.

65. David R. Mapel, "Realism and the Ethics of War and Peace," in Terry Nardin, ed., *The Ethics of War and Peace: Religious and Secular Perspectives* (Princeton, NJ: Princeton University Press, 1996), 59–60. Generalizing about the "realists" is not easy. Alex Bellamy stresses that Morgenthau's intention was not to rule out morality in guiding state decisions and behavior. However, Morgenthau was deeply troubled by the lack of restraint on state behavior and the growing destructiveness of modern war. He wanted restraints on war and its conduct. See Bellamy, *Just Wars,* 105–6.

66. Walzer, "The Triumph of Just War Theory," 9–11.

67. Fletcher, *Romantics at War,* 7.

68. Walzer, "The Triumph of Just War Theory," 10–11.

69. Tony Smith examines this model in "Good, Smart, or Bad Samaritan: A Case for U.S. Military Intervention for Democracy and Human Rights," in Brand, ed., *The Use of Force after the Cold War,* 36–37.

70. This discussion and quote comes from Oliver O'Donovan, *The Just War Revisited* (Cambridge: Cambridge University Press, 2003), 9.

71. Paul Christopher, *The Ethics of War and Peace: An Introduction to Legal and Moral Issues,* 2nd ed. (Upper Saddle River, NJ: Prentice-Hall, [1994] 1999), 8–15; James Turner Johnson, "Conflicts Inflamed by Cultural Difference," in James Turner Johnson, *Morality and Contemporary Warfare* (New Haven, CT: Yale University Press, 1999), 166–90; chapters by Michael Walzer, Aviezer Ravitzky, Bassam Tibi, and Sohail Ishmi in Nardin, ed., *The Ethics of War and Peace,* 95–166.

72. Herfried Münkler, *The New Wars,* translated from the German by Patrick Camiller (Cambridge: Polity Press, 2005), 62–64, originally published as *Die Neuen Kriege* (Reinbek bei Hamburg: Rowohlt Verlag GmbH, 2002); Christopher, *The Ethics of War and Peace,* 47–60.

73. Münkler, *The New Wars,* 64; Johnson, "Conditions for Just Resort to Armed Force: Just Cause, Competent Authority, and Right Intention in Historical and Contemporary Context," in Johnson, *Morality and Contemporary Warfare,* 54–55.

74. The quote is from Yoram Dinstein, *War, Aggression, and Self-Defence,* 2nd ed. (Cambridge: Cambridge University Press, 1994), 73. Also see Michael Byers, *War Law: Understanding International Law and Armed Conflict* (New York: Grove Press, 2006), 54–55.

75. The agreement is quoted from Reisman and Antoniou, *The Laws of War,* 4–5; Byers, *War Law,* 55; and Robert H. Ferrell, *Peace in Their Time: The Origins of the Kellogg-Briand Pact* (New Haven, NJ: Yale University Press, 1952).

76. UN Charter as reprinted in Reisman and Antoniou, *The Laws of War,* 6.

77. Alex J. Bellamy, "Ethics and Intervention: The 'Humanitarian Exception' and the Problem of Abuse in Iraq," *Journal of Peace Research,* vol. 41 (March 2004), 132–33, 142; O'Donovan, *The Just War Revisited,* 28–29.

78. Paul Ramsey, "The Ethics of Intervention," in Paul Ramsey, *The Just War: Force and Political Responsibility* (Lanham: University Press of American, 1983), 31, originally published in *The Review of Politics,* vol. 27 (July 1965), 287–310; Ramsey, "How Shall Counter-Insurgency War be Conducted Justly," in Ramsey, *The Just War,* 430; Johnson, "Just War Thinking in Recent U.S. Religious Debate," in Reed and Ryall, eds., *The Price of Peace,* 87.

79. For discussions of Ramsey, see Johnson, "The Question of Intervention," in Johnson, *Morality and Contemporary Warfare,* 76–81; Walzer, *Just and Unjust Wars,* 278–83.

80. Damon Linker, *The Theocons: Secular America Under Siege* (New York: Doubleday, 2006), 123–29.

81. Gregory Reichberg and Henrik Syse, "Humanitarian Intervention: A Case of Offensive Force?" *Security Dialogue,* vol. 33 (September 2002), 309.

82. Ibid., 315–17. The discussion above enters into reprisals, which are defined as "illegal acts of retaliation carried out by one party to a conflict in response to illegal acts of warfare and intended to cause the enemy to comply with the law." Quotation is from Roberts and Guelff, *Documents on the Laws of War,* 32. If they fall within the right of

self-defense recognized in Article 51 of the UN Charter, some scholars recognize their legality. Yoram Dinstein states that for them "to be defensive, and therefore lawful, armed reprisals must be future-oriented, and not limited to a desire to punish past transgressions." See Dinstein, *War, Aggression and Self-Defence,* 222. Also see Michael J. Kelly, "Time Warp to 1945—Resurrection of the Reprisal and Anticipatory Self-Defense Doctrines in International Law," *Journal of Transnational Law and Policy,* vol. 13 (Fall 2003), electronic edition, http://web.lexis-nexis.com/universe.

83. A good study of this pattern is Dominic D.P. Johnson, *Overconfidence and War: The Havoc and Glory of Positive Illusions* (Cambridge, MA: Harvard University Press, 2004).

84. Christopher, *The Ethics of War and Peace,* 12–13, 51.

85. Ibid., 85–86.

86. Laurie Calhoun, "Legitimate Authority and 'Just War' in the Modern World," *Peace and Change,* vol. 27 (January 2002), 39–41.

87. See Chapter 6, this volume.

88. Peter S. Temes, *The Just War: An American Reflection on the Morality of War in Our Time* (Chicago: Ivan Dee, 2003), 84.

89. As quoted by Williamson Murray in "Not Enough Collateral Damage: Moral Ambiguities in the Gulf War," in Mark Grimsley and Clifford R. Rogers, eds., *Civilians in the Path of War* (Lincoln: University of Nebraska Press, 2002), 255.

90. Harlan Ullman and James Wade, Jr., with L.A. Edney, et al., *Shock and Awe: Achieving Rapid Dominance* (Washington, DC: National Defense University Press, 1996), 45, 64.

91. As quoted in Christopher Jochnick and Roger Normand, "The Role of Law in the Gulf War: Protection of Civilians or Legitimation of Violence," in John O'Loughlin, Tom Mayer, and Edward S. Greenberg, eds., *War and Its Consequences: Lessons from the Persian Gulf Conflict* (New York: Harper Collins, 1994), 59.

92. See the expansion of the above chapter by Christopher Jochnick and Roger Normand in a two-part series of articles titled, "The Legitimation of Violence: A Critical History of the Laws of War," in *Harvard International Law Journal,* vol. 35 (Winter 1994) and vol. 35 (Spring 1994), electronic edition from lexisnexis@prod.lexix nexis.com. Also see Thomas W. Smith, "The New Law of War: Legitimizing Hi-Tech and Infrastructural Violence," *International Studies Quarterly,* vol. 46 (2002), 355–74.

93. Christopher B. Puckett, "In This Era of 'Smart Weapons' Is a State Under an International Legal Obligation to Use Precision-Guided Technology in Armed Conflict?" *Emory International Law Review,* vol. 18 (Fall 2004), electronic edition, lexis-nexis@prod.lexisnexis.com.

94. Adrian R. Lewis, *The American Culture of War: The History of U.S. Military Force from World War II to Operation Iraqi Freedom* (New York: Routledge, 2007), 412–35; Frederick W. Kagan, *Finding the Target: The Transformation of American Foreign Policy* (New York: Encounter Books, 2006), 327–35; Max Boot, *War Made New: Technology, Warfare, and the Course of History, 1500 to Today* (New York: Gotham Books, 2006), 384–418.

95. *The National Security Strategy of the United States of America* (March 19, 2006), 18, electronic edition, http://whitehouse.gov/nsc/nss/2006.

96. Ibid., 30–31.

97. Byers, *War Law,* 73–74; Dershowitz, *Preemption,* 164–65. See Bellamy, *Just War,* 158–79, for a good overview of the different schools of thought on preemption.

98. Michael Garcia and Arthur Traldi, *International Law and Agreements: Their Effect Upon U.S. Law,* RL 32528 (Washington, DC: Congressional Research Service, Library of Congress, August 16, 2004).

99. Louis Henkin, *Foreign Affairs and the U.S. Constitution,* 2nd ed. (Oxford: Clarendon Press of Oxford University Press, 1996), 233–35.

100. John Yoo, *The Powers of War and Peace: The Constitution and Foreign Affairs After 9/11* (Chicago: University of Chicago Press, 2005), 172.

101. John F. Murphy, *The United States and the Rule of Law in International Affairs* (Cambridge: Cambridge University Press, 2004), 74.

102. United National General Assembly Resolution 3314 (XXIX), *Definition of Aggression,* electronic edition, http://jurist.law.pitt.edu/3314; Ingrid Detter De Pupis, *The Laws of War* (Cambridge: Cambridge University Press, 1987), 60–61.

103. See excerpts from *Nicaragua v. United States of America* in Reisman and Antoniou, *The Laws of War;* Murphy, *The United States and the Rule of Law in International Affairs,* 255–66; and W. Michael Reisman, "Assessing Claims to Revise the Laws of War," *The American Journal of International Law,* vol. 97 (January 2003), 83–84.

104. See David M. Ackerman, "International Law and the Preemptive Use of Force Against Iraq," CRS Report for Congress, RS21314 (March 17, 2003), 2, electronic edition, www.house.gov/htbin/crsprodget?rs/RS21314; Abraham D. Sofaer, "On the Necessity of Pre-emption," *English Journal of International Law,* vol. 14 (2003), 214–19; Robert H. Ferrell, *American Diplomacy: A History,* 3rd ed. (New York: W.W. Norton & Co., 1975), 207–8.

105. Sofaer, "On the Necessity of Pre-emption," 220.

106. Mary Ellen O'Connell, "The Myth of Pre-emptive Self-Defense" (Washington, DC: The American Society of International Law Task Force on Terrorism, August 2002), 9–10.

107. Walzer, *Just and Unjust Wars,* 2nd ed., 74–76.

108. Keller and Mitchell, "Preemption, Prevention, Prevarication," in Keller and Mitchell, eds., *Hitting First,* 19.

109. John Yoo, "Using Force," *The University of Chicago Law Review,* vol. 71 (Summer 2004), 752–60, and Mark L. Rockefeller, "The 'Imminent Threat' Requirement for the Use of Preemptive Military Force: Is It Time for a Non-Temporal Standard?" *Denver Journal of International Law and Society,* vol. 33 (Winter 2004), electronic edition, lexisnexis@prod.lexisnexis.com.

6 Why Challenges to Accountability Will Grow

1. Richard Szafranski, "A Theory of Information Warfare: Preparing for 2020," *Airpower Journal* (Spring 1995), 2, electronic edition, http://132.60.50.46/airchronicles/apc/szfran.

2. The terms "postmilitary" and "postmodern" come from the following: Martin Shaw, *Post-Military Society: Militarism, Demilitarization and War at the End of the Twentieth Century* (Philadelphia: Temple University Press, 1991), 184–89; and Charles C. Moskos, John Allen Williams, and David R. Segal, "Armed Forces after the Cold War," in Moskos, Williams, Segal, eds., *The Postmodern Military: Armed Forces after the Cold War* (New York: Oxford University Press, 2000), 2. The acceptance of civilian

methods, but without some of the above interpretation, is examined in Morris Janowitz, *The Professional Soldier: A Social and Political Portrait* (New York: Free Press of Glencoe, 1960), 32–33. The last comment about the founders relies on Richard H. Kohn, *Eagle and Sword: The Beginnings of the Military Establishment in America* (New York: Free Press, 1975), 282.

3. The point about less traditional operations comes from Moskos, Williams, and Segal, "Armed Forces After the Cold War," 2.

4. See the most recent national security strategy document released in March 2006, which emphasizes the importance of special operations; electronic edition, http://www.whitehouse.gov/nsc/nss/2006.

5. Lori Fisler Damrosch, "Covert Operations," *The American Journal of International Law,* vol. 83 (October 1989), 797.

6. Ibid., 798–99. Also see Jennifer D. Kibbe, "The Rise of the Shadow Warriors," *Foreign Affairs,* vol. 83 (March/April 2004), 105.

7. See Loch K. Johnson, "Covert Action and Accountability: Decision-Making for America's Secret Foreign Policy," in Loch K. Johnson and James J. Wirtz, eds., *Strategic Intelligence: Windows into a Secret World: An Anthology* (Los Angeles: Roxbury Publishing Company, 2004), 370; and Johnson, "Accountability and America's Secret Foreign Policy: Keeping a Legislative Eye on the Central Intelligence Agency," *Foreign Policy Analysis* (March 2005), 112–13, 116.

8. Personal discussions and seminar presentations by congressional staff in 2001–2003. Also see William J. Daugherty, "Approval and Review of Covert Action Programs Since Reagan," *International Journal of Intelligence and Counterintelligence,* vol. 17 (Spring 2004), 76.

9. *The 9/11 Commission Report: Final Report of the National Commission on Terrorist Attacks Upon the United States* (New York: W.W. Norton and Co., 2004), 420.

10. Kathryn Stone, "'All Necessary Means'—Employing CIA Operatives in a Warfighting Role Alongside Special Operations Forces" (paper prepared for a U.S. Army War College Research Project, 2003), 4; Kibbe, "The Rise of the Shadow Warriors," 108.

11. As quoted in Stone, "All Necessary Means," 5–6.

12. Barton Gellman, "Secret Unit Expands Rumsfeld's Domain," *The Washington Post,* January 23, 2005, p. A10; Linda Robinson, *Masters of Chaos: The Secret History of the Special Forces* (New York: Public Affairs, 2004), 367.

13. Gellman, "Secret Unit Expands Rumsfeld's Domain," p. A10.

14. See *The 9/11 Commission Report,* 415–16. Also discussed in Robinson, *Masters of Chaos,* 367–68. Examples of covert operations that would not be paramilitary could include those to seek influence, placement of operatives in the press, or operations to assist escape or defection. See Stone, "All Necessary Means," 11.

15. Kibbe, "The Rise of the Shadow Warriors," 102–109.

16. Stone, "All Necessary Means, 11–12, 15–16.

17. See Eugene B. Smith, "The New Condottieri and US Policy: The Privatization of Conflict and Its Implications," *Parameters,* vol. 32 (Winter 2002–2003), 104–19, to illustrate how this historical term is used for today's situation.

18. Deborah Avant, "Mercenaries," *Foreign Policy* (July/August 2004), 20.

19. The reason the United States has not ratified Protocol I is that it believes two of the provisions may encourage terrorism because they treat terrorists as combatants rather than criminals. See fn. 11 in Ryan Goodman and Derek Jinks, "International Law, U.S.

War Powers, and the Global War on Terrorism, *Harvard Law Review,* vol. 118 (2005), 2655.

20. Adam Roberts and Richard Guelff, *Documents on the Laws of War,* 3rd ed. (Oxford: Oxford University Press, 2004), 447, and also concluding notes relating to both Geneva Protocols I and II, 493–512.

21. Ibid., 36–37.

22. Kim Richard Nossal, "Global Governance and National Security Interests: Regulating Transnational Security Corporations in the Post–Cold War Era," *Melbourne Journal of International Law,* vol. 2 (2001), 471–72.

23. Juan Carlos Zarate, "The Emergence of a New Dog of War: Private International Security Companies, International Law, and the New World Disorder," *Stanford Journal of International Law,* vol. 34 (Winter 1998), 26–28, electronic edition, lexisnexis @prod.lexisnexis.com.

24. P.W. Singer, *Corporate Warriors: The Rise of the Privatized Military Industry* (Ithaca, NY: Cornell University Press, 2003), 88–100; Deborah D. Avant, *The Market for Force: The Consequences of Privatizing Security* (Cambridge: Cambridge University Press, 2005), 16–22. Also see Thomas K. Adams, "The New Mercenaries and the Privatization of Conflict," *Parameters,* vol. 29 (Summer 1999), 103–16.

25. P.W. Singer, "Corporate Warriors: The Rise of the Privatized Military Industry and Its Ramifications for International Security," *International Security,* vol. 26 (Winter 2001/02), 193–94.

26. Avant, *The Market for Force,* 33; Singer, *Corporate Warriors,* 5–6.

27. Singer, *Corporate Warriors,* 194–95.

28. Ibid., 195–96.

29. Ibid., 197–98; Avant, *The Market for Force,* 35.

30. U.S. Department of Defense, "Improving the Combat Edge Through Outsourcing," *Defense Issues,* vol. 11 (March 1996), electronic edition, http://www.defenselink .mil/cgi-bin/dlprint.cgi?http://www.defenselink.mil/speeches/1996/s19960301-report.

31. See some of the report summaries in Ann Markusen, "The Case Against Privatizing National Security," *Dollars and Sense* (May/June 2004), 25–26. Also see Avant, "Mercenaries," 22.

32. Steven J. Zamparelli, "Contractors on the Battlefield: What Have We Signed Up For?" (research report submitted to the Faculty at the Air War College, Air University, Maxwell Air Force Base; Montgomery, AL, March 1999), 8; Jennifer K. Elsea and Nina M. Serafino, *Private Security Contractors in Iraq: Background, Legal Status, and Other Issues,* CRS Issue Brief for Congress (Washington, DC: Congressional Research Service, Library of Congress, updated July 11, 2007), 3.

33. Singer, *Corporate Warriors,* 58–60. The Darfur crisis in the Sudan developed after the publication of Singer's book.

34. This point is raised by Thomas K. Adams, "Private Military Companies: Mercenaries for the 21st Century," *Small Wars and Insurgencies,* vol. 13 (Summer 2002), 63. Also see Sarah Percy, *Regulating the Private Security Industry,* Adelphi Paper 384, International Institute of Strategic Studies (London: Routledge, 2006), 17.

35. The example is from Adams, "Private Military Companies," 62.

36. Singer, *Corporate Warriors,* 206–209, 218–19. Also see Percy, *Regulating the Private Security Industry,* 16.

37. See discussion in Chapter 1, this volume; and C. Kevin Marshall, "Putting Privateers in Their Place: The Applicability of the Marque and Reprisal Clause to Unde-

clared Wars," *University of Chicago Law Review,* vol. 64 (Summer 1997), 8, electronic edition, http://web.lexis-nexis.com/universe.

38. For this point see Matthew J. Gaul, "Regulating the New Privateers: Private Military Service Contracting and the Modern Marque and Reprisal Clause," *Loyola of Los Angeles Law Review,* vol. 31 (June 1998), 7, electronic edition, http://web.lexis-nexis .com/universe.

39. A solution advocated, for example, by Nikolas K. Gvosdev and Anthony A. Cipriano in *A New Resource in the War Against Terrorism* (Washington, DC: The Nixon Center, July 9, 2002), http://www.nixoncenter.org/publications/articles/070902privateer.

40. Roberts and Guelff, *Documents on the Law of War,* 46–51. The premise of a bounty is not unlike the reward money offered by the United States for information that would contribute to the capture of Osama bin-Laden and other terrorists.

41. Smith, "The New Condottieri and U.S. Policy," 7–8, electronic edition, http://carlisle-www.army.milusawc/Parameters/02winter/smith.

42. As quoted in Carlos Ortiz, "Regulating Private Military Companies: States and the Expanding Business of Commercial Security Provision," in Libby Assassi, Duncan Wigan, and Kees Van Der Pihl, eds., *Global Regulation: Managing Crisis After the Imperial Turn* (Houndmills, Basingstoke: Palgrave MacMillan, 2004), 212. For the Arms Export Control Act (AECA), see U.S. Code Title 22, Chapter 3, at http://wwwlaw cornell.edu/uscode/22/usc_sup_01_22_10_39.html.

43. Ibid., 213–14. Also see AECA.

44. Percy, *Regulating the Private Security Industry,* 26.

45. Gaul, "Regulating the New Privateers," 17.

46. See Gordon L. Campbell, Presentation to Joint Services Conference on Professional Ethics 2000 (Springfield, Virginia, January 27–28, 2000), http://www.usafa.af .mil/jscope?JSCOPE00/Campbell00.html; and Karen L. Douglas, "Contractors Accompanying the Force: Empowering Commanders with Emergency Change Authority, *The Air Force Law Review* (Spring 2004), 135. A very critical depiction of Blackwater USA is in Jeremy Scahill, *Blackwater: The Rise of the World's Most Powerful Mercenary Army* New York: Nation Books, 2007); see House Committee on Oversight and Government Reform, Memorandum to Members of the Committee on Oversight and Government, October 1, 2007, 110th Cong., 1st sess. (copy provided to author). "Management of DoD Contractors and Contractor Personnel Accompanying U.S. Armed Forces in Contingency Operations Outside the United States," Memorandum for Secretaries of the Military Departments, September 25, 2007, available at http://www.mclatchydc .com/status/pdf/092507_contract_memo.pdf.

47. Dustin M. Tipling, "The Military Extraterritorial Jurisdiction Act and Its Implications for Private Military Companies," Working Paper 1393, *bepress Legal Series* (May 26, 2006), 15–33, http://law.bepress.com/expresso/eps/1393. A more recent examination of this issue is in Marc Lindemann, "Civilian Contractors under Military Law," *Parameters,* vol. 37 (Autumn 2007), 83–94.

48. This is examined at length in William C. Peters, "On Law, Wars, and Mercenaries: The Case for Courts-Martial Jurisdiction Over Civilian Contractor Misconduct in Iraq," *Brigham Young University Law Review,* no. 367 (2006), 395–97, electronic edition, lexisnexis@prod.lexisnexis.com.

49. Griff Witte, "New Law Could Subject Civilians to Military Trial," *The Washington Post,* January 15, 2007, pp. A1, 11.

50. See H.R. 369 and S. 674, the Senate counterpart. See The Transparency and Ac-

countability in Security Contracting Act of 2007, http://gvtrack.us/congress/billxpd
?bill=h110–369. Davie Herszenhorn, "House Iraq Bill Applies U.S. Law to Contractors," *The New York Times,* October 5, 2007, pp. A1, 12.

　　51. Douglas, "Contractors Accompanying the Force," 136.

　　52. Goodman and Jinks, "International Law, U.S. War Powers, and the Global War
on Terrorism," 2656–57.

　　53. P.W. Singer, "Peacekeepers, Inc.," *Policy Review,* vol. 119 (June–July 2003), 67.

　　54. Michael O'Hanlon, *Saving Lives with Force: Military Criteria for Humanitar-
ian Intervention* (Washington, DC: Brookings Institution, 1997), 8; Todd S. Milliard,
"Overcoming Post-Colonial Myopia: A Call to Recognize and Regulate Private Military
Companies," *Military Law Review,* vol. 176 (June 2003), 16–19.

　　55. See the arguments by Milliard, "Overcoming Post-Colonial Myopia," 77–79;
Zamparelli, "Contractors on the Battlefield," 26–27, and Charles J. Dunlap, Jr., "Technology: Recomplicating Moral Life for the Nation's Defenders," *Parameters,* vol. 29
(Autumn 1999), 7, electronic edition, http://www.carlisle.army.mil/usawc/Parameters/
99autumn/dunlap.htm.

　　56. Caroline Holmqvist, "Private Security Companies: The Case for Regulation,"
SIPRI Policy Paper No. 9 (Stockholm: Stockholm International Peace Research Institute, January 2005), 54.

　　57. The thrust of these questions is drawn from Charles J. Dunlap, Jr., "Technology
and War: Moral Dilemmas on the Battlefield," in Anthony F. Lang, Jr., Albert C. Pierce,
and Joel H. Rosenthal, eds., *Ethics and the Future of Conflict: Lessons from the 1990's*
(Upper Saddle River, NJ: Pearson Prentice Hall, 2004), 132.

　　58. This interpretation draws from Daniel Pick, *War Machine: The Rationalization
of Slaughter in the Modern Age* (New Haven, CT: Yale University Press, 1993), 165–67.

　　59. For a discussion of this, see "The Pendulum between Perfect and Imperfect
War," Chapter 4, this volume.

　　60. Robert Mandel, *Security, Strategy, and the Quest for Bloodless War* (Boulder,
CO: Lynne Rienner Publishers, 2004), 48.

　　61. The pattern of this approach during the Cold War is evident in reading Odd Arne
Westad, *The Global Cold War: Third World Interventions and the Making of Our Times*
(Cambridge: Cambridge University Press, 2005). Of course, the Soviets did the same
thing, as Westad shows.

　　62. Andrew Latham, "Warfare Transformed: A Braudelian Perspective on the 'Revolution in Military Affairs,'" *European Journal of International Relations,* vol. 8 (2002),
240–47.

　　63. J. Marshall Beier, "Discriminating Tastes: 'Smart' Bombs, Non-Combatants, and
Notions of Legitimacy in Warfare," *Security Dialogue,* vol. 34 (December 2003), 413.
For the decrease in public support of military force, see Scott Bittle and Jonathan Rochkind
with Amber Ott, "Confidence in U.S. Foreign Policy Index: Anxious Public Pulling Back
from Use of Force," *Public Agenda,* vol. 4 (Spring 2007), 10, electronic edition, www
.publicagenda.org.

　　64. Beier, "Discriminating Tastes." 419–23.

　　65. John Leech, *Asymmetries of Conflict: War without Death* (London: Frank Cass,
2002), 14.

　　66. See his *Virtual War: Kosovo and Beyond* (New York: Metropolitan Books, 2000).

　　67. Emphasis is Der Derian's. See James Der Derian, "The War of Networks,"
Theory & Event, vol. 5 (2002), 2–3, electronic edition, http://muse.jhu.edu/journals/

theory_and_event/v005/5.rderderian.html; and Der Derian, *Virtuous War: Mapping the Military-Industrial-Media-Entertainment Network* (Boulder, CO: Westview Press, 2001).

68. The point about the limits of technology is a theme in Max Boot's recent book, *War Made New: Technology, Warfare, and the Course of History* (New York: Gotham Books, 2006), 417.

69. See Daniel R. Headrick, *The Invisible Weapon: Telecommunications and International Politics, 1851–1945* (New York: Oxford University Press, 1991).

70. James R. Hosek, "The Soldier of the 21st Century," in Stuart Johnson, Martin C. Libicki, and Gregory F. Treverton, eds., *New Challenges New Tools for Defense Decisionmaking* (Santa Monica, CA: RAND Corporation, 2003), 182–83; "'Land Warrior' and Beyond," *Military Technology* (November 2004), 66–70; David D. Perlmutter, *Visions of War: Picturing Warfare from the Stone Age to the Cyber Age* (New York: St. Martin's Griffin, 1999), 214–15.

71. Manuel DeLanda, *War in the Age of Intelligent Machines* (New York: Zone Books, 1991), 127, 177.

72. Christopher J. Bowie, Robert P. Haffa, Jr., and Robert E. Mullins, "Trends in Future Warfare," *Joint Force Quarterly* (Summer 2003), 131.

73. David C. Gompert, Irving Lachow, and Justin Perkins, *Battle-Wise: Gaining Advantage in Networked Warfare* (Washington, DC: Center for Technology and National Security Policy, National Defense University, January 2005), 3.

74. See section titled "Imperfect War, Technological Superiority, and Special Mission," Chapter 4, this volume.

75. For an optimistic scenario written before either of these campaigns, see Admiral Bill Owens with Ed Offley, *Lifting the Fog of War* (New York: Farrar, Straus, and Giroux, 2000), 136–49.

76. See Wayne Michael Hall, *Stray Voltage: War in the Information Age* (Annapolis, MD: Naval Institute Press, 2003), 14–42.

77. See Nick Cullather, "Bombing at the Speed of Thought: Intelligence in the Coming Age of Cyberwar," *Intelligence and National Security,* vol. 18 (Winter 2003), 144.

78. Quotation of General William F. Kernan, Commander in Chief of the U.S. Joint Forces Command, in John Stone, "Politics, Technology and the Revolution in Military Affairs," *The Journal of Strategic Studies,* vol. 27 (September 2004), 418.

79. Ibid., 418.

80. MacGregor Knox and Williamson Murray, "The Future Behind Us," in MacGregor Knox and Williamson Murray, eds., *The Dynamics of Military Revolution: 1300–2050* (Cambridge: Cambridge University Press, 2001), 179.

81. Williamson Murray and Major General Robert H. Scales, Jr., *The Iraq War: A Military History* (Cambridge, MA: Belknap Press of Harvard University Press, 2003), 57, 236.

82. See Lee Braudy, *From Chivalry to Terrorism: War and the Changing Nature of Masculinity* (New York: Alfred A. Knopf, 2003), 278–79.

83. See the discussion in William Church, "Information Warfare," *International Review of the Red Cross* (March 31, 2000), 1–2, electronic edition, http:///icrc.org/web/eng/siteeng0.nsf/iwpList356/0A7FEC8D33249CDAC1256B6600.

84. Martin Libicki, *"What Is Information Warfare?"* (Washington, DC: National Defense University Press, 1995), x.

85. John Arquilla, "Ethics and Information Warfare," in Zalmay Khalilzad, ed., *Strategic Appraisal: The Changing Role of Information Warfare* (Santa Monica, CA:

RAND Corporation, 1999), 384. The problem of altered computer chips is reviewed in Julien Pretorius, "Ethics and International Security in the Information Age," *Defense & Security Analysis,* vol. 19 (June 2003), 169.

86. This point is drawn from Arquilla, "Ethics and Information Warfare," 385–86. The difficulty of tracing the origin of the attack is explored, too, in Mark R. Jacobson, "War in the Information Age: International Law, Self-Defense and the Problem of 'Non-Armed' Attacks," *The Journal of Strategic Studies,* vol. 21 (September 1998), 8; and in Martin C. Libicki, *Defending Cyberspace and Other Metaphors* (Washington, DC: National Defense University Press, 1997), 49–51.

87. Tim Cathcart, "Standoff Ethics: Policy Considerations for the Use of Standoff Weapons" (Joint Services Conference on Professional Ethics, 2004), 2, http://www.us afa.ag.mil/jscope?JSCOPE0r/Cathcart04.html.

88. Michael Fitzsimmons, "The Importance of Being Special: Planning for the Future of U.S. Special Operations Forces," *Defense & Security Analysis,* vol. 19 (September 2003), 210.

89. The figure comes from Robert H. Scales, *Yellow Smoke: The Future of Land Warfare* (Lanham, MD: Rowman & Littlefield, 2003), 159.

90. John A. Gentry, "Doomed to Fail: America's Blind Faith in Military Technology," *Parameters,* vol. 4 (Winter 2002–2003), 90.

91. Douglas A. MacGregor, *Transformation Under Fire: Revolutionizing How America Fights* (Westport, CT: Praeger Publishers, 2003), 54.

92. Scales, *Yellow Smoke,* 76.

93. Discussed in James Adams, *The Next World War: Computers Are the Weapons and the Front Line Is Everywhere* (New York: Simon and Schuster, 1998), 124–25.

94. See Steven Metz, *Armed Conflict in the 21st Century: The Information Revolution and Post-Modern Warfare* (Carlisle, PA: Strategic Studies Institute, U.S. Army War College, 2000), 46–47; 65–66.

95. Hall, *Stray Voltage,* 83.

96. This discussion, while not literally derived from the following book, owes much to questions raised by H.G. Wells and examined in Christopher Coker, *The Future of War: The Re-Enchantment of War in the Twenty-First Century* (Oxford: Blackwell Publishing, 2004), 45.

97. Robert D. Kaplan, *Warrior Politics: Why Leadership Demands a Pagan Ethos* (New York: Random House, 2002), 117–18.

98. Hall, *Stray Voltage,* 81; Coker, *The Future of War,* 95–100. Also see John B. Alexander, *Winning the War: Advanced Weapons, Strategies, and Concepts for the Post-9/11 World* (New York: Thomas Dunne Books, St. Martin's Press, 2003), 72–73.

99. Coker, *The Future of War,* 100–109.

100. Metz, *Armed Conflict in the 21st Century,* 71; Tim Weiner, "A New Model Army Soldier Rolls Closer to the Battlefield," *The New York Times,* February 16, 2005, pp. A1, C4. Also see Alvin and Heidi Toffler, *War and Anti-War: Survival at the Dawn of the 21st Century* (Boston: Little, Brown and Co., 1993), 108–17.

101. Serge Schmemann, "For Tomorrow's Army, Cadets Full of Questions," *The New York Times,* July 8, 2001, 4.1, electronic edition, http://www.nytimes.com/2001/07/ 08/weekinreview/08SCHM.Html?pagewanted+all. Also see Jeremy Black, *War and the New Disorder in the 21st Century* (New York: Continuum, 2004), 165.

102. Report to the President's Commission on Critical Infrastructure Protection, "A

'Legal Foundations' Study," Report 6 of 12, 16–18, electronic edition, http:///www.pc cip.gov.

103. Sean P. Kanuck, "Recent Development: Information Warfare: New Challenges for Public International Law," *Harvard International Law Journal,* vol. 37 (Winter 1996), 8, electronic edition, lexisnexis@prod.lexis.com; Bruce Berkowitz, *The New Face of War: How War Will Be Fought in the 21st Century* (New York: Free Press, 2003), 152–53.

104. Office of General Counsel, Department of Defense, "An Assessment of International Legal Issues in Information Operations" (June 15, 1999), 12, electronic edition, http://www.infowar.com/info_opsinfo_ops_061599a_j.shtml; David J. DiCenso, "IW Cyberlaw: The Legal Issues of Information Warfare," *Airpower Journal* (Summer 1999), 95.

105. See the pertinent sections of the UN Charter in W. Michael Reisman and Chris T. Antoniou, *The Laws of War: A Comprehensive Collection of Primary Documents on International Laws Governing Armed Conflict* (New York: Vintage Books, 1994), 5–6.

106. Office of General Counsel, Department of Defense, "An Assessment of International Legal Issues in Information Operations," 13–14.

107. Lawrence T. Greenberg, Seymour E. Goodman, and Kevin J. Soo Hoo, *Information Warfare and International Law* (Washington, DC: National Defense University Press, 1997), 84–85.

108. William Yurcik, "Information Warfare: Ethical Challenges of the Next Global Battleground," Proceedings of the Second Annual Ethics and Technology Conference, Loyola University, Chicago, June 6–7, 1997, http://www.math.luc.edu/ethics97/papers/Yurcik.txt. Also see Gregory D. Grove, Seymour E. Goodman, and Stephen J. Lukasik, "Cyber-Attacks and International Law," *Survival,* vol. 42 (Autumn 2000), 93.

109. Greenberg, Goodman, and Soo Hoo, *Information Warfare and International Law,* 87.

110. Ibid., 89–90.

111. DiCenso, "IW Cyberlaw: The Legal Issues of Information Warfare," 92.

112. Grove, Goodman, and Ludasik, "Cyber-Attacks and International Law," 95

113. DiCenso, "IW Cyberlaw: The Legal Issues of Information Warfare," 94; Daniel M. Vadnais, "Law of Armed Conflict and Information Warfare—How Does the Rule Regarding Reprisals Apply to an Information Warfare Attack?," paper presented to the Research Department, Air Command and Staff College, March 1997, 22, electronic edition, http://research.airuniv.edu/papers/ay1997/acsc/97-0116.pdf.

114. For a good and accessible overview to many of these weapons and their application see John B. Alexander, *Future War: Non-Lethal Weapons in Twenty-First Century Warfare* (New York: Thomas Dunne Books, St. Martin's Press, 1999).

115. Christopher Coker, "On Humanizing War," *Totalitarian Movements and Political Religions,* vol. 1 (Autumn 2002), 80–82; Victor Wallace, "Non-Lethal Weapons: R2IPE for Arms Control Measures," in Nick Lewer, ed., *The Future of Non-Lethal Weapons: Technologies, Operations, Ethics and Law* (London; Frank Cass, 2002), 146–48; Alexander, *Future War,* 24–25.

116. Alexander, *Future War,* 24–25.

117. Ibid., 17; Stephen R. Bowers and Pamela A. Mielnik, "Making Warfare Acceptable: Nonlethal Strategies," *The Journal of Social, Political, and Economic Studies,* vol. 23 (Spring 1998), 18.

118. As pointed out in Yurcik, "Information Warfare," 6.

119. David P. Fidler, "'Non-Lethal' Weapons and International Law: Three Perspectives on the Future," 34, in Lewer, ed., *The Future of Non-Lethal Weapons,* 34.

120. David P. Fidler, "The International Legal Implications of 'Non-Lethal' Weapons," *Michigan Journal of International Law,* vol. 21 (Fall 1999), 67–68. The text and all the protocols, including amendments, are reproduced in Roberts and Guelff, *Documents on the Laws of War,* 3rd ed., 513–60.

121. Roberts and Guelff, *Documents on the Laws of War,* 516–18, 551. In the case of incendiary devices, the United States wanted to retain the ability to use such weapons, like napalm, in instances requiring close air support; ibid., 517. It is important not to confuse Protocol II dealing with land mines with the Ottawa Convention (The Convention on the Prohibition of the Use, Stockpiling, Production, and Transfer of Anti-Personnel Mines and on Their Destruction signed in December 1997), which the United States did not sign. See Department of the Army Pamphlet 27–50–313, "Antipersonnel Land Mines Law and Policy," reproduced in *Army Lawyer* (December 1998), electronic edition, http:///www.lawofwar.org/Barfield_landmines_army_lawyer.htm.

122. See endnote 69 in Fidler, "International Legal Implications of 'Non-Lethal' Weapons," which cites discussion in Marian Nash Leigh, "Contemporary Practice of the United States Relating to International Law," *American Journal of International Law,* vol. 91 (1997), 325, 332.

123. DiCenso, "IW Cyberlaw: The Legal Issues of Information Warfare," 88–90.

124. See the discussion in Christoph Seidler, "Ruestungskontrolle im Cyberspace" (paper submitted in the Institut fuer Politikwissenschaften, Technische Universitaet Dresden, August 2003); Olivier Minkwitz and Georg Schoefbaenker, "Information Warfare: Die neue Herausforderung fuer die Ruestungskontrolle (May 31, 2000), electronic edition, http://www.heise.de/bin/tp/issue/r4/dl_artikel2cgi?artikeln=6817&zeilenlaenge =72&mode. Seidler draws from this paper. The authors work at the Frankfurt Peace Research Institute, where the paper was written.

125. Much of this discussion draws from papers prepared for an international conference in Berlin, Arms Control in Cyberspace: Perspectives for Peace Policy in the Age of Computer Network Attacks, June 29–30, 2001, arranged by the Heinrich Boell Stiftung, the Green Party institute. See in particular Christian Moelling and Goetz Neuneck, "Praeventive Ruestungskontrolle und Information Warfare"; Berthold Johannes, "Arms Control in Cyberspace"; and Olivier Minkwitz and Georg Schoefbaenker, "Information Warfare: Die Ruestungskongrolle steht vor neuen Herausforderungen." All are available at the Website of the Heinrich Boell Stiftung, http://www.boell.de.

126. Szafranski, "A Theory of Information Warfare," 8.

127. Ibid.

Conclusion

1. See Alexander DeConde, *Presidential Machismo: Executive Authority, Military Intervention, and Foreign Relations* (Boston: Northeastern University Press, 2000).

2. Charlotte Ku and Harold K. Jacobson, "Broaching the Issues," in Ku and Jacobson, eds., *Democratic Accountability and the Use of Force in International Law* (Cambridge: Cambridge University Press, 2003), 12.

3. A point developed by Jed Rubenfeld, "Commentary: Unilateralism and Constitutionalism," 79, *New York University Law Review* (December 2004), 1972–76.

4. This is from Lori Fisler Damrosch, "The Interface of National Constitutional Systems with International Law and Institutions on Using Military Forces: Changing Trends in Executive and Legislative Powers," in Ku and Jacobson, eds., *Democratic Accountability and the Use of Force in International Law* (Cambridge: Cambridge University Press, 2003), 40. The author also briefly explored this theme in the context of German–American relations in *Constitutions, Military Force, and Implications for German–American Relations,* SWP Comments 56 (Berlin: Stiftung Wissenschaft und Politik, December 2005), available at http://www.swp-berlin.org/.

5. See Yves Boyer, Serge Sur, and Olivier Fleurence, "France Security Council Legitimacy and Executive Primacy," and Nigel D. White, "The United Kingdom: Increasing Commitment Requires Greater Parliamentary Involvement," in Ku and Jacobson, eds., *Democratic Accountability and the Use of Force in International Law*, 280–99 and 300–22, respectively.

6. See Andrew Kohut and Bruce Stokes, *America Against the World* (New York: Times Books, Henry Holt and Company, 2006), 193–205.

7. See the discussion of legislation introduced by Senators John Mitchell, Sam Nunn, John Warner, and Robert Byrd, as well as Representative Lee H. Hamilton in the House, in Richard F. Grimmett, *The War Powers Resolution: After Twenty-Eight Years,* CRS Report for the Congress, Order Code RL31185 (Washington, DC: Congressional Research Service, Library of Congress, November 15, 2001), 49–50.

8. As any resolution providing a president the authority to use force is an act signed into law, a resolution seeking the repeal of the resolution and the recall of U.S. forces should also be subject to presidential signature or veto.

9. *Deciding to Use Force Abroad: War Powers in a System of Checks and Balances,* An Initiative of The Constitution Project (Washington, DC: The Constitution Project, 2005), 41, electronic edition, http://www.constitutionproject.org.

10. See sections titled "Who Respects the War Powers Resolution?" and "When War Is Not War: The Continued Diminishment of the War Powers Resolution," Chapter 3, this volume.

Index

Abrams Doctrine, 130
absolute wars, 30
The Absolute Weapon (Brodie), 126
Abu Ghraib, 8, 146, 181, 196
Accessory Transit Company, 58
accountability, 8–9, 183–215;
congressional and presidential
diminishment of, 6–7, 110–11; and
congressional power of the purse,
37; of Congress to citizenry, 41;
and covert actions, 83, 184–87;
creation of system of, 18, 36, 39;
and executive-congressional
relationship, 42, 84, 181, 182; and
information technology, 198–204;
and information warfare, 204–11,
213–15; and limited war, 20; and
National Security Council, 108;
and non- and less-lethal weapons,
212–15; for presidential action,
40, 55, 108; and preventive use of
force, 180; and private military
firms, 187–98; and reliance on
surrogates, 81; and war powers, 9,
223
Acheson, Dean, 78
Adair, Douglas, 6
Adams, John: and Barbary pirates, 51;
and limited war, 116; and Mexican
War, 61; and Quasi-War

(U.S./France), 49–50, 183; and War
of 1812, 52
Aidid, Mohammed Farrah, 138
Adler, David Gray, 24
advice and consent of Senate, 36, 84,
213
Afghanistan: Al-Qaeda operating in,
102; Cold War conflict in, 220; and
covert operations, 185; funding
of war in, 38, 110; low-casualty
war in, 200, 201; military force
as a policy instrument in, 143;
operation's initial name, 166; post-
9/11 war in, 1, 2, 5; and precision-
guided munitions, 205–6; and presidential authority to use force, 182,
224; and reprisals, 59, 172; technological warfare in, 144–45, 201
aggression and aggressive war: and
(George W.) Bush, 153; and
Clinton, 101; and covert operations,
187; definition of, 211; and
humanitarian intervention, 158; and
information warfare, 215; in
international law, 172; and
preemption, 178–79; rejection of,
75; and UN Charter, 168, 171, 177,
209; UN's authority to use force to
stop, 76–77, 159; U.S. response to,
77, 86

277